JOURNEYS
from
SCANDINAVIA

JOURNEYS *from* SCANDINAVIA

Travelogues of Africa, Asia, and South America, 1840–2000

ELISABETH OXFELDT

University of Minnesota Press
Minneapolis
London

The University of Minnesota Press gratefully acknowledges the financial assistance provided for the publication of this book from the Department of Linguistics and Scandinavian Studies at Oslo University.

Chapter 2 was previously published in Danish as "Mellem orientalisme og feminisme: Bindestregs-kvinden Elisabeth Jerichau-Baumanns konstruktioner af nationaltyper i *Brogede Reisebilleder*," *Spring* 22 (2004): 196–224. Chapter 3 was previously published in Danish as "*Ingen-steder* i Hamsuns orientalske rejseskildringer," in Even Arntzen and Henning H. Wærp, eds., *Hamsun i Tromsø III. Rapport fra den 3. Internasjonale Hamsun-konferanse, 2003* (Hamarøy: Hamsun-Selskapet, 2004), 129–48, and as "Orientalske rejseskildringer," in Ståle Dingstad, ed., *Den litterære Hamsun* (Bergen: Fagbokforlaget, 2005), 105–23.

Copyright 2010 by the Regents of the University of Minnesota

All rights reserved. No part of this publication may be reproduced, stored in a retrieval system, or transmitted, in any form or by any means, electronic, mechanical, photocopying, recording, or otherwise, without the prior written permission of the publisher.

Published by the University of Minnesota Press
111 Third Avenue South, Suite 290
Minneapolis, MN 55401-2520
http://www.upress.umn.edu

Library of Congress Cataloging-in-Publication Data

Oxfeldt, Elisabeth.
    Journeys from Scandinavia : travelogues of Africa, Asia, and South America, 1840–2000 / Elisabeth Oxfeldt.
        p.   cm.
    Includes bibliographical references and index.
    ISBN 978-0-8166-5634-9 (hc : alk. paper) — ISBN 978-0-8166-5635-6 (pb : alk. paper)
    1. Travelers' writings, Scandinavian—History and criticism.   2. Travel in literature.
3. Travelers in literature.   4. Postcolonialism in literature.   5. Other (Philosophy) in literature.   6. Exoticism in literature.   7. Africa—In literature.   8. Asia—In literature.
9. South America—In literature.   I. Title.
    PT7073.T73O94   2010
    839.7'355—dc22   2010017035

Printed in the United States of America on acid-free paper

The University of Minnesota is an equal-opportunity educator and employer.

16 15 14 13 12 11 10   10 9 8 7 6 5 4 3 2 1

To Sara Elise

Contents

INTRODUCTION *xi*

Part I
Romantic Journeys to the Orient 3

ONE
Discovering His Inner Turk:
Hans Christian Andersen's Commodification of the Exotic 6

TWO
The Hyphenated Woman:
Elisabeth Jerichau-Baumann's Juggling Categories
of Gender, Nation, and Ethnicity 31

THREE
The Ironic Traveler:
Danger and Identity in Knut Hamsun's Oriental Travelogues 58

Part II
Modern Primitive Travel 81

FOUR
Savage Science:
Johannes V. Jensen in the Malay Jungle 87

FIVE
Humor, Gender, and Nationality:
Isak Dinesen's Encounter with Africa 106

SIX
The Traveler and the Tourist:
Axel Jensen's Desperate Frolic in the Sahara   143

Part III
Late and Postmodern Travel   173

SEVEN
From the Personal to the Universal—and Back:
Carsten Jensen around the World   176

EIGHT
Futile Journeys:
Parody, Postmodernism, and Postnationalism in
Erlend Loe's Traveling   204

CONCLUSION   233

NOTES   243
BIBLIOGRAPHY   287
INDEX   295

Georg Wilhelm Baurenfeind, *Depiction of Dancers and Their Musicians on the Way to Cairo*, from *Reisebeschreibung nach Arabien und andern umliegenden Ländern* by Carsten Niebuhr (1774)

Introduction

THE DANISH-GERMAN EXPLORER Carsten Niebuhr's *Reisebeschreibung nach Arabien und andern umliegenden Ländern* (Travel Depiction from Arabia and Other Surrounding Countries, 1774) includes a copper etching by Georg Wilhelm Baurenfeind of seminude Egyptian women dancing in the sand to the sound of strings and cymbals.[1] The composition consists of seven figures, including two women dancing in the middle and two similar female figures in the lower left corner whose turn to dance it might be next. The lower right corner shows an entirely veiled woman smoking a long pipe, and in the right top corner are two musicians, including the etching's only male figure located farthest away. This man attentively accompanies the dancers on his stringed instrument, his monitoring stare redirecting the onlooker's gaze back to the dancers in the middle. In the background is a cluster of palm trees.

The picture exudes exoticism—in this context, geographic exoticism coupled with historic exoticism. That may be part of the reason it was reproduced on the front page of the book section of Denmark's leading cultural paper, *Weekendavisen*, in August 2003, when Niebuhr's travel depiction was first translated from German into Danish.

The attention surrounding the publication is a clear indication of present-day interest in travel literature. It also signals nostalgia for a greater and simpler time when political correctness did not interfere with the urge to explore and depict foreign—and especially Arabic—lands. The review accompanying the picture in *Weekendavisen* is a shortened version of Danish literary scholar Frits Andersen's article on Carsten Niebuhr's travelogue arguing precisely this point. Whereas Renaissance travelogues focus on the cultural Other as simply bizarre, those from the late seventeenth century and beyond reveal an equally problematic romanticizing and Orientalizing view of the Other. In contrast, the pre-Herderian Enlightenment period allegedly holds up a few "honest" travelers and travel depictions.[2]

Niebuhr thus ends up playing a reassuring role, representing guilt-free Danish prominence. He is a scientific and literary national hero. His cartographic work was of international caliber and importance, and his travelogue can be considered "Danish world literature."[3] At the same time, his method was allegedly impartial and politically innocent. In short, Niebuhr is presented as a role model for how Westerners could—and still could learn to—interact with Easterners.[4]

Returning to Baurenfeind's eighteenth-century copper etching, we may see it as illustrating some of the ethical and political issues—emphasized by postcolonial theory—involved in representing the cultural Other. Its focal point is the woman dancing in the middle. Although she is looking straight at the beholder (and is the only one of the etching's seven figures doing so), she cannot be said to establish eye contact. Her gaze, soberly registering the beholder, is far less eye-catching than her rounded, right breast, peeking out above her robe. Her dancing—leaning, with outstretched arms—has caused her garment to drop, exposing her nipple. This seemingly inadvertent exposure is the composition's true focal point—or rather, the tension between the emotionless gaze and the erotically revealed breast comprises the focal point.

What is one to make of the discrepancy between the attentiveness of the facial expression and the eroticism of the perky breast? What is the woman's attitude to being exposed? What is the beholder's? Is *her* sober gaze to reflect *his* presupposed impartial, unemotional, scientific, and thus innocent attitude? Is the relationship between Baurenfeind and the dancer—and subsequently the reader and the dancer—in any way mutual, reciprocal, and equal?

Baurenfeind's etching may be read as an emblem of cross-cultural representation with all the ethical and political issues this practice raises. The dancer's undermined attempt at establishing eye contact is only too representative of the unequal relationship between subject and object. Mary Louise Pratt's notion of a contact zone where "disparate cultures meet, clash, and grapple with each other, often in highly asymmetrical relations of domination and subordination" seems relevant.[5] While the object in this case attempts to establish a relationship of reciprocal straightforwardness through her steady gaze, she is betrayed by the artist's interest in her breast—or, we may choose to believe, by her own body and gender. Or perhaps she is not betrayed at all.

The text accompanying the etching in Niebuhr's travelogue explains that the Egyptian dancers are Gypsies dancing for anyone willing to pay and that they have a reputation for lacking in virtue. The woman's attentive gaze coupled with the exposed breast may reflect power and calculation. Unlike later exoticist depictions (such as Paul Gauguin's Tahitian women), this woman does not appear a child of nature who is fully absorbed in her own culture and unaware of the onlooker's interest.

The picture, in itself, thus raises a myriad of questions without providing definitive answers. In addition, its insertion in the travelogue—as illustration—creates fissures and discontinuities in the text. Image and narrative clearly contradict each other, as in this case, where Niebuhr—depicting the same scene as the etching—writes that the women's faces, arms, and chests were decorated with black and blue lines and that they wore large rings around their ankles and in their ears and noses (Niebuhr, 215–16). There are no black and blue lines, nor large rings, in the etching, and in the end the reader is uncertain of his understanding of both text and image. This uncertainty is one the reader of travelogues has had to accept—and preferably enjoy—at least since Marco Polo recounted his journey to China in the late 1200s. Once the experience of a journey far away is turned into a travelogue, the text becomes the site not only of grappling with the unknown but also of entertaining a home audience. Observed facts are lodged within a narrativized, dramatized, and fictionalized account, and the genre itself demands its share of extraordinary encounters and tension.

Danish and Norwegian Travelogues

Journeys from Scandinavia provides a closer examination of cross-cultural representation in a specific historical and geographic context. Its object of study is Danish and Norwegian travelogues based on journeys made beyond the European continent between 1840 and the present.

It discusses eight authors: Hans Christian Andersen, Elisabeth Jerichau-Baumann, Knut Hamsun, Johannes V. Jensen, Karen Blixen/Isak Dinesen, Axel Jensen, Carsten Jensen, and Erlend Loe.

The word "Scandinavia" might suggest that Swedish travelogues are included. When they are not, it is for historical and personal reasons. That Denmark and Norway shared a common language and literary culture until the early 1900s makes it natural to regard the romanticist and early modern literature of the two nations from a common perspective. In the twentieth century Norwegians began to publish in Norway for a specifically Norwegian audience, yet the written languages are still so similar that if one can read Danish, one can read Norwegian, and vice versa. On a more personal note, the two national literatures happen to fall under my area of expertise in a way that Swedish literature does not. When I have chosen to downplay the national divide between Denmark and Norway instead of contrasting Danish and Norwegian literature, it is also because I have grown up partly in Scandinavia, partly in the United States—with a Danish father and a Norwegian mother—and I do not experience the two cultures as significantly different (especially not when viewed from across the Atlantic). Although Norway did not gain independence until 1905 and wealth until the 1970s, Denmark and Norway share a common cultural history and form similar small welfare states whose inhabitants tend to enjoy a high standard of living, share similar values, and—more important for this study—view themselves as minority cultures in a European context. When abroad, they represent themselves on the terms of more domineering nations, speaking foreign languages and referring to the cultural achievements of European nations greater than their own.

Aesthetic as well as thematic criteria have influenced the selection of the eight travelogues. They are all literary in the sense that they are written by people who emphasize their status as artists rather than as historians, journalists, or scientists. In their writing, this perspective emerges through narratives centered on a strongly autobiographical, interpreting, traveling "I"—more similar to the protagonist of a novel than to the withdrawn narrator of a report or a documentary. The literary writers rarely hold back when it comes to entering other people's minds, recounting events from others' perspectives through inner dialogue or *style indirect libre* (free indirect speech). They indulge in poetic language such as metaphors and alliteration. They project their own fantasies onto the observed through personification, and they dramatize and create narrative wholeness through their choices of genres and subgenres. The subgenres include fairy tales, allegories, and recounted dreams, whereas the main genre tends to border on the novel, stressing the inner development of the traveler. The twentieth-century novelization of the travelogue is furthermore an integral part of the literary travelogue's historical development. In this study, Axel Jensen's *Ikaros* constitutes the exemplary Scandinavian mid-twentieth-century travelogue turned bildungsroman.

Thematically the travelogues depict a journey to a non-European country—with the term "journey" referring to real (rather than imaginary) travel to places the travelers are interested in seeing, but in which they do not intend to settle down. An exception to this definition of a travelogue journey is Isak Dinesen's *Out of Africa,* depicting the author's seventeen years of settlement in Kenya. I have made a special case for Dinesen as I have wanted to take into consideration issues of gender, nationality, and history in each of this book's three parts. Aside from being a personal favorite, *Out of Africa* lends itself only too well to questions of gender and national belonging for it to be omitted. In addition it appears, both nationally and internationally, to be the most frequently discussed Scandinavian work of literature in a postcolonial setting.

Since the main premise for this book is based on a postcolonial view of the world as divided into a "first" and a "third" world, journeys to non-European countries do not include countries such as the United States. Although American Indians may be regarded as cultural Others, the United States did not form part of Europe's colonial Other—and was not the object of European imperialism—in the nineteenth and twentieth centuries treated in this study.

This type of study, of course, invites objections against periodization. Admittedly, depicting the passage of time as falling into distinct eras contains an element of arbitrariness. Furthermore, when it comes to the specific periodization, scholarship on travelogues often relies on World War I, rather than the turn of the century, as a main boundary marker.[6] Yet, arguing for my choices of historical parameters allows, I think, for meaningful and necessary discussions of the individual travelogues, with this historicizing aspect ultimately constituting a significant part of the analyses throughout the book.

Picking eight travelogues for the study of more than a century and a half of travel is also problematic. An alternative method could have been to include more text examples in my study, but I have chosen quality over quantity in the sense that I have wanted to be more thorough rather than cursory with each particular literary text. In terms of quality, I have to a high degree granted representative status to texts whose authors are already canonized—through Scandinavian literary histories, canonization lists, and literary awards (such as the Nobel Prize, won by Hamsun and Johannes V. Jensen and for which Isak Dinesen was nominated). A primary desire behind using the canon as a point of departure is wanting to emphasize the degree to which national literature exists in a global, geopolitical context where colonialism and imperialism play an important part—also in the case of Danish and Norwegian literature. This interrelatedness need not be pointed out through travelogues—it can, as Homi K. Bhabha has shown, be read into domestic novels as well—but the travelogue is nonetheless a genre par excellence when it comes to emphasizing a national author's involvement with the world outside Europe.

The one exception to focusing on canonized authors is Elisabeth Jerichau-Baumann. It is no coincidence that both women writers treated here ultimately constitute exceptions. Women writers have, as Anka Ryall points out in *Odyssevs i skjørt* (Odysseus in a Skirt), influenced the Western travelogue since the latter half of the nineteenth century, but neither women nor travelogues are commonly canonized.[7]

Postcolonial Theory

Viewed from a Foucauldian discourse analytical perspective, Niebuhr's project was anything but politically innocent. In *Imperial Eyes,* Mary Louise Pratt argues that it was indeed the scientific expeditions of the Enlightenment era that brought about a paradigmatic change in European epistemology, facilitating Western imperialism. A new form of Eurocentered "planetary" consciousness arose with scientific projects and journeys, such as those of Swedish naturalist Carl Linnaeus and French geographer Charles Marie de la Condamine (Pratt, 5). Linnaeus's botanizing, for instance, forced a Western classificatory scientific order upon the entire planet, one that allowed Europeans to disregard the "vernacular peasant knowledge" of non-European cultures (ibid.). According to Pratt, the scientific and sentimental travelogues that replaced older survival literature not only register but also contribute to this structural shift in knowledge and power. In her analysis of travel writing covering the period from 1750 to 1980, Pratt's predominant theme is "how travel books by Europeans about non-European parts of the world went (and go) about creating the 'domestic subject' of Euroimperialism" (4).

Pratt's points are similar to those of Edward Said in *Orientalism*. Said, too, argues on Foucauldian discourse theoretical terms, emphasizing the relationship between knowledge and power, and between scientific expeditions, travelogues, and imperialism. Said's prime example in this context is the Napoleonic invasion of Egypt in 1798, which he sees as "in many ways the very model of a truly scientific appropriation of one culture by another" (42). The scientific efforts accompanying the invasion resulted in the comprehensive account, the *Description de l'Égypte* (1809–23), which can be read as a scientific travelogue, similar to those of Niebuhr and Linnaeus. In addition it served, claims Said, as a discursive model setting the parameters for subsequent Orientalist literature, including real and imaginary travel accounts (Said, 88). Thus, Said and Pratt argue according to the same logic, although their geographical and generic interests vary. Said discusses an Orientalist consciousness, whereas Pratt discusses a planetary consciousness; Said divides the world into Europe and the Orient, but Pratt divides it into the West and the rest (allowing her to focus on Africa and South America); and although Said tends to read all texts as constituting one common discursive practice, Pratt zooms in on the literary travelogue, its historical development, and its oppressive power vis-à-vis its depicted objects.[8]

Generally, postcolonial discourse theory proves problematic when held up against polyphonic texts. In addition, both Said's and Pratt's arguments—like those of many other postcolonialists—are vulnerable to criticism owing both to their reliance on and their reification of simple binaries. In her introduction Pratt admits that a totalizing view of the travelogues—

already dubbed "narratives of European superiority" (xi) and texts of "Euroimperialism" (2)—"would reaffirm metropolitan authority in its own terms" (5). In her subsequent considerations of heterogeneity and possible contestatory genres within the travelogues, her readings are finely nuanced, yet she constantly concludes with the same two categories suggested by her point of departure: empire and colony. Thus, her readings may also well prompt accusations that the violence she exerts on the literary texts as a reader is similar to the violence she accuses Western travelers (and travel writers) of exerting on non-European cultures. With *theoretical eyes,* she plows through the texts with only one purpose in mind: finding the relevant (for her thesis) aspects of each text. Ultimately, this reading allows her (rather tautologically) to place the travelogues within a single category of her binary system: the imperialistic, consisting of the West and the rest.

The strict postcolonial point of departure presupposes that Europe constitutes one homogeneous mass and that all Westerners are equally imperialistic. Gender and nationality allow only for subcategories within this system. When for instance a woman's writing is found to differ from that of a man, the feminine discourse is ultimately regarded as complementary. Similarly, when travelers of the 1970s write critically about the third world, describing it as ugly and monotonous, this is but the inverse of those claims to beauty, potential, and the need for Western civilization and interference that romanticist writers made two centuries earlier as the descriptions build on the same dichotomies. Pratt's postcolonial theoretical point of view in a sense "produces" the travel narratives in the same manner that, according to her main argument, European travel writing "produces" the colonial subject.

As a corrective to the binary point of view, one may draw on postcolonialists such as Homi K. Bhabha. Bhabha points to hybridity, in-betweenness, borders, and peripheries in terms of geography, race, and ethnicity. Often these "third spaces" constitute a privileged point of view from which Western narratives about history, modernity, and nationality may be deconstructed.[9] While Bhabha applies these categories to the colonized world, they also pertain to peripheral European nations such as Denmark and Norway—not least Norway, which did not gain political independence until 1905.

INTRODUCTION xix

Pratt operates with more stable dichotomies than Bhabha, especially when it comes to the West. Yet, if one applies her notions of "contestatory" and "autoethnographic" expressions to Denmark and Norway, and not only to non-Western countries, one may also gain a more insightful understanding of Scandinavian travelogues in particular. Hence, it is this book's argument that Pratt's thought-provoking interpretations form an innovative point of departure for an analysis of Danish and Norwegian travelogues, not only as texts building on and contributing to a European hegemonic discourse concerning the cultural Other, but also as "contestatory expressions" vis-à-vis the binary models upon which much postcolonial theory relies. Just as Pratt presents oral histories and *testimonios* as "contestatory expressions from the site of imperial intervention, long ignored in the metropolis" (2), Danish and Norwegian travelogues may be viewed as a type of literary expressions from the European periphery that problematize the category of "Europe" or "the West." The travelogues are what Pratt calls "autoethnographic expressions" in that their self-representational aspects are in dialogue with the European metropolis/center (7).[10] Not only is the Danish and Norwegian gaze directed at the non-European cultural Other determined by the *imperial eyes* of such European cultural and political powers as France and England, but so is the gaze directed at the Self. Scandinavians often identify with their British and French counterparts vis-à-vis the cultural Other. But they also often identify with the cultural Other vis-à-vis domineering European powers.

As Pratt points out, autoethnographic texts often "constitute a group's point of entry into metropolitan literate culture" (7–9). This aim and hope becomes clear when, as cited earlier, Niebuhr's travelogue rather oxymoronically is celebrated as "Danish world literature." Similarly, Norwegian social anthropologist and cultural critic Thomas Hylland Eriksen, in a recent article on Norwegian travel literature, calls on his compatriots to immerse themselves in, and reach for the standards of, English travelogues.[11] These are indications of how Scandinavians constantly read and write themselves into a European context. In the literary realm, they have in a sense been left out since Europe—or the West—hardly has considered Scandinavian literature part of "world literature" since the Modern Breakthrough of the late nineteenth century produced writers like Henrik Ibsen and August Strindberg.[12] The peripheral status granted to

Scandinavian literature, however, is ambiguous. In terms of literary quality one wishes to produce "world literature" and enter into a two-way dialogue with the metropolis. Yet, in terms of self-representation, the travelogues also express a need for a separate Nordic identity. An ongoing source of frustration expressed in Danish and Norwegian travel literature is that the traveling subject is assumed to be French, English, or American.

The Field in Denmark and Norway

In terms of earlier research on the topic of Nordic literary travel depictions, Lars Handesten's *Litterære rejser* (Literary Journeys) constitutes an impressive examination of Danish travel literature written between 1790 and 1980. *Litterære rejser* is a national literary history of travelogues, focusing on the texts' existential and poetic dimensions (as indicated by Handesten's subtitle: *Poetik og erkendelse i danske digteres rejsebøger*). Arne Melberg's more recent essay *Å reise og skrive* (To Travel and Write) covers more than sixty modern travelogues.[13] Using Friedrich Nietzsche as his point of departure, Melberg reads travel literature as individual expressions in which each traveler represents the modern person, trying to make sense of his or her experiences in the world. Thus categories of gender, class, nationality, generation, and age largely remain unexplored.

Both Handesten's and Melberg's studies are seminal within the field in a Scandinavian context. In contrast to Handesten's book, however, it is the aim of this book to read Danish and Norwegian travelogues within a broader context of Western travelogues and postcolonial theory. The national aspect is still constitutive, albeit relativized and problematized. And as opposed to Melberg's essay grouping Scandinavian travel literature with that of other Western nations, anchoring his readings in a general philosophical discussion of European modernity (1900–today), this study sets out to distinguish between travelogues along axes of time and place. Throughout, I will point out what might be particularly characteristic of Danish and Norwegian literature and what the authors themselves found to characterize their own nations—not just in opposition to non-European nations, but also in opposition to central European or Western nations.

Journeys from Scandinavia, then, is a comparative and postcolonial study that is interested less in ontological questions than in questions pertaining to cultural studies, placing the travelogues not only in relation to the author as an individual but in relation to a historical, sociopolitical reality. In terms of historical specificity, I distinguish between various epochs of modernity, comparing and contrasting (1) nineteenth-century romanticist, Orientalist travelogues, (2) early-modern twentieth-century primitivist travelogues, and (3) twentieth-century late-modern, or postmodern, travelogues. In terms of national specificity I seek to point out fraught positions arising as the travelers' native countries are located on the European periphery rather than to establish a core Danish or Norwegian national identity. In this sense, my study is postnational.[14]

The Genre

Travel literature is a hybrid genre containing autobiographical, novelistic, essayistic, and journalistic elements. In terms of disciplines, it has anthropological, psychological, political, historical, and literary ambitions. And as indicated by my chronological presentation and periodization, the genre is in constant flux, responding to ever-changing ideologies and market contours. For literary scholars, the relationship between the travelogue and the novel—between factual prose and fiction—constitutes a recurring field of investigation. As Percy G. Adams puts it in his extensive study of the mutual evolution of travel literature and the novel, one could argue that both genres have become exhausted literary forms. Yet: "By no means... have the novel and the *récits de voyage* ceased to evolve, or to evolve together; for the journey motif—real or fictional—is still the most significant, whether geographical, spiritual, psychological, or intellectual."[15]

In their introduction to *The Cambridge Companion to Travel Writing*, Peter Hulme and Tim Youngs present the relationship between the genres as "close and often troubling" (6). On the one hand, they point out, the two genres have always shared certain similarities: "Travel writing and the novel, especially in its first-person form, have often shared a focus on the centrality of the self, a concern with empirical detail, and a movement through time and place which is simply sequential" (ibid). On the other hand, as several articles in Hulme and Youngs's anthology show, it is possible to historicize the convergences and divergences between the travelogue and the novel. Tracing the development of travelogues written between 1880 and 1940, British literary scholar Helen Carr, for instance, notes that during this period, the travelogues became increasingly subjective, often functioning as "an alternative form of writing for novelists."[16] At the same time, she views travelogues written between 1880 and 1900 as falling into a realist tradition, and those written between 1900 and World War I as turning less didactic and increasingly literary. During the interwar years, finally, "the literary travel book had become the dominant form" (75).

At a most basic level of representation it is, of course, impossible to draw a distinct line between reality and fiction, between, for instance, the autobiographical novel and the literary autobiography. On the one hand nonfictional genres—documentaries, reports, journals, and the like—are always literary constructions, building on the same narrative strategies as fictional genres, a point that has been made rather convincingly by Hayden White in *Metahistory*. Viewed from the point of view of the novel, one could also argue that fictional genres constantly explore their own boundaries. As Mikhail Bakhtin has shown, it is in the nature of the novel to *remain* novel by pushing on the dichotomy between fact and fiction, by parodying itself, and by parodying other genres, including the travelogue.[17]

In a Scandinavian context extending more broadly than the period Helen Carr discusses, I see the relationship between travel literature and the novel as having come full circle. In its first phase—through the nineteenth century—the novel absorbed and parodied other genres while centering on the development of a main character. Meanwhile the travelogue sought to relate information about distant places only the travel writer had had the privilege to visit. When pointing to the author's own person, it was to illustrate his or her genius in turning the seen into a poetic or ethnographically enchanting picture. Its aim was *not* to claim that the author-traveler had developed into a full-fledged individual during the course of his journey. During a second, modernistic phase, the novel receiving most critical attention turned autonomous, experimentally dwelling on its own aesthetics. During this twentieth-century phase, the literary travelogue increasingly took on the role of the premodernist novel—the bildungsroman—presenting the linear development of a main character's inner and outer journey.

In the third and current postmodern phase, the novel has once again turned outside its autonomous realm, annexing and problematizing "reality." The genres of novel and travelogue merge, and traditional (modernist) genre definitions become problematic.

A final generic consideration is that of the relationship between text and paratext. As Gérard Genette has pointed out in *Palimpsests,* a paratextual label does not necessarily determine whether a text is read as fact or fiction, as autobiographical or not: "Determining the generic status of the text is not the business of the text but that of the reader, or the critic, or the public. Those may well choose to reject the status claimed for the text by the paratext" (4).

From the author's side, the tension possibly arising between text and paratext may be intentional or unintentional. Norwegian author Erlend Loe's postmodernist project *L* seems to warrant a deliberate play with genres, but it could also be a matter of novels selling better than travelogues[18]—just as travelogues traditionally have sold better than essay collections.[19]

In an attempt to tackle the problem of distinguishing between fact and fiction, I have, in choosing a text corpus for this project, used Philippe Lejeune's notion of an autobiographical contract.[20] If the narrator, the protagonist, and the author are the same person, and this person describes a journey he or she has made, I consider the work an autobiographical travelogue. Whether the text, then, is labeled as a novel or a travelogue—as fiction or fact—becomes one of many factors pointing to a crisis in epistemology and representation at given historical moments.

Textual Organization

The book is divided into three parts based on literary historical chronology: romanticism, modernism, and postmodernism. Each part, in turn, analyzes two or three travelogues. In addition, each part begins with a brief discussion of the travel destinations and types of travelogues characterizing that particular time period.

Part I treats Romantic travelogues written by artists who admittedly went to Constantinople to satisfy an Orient-craving market of readers at home. Both Hans Christian Andersen and the painter Elisabeth Jerichau-Baumann present themselves as artists in search of exotic, marketable motives. Being of Polish descent, Jerichau-Baumann furthermore allows us to explore questions of hybridity. As a subject who cannot take her national identity for granted, Jerichau-Baumann spends as much effort defining herself in terms of stereotypical ethnographic terms as she does defining her Oriental objects. Finally, in the context of romanticism, I place Knut Hamsun's travelogues—written at the turn of the century—as the culminating point within this paradigm. Hamsun taps into the romanticist tropes and traditions with irony, using and inverting them at the same time. And as he exhausts them, he opens up the European Self for discussions and criticism, of its presence in other parts of the world, and of its means of constructing and (mis)representing the Orient.

Part II provides a view of early-twentieth-century primitivist travelogues. Unlike their nineteenth-century counterparts, Johannes V. Jensen, Isak Dinesen, and Axel Jensen depict travelers leaving their civilized homelands, not in search of poetic material, but in search of their own authentic selves. The two Jensen travelogues depict macho men attempting to get in contact with their own identities, bodies, and desires through exposure to danger, sun, and exotic women. As the modern travelers dig deeper into their existential selves, their journeys also extend farther away than those of their romanticist predecessors—toward the Far East and the African heartland. Humor, irony, and sarcasm play a great part in these travelogues. The two Jensens further develop the tradition of Hamsunian irony, playing up the distance between themselves as narrators, protagonists, and implied authors. Dinesen, on the other hand, uses humor to establish not distance but proximity between herself and the natives. In her text, the same humor brings together the narrator and her reader while it also seeks to establish a distinct Nordic national trait exempting her from accusations of British colonial injustice in Kenya.

Part III focuses on modern, postcolonial travel literature with "postcolonial" serving not only as a term emphasizing a theoretical perspective on literature but also as a historical term, referring to the world as it appears after the decolonization of the 1950s and 1960s. Clearly, it is in the nature of a study written in the beginning of the twenty-first century to ask in what ways recent postmodern travel writing has responded to postcolonial criticism. The travel narratives written after the 1980s respond not only to a sense of postcolonial, imperialistic, and nationalistic guilt and complicity but also to the challenge that there are supposedly no more blank spots on the map. What, at a point in time of globalization and political sensitivity, can the travel writer explore and depict that has not already been described—and that will not come across as politically insensitive? Some of the strategies travel writers have developed to tackle these issues are increased self-reflectivity, estrangement tactics, and parody.

The questions this study poses in a postcolonial theoretical context, then, revolve around travelers stemming from what might be considered minority, or peripheral, nations within Europe. Based on this peripheral status, one of the most important issues regarding Scandinavian writers becomes the degree to which Pratt's notion of "transculturation" plays a role, not just in case of the depicted Other, but also in case of the writing Self.[21] Exploring this question, I situate postcolonial theory within a broader field of both anthropology and narratology. Often, as we shall see, the authors write *about* journeys and peoples abroad, while writing themselves *into* particular national or international traditions and communities at home.

Postcolonial theory builds on the assumption that modern Europeans are engaged in a constant process of defining our national, European Self in opposition to a non-European Other. We are permanently trapped in a web of hegemonic discursive practices and are able to see the cultural Other only as a stereotype. The point made by those propagating Niebuhr's Enlightenment style, by contrast, is that Niebuhr avoids the synthesizing involved in cultural representation, whether it be done in the name of cultural relativism or condemnation. Instead, he reacts with sincerity and openness to every encounter and experience. In his descriptions, he postpones judgment, viewing things from different angles and allowing them to have an impact on his initial prejudices. Still, he is part of an expedition that set out to categorize all aspects of the world based on a European encyclopedic and taxonomic framework. His *Reisebeschreibung nach Arabien und andern umliegenden Ländern* contains numerous of Baurenfeind's etchings illustrating how many different types of a certain object the Arabs have—whether headgear, board games, or musical instruments.

The impetus behind postcolonial theory is to alter a current state of affairs through criticism. Although it is impossible for people to completely disregard the epistemological paradigms that constitute their world, they may confront these cultural categories with questions of construction and complicity. It is the argument of this book that travel writers have done so—to various extents—also after the Enlightenment. Their tendency to confirm or reject stereotypes have varied, and close readings of their texts reveal a wide range of strategies allowing them to order, systematize, and poeticize their experiences. In my readings of each travelogue, I focus on four aspects in particular: (1) the overall structure of the travelogue and its generic placement vis-à-vis the novel; (2) the construction of the travelogue's "I" and the three positions this "I" holds as the traveling protagonist, the narrator, and the implied author; (3) depictions of encounters with the cultural Other in what Pratt calls "contact zones" and the stylistics used in these depictions (the encounters, I might add, include people *and* landscapes—not least in arrival scenes); and (4) depictions of the Self in autoethnographic representations aimed at the author's reading audience back home.

A final glance back at Baurenfeind's etching regards its emplacement as it graces *Weekendavisen*'s front page in 2003—accompanied by the rather self-congratulatory article (with "self" here referring to the perceived national Self). In this situation, the Danes drinking their morning coffee, looking at the exotic depiction, have a choice between several viewing positions. They may look at the etching and simply find it amusing, exotic, and reassuring. Like the etching's male figure, they may be absorbed in the activity and *play along*. After all, the etching's context, in this case, is a newspaper, which—according to Benedict Anderson in *Imagined Communities*—is one of the main media constituting the imagined community that is the nation.

It is, however, this book's aim to assume a different *questioning* viewing position. With typical postcolonial ambivalence, the study operates within the categories it claims to deconstruct. It reinstates the categories of the Danish, Norwegian, European, and Western, and on top of that it focuses on canonized writers. This, however, is done to destabilize the known and taken for granted by viewing the national canons from a new angle, emphasizing in particular the intercultural relations that contribute to establish modern identities. This is in part achieved by holding the national literature up against postcolonial theory and the literature of other nations. The goal of the project, then, is to emulate the woman in the middle of Baurenfeind's etching: dancing along while confronting the viewer with an open gaze. Her position is one of both–and—unabsorbed, she is simultaneously *in* and *out* of the etching. She no doubt participates in the group's praxis, but she also tries to gain an outside perspective upon it—through the gaze of the Other.

PART I

ROMANTIC JOURNEYS TO THE ORIENT

Romantic Journeys to the Orient

A Brief History of Travel

When it comes to the genealogy of Western travel and travelogues, literary scholars tend to regard Homer's *Odyssey* and mediaeval pilgrimages as prototypical examples.[1] Marco Polo's journey to China in the 1200s marks a late-medieval budding interest in foreign ways of life, while Christopher Columbus's voyage to America in 1492 constitutes yet another turning point, reflecting both a new type of travel writing and a new type of scientific endeavor, the goal of which was the exploration and mapping of the world (Hulme and Youngs, 3). In the seventeenth century, Grand Tour travelers emerged as a group of young men leaving northern Europe (especially England) to travel southward through continental Europe on an educational journey. In France, Germany, Austria, and Italy—not least in classical Rome—the Grand Tourist sowed his wild oats, refined his manners, and explored and discovered his cultural roots whereupon he could return back north as a full-fledged European adult.[2]

Overlapping with Grand Tourism, the eighteenth century gave rise to a new type of scientific travel, with scientists such as Carl Linnaeus and his disciples exploring the interior parts of non-European continents. Together, toward the end of the eighteenth century, the scientific and the Grand Tour traveler gave way to the sentimental traveler and the travelogue. What may be regarded as early romanticist travelers and travelogues tend to focus not only on the outward world but also on the emotions its sights and experiences evoked in the traveler himself. What emerges is a subjective, emotional traveler eager to render the picturesque, the sublime, and the beautiful.[3]

Since the focus of this study is the *literary* travelogue, I will begin by studying the descendants of the sentimental traveler: the nineteenth-century romantic travelers Hans Christian Andersen, Elisabeth Jerichau-Baumann, and Knut Hamsun. As opposed to the sentimental traveler of the late 1700s who made a Grand Tour to what was perceived as the cradle of European culture and civilization, the romantic traveler of the latter half of the nineteenth century went *beyond* Europe.

The year 1840 generally marks the beginning of tourism and the *voyage en Orient*, when increased mobility coupled with the decline of the Ottoman Empire placed countries such as Turkey and Egypt within the European traveler's reach. Andersen, Jerichau-Baumann, and Hamsun represent three stages of romantic Orientalism: Andersen the stage at its very beginning, when it is still deeply rooted in the classical Grand Tour tradition; Baumann at a stage capturing both national romanticism and a modern form of realism; and Hamsun at a neoromantic stage, when his writings become based on an ironic worldview, indicating contempt as well as nostalgia for bygone days of romanticism.

The Travelogue Genre

Generically, the romanticist travelogues discussed in Part I carry several common features. They are centered on an artist subject traveling through a landscape over time, compiling impressions to be represented to a home audience. The depictions of foreign landscapes, cityscapes, peoples, and cultures are to serve as evidence both of the foreign cultures themselves and of the traveler's sensibility. Arranged in various subgenres—from fairy tale to political discourse—within the travelogue, they point to the artist's capacity to absorb impressions and represent them in an engaging format, evoking laughter, tears, and awe. Andersen's, Jerichau-Baumann's, and Hamsun's depictions point to the travel writer's emotional and intellectual capacity—whether this be presented as naive, cunning, or self-deprecating. Yet, in none of these romanticist cases does the traveling protagonist develop and change along the journey. His or her identity is regarded as a stable core identity. Not until Hamsun do we detect a shift toward this type of modern sensibility. In terms of inner development, Constantinople prompts Hamsun's traveler to gain new and surprising insight into the world. In terms of the literariness of the travelogue, Hamsun's narrator moves toward the linear form of a nineteenth-century novel as well as a modern epistemological uncertainty. While his travelogue still, to a large extent, consists of fragmented impressions gathered along the journey, Hamsun uses various fictional strategies to create suspense, climactic turns, and overall linearity. Whenever he does so, he bases these linear trajectories on his own inner imagination—on paranoia and dream imagery—a strategy that will be further developed by the travel writers of the twentieth century.

ONE

Discovering His Inner Turk
Hans Christian Andersen's Commodification of the Exotic

ANDERSEN ABSORBED LIKE A SPONGE. His entire oeuvre—from fairy tales to drama to travel accounts—reflects his uncanny ability to soak up the mental, material, and cultural preoccupations of his era. Even in the shortest of depictions, one has the sense that Andersen squeezes his sponge and lets out an entire epoch's cultural and aesthetic issues—never reducing their complexity, but leaving opposite standpoints unresolved and ending his accounts on an ambivalent note. Søren Kierkegaard may well have launched his writing career by expressing his contempt for Andersen's lack of a coherent worldview, but readers today, emphasizing his premodernist aesthetic, find Andersen's tendency to absorb the various discourses of his age less problematic than intriguing.[1]

In Andersen's life and oeuvre, traveling occupies a predominant position. "At rejse er at leve" (to travel is to live), he declared, and the romanticist author lived up to this dictum, embarking on approximately thirty journeys during his seventy-year life span, spending a total of ten years abroad.[2] Beginning with domestic journeys, moving on to neighboring Scandinavian countries, heading down through Europe, and eventually moving beyond the European continent, Andersen in the end traveled as far east as Constantinople and Smyrna (present-day Istanbul and Izmir) and as far south as Tangier in North Africa. These journeys have resulted in such a wealth of travel accounts that one may conclude that for Andersen, to travel was not only to live but also to write—or maybe writing should be placed as an intermediary term: to travel is to write, which in turn is to live.

The focus of this chapter is *En Digters Bazar* (A Poet's Bazaar, 1842) depicting Andersen's first journey beyond the European continent to Turkey. The travelogue's title has previously been regarded as a well-chosen indicator of the text's content and form. In terms of content it conjures up a sense of the exotic and sensual; with regard to genre, it suggests a series of unconnected portraits and impressions. As noted in one Danish literary history, "Systematization is of no concern for this traveler."[3] Yet, what tends to be overlooked is the degree to which Andersen—through this title—signals a commercialization and commodification not only of art but also of the cultural Other. The first part of this chapter will thus regard the text from a nineteenth-century point of view—that is, within its own historical horizon—and focus on what I will call Andersen's bazaar poetics.

The second part of this chapter is inspired by Andersen's bicentennial. In the case of "Andersen 2005" and the so-called worldwide celebration, commodification remains a relevant focus for this chapter. Now, however, it must be applied to Andersen himself. Since 2004, the Danish media have held up Andersen as a cultural icon symbolizing innocence and cross-cultural openness. *En Digters Bazar*, in particular, has been promoted as a model and inspiration for attaining friendship and understanding between Danes and Arabs. Yet, one could just as well read the text concentrating on its Orientalist and Euroimperialist aspects. The second part of this chapter, then, situates *En Digters Bazar* in the ideological landscape emerging between two poles: between that of a radical postcolonial stance in which all white, European, male travelers are seen as suspect imperialists, on the one hand; and that of a national, excessively self-congratulatory project, on the other. Finally, I will consider the use of Andersen's sketches as illustrative material in his travelogues—a practice dating back to the middle of the twentieth century.

Bazaar Poetics

En Digters Bazar covers nine months of travel during which Andersen—in 1840 and 1841—journeyed from Denmark, down through Germany to Italy, Greece, and Turkey, and returned up the Danube River to Budapest, Vienna, and Prague, and finally back to Denmark through Germany. The travelogue is divided into six geographical sections presenting the journey chronologically. Each section, in turn, is composed of short chapters containing a hodgepodge of genres, ranging from lyrical depictions to fairy tales, poetry, prose poems, short stories, and dialogues. Andersen, in fact, makes an explicit point of his romanticist goal of breaking through previously established genre conventions. Whereas his diaries reflect pecuniary and physical concerns—referring to hotel prices, toothaches, and a sore penis—his travelogue focuses enthusiastically on what he has seen and experienced, leaving us with the impression of an upbeat, sensitive artist.[4]

In terms of content Andersen is up against earlier travel accounts; Goethe, for instance, he muses, has already described the Roman carnival to completion, rendering a new depiction superfluous.[5] Andersen, in turn, provides but a *sketch* on this subject—a solution pointing to *form* as one of his main strategies for originality. A few pages later he introduces a chapter subtitled "En Dialog" (A Dialogue) with the following claim to originality: "One has gotten travelogues in so many forms, but still not as dialogue, I believe." He then depicts a day trip from Rome to the countryside from the point of view of the horses drawing the carriage (1:178).[6]

Clearly, the travel account is to prove Andersen's status as a romantic poet, engaging the reader in constant games of formal experimentation, changing points of view, and temporal shifts. Brimming with metapoetic reflections, Andersen also emphasizes his aim of embracing modernity. *En Digters Bazar* is ultimately situated at the intersection of fantasy, feeling and reason; West and East; tradition and modernity; poetry and prose; art and commerce. In each of these constellations, it is the latter concept that breaks with earlier romanticism, that is, the emphasis on reason, travel to the Orient, modernity, prose, and commerce.

When it comes to a modern aesthetic, one of the most commonly cited passages in *En Digters Bazar* is Andersen's enthusiastic depiction of his first railroad journey.[7] Various scholars have pointed to this textual celebration of the steam engine and the newly constructed railroad.[8] Andersen describes seeing a railroad for the very first time in Magdeburg, Germany, experiencing what he calls railroad fever. Merely entering a bustling railway station prompts excitement, while the sound of the train's departure signal evokes death imagery: "The signal whistle does not sound beautiful, it has much in common with the swan song of a pig at the moment when a knife forces its way through its throat" (1:42).[9] Aboard the train, Andersen declares that riding on "Tryllebaandet" (the magic rail) is as he expects flying would be, albeit much more comfortable. Looking out the window, he finally comments on what it is like to look at a moving depth perspective. While objects at a distance seem to be standing still, those closest to the train are but a blur, causing an aching or straining of the eye (ibid.). The depiction culminates in poetic insight, with the narrator contemplating the role reason must now play in poetry: "In the kingdom of poetry, feeling and fantasy are not the only rulers, they have a brother, equally powerful, called reason" (1:44).[10]

Yet, in order to illuminate a broader range of aspects of Andersen's poetics, I would like to move on to the metapoetic reflections the author derives from modern, romanticist music. Franz Liszt's concerts in Hamburg constitute an aesthetic frame in the travelogue, with Andersen attending them on both his outward- and homeward-bound journey. Liszt's boundary-breaking artistry thoroughly impresses Andersen, who sees and hears in the composer's performance of "Valse Infernale" the need to combine genius with technical skill:

> Our era is no longer that of fantasy and feeling, but that of reason. Technical skill in every art form and in every trade is now a common prerequisite for their execution... Everything technical—both materially and spiritually—is at its highest point of development in our era. (1:36)[11]

This statement recaptures the emphasis on rationality in the railroad conclusion, but Andersen then goes on to establish a link between art and geography implicating the modern poet's reliance on travel. Europe and the Orient, we find out, are of equal importance for the artist. They always have been, one may argue, but that to which Europe and the Orient refer has changed. Rather than emphasizing Europe's cultural cradle in the South—especially Rome—Andersen's reference is to Europe's industrial and economic centers in the North. Liszt's capacity to boldly define the limits for the art of his time is tied to his visits to London, "this great world-city of machines," and Hamburg, "this European trade office" (1:35–36). The Orient, on the other hand, is slipping from a realm of pure fantasy—that of *A Thousand and One Nights*—to one the traveler will visit and experience as reality.

Andersen's interpretation of Liszt's music captures this ambivalence toward the Orient as a geographical site as well as a state of mind. As a means of introducing the reader to his text, Andersen the narrator presents

Liszt's performance as an overture to Andersen the traveler's journey. In Liszt's "Tone-Billeder" (tonal images), he foresees the entire journey, from leaving the well known to arriving in the unknown: "Tones I did not know, tones for which I have no words, indicated the Orient, the land of fantasy, the poet's second homeland!" (1:38).[12] Thus, the modern romanticist poet is one who travels, and in opposition to his Grand Tour predecessor, he does not seek out the great sites of antiquity. Rome and Athens no longer function to educate the traveler by showing him what he perceives as his own cultural heritage—his historical Self. Instead, the traveler seeks out his modern Self in Europe's big cities, as well as his cultural Other in the Orient. Technology, trade, and fantasy combine as the traveler, in short, absorbs the influences from the geographical sites representing each. This is the new, and I am admittedly misrepresenting the situation by presenting it as an either-or when it is, in fact, a both-and. Andersen travels during a time of transition and he pursues both the traditional and the modern, the European historical Self as well as the European modern Self *and* cultural Other. The mid-nineteenth-century means of transportation alone would make it impossible to skip the Grand Tour aspect of his journey.[13]

The development of Andersen's travelogue titles similarly captures a shift in emphasis, from insisting on the newest aspect of his travels to more sober-mindedly considering their in-between status. His original working title for the travelogue was "Orientalske Aftener" (Oriental Evenings)[14]—a title that seems overzealous if not preposterous for a journey lasting a total of nine months, of which eleven days were spent outside Europe, in the so-called Orient. It could of course be justified by the notion that the Orient represents a state of mind: the actively poeticizing fantasy accompanying Andersen throughout his journey. Andersen's final title, though, with its emphasis on the bazaar, captures the extent to which *En Digters Bazar* is situated in a transitional era, emphasizing the Orient as both a mental and as a geographical site for him to explore as a real place entirely new to him and his readers. In the 1840s we are still far from the nostalgia setting in toward the turn of the century. With a reference to William Butler Yeats, we may say that Andersen is no old man "sailing to Byzantium"; instead, he is a man of his time embracing the reality of modern steam travel to Constantinople.

Traditionally, critics have focused on the exotic aspect of the bazaar—on how "the image of the bazaar prompts associations to a distant, exotic market with all its sensual experiences."[15] Yet, according to the text itself, the bazaar is not merely an exoticist Other located in opposition to the European Self. Rather, it is a site where East meets West, and where each nation has its own quarter. In the end, the bazaar is seen as functioning as a world of graspable dimensions lending itself to a comparative ethnographic study.[16]

In signifying a meeting ground between East and West, a "bazaar" reveals the preconditions for this meeting, namely, trade. A bazaar is, after all, a market where people come to buy and sell goods. In using this as his title, Andersen suggests not only how his own work is *like* a bazaar, containing a vast variety of literary goods, but also how it is the object *of* a bazaar—a commodity for sale in and of itself. At the time of publication, this implication prompted aesthetic annoyance. Noting the unpoetic aspect of the term, *Fædrelandet*'s critic insisted that "bazaar" was no suitable name for a poetic work, "for industry and poetry are of incongruous dimensions and cannot be brought under a common term."[17]

However, as the previous reference to Liszt shows, Andersen saw modern technology *and* financial trade as components of a modern romanticist aesthetic. And at Constantinople's Grand Bazaar he saw the poetic aspect of commerce, as well as the commercial aspect of poetry. This latter point—the commercial aspect of poetry—would remain a point of deliberation in Andersen's oeuvre. We recognize the theme from his "Skyggen" (The Shadow, 1847), for example, in which poetry—in the shape of a woman—lives isolated, atop a row of shops. This depiction, too, points to the commercialization of poetry, which has to pass through a type of marketplace to get out and find an audience.

Finally, with regards to the commercial aspect of the bazaar title, Andersen's own opportunity to travel to the Orient depended entirely on modern economics and trade interests. When he visited Constantinople, the Ottoman Empire had just become an open market through the Anglo-Turkish Commercial Treaty of 1838.[18] In the following years, similar agreements were made with other European countries, including Denmark—a fact of which Andersen was entirely aware and of which he informs his reader in a footnote: "During my stay in Constantinople, the trade agreement between His Majesty the King of Denmark and the Ottoman Port was signed" (2:109).[19]

Thus Andersen's travels and texts are embroiled in nineteenth-century economics and politics and may be read as products of—and as contributions to—European imperialism and Orientalism. This is the point at which I want to move on to the second part of this chapter in order to look at *En Digters Bazar* from a late-twentieth- and early-twenty-first-century point of view, emphasizing recent concerns with cross-cultural meetings.

The National Hero

The narrator of *En Digters Bazar* has the potential of being read as tolerant *and* prejudiced, honest *and* dishonest, politically innocent *and* politically implicated. To illustrate the span of these ideological readings, I will first consider the celebratory hype emerging in Denmark with Andersen's being launched as a worldwide icon by the Hans Christian Andersen 2005 Foundation, and more popularly being elected as "Alle Tiders Største Dansker" (The Greatest Dane of All Times) by the readers of *Berlingske Tidende* in 2004.

Especially since the publication of his two-volume Andersen biography in 2003, Jens Andersen has emerged as a natural Andersen expert in the public arena. In this context he often emphasizes Andersen's open and friendly attitude toward the Arab world based on a scene in *En Digters Bazar*. The scene is one in which Hans Christian Andersen is approaching Turkey aboard a series of steamships. First, on a ship taking him from Italy to Greece, Andersen spots a Persian on deck during nightfall. This and subsequent encounters with the Persian eventually function as a leitmotif in the text, leading the reader ever further toward the Orient, signaling this continent's appearance in the text long before the traveler actually gets there. Leaving from Malta, Andersen once again depicts a deck scene with the Persian, this time referring to him as "our" Persian. We are told he is lonesome, playing with his earrings and saber. Nobody talks to him, and he talks to nobody. Yet, the observant Andersen occasionally catches a smile about his lips and projects thoughts of a happy homecoming onto him.

The final encounter gains in momentum as it takes place on a new ship upon which Andersen and the Persian are the only passengers from the previous stretch. The two immediately recognize each other and feel a sense of comradeship. They exchange fruits, then phrases. Andersen points to the starry sky and recites the first line of Genesis in Hebrew. The Persian, in turn, answers in English: "Yes sir! Verily! Verily!" Andersen concludes the depiction of this scene with the following words: "That was our entire conversation. Neither one of us knew more; but we were good friends!" (1:236).[20]

In the depiction, the key ingredient is reciprocity: the exchange of objects, words, greetings, and the conclusion that the two are friends. Jens Andersen's conclusion is that Andersen (much like Niebuhr, as we saw in the introduction) is a person from the nation's past whose historical example can be held up as an ideal for cross-cultural understanding, openness, and communication. In his article in *Berlingske Tidende* celebrating Hans Christian Andersen's being voted "Alle Tiders Største Dansker," Jens Andersen sums up the meeting with the Persian—referred to as a "kærligt kulturmøde" (an affectionate cultural encounter)—with a plea to the rest of the nation: "We are, after all, able to understand each other—and meet despite cultural, political and religious differences. If we dare, that is. Hans Christian Andersen dared."[21]

While I find celebrating Andersen and inspiring Danes to be open in their encounters with Arabs and the rest of the world entirely commendable, the reading of the preceding scene strikes me as odd. Andersen no doubt captures the traveler's momentary goodwill and eagerness for friendly and somewhat meaningful exchanges. But the abundance of exclamation points—in the Persian's line and not least Andersen's concluding remark—also suggests irony, and an understanding that the two are but momentarily staging or playing at something that can be called a friendship. As Andersen so openly admits, after the exchange neither of them knew more. Andersen knows nothing about the Persian, and nothing about Persian culture, history, or language. Nor has the Persian gained any insight into Andersen's culture. And neither one feels bad about it. Promoted as a model for cross-cultural openness and understanding, the scene functions well as a feel-good anecdote when presented to a Danish audience at the beginning of the twenty-first century. Yet, as an example, it hardly leads to a greater understanding of the Arab world—neither for Andersen then, nor for Danes today.

The Seeing Man

Postcolonial theory provides a corrective to what may appear too unilaterally as a heroic traveler's innocence and openness abroad. For this, I will turn to Edward Said's *Orientalism* and Mary Louise Pratt's *Imperial Eyes*. Andersen is often depicted as "et se-menneske"—a man with the ability to absorb his surroundings visually and turn these scenes into writing.[22] According to *En Digters Bazar*'s traveler himself, the main purpose of his travel *is* seeing. On his return journey along the Danube, an exhausted traveler reflects on his writing process:

> While traveling I have to romp about from morning to evening, I must see, and always see! One cannot but wrap entire cities, peoples, mountains, and oceans into one's thoughts; always take, always store. There is no time to sing a single song! (2:158)[23]

In *Imperial Eyes,* however, Pratt stresses how "seeing" is never an innocent act, whether the traveler presents himself as a scientist observing nature or as a sentimental traveler taking in nature scenes for poetic inspiration. The position of traveling outside Europe to see, she insists, is inextricably linked to imperial conquest: "Only through a guilty act of conquest (invasion) can the innocent act of the anti-conquest (seeing) be carried out" (66). Pratt's point is that anti-conquest and seeing rather than constituting innocent acts, are strategies used by travel writers in an attempt to distance themselves from the project and guilt of empire. "Anti-conquest" refers to "the strategies of representations whereby European bourgeois subjects seek to secure their innocence in the same moment as they assert European hegemony" (Pratt, 7). To what degree then, we may ask, do Andersen and his traveling protagonist assert European hegemony in Turkey? To what degree is Andersen Pratt's "seeing man" defined by Pratt as "the European male subject of European landscape discourse—he whose imperial eyes passively look out and possess" (ibid.)?

Given that world trade and capitalism are viewed as pillars of European imperialism, Andersen is, of course, guilty. He would not be traveling to Turkey were it not for Europe's interest in the Ottoman Empire as a trading partner. The European representatives would not be there to host him. Similarly, he would not be in a position to bring knowledge about the Orient to a European reading audience if Europeans did not view the Orient as something to be known and that could be known.

Pratt argues, further, that not only passively possessing eyes but also the depiction of reciprocal vision—that is, the exchange of curious glances—is fundamentally imperialistic. Reciprocity, she argues, "has always been capitalism's ideology of itself" (ibid., 84). Thus any kind of reciprocal gesture, such as Andersen's exchange of glances, fruits, and phrases with the Persian, is rendered suspect. In her chapter on sentimental travelers, subtitled "The Mystique of Reciprocity," Pratt writes about Mungo Park's *Travels in the Interior Districts of Africa* (1799), a travel account she holds up as her exemplary text in the sentimental travel genre (ibid., 74–75). In her reading of this text and its narrative strategies, she arrives at the conclusion that "Park's everyday struggles, then, consist mainly of attempts to achieve reciprocity between himself and others," and her subsequent suggestion is that "his account figures the commercial expansion in whose name he traveled and wrote" and that, ultimately, "Park's expansionist commercial aspirations idealize themselves into a drama of reciprocity" (ibid., 81). Thus, she establishes a link between sentimental travel literature and Euroimperialism; sentimental travel literature is structured around a narrative of reciprocal exchanges, which in turn mirrors capitalist ideology. Again a link between art and commerce is established—this time by the postcolonial theorist associating European travelogues with imperialism.

Pratt's reading is full of sharp observations and her material is historically relevant and interesting. The problem, however, is the level of generalization. As Mungo Park's *Travels* is presented as the quintessential European sentimental travel account, we are led to believe that *En Digters Bazar* should be read in the same way. Pratt's insinuation—or suggestion—ends up turning every sentimental traveler and travel writer into a suspect, exploitative capitalist based on the argument that this is what the traveler is, if he—in his narrative—presents himself as someone aiming for reciprocity in the contact zone. In Andersen's case this seems extremely reductive, moralistic, and in need of a less monolithic, historicizing corrective. Reading Andersen, one is best served, I think, by finding a nuanced position that allows for a twenty-first-century critical perspective placing his text in a greater global context, while also allowing for an understanding of Andersen, in particular, as a nineteenth-century *Danish* artist.

Cosmopolitanism and Nationalism

In terms of nationality, the Scandinavian traveler's attitude changes during the course of the nineteenth century, moving along a trajectory from universalism to particularism—from cosmopolitanism (a.k.a. Europeanism) to nationalism.[24] While travelers at the turn of the century (as we shall see in chapter 3) wish to distinguish themselves from the French and English, Andersen finds it entirely natural to disregard his Danishness abroad. When he is taken for a German or an American, despite the fact that he tells people he is Danish, he notes this without further commentary or annoyance (2:55). In Constantinople Andersen lives at the Hôtel de la France, where he feels at home since it offers "European convenience and luxury" and German, French, and English newspapers (2:106). He refers to other Europeans as *Frankere* (Franks) and clearly identifies with, and accepts, all expressions of French culture. He compares the Grand Bazaar to the Palais-Royal in Paris; he notes that Sultan Mahmud overthrew the Janissaries and established French discipline and clothing (2:86); and he discusses Lamartine's *Voyage en Orient* with Europeanized Turks (2:108). Furthermore, he communicates with Italian- and French-speaking Turks (2:104), and he refers to "our" Danish consul—who is Italian (2:106).

It never occurs to Andersen to make a special case of his Danishness or to insist that the Turks approach him as a Dane. This is not to say that Andersen does not present himself as a Dane to his Danish reading audience. His travelogue abounds with references to Danish and Nordic objects used to relate the foreign to the known. Sometimes the comparisons are as straightforward as Turkish cypresses being likened in size to

Danish poplars (2:64). Other times the comparisons are more bizarre, as when Andersen describes Armenians as wearing hats that look like upside-down "Jydepotter" (Jutland pottery; 2:65). In general, his descriptions are comical in their striking particularity. Smyrna's streets come alive when Andersen describes them as so narrow that "the neighbor across could conveniently reach out from his window and grab a pinch of snuff from his neighbor's tin across the way" (2:64).[25] Aside from imagining what could happen, Andersen also has a sharp eye for the inanimate object as living body and, conversely, the living body as a thing. In Smyrna's main street, each of two ostriches is likened to "a worn suitcase on stilts upon which a bloody swan's neck was attached" (2:66).[26] Andersen is aware of his audience and knows that with a Danish audience he can draw on Danish culture but that for a non-Danish audience, he has to tap into a common European culture. We may say that Andersen in the 1840s is subject to the same marginalizing logic that governs present-day postcolonialism. Yet, the purpose of downplaying the European periphery is different.

Part of Andersen's undertaking is to travel and write himself into a European context. His dedications at the beginning of each section of his travelogue strongly indicate this legitimizing project. Yet, again Andersen is caught in a time of transition. Fraternizing with great European men may have been a natural feature of the classical Grand Tour during the age of high romanticism, but by the time Andersen travels and writes, references to Johann Ludwig Tieck, Felix Mendelssohn-Bartholdy, and Franz von Liszt as "my friends" were frowned upon by a Danish reading audience. The cosmopolitan project clashes with that of nationalism, and viewing oneself from the center rather than from the periphery simply comes across as conceited.

The second aspect of Andersen's identity upon which I want to comment is his profession as a poet. Pratt's exemplary sentimental traveler, Mungo Park, was commissioned (by the London-based Association for Promoting the Discovery of the Interior Parts of Africa) to explore West Africa as a potential market for British goods (Pratt, 69). Officially, then, Park traveled as an economic explorer, with the connection between art (his travelogue) and commerce being entirely overt. Andersen, on the other hand, traveled as a literary explorer and was not instructed or paid by anybody to search out a market for Danish goods. While Mungo Park may be exemplary of British colonial adventurers, Andersen may at best be exemplary of peripheral European travelers.

Andersen's Poeticizing Strategies

Finally, with regards to Andersen the poet, I want to make a point of his poeticizing strategy and insist on the reader's responsibility with regard to ambivalent texts. Andersen's method in writing what is often termed poetic realism consists of seeing and remembering. Seeing supplies the realistic aspect of his travelogue and is the main purpose of his travels, as we read in the earlier quotation about his manic seeing. The quote, however, continues with a reflection on the second aspect of his writing process—his remembering:

> It [the poetry] will come, I know! Inside things are seething and brewing, and when I am back in the good city of Copenhagen and have some cold compresses applied to my body and soul, then the flowers will shoot forward. (2:158)[27]

Writing in the romanticist vein is described as a threefold process consisting of seeing, inner seething and brewing, and applying cold compresses. While the final cold compresses function as a metaphor for applying cold reason and structure to the amassing of visual material, the feverish state of inner seething and brewing refers to Andersen's remembering. The memory associations may be factual or fictional, and may be of a personal or historical kind. In southern Europe, remembering often consists of projecting figures from classical literature onto Italian or Greek landscapes, while in Turkey it consists of recalling scenes from the Old Testament, from classical Greek literature, and from *A Thousand and One Nights*. Andersen's first view of the Asian coastline outside Smyrna, for instance, activates memories of Moses's and Jesus's lives, Homer's songs, and Oriental fairy tales (2:64). When applied to the Orient, this memory process constitutes what Said, in short, has termed Orientalism.

According to Said, "Every writer on the Orient...assumes some Oriental precedent, some previous knowledge of the Orient, to which he refers and on which he relies" (Said, 20). Said's criticism is that this process allows the nineteenth-century European traveler to claim authority over the Orient in its present state: "At most, the 'real' Orient provoked a writer to his vision; it very rarely guided it" (ibid., 22). Andersen no doubt Orientalizes the Orient—just as he Hellenizes Greece—yet, it is also worthwhile noticing his moments of surprise when the "real" Orient in fact does guide his description. Sailing to Constantinople, for example, he observes a young, animated storyteller on deck and concludes: "here was merriment quite different from what I had imagined regarding the solemn Turk" (2:72).[28] The Turks similarly surprise Andersen with their honesty in financial matters: "The Turks are the most good-natured, the most honest of people" (2:77).[29]

If we compare Andersen's associative process in the Orient with that in southern Europe, we find that the Orient activates memories and projections linked to notions of Oriental eroticism and Mohammedanism (the nineteenth-century term for Islam). Time and again, realistic depictions of poverty, brutality, death, and the grotesque are suspended by harem and houri fantasies. A chapter titled "En Tyrkisk Skizze" (A Turkish Sketch) includes a reflection upon this aestheticizing process and serves as a particularly illustrative example of Andersen's poetic realism. Over the course of one page, a scene of poverty metamorphoses into an erotic fantasy. Specifically, the poet turns the poverty-stricken street—with dogs fighting and ripping at a carcass, and with little children running around half naked, playing on the corpse of a bloody, skinned horse—into a turban-clad Turk's fantasy about his extreme sexual vigor, his harem, and his climactic praise of Allah (2:94–95).

Andersen is well aware of the challenge this aestheticizing project has presented, and he proudly delivers a metapoetic reflection, laying his poetics out as a three-step process. First, he presents what he has seen: "I render the picture as I have seen it." Second, he struggles to demonstrate his poetic genius by finding beauty even in this scene: "But is there no ray of poetry in this entire abomination!" he asks rhetorically, significantly ending his question with an exclamation point rather than a question mark. Third, after having activated his memories, he is able—in true romanticist fashion—to evoke nature's capacity to create an organic whole: "Yes, for I recall the great vines that stretch their thick stems up along the wooden wall of the individual houses, spreading like a roof of leaves across the street to the neighboring house, which it then decorates with its greenery!"

(2:94–95).[30] The natural aspects creating harmony are of an outer and an inner kind. While the trees create a physical connection between the houses, the gazes from young Turkish women create an erotic link between the street's inhabitants and the traveler: "I recall the thoroughly barred, higher floor, surrounding the women, hiding them from the stranger's view. Here is poetry!" (2:95).[31] The phrase clearly reveals that "recalling" for Andersen means fantasizing and *not* recalling facts—*not* seeing; after all, he never saw the women who may or may not have been hidden from his gaze.

The scene is telling for Andersen's poetic realism in which two seemingly incommensurable narratives coexist: that of a cruel, everyday reality, and that of a kind, metaphysical eternity. His equally short tale, "Den lille Pige med Svovlstikkerne" ("The Little Match Girl," 1845), shows how common this antithesis is for Andersen's poetics, but it also points to the distancing mechanism applied to the Oriental variants. Telling two stories simultaneously in "The Little Match Girl," the narrator ends up leaving a double imprint upon the reader's retina: that of a girl dying in Copenhagen's streets and that of the same girl being reunited with her grandmother in heaven. This is similar to the narrative strategy in "En Tyrkisk Skizze." As readers we are left with an image of everyday poverty and one of eternal bliss. In the context of Orientalism, however, an important difference between the two tales is a shift in perspective. The two stories in "The Little Match Girl" are told by the same narrator. "En Tyrkisk Skizze," on the other hand, relies on a disavowing shift in perspective. In the final paragraph, the original poet-narrator's voice slips into a Turk's fantasy, rendering this in quotation marks. The quotation marks serve to further reinforce the distance between the fictional Turk and the autobiographical narrator—a distance that nonetheless comes across as strained.

Throughout the Orient section, Andersen uses the Turk's thoughts, dreams, intoxications, and poetry as narrative vehicles for his erotic fantasies. It is as if the Orient allows—or forces—Andersen to play with his own inner Turk. Often, Andersen simply comes across as a dirty old man viewed with current eyes. An encounter with a six-year-old Turkish girl turns into a fantasy about riding away with her on a horse once she has turned into a grown virgin (2:75). The aforementioned sight of the impoverished, opium-smoking Turk turns into thoughts of entering his

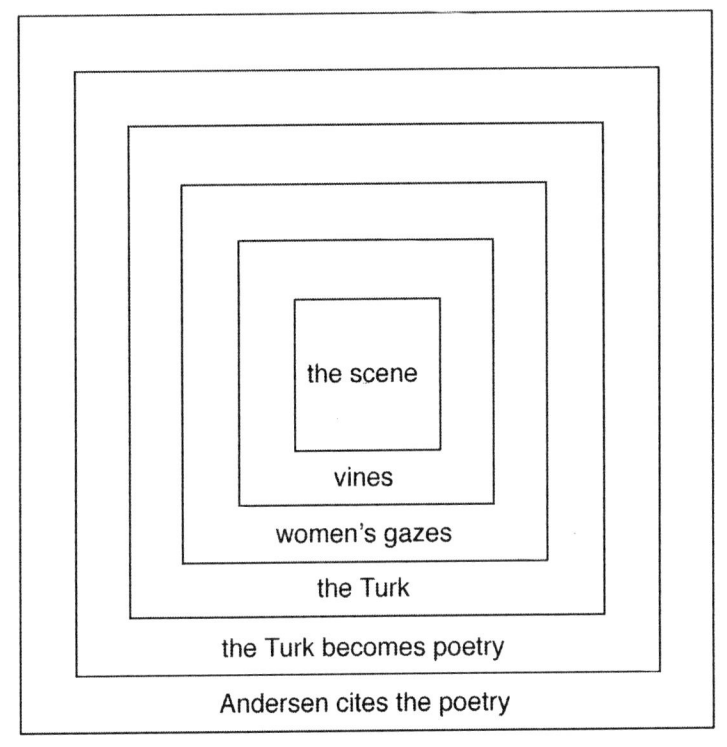

```
┌─────────────────────────────────────────┐
│  ┌───────────────────────────────────┐  │
│  │  ┌─────────────────────────────┐  │  │
│  │  │  ┌───────────────────────┐  │  │  │
│  │  │  │  ┌─────────────────┐  │  │  │  │
│  │  │  │  │    the scene    │  │  │  │  │
│  │  │  │  └─────────────────┘  │  │  │  │
│  │  │  │         vines         │  │  │  │
│  │  │  └───────────────────────┘  │  │  │
│  │  │       women's gazes         │  │  │
│  │  └─────────────────────────────┘  │  │
│  │            the Turk               │  │
│  └───────────────────────────────────┘  │
│         the Turk becomes poetry         │
└─────────────────────────────────────────┘
        Andersen cites the poetry
```

In "Tyrkisk Skizze," Hans Christian Andersen achieves his move from reality to fantasy in a six-step process relying on visual and verbal associations and metamorphoses. The first level is the scene. The next three levels consist of poetic intensification as Andersen adds vines (which he might have seen), then women's gazes (which he could not have seen but nonetheless "senses"), and finally the Turk (who seems a figment of his imagination). While the three levels of adding the unseen to the seen are accompanied by the interjection "Her er poesi," the fifth step literally turns the Turk into poetry: he becomes "et levende Digt"—a figure of speech rendered literal by Andersen's reliance on visual and verbal similarity. The Turk's "zittrende Læber" are turned into "zittrende Blade" in the fifth step. Finally, Andersen reads the Turk's lips/sheets, creating and entering a sixth level of fictional reality.

intoxicated imagination in which the Turk gets ever more excited, wanting to embrace not just his wife but ten or twelve of them (ibid.). At the cemetery in Scutari Andersen cannot see an old man without projecting Orientalist thoughts of harem lust onto him. Moments later, an allegedly passionate young man passes by, and of course his thoughts are the same.

He, too, must be insatiable and dream of nonstop lovemaking ("elskov"): "What thoughts flutter through his soul—! Indeed, that is a Turk!" (2:98).[32] Through whose soul, one may ask, and who, here, is a "Turk"?

The Erotics of Slavery

As other scholars have pointed out rereading Andersen in recent years, the most upsetting and inappropriate poeticizing moment in *En Digters Bazar* occurs when Andersen visits a slave market in Constantinople.[33] Andersen soberly registers that at a market not far from the Grand Bazaar, the goods sold are human beings: black and white female slaves (2:82). As in the Turkish sketch, Andersen seems intent on pointing out the slave market's positive qualities: the sun is shining, the trees are green, and "Asiens Døttre" (the daughters of Asia) seem happy. A mother is nursing her child, and according to Andersen, the two will be able to remain together instead of being sold separately. A naked fourteen-year-old black girl smiles and flashes her white teeth at an old Turk grabbing at one of her legs. Four Circassian slaves are about to sing and dance for a Turk "with a passionate gaze!" before he will decide on his purchase (2:83). Finally some white Circassian women are placed in a cage. Andersen's only lament is that he does not get to look at the beautiful women: "Do not cover up the beautiful, white women, you old disgusting man. We just wanted to look at them. Do not force them into the cage. We would not, as you believe, hurt them with evil eyes!" (2:83).[34] Here is a direct and absolutely disconcerting claim to innocent eyes.

Andersen's reaction seems particularly naive considering that just before leaving on his trip, he had written the abolitionist drama *Mulatten* (The Mulatto, 1840). In fact, the revenues from the sales and from the performance of this play at Copenhagen's Royal Theater facilitated Andersen's travels. Two things can be said about this. The first is that slaves were not viewed as a homogeneous group. While colonial enslavement of Africans prompted thoughts of physical violence and cruelty in the mid-nineteenth century, Oriental slavery of Circassians prompted only harem fantasies. As Birgitte von Folsach has pointed out, paintings of Oriental female slaves were, at the time, deemed entirely *fit for society* (Folsach,

81). Second is the Danish audience's reaction to *Mulatten* and its final slave scene in particular. *Mulatten* also constitutes a case of poetic realism in which the audience can choose to focus on the exoticism and romanticism of the drama rather than its political setting. Interestingly, *Mulatten* was accepted at the Royal Theater precisely for its depiction of a slave scene in the final act—a scene that was found entertaining, exotic, and appealing.[35] Aside from the fact that the heroic mulatto ends up being liberated rather than sold as a slave, Copenhageners evidently found slave-market scenes attractive from a purely exoticist point of view. Given this context, Andersen's rosy depiction ends up saying as much about its intended audience as it does about his own callousness.

Still, Andersen's decision to focus on the erotics and not the politics of human oppression, in this case, ultimately calls for an even stronger distancing mechanism than the one discussed in connection with the Turkish sketch, and as such, it seems to point to a considerable level of discomfort. Andersen's narrator begins by suggesting we enter the mind of the young Turk watching the Circassian slaves: "he could supply us with a depiction of a female slave market that we could not" (2:83).[36] Yet, rather than dissolving the slave scene into the fantasy or experience of the "Turk"—a narrative strategy that easily comes across as the travel writer's own projected fantasy—Andersen resorts to Ottoman poetry and simply ends this section by citing Ibn al-Katib's poem about houris who can "kysse og omfavne" (kiss and embrace), pointing out that the models for these heavenly houris must be found among the earthly ones (the ones the Turk has seen) (ibid.). Thus Andersen once again creates poetic realism by first depicting a real scene and then creating a transition to what he considers Mohammedan religion and eroticism—this time, however, without thematizing his poetic skill. He seems less proud, and more distanced from, a politically loaded issue, opting to present the Oriental world as self-contained.

When it comes to poetic realism, Andersen's romanticizing tour de force may at times seem nauseatingly escapist. Yet, as indicated earlier, the reader is informed of Andersen's aestheticizing project and is able to judge for him- or herself. In the reader's mind, Andersen has planted dual images of social outrage and faith in a higher sense of justice, and even if the harmonizing image always leaves the last impression and thus has the advantage of greater impact, Andersen cannot be accused of being blind to reality. Still, as the comparison between the Constantinople and the Copenhagen cases of poetic realism shows, the poverty and oppression Andersen witnesses in Turkey end up being situated within an organic, Oriental fantasy or literary space set off entirely from that of the Christian West. Ultimately, one may criticize him for cultural relativity.

Mohammedanism and Christianity

The underlying tenet of Said's Orientalism and Pratt's Euroimperialism is that people understand the world in binary structures that end up functioning as opposing, unequal terms. Hence, the superior European Self is understood in contrast to the inferior Oriental Other, or the imperial Self is understood in contrast to the colonial Other. The depictions in *En Digters Bazar* admittedly tend to be structured around antithetical pairs: the historical past versus the present, personal memories versus their current reality (especially in Italy), the North versus the South, and Europe versus the Orient. These opposing categories are, however, slippery and change throughout the journey. As Andersen approaches the Orient, the South (southern Europe) slowly shifts from the category of cultural Other to that of cultural Self, so that Catholicism and Protestantism stop functioning as opposing terms and are rather joined conceptually under the category of Christianity—now a contrast to the category of Islam—or Mohammedanism, as Andersen calls it.

Once in the Orient, Andersen clearly sees himself as a representative of Christianity—even if this may be his own romanticized and unorthodox version of Christianity. The hostile relationship between Orient and Occident is eroticized, in the traditional manner of feminizing the Orient— here as an impotent male rather than a female: "here [at Bosphorus] the Orient courts Europe and dreams of being the ruler" (2:114).[37] And, there is no doubt in Andersen's mind of Europe's—including Denmark's— capacity to conquer the Orient. Leaving Turkey on the Bosphorus, he passes by the consuls' summer residences and rejoices at the sight of a Danish flag, triumphantly noting that "Denmark has planted its white cross of Christ in the land of the Turk" (2:121).[38]

An episode—like that of the encounter with the Persian Arab—often used to emphasize Andersen's considerate attitude toward Islam and Turkish culture is his visit to a Dervish monastery.[39] Here, his travel companion arouses anger by refusing to take off his boots. Andersen, on the other hand, resolutely cuts asunder the straps sewn onto his pants, removes his boots, and claims that "one ought to follow the ways of a country or leave it" (2:89).[40] In response, a Turk tells him he is a good human who respects religion and deserves to be a Turk—a statement Andersen takes as a compliment (ibid.). Yet, Andersen is not always equally considerate, and he certainly falls under Pratt's accusation of European expectations of *disponibilité*—the attitude that the non-West must lay itself open, be available to the European visitor.

At Sultan Mahmud's grave and in the Aya (Hagia) Sophia, Andersen describes receiving angry looks from Muslims who find it inappropriate that a Christian enters their sanctuary as a tourist. In reporting this, Andersen apparently feels no shame and conveniently trades in his Christian view for an all-embracing romanticist standpoint. In Aya Sophia, he exclaims, "Do not look at us so angrily, you old priest, your God is also our God! Nature's temple is our common house of God, you kneel toward Mecca, we toward the East" (2:84–85).[41] This claim to romanticist universality would not come across as suspect were it not for Andersen's preceding apostrophe to Aya Sophia. In the spirit of nineteenth-century romanticism, Andersen personifies what he calls the Sophia *church,* dramatizing a battle between Christians and Muslims while expressing a strong underlying imperialistic and missionary desire that the Christians once again prevail:

> The church...dreams of that night of terror when its gates were burst open and the Christian altars were desecrated...that night when it was turned into a mosque...Do you, perchance, also dream about the future, *Aya Sophia*! Harbor a premonition related to the one stirring in the people present inside; might the scratched-out Christian crosses on the door be renewed? Shall the altar be moved from the corner facing Mecca and once again assume its position toward the East?...Through the church, the Christian hymns reverberate. (2:84)[42]

Here, there is no doubt that Andersen finds Europe and Christianity superior to the Orient and Islam. He is convinced that the Muslims inside Aya Sophia feel threatened by the European's presence and that they harbor a premonition of the defeat awaiting them.

As Folsach has pointed out, Andersen seems ambivalent in his overall attitude toward the Orient. While describing Turkey and its inhabitants with much enthusiasm in his travelogue, back in Vienna, he notes in his diary that the Turks are barbarians whose hope for improvement lies in European culture: "what could Constantinople not become with European culture" (quoted in Folsach, 80).[43] Andersen is a traveler at a point in time when the Ottoman Empire's modernization is taken for granted. Since the Tanzimat (reorganization) and other Westernization projects have not had much impact yet, Andersen encounters an Orient that mainly lives up to his *Arabian Nights* expectations. At the same time he takes its turn toward the West for granted and feels no need to engage politically or religiously—nor does the thought that the Orient may evolve into something different from what he sees and enjoys occur to him.[44] To Andersen, traveling to the Orient presents an opportunity to see something new and different, to activate his fantasy, and to commodify the cultural Other, turning it into poetic, exoticist imagery in his *Digters Bazar*.

Innocent Drawings

It has become the practice to publish the travel sketches Andersen drew in his autobiographical novels and travel accounts. The 1975 edition of *En Digters Bazar* thus includes eighty-six of his drawings. While they illustrate Andersen's self-taught drawing technique to an audience that is increasingly interested in this artist's overall skills, they also serve as markers of authenticity. More important, the illustrations reinforce the prevailing notion of Andersen's innocence, childishness, and naïveté. Andersen draws things as he sees them, with no regard for classical conventions. And yet, as Heltoft points out in his discussion of the drawings, the issue of the naive versus the naivistic presents itself (Heltoft, 14). As with Andersen's verbal depictions, one can never be sure of his level of intent.

In this discussion, I point to a series of similarities between Andersen's verbal and visual portraits in order to further discuss Andersen's aesthetics. In my previous look at Andersen's poetic realism, I emphasized his narrative moves from reality to fantasy. Here I want to dwell a bit more on the "reality" side of the equation, expounding upon how Andersen animates the seen and on how this relates to Orientalism and Euroimperialism—or accusations thereof.

The view over Constantinople from the Austrian Ministerial Palace (2:107) shows houses, trees, and a minaret. Compositionally the ground is divided into three horizontal planes. Farthest away is a cluster of undistinguished houses—rooftops mainly, with a few cypresses in between them. Closer to the foreground is a minaret, extending from its base—a mosque, presumably—in the middle of the drawing, through the sky, to the top edge of the drawing. And finally, the foreground is divided in two, with a couple of cypresses setting the right side off from the left. The perpendicular growth of these cypresses creates continuity with the minaret and the drawing's other cypresses. In the right foreground is a large hardwood tree, and finally, on the left are three houses built on a hillside and resting partly on stilts. Andersen seems particularly interested in this stilt construction, and this is where he most clearly breaks with post-Renaissance rules of perspective. The house on the left, in particular, shows an unfolding of a three-dimensional surface, allowing the viewer to see the side and front of the building simultaneously. In fact, the line that ought to be the shortest if the viewpoint were limited by realistic human grounded perception is the longest. Basically, Andersen allows himself a change in perspective that reflects his fantasy and his ability to animate objects. With its unbalanced proportions, the house on stilts ends up looking like it is turning toward the viewer—as if it is looking at him, and may soon approach him upon stilt legs.

This understanding of Andersen's animated drawing is supported by the poet's verbal renditions of similar views of Constantinople.[45] Andersen consistently adds animation through anthropomorphization, metaphors, and dramatization. Describing his arrival to Constantinople from the sea, he romantically exclaims:

> Black cypresses and light green hardwood trees peeked arabesque-friendly out from between this stone sea of dark red buildings, where the copulas of the mosques with golden spheres and crescent moons each rested like a Noah's ark; and where hundreds of tall, columnlike minarets, with their sharp towers, shone against the gray, cloudy air. (2:75–76)[46]

The verbal rendition is, of course, in color, with the scenery building on a palette of black, light green, dark red, gold, and gray. In addition, the

Drawing by Hans Christian Andersen from the Austrian Ministerial Palace, 28 April 1841. Courtesy of Hans Christian Andersen Museum/Odense City Museums.

trees have been anthropomorphized with the ability and eagerness to *peek* at the viewer. Through the metaphor of the city as a *stone sea,* Andersen creates a harmonic unity of the elements of his own position (on the water) and that of the scenery (on land): the sea is projected onto the city, creating an image of the whole and organic, as the city (a sign of civilization) is viewed as an element of nature.

Verbally describing and filling out a visual impression in this way relies on what Pratt calls "density of meaning." Pratt describes this technique as a typical element of "imperial stylistics," explaining that "the verbal painter must render momentously significant what is, especially from a narrative point of view, practically a non-event" (202). The three main elements of imperial stylistics, according to Pratt, are (1) aestheticization (looking at a landscape as a painting), (2) density of meaning, and (3) mastery (depicting the scenery as if one has full access to it) (204). "Density of meaning"—the most interesting aspect in Andersen's case—is attained through adjectival modifiers and by introducing additional objects—objects not present in the scenery—into the discourse. The passage of text Pratt uses to illustrate "density of meaning" is Richard Burton's depiction from 1860 of Lake Tanganyika, which he has just discovered in Central Africa. In this description, Pratt points out, Burton's references to objects outside the landscape all tie it imperialistically to his home culture by "sprinkling it with some little bits of England" (204).

In Andersen's case, he does not introduce Danish elements into his depiction of Constantinople. Rather than late-nineteenth-century imperial stylistics, we may speak of midcentury romanticist, Orientalist stylistics. As Said has pointed out, Westerners have tended to accentuate the Orient as a *biblical* landscape, and Andersen achieves this effect through simile: the mosques' cupolas rest *like* Noah's ark. As Pratt might have pointed out, though, the scene also conjures up a reciprocal relationship between the European traveler and the destination. The trees return the traveler's curious glances and seem as eager to meet him as he is to meet them.

In Andersen's fantasy, and subsequently in his travelogue *En Digters Bazar,* buildings, trees, and stones come alive. His challenge as a Biedermeier romanticist poet lies in his constant ability to animate objects, change perspectives, and present objects from both a phenomenological and an ideal point of view. In the Orient in particular, he is on the lookout for exoticist imagery, turning on his "inner Turk" while also commenting on a social and political reality. Seen with contemporary eyes, Andersen is not as politically correct as many of those celebrating Andersen's bicentennial would have it. He eroticizes human oppression, takes Western and Christian superiority for granted, and expects foreign sanctuaries to be available to his tourist eyes. Still, his travelogue cannot be reduced to an example of Orientalism and Euroimperialism either. As the title suggests, *En Digters Bazar* reflects the polyphony of a marketplace. These voices have different geographical origins but cannot transcend time. And like his idol, Franz Liszt, Andersen can go up against the conventions of his time—he can strike many chords, but given the restrictions of history, most of these will sound somewhat familiar even if played with unprecedented virtuosity.

TWO

The Hyphenated Woman
Elisabeth Jerichau-Baumann's Juggling Categories of Gender, Nation, and Ethnicity

IN 1869-70 AND 1874-75, the painter Elisabeth Jerichau-Baumann embarked on two journeys to the Orient with Cairo and Constantinople serving as exotic end points. She went to collect motifs appropriate to contemporary taste and its penchant for ethnographic, national, and exotic material. Her paintings had already won great acclaim, and at the Paris Exposition in 1867, Jerichau-Baumann was the best-represented Danish artist. Later in life, she wrote several memoirs of which her account of her Oriental journeys, *Brogede Reisebilleder* (Colorful Travel Pictures, 1881), was her last publication.[1] It was published the year she died, and it is the product of a reflection and writing process that, in her own words, constitutes her "Spejlbillede" (mirror image).[2] A wide variety of impressions is gathered to form a Romantic, aesthetic whole through her subjective understanding and interpretation.

Jerichau-Baumann turns out to be an amusing, sharp, reflective writer who certainly cannot be accused of hiding her light under a bushel. One can only wonder why *Brogede Reisebilleder* has not been reissued since the original publication.[3] Nevertheless, Jerichau-Baumann did become an object of revival in the 1990s, when Orientalism and the relationship between Denmark and the Islamic world was particularly scrutinized in connection with Copenhagen's role as *Kulturby* (cultural city) in 1996. When the National Museum, Moesgård Museum, and the David Collection arranged joint Islamic art exhibitions, Jerichau-Baumann's paintings, mostly in the possession of private owners, were exhibited at the David Collection. In 1996 Birgit Pouplier published a weighty biographical novel, *Lisinka*, about the painter in which she emphasizes her problematic artist and female role. Being married to the mentally unstable Danish sculptor

Jens Adolf Jerichau; moving from Poland to Denmark and learning Danish; and having the responsibility for nine children, while at the same time wanting to travel and develop as an artist, was not exactly easy. Jerichau-Baumann traveled both in order to collect motifs and to sell her paintings at the courts of Europe and the Middle East.

In recent scholarship, women academics have used Jerichau-Baumann to object to Edward Said and the fact that he does not distinguish between feminine and masculine representations of the Orient in his 1978 book, *Orientalism*. In *Women's Orients,* professor of English history Billie Melman depicts women's alternative view of the Orient as it appears in English women's harem literature and travelogues emerging in the eighteenth century. In *Gendering Orientalism,* Reina Lewis transfers the search for a feminine counterdiscourse to Orientalism to the realm of the visual arts. Here Elisabeth Jerichau-Baumann is included as a problem for Lewis. Although she is interested in women's intimate sphere, several of her paintings "contain a level of nudity that seems surprising for a woman artist of this period" (Lewis, 119). Lewis refers to her depictions of Turkish and Egyptian odalisques as "semi-naked," "unfeminine," and "potentially improper" (119, 166). Why, she asks, did Jerichau-Baumann choose to depict the other woman in this masculine manner? And how could this artist, despite the indecency of her paintings, gain entry into European bourgeois homes? In her search for an answer, Lewis discovers the decisive role ethnography and national identity played in the latter half of the nineteenth century. Jerichau-Baumann's contemporaries considered her paintings splendid depictions of ethnic and national characteristics, and as such they were allowed to wallow in eroticism.

Whereas Lewis barely touches upon the question of national identity and ideology in a study that otherwise focuses on race and gender, I want to focus on a series of questions regarding Jerichau-Baumann's Orientalism and her ability to construct national stereotypes—her verbal and visual representations not just of Oriental women but also of Danish women, and especially herself. The extremely colorful and mixed aspects of Jerichau-Baumann's oeuvre will constitute this chapter's main axis: the colorful travelogue, its mixed reading audience, and its diverse protagonist. By analyzing these three aspects of the travelogue, I want to demonstrate how Jerichau-Baumann weaves nineteenth-century discourses of

Orientalism, feminism, and nationalism into a text that establishes her own unusual identity as an acceptable hyphenated being. But before arriving at this point, I want to lay out a theoretical background.

Postcolonialism and (Feminist) Orientalism

Although gender is excluded from the first phase of postcolonial theory, feminist scholars such as Gayatri Spivak and Chandra Talpade Mohanty have reflected on women's particular experience of colonization in a later phase of postcolonial studies (see Melman, xii). Within the field of Orientalism, feminist academics have, as mentioned, criticized Said's notion of Orientalism for not including women's experiences and representations of the Oriental Other. In a preface to her second edition of *Women's Orients,* Melman accuses Said's *Orientalism* of being "gender-blind": "One example of 'gender-blindness' is Edward Said's epochal *Orientalism,* from which women are absent and which, moreover, bases its analysis of imperialism/orientalism on an analogy between orientalism and patriarchalism" (xxii).[4] In *Women's Orients,* Melman's point of departure and conclusion is that European women, starting with Lady Mary Wortley Montagu in her *Embassy Letters* (written 1717–18; published posthumously in 1763), do not regard and portray Oriental women as their opposites, but rather express a sense of sympathy, identification, intimacy, and women's solidarity by emphasizing similarities rather than differences.

Women's Orients is one of several works appearing in the 1990s that focuses on a feminist Orientalist discourse and on women's particular experiences of and in the Orient. This feminist strand of Orientalism tends to fall into two camps. On the one side are those scholars who, like Billie Melman, claim that women's representations of the Orient make up an alternate discourse—or even a counterdiscourse—to the dominating, hegemonic (male) Orientalism. On the other side are those academics who maintain that the feminist discourse is subordinate to, and ultimately supports, the male, Orient-subjugating discourse. With *Imperial Eyes,* Mary Louise Pratt falls into this latter category.

In *Discourses of Difference,* Sara Mills analyzes English women's travelogues from the colonial period. Like Pratt, she focuses on imperialism (rather than Orientalism), but like Melman she draws the conclusion that the feminist texts constitute "counter-hegemonic voices within colonial discourse" (23). Women, Mills claims, are subject to the oppressive power of both patriarchism and colonialism (18), and their unease with discourses of femininity and imperialism emerges in wavering texts that are often judged as "bad writing" (3). Mills inverts this judgement by emphasizing the texts' ability to reveal hegemonic discourses: "What are generally regarded as limitations on women's writing...can in fact be seen to be discursively productive, in that these constraints enable a form of writing whose contours both disclose the nature of the discourses and constitute a critique from its margins" (29). Elisabeth Jerichau-Baumann's text is clearly marked by having to negotiate patriarchal gender demands as well as Orientalism's expectations of a subordinate Other. Furthermore, it is also clearly influenced by the nationalist discourses of the time.

Postcolonial scholars generally base their arguments on French and English texts, which makes the connection between travelogues and imperialism more clear-cut than in the case of Scandinavian literature. In addition, their theories are based on authors whose own nationality tends to be taken for granted. Elisabeth Jerichau-Baumann, however, was not just a woman from a peripheral colonial power—Denmark—but also a person located on the margins of what could be considered Danish. As a constantly hyphenated woman (first Polish-German, then Polish-Danish), Jerichau-Baumann had to demonstrate her national belonging and patriotism in an extremely constructed and self-conscious manner—in the same manner that she constructed her Oriental women. It seems as if her own origins and desire for integration into a foreign culture provided her with a measure of distance and pragmatism vis-à-vis the portraiture of ethnographic types. Thus her *own* nationality (and not just that represented in her paintings) explains her break with the French and English material Reina Lewis analyzes in *Gendering Orientalism*. As Melman points out, not all women are alike: "The category of gender cannot be a totalising one and...must be modified by difference of class, ethnicity and culture" (xxviii). In the case of Elisabeth Jerichau-Baumann, her unusual ethnic and cultural Polish-Danish background together with her unconventional artist role contributes to the discursive constraints that, in the end, leave us with a text serving as a revelatory, indirect critique of the late nineteenth century's discourses of Orientalism, nationalism, and feminism.

The Colorful Travelogue

Travelogues are naturally colorful. As mentioned in the introduction, they belong to a genre comprised of a series of subgenres such as personal anecdotes, historical and political accounts, essayistic features, and intertextual recountings of previous travelers' experiences. What creates coherence and narrative drive across the subgenres is the traveling subject and his or her itinerary. Jerichau-Baumann, however, claims her travelogue is colorful and diverse based on an ethnographic rather than generic point of view:

> Thus, the paintings I shall paint will be very colorful and diverse and in advance I must beg the strict critics' pardon, their mercy even, should I here and there transgress some boundaries; for Egyptians, Turks, Greeks, and Italians are elements much too diverse to create a whole, except if I should succeed in joining them like sunbeams that all emit from the same point, from one and the same focal point, namely, artistic unity. (2)[5]

A potential vice is turned into a virtue: if the travelogue's twenty-four chapters come across as incoherent, it is because Jerichau-Baumann has succeeded in capturing the particular national characteristics of various peoples. The quotation is a verbal reinstatement of the visual point made on the book's cover. As a focal point surrounded by twelve drawings, we find the portrait of the artist. As she points out in a later metapoetic comment:

> This depiction of mine is a reflection of myself; I am the center of the ever-changing kaleidoscope and of these figures whose origin, cause, and understanding is literally I: thus it is all entirely subjective, individualizing, but arabesque; it consists of constantly changing pictures. (62)[6]

Ten of the pictures along the edge of the cover indicate the changing experiences Jerichau-Baumann has had in the various countries she visited, while the pictures in the two lower corners point to her status as an artist. The picture on the right shows the painter while that on the left shows the writer. Thus the illustrated travelogue is artistic on two levels. As opposed to the type of literary travelogue in which the author—like Andersen in *En Digters Bazar*—constantly alternates genres, narrative techniques, and points of view to create variation, *Brogede Reisebilleder* mainly relies on the juxtaposition of text and illustrations to create formal diversity.

Brogede Reisebilleder contains twenty wood engravings based on Elisabeth Jerichau-Baumann's and her son, Harald Jerichau's, paintings and

Original cover of *Brogede Reisebilleder* by Elisabeth Jerichau-Baumann. Courtesy of The Royal Library, Copenhagen, Denmark.

sketches. The division of labor is typical: the man paints exteriors, and the woman devotes her time to portraits and a feminine intimate sphere. According to Reina Lewis, it was more permissible for the female artist of the nineteenth century to transgress professional boundaries, if she dedicated her art to the female, private sphere.[7] Jerichau-Baumann largely lives up to this demand. She paints portraits, and in her text she claims to depict what she refers to as her "Opfattelse af det private Livs forhold" (impression of the conditions of private life) (2). The subsequent discussions of politics and the public sphere, however, make this declaration of intimacy appear rather rhetorical. In the same deceptive vein, the author defends her position as a female artist by apparently complying with contemporary feminist and Orientalist discourses. Underneath the apparent compliance lurks the rebellion of a radical individual.

The Pragmaticist

Jerichau-Baumann is in constant danger of coming across as a bad mother, but ends up taking advantage of her maternal role to defend her artistic project. As a mother she has to do what she can to feed her many children: "After all, the purpose of the journey was—aside from carrying out Oriental studies—to bring treasures to my home, otherwise I would hardly, as a mother, have left it for such a long period of time" (42).[8] As Lewis has pointed out, nineteenth-century women artists generally excused their transgression of the boundary between the private and the professional by claiming they did so for the sake of their families.[9] Thus the artist role is presented as being subjugated to the maternal role in a situation that otherwise easily could have indicated the opposite.[10] Jerichau-Baumann expresses this type of suspension between a pragmatic and a romantic-idealistic view of the artist in several places of her text.

If we compare Jerichau-Baumann to Hans Christian Andersen, who happened to be a friend of hers, we may note that both travel to the Orient as artists seeking out Oriental motifs. Yet while Andersen's traveler is constructed as a sentimental poet showing us the extent to which he can feel and fantasize, Jerichau-Baumann's traveler constructs herself as a calculating pragmatist emphasizing the degree to which she can make money. The difference between the two may be a matter of both gender and history. While Andersen travels and writes during the period of romanticism, Jerichau-Baumann writes after the Modern Breakthrough.[11] According to Dennis Porter, the year 1857—with the publication of Flaubert's *Madame Bovary* and Baudelaire's *Fleurs du Mal*—marks a new epoch and what he terms "the end of the dream of travel." The romanticist belief in the transcendental potential of a journey is replaced by aesthetic modernism—or modern aestheticism—allowing for an escape from worldly ennui only through art.[12] True to Porter's argument, Jerichau-Baumann's traveler does not harbor a dream of transcending the everyday through the power of travel. To the contrary, she wishes to create an everyday—as an artist—in the Orient. The woman artist, we may say, is less preoccupied with *the end of the dream of travel* than with *the beginning of the reality of work.*

The Aestheticist

Aside from having to explain that she, as a woman and a mother, travels to paint, it also becomes incumbent upon Jerichau-Baumann to explain her eroticizing gaze. This she does by using an aestheticist and Orientalist discourse, defining the Oriental woman as erotic. When it comes to her ability and duty to observe, Jerichau-Baumann, in the travelogue's opening pages, strongly distinguishes between her role as a human being and that of artist. Clearly, it is her gender that requires this distinction between "human being" and artist. From the moment she leaves Pest by steamship on the Danube, Jerichau-Baumann enters what she emphasizes as an *Oriental* world. With her sketchbook she places herself half hidden in the first-class salon, decorated with soft cushions and Oriental rugs. The flirtatious behavior of the other guests immediately causes her to consider the demimonde of Paris. Using the Bal Mabille as her point of reference, she discusses the relationship between aesthetics and ethics, emphasizing that as a human being she despises the expression of passion, but that as an artist, she finds it justified. She especially finds it justified within the art of painting, the essence of which is sensual perception. Visual representation is dedicated to "the representation of sensual beauty" (4), and it is important to establish this fact, since otherwise, the beauty of the Oriental woman could not be reproduced at all—for, as Jerichau-Baumann says, "the only meaning of the Oriental woman is sensual existence" (ibid.).[13]

The argument is typically Orientalist; as Said has pointed out, some of the most common notions about the Orient are "Oriental despotism, Oriental splendor, cruelty and sensuality" (4). Jerichau-Baumann's standard Orientalism, however, loses some of its credibility, as she is also critical of the Oriental women's harem situation. Alternating between a view of the Oriental woman as "the lazy, indolent, Oriental being" (85)[14] and as an enterprising and freedom-loving human being, Jerichau-Baumann's argument turns unstable, supporting Sara Mills's thesis that women travel writers are drawn in different textual directions, revealing the unstable foundation upon which their texts are constructed (Mills, 3). At the same time, it is also this pattern of negotiation in the texts that brings the Orientalism of the time into focus. Similarly, the conflicting discourses of Orientalism and feminism emerge in the contradictions between word and image, text and illustration.

Erotic Excitement and Political Indignation

In *Brogede Reisebilleder* the author constantly reveals the constructedness of her ethnographic portraits. She describes, for instance, how she rejects a blond, blue-eyed Jewish girl as a model by asserting that the market in Europe is for dark Jewish women.[15] She provides us with several examples of having to convince Orientals to change from their Parisian fashions to ethnic clothing and national costumes, and often she complains of the many hours of preparation required to create the women's exotic *look*. Thus the travelogue often functions as a counterdiscourse to the text's visual illustrations. I will furthermore suggest that Jerichau-Baumann's constructions *as* constructions—of both femininity and Orientalism—become apparent in her so-called indecent paintings. They do so through the models' extremely self-conscious, performative gazes.[16]

If we employ Michael Fried's notions from *Absorption and Theatricality*, the paintings are based on the latter rather than the former (i.e., on theatricality). The women are not portrayed as being absorbed in their own activities. On the contrary, their attention is directed toward the European onlooker—whether this be the painter herself or the European audience for whom she paints. The book's centerfold is exemplary. Sprawled on a rug, the Egyptian pot seller poses comfortably with her goods, but what kind of goods, we may ask, is she actually selling? In the background there are fourteen pots, while the fifteenth vessel establishes the connection between pot and seller. Its placement as an extension of the woman's body highlights the body as merchandise, and it is hardly coincidental that the pot is placed on its side with its big mouth gaping at the onlooker. The alignment of the hole with the woman's slightly parted

Elisabeth Jerichau-Baumann, *Female Pot Seller.* Courtesy of The Royal Library, Copenhagen, Denmark.

legs indicates a certain self-consciousness concerning the function of the painting. This is no case of Keats's "Grecian Urn"—the silent, mysterious, "still unravish'd bride." Rather, romanticism's shy, enigmatic female ideal is turned upside down. Inverted, it is emptied out as it is evoked. The pot shows us what it contains—and what it does not contain; thus the depiction's ultimate theme, rather than being romanticist-Orientalist, is revealing in its self-conscious performativity, staging, and theatricality. The Egyptian pot seller, we may say, is jarringly exhibitionist—portrayed as a poser who is well aware of her position as a marketable good. In this context, the fabric draped to the side in the back ends up coming across more as a theatrical backdrop than as a sunshade.

In *Brogede Reisebilleder* the notion of the Oriental human being as a constructed object of circulation in a European culture industry is underscored by the author's repeated accounts of her searches for particular human types—accounts that also highlight her pragmatic role and remind the reader that Jerichau-Baumann travels in order to make Oriental studies and to bring these "Skatte" (treasures) back to Denmark (42). The reader is never left in doubt as to the great amount of work required of the artist to create paintings exuding the laid-back bordering on the indolent. The main theme of the Cairo chapter is "menneskejagten" (the manhunt)—Jerichau-Baumann's own term used to describe her problem finding models (45). It is on a manhunt that Jerichau-Baumann, who throughout the journey has placed herself in numerous dangerous positions, exposes herself to the journey's greatest danger. This takes place in an episode indirectly connecting selling one's body as a model to common prostitution. An Indian man offers to be the artist's unofficial guide and to lead her to what he calls "laban-madamizeller" (ibid.). Jerichau-Baumann knows enough Arabic to connect "laban" with milk, and believes she will be taken to some local milkmaids—a favored motif for an artist interested in depicting society's highest and lowest classes: royalty and peasantry. The Indian leads Jerichau-Baumann through crooked, narrow, dirty streets—farther and farther away—and finally pulls her into a house where she is met by "raw laughter, women's voices and the sight of several women and soldiers" (46).[17] Having ended up in a red-light district, Jerichau-Baumann describes the episode as "the most dangerous situation I have ever been in; it is a fact that I never ventured on another manhunt in Cairo" (ibid.).[18] Understandably, nothing more is made of the connection between models and prostitutes. Linking the two types of human categories would only place Jerichau-Baumann in a bad light as she, within a whorehouse metaphor, would be comparable to the brothel owner offering up other women's bodies for sale.

Jerichau-Baumann's aggressive gaze and painting activity often lead to situations in which she and her models, too, risk a beating. In Constantinople's grand bazaar, she entertains herself by looking at "the real, old-fashioned, Turkish hanums, accompanied by their white or black female slaves" (19).[19] Her beginning to sketch one of them nearly causes a fistfight: "woe be to those who observe them sharply! I was nearly punched in the face by one of these barbaric housewives" (ibid.).[20] Jerichau-Baumann clearly feels entitled to her objectification of the Oriental Other. Viewed with contemporary eyes, this is an unsympathetic, imperialistic trait recurring in several of the manhunt scenes. In Egypt she paints women and children while the man of the house is out, but when "Babba" unexpectedly shows up, everybody panics: "'Away with the infidel!' 'He will kill us!'" (45).[21] Nevertheless, Elisabeth Jerichau-Baumann never suggests that her depicting Muslims might be a questionable activity. In her view, it is merely a matter of her, and art in general, conquering Muslim prejudices (25). Her painting activity, that is, is justified from a personal, pragmatic point of view as well as from a universal, civilizing standpoint. In this manner, she carries an attitude similar to that of Hans Christian Andersen, who takes his admittance to Muslim mosques and cemeteries for granted.

I do not intend to judge Jerichau-Baumann as either moral or immoral. What I wish to point out is her own disclosure of the unethical aspect of the aestheticist's endeavors and how this tends to come across in her paintings—perhaps even unintentionally. One more example serving to illustrate this pattern is the portrayal of the Egyptian water carriers. Characteristically in terms of Jerichau-Baumann's verbal depictions, they—like so many of her depictions of Oriental women—culminate in a critique of women's oppression. The water carriers, according to the artist, are innocent, chaste, and ignorant of their own bodily beauty. With regards to the figure in the foreground, Jerichau-Baumann writes:

> One of the women let her black, sheer cloth fall down for a moment because it was so monstrously hot; she thought she was unnoticed, and her abundantly beautiful body was revealed to me, further enhanced by her rich, Nubian, fringed bridal ornamental belt—the only thing a man is compelled to give his wife when he repudiates her.[22]

Seen together with the text, the engraving ends up *also* thematizing women's oppression. On the one hand, the beholder is offered the position of the voyeur: the water carrier is unaware of the gaze resting on her seminude body; she is fully absorbed by her own thoughts and activities, and the onlooker can uninhibitedly dwell on his own desire and project it onto the woman whose body can be the object of several isms: eroticism, exoticism, primitivism, Orientalism. At the same time, the verbal depiction insists on the sad fact that the only thing the woman owns is the belt, tying her to her husband as well as to an oppressive patriarchal social structure. Thus, the lowered gaze ends up signifying oppression, poverty, and submission as much as it signifies absorption. Visually the potential for the onlooker's limitless projection, as in the previous engraving of the

Elisabeth Jerichau-Baumann, *Female Water Carriers.* Courtesy of The Royal Library, Copenhagen, Denmark.

woman selling pots, is hindered not only by the text's resistance but also by the next woman's gaze. As a secondary focal point, the gaze of the clothed water carrier behind the main figure breaks through the frame, involving the beholder. As the depiction, ultimately, indicates a serial event, it is tempting to interpret the dressed woman as the next phase in a series of events in which woman number two approaches as a more self-aware woman, entering into a relationship with the Western beholder. The Western beholder is kept in suspense as to the outcome of this process; the third woman is barely visible, and it is impossible to conclude anything about her.

In the textual universe, Jerichau-Baumann's narrating "I" is clearly suspended between two extreme positions: that of the aestheticist's erotic excitement and that of the ethical person's political indignation (the latter of which, we may note, was entirely lacking in Andersen's account). The harem, Jerichau-Baumann's specialty—an area she can proudly declare that she is the first European painter to enter—constitutes a topos in which political and erotic discourses alternate from paragraph to paragraph until finally reaching a point of transcendence. Nazili Hanum, for instance, is Jerichau-Baumann's favorite princess. She stands forth as a mixture of the Oriental and the European. In almost all other parts of the travelogue this combination is described as a barbaric bastardization, but Nazili Hanum is evidently the exception who knows how to apply an ethnic, Oriental content to proper, European taste and form: "She was a remarkable mixture of Oriental and European influence" (22).[23] Nazili Hanum is civilized *and* wild: "Thus her movements were graceful, soft, slow, supple and yet also sneaky and strong like those of a panther. Her oblong, almond-shaped, black-fringed eyes were light blue, languid and wild" (ibid.).[24] For the painter, the result is aesthetically divine (ibid.); consequently Jerichau-Baumann made three paintings of her. For the model, however, the result of being mixed is devastating; according to the travelogue, Nazili Hanum is a split human being for whom real life constitutes an either-or, rather than a harmonic whole. Jerichau-Baumann recounts that on excursions, the princess secretly replaces her Oriental dress with an English "Amazon suit" in order to gain a little time "as a free Englishwoman," only to return to "her golden prison" (23–24). The conclusion, then, is that Nazili perhaps would have been happier "had she never been touched by Euro-

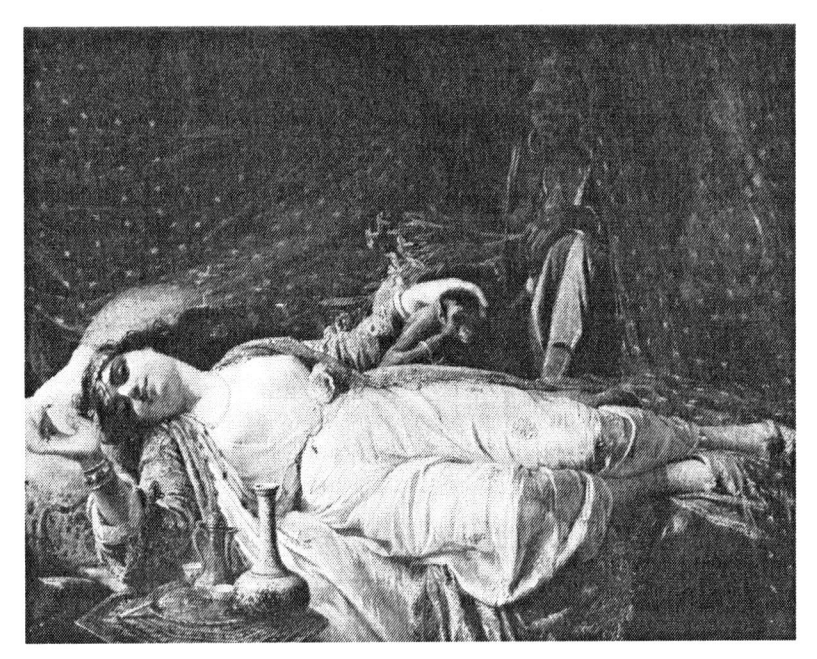

Elisabeth Jerichau-Baumann, *Princess Nazili Hanum*, 1875. From Birgitte von Folsach, *I Halvmånes Skær* (Copenhagen: *Davids Samling*, 1996). The original painting is owned by the Sultan of Brunei.

pean culture" (24).[25] This doubt and uncertainty contribute to the text's inner contradictions and to the reader's having to consider the unfortunate consequences the Europeans' civilization projects can have abroad.

Jerichau-Baumann's confidence as a European and an aestheticist was not entirely unshakable, and to illustrate this I will point to a final breakdown. Asserting her right to seek out and paint the Other's erotic, female sphere according to the stereotypical conventions of ethnography, she tolerates almost everything in the name of her calling: from being bombarded with orange peels to having her head pressed against "Mama's" big, greasy bosom (45). Still, Smyrna turns into the journey's liminal site where her aestheticism collapses. Jerichau-Baumann introduces the Smyrna chapter with some reflections on how threatened the European's identity is in the Orient:

> Nowhere is the individuality of different nationalities neutralized as much as in the Orient—probably due to the relaxing, pleasure-inducing climate and the

slow pace of business as well as the association with lethargic, demoralizing, Turkish authorities and the stultified, oppressed population.[26]

According to Jerichau-Baumann, a European can "swim against the current" for a short while, but then he will become part of "the vicious race" (84). This general introduction leads up to the chapter's final scene in which the author is so shaken by the sensuality to which she exposes herself that, for the first and only time in the travelogue, she loses her composure; as an artist and a European she simply has to avert her gaze:

> They [four Jewish female dancers] turned in circles, they circled about each other with their lowered eyes passionately aflame, and even when they stood still in one place, they bent over and turned so that their entire bosoms and upper bodies shimmied. Although the dancers were clothed—which is not the case for Turkish peasant dancers—these movements were marked by such a degree of sensuality that I had to turn away.[27]

At this point, Jerichau-Baumann is no longer capable of separating the aesthetic from the ethic. As she experiences the dance moves as sexual rather than erotic, aesthetic and ethical disgust conflate. Nonetheless, she quickly saves face by replacing her eroticizing gaze with a political message. Thus, if Jerichau-Baumann cannot use the scene for a visual representation, she can verbally insist on it being "a very interesting sight" (90). Suddenly she uses the four Jewish female dancers to generalize about the entire Orient:

> Not until this point did I experience the degradation of Oriental women, which due to the past, due to habit, and even to law has become her second nature. This may well serve as her excuse, but it is also the source of the Orient's demoralization and fall.[28]

Where Jerichau-Baumann momentarily seems to have lost control, she immediately recuperates and masters the situation by tapping into an Orientalist discourse, establishing the strong lines of division between East and West and thus also fixing her own identity. With regards to Orientalism and feminist Orientalism, the conclusion contains an element of political revolt and female identification. Jerichau-Baumann protests against the negative social effects of women's oppression while she excuses the Oriental woman. On the whole, though, the argument is an example of

Saidian Orientalism. A single event is Orientalized by drawing on a prejudice based on European "knowledge" about the Orient, rather than the isolated event the traveler actually experiences in the Orient.

The Mixed Audience

Although Jerichau-Baumann in the preceding example seems unaware of switching between Orientalist, feminist and aestheticist discourses, she often seems to choose her modes of address and expression very consciously. Part of the colorful aspect of *Brogede Reisebilleder* arises because Jerichau-Baumann so clearly aims the book at a mixed audience. Figuratively speaking she acts as the text's host tending to everybody's needs. As a narrator, she maintains a tight grip on her guests' experiences, often addressing them directly, predicting their objections, and striving to accommodate their needs before they even arise. Graciously, Jerichau-Baumann provides her readers with a preview of where they will be going and explains, from the onset, how she intends to join together two journeys in one narrative (2). Not that addressing the reader directly is an uncommon narrative strategy in nineteenth-century travelogues—we recognize it from Hans Christian Andersen's *En Digters Bazar*—but what characterizes Jerichau-Baumann's position as host in particular is the attention she pays to *different* readers. While Hans Christian Andersen addresses a homogeneous group, Jerichau-Baumann clearly distinguishes between her male and female readers. She comes across as operating in a textual space where the men and the women have retired into separate salons after a good dinner, while she—as their host—has to tend to both groups.

Jerichau-Baumann flirts with her "gentleman readers" (17), while she makes sure her "sweet" maiden readers do not feel jealous when, for instance, she describes the beautiful Greek ladies (37). Addressing the readers directly contributes to the travelogue's immediate, oral tone. In addition, it reveals Jerichau-Baumann's awareness of a split reading audience, whom she imagines as posing different demands and possessing different levels of tolerance. Her expectation is that her male audience wants erotic entertainment rather than political remarks, while her female audience demands the political engagement of an adult woman.[29] Jerichau-Baumann employs three narrative strategies in order to attain a balance between the two sets of expectations: she eroticizes politics, she holds up Europe as an ideal, and she interrupts her own account with imagined reprimands. She employs the first strategy in her depiction of Nazili, when she concludes her evaluation of the real Nazili's problems with a synthesizing, apostrophic, and ekphrastic depiction of her Nazili painting (which otherwise is not included as an illustration in the travelogue). In the painting, Jerichau-Baumann creates a transcendental whole by politicizing the erotic, or—conversely—by eroticizing the political. "Oh, Nazili, having to languish among barbarians! You burgeoning rosebud, surrounded by thorns, you, who live a dream of all the unknown; when it comes to this world, you have only a vague notion" (24).[30] The rosebud metaphor conflates the question of Nazili's social, political, and erotic potential into a single discourse recognizable from the Modern Breakthough's literature on women's issues.[31] As opposed to such texts as Amalie Skram's *Constance Ring* (1885) and Christian Krohg's *Albertine* (1886), however, Nazili's oppression is presented as a consequence of having grown up in the Orient rather than in Europe—a point that takes us to the narrator's second strategy.

According to Joyce Zonana, the strategy of indirectly presenting Europe as an ideal characterizes transgressive female artists in the nineteenth century. To gain access to her audience at home, the otherwise dubious traveling artist had to overtly endorse the European way of life. Yet, she could also criticize domestic conventions by Orientalizing them—primarily through the use of harem metaphors.[32] Zonana's argument, like that of Billie Melman, is rooted in the travelogue of an eighteenth-century traveling Mary—in this case Mary Wollstonecraft. According to Zonana, a feminist Orientalism (i.e., the aforementioned rhetorical strategy subordinating the issue of gender to that of Orientalism) has flourished since Wollstonecraft's *Vindication of the Rights of Woman* (1792). Through this discourse, European women criticized the West's patriarchy throughout the nineteenth century by arguing that women's rights were Western, whereas women's oppression was Oriental. In her article, Zonana focuses on the use of harem metaphors in Charlotte Brontë's *Jane Eyre* (1847), but also mentions women's travelogues such as Florence Nightingale's letters from Egypt (1849–50). Yet, while Nightingale views the harem as hell on earth, mostly because it is monotonous and boring (Zonana, 605), Jerichau-Baumann is attracted to it as a sensual female space, although she is also repelled by its oppressive function.

Feminist Orientalism, however, constitutes but one of several discourses reflected in *Brogede Reisebilleder*. The third conspicuous strategy is a strategy of innocence described by Mary Louise Pratt in *Imperial Eyes*. It pertains to women like Mary Kingsley, who depict their traveling female "I" with irony and comic innocence. An example of this strategy in Jerichau-Baumann's text is her self-ironic admonishments as they appear, for instance, in her chapter on St. Petersburg. Here she criticizes the country's "stagnant disparities" (56) and the oppression of the Slavs (58). In the same chapter, though, she interrupts herself with imaginary readers' objections, such as: "'But, Mrs. Jerichau, it is in no way for you to judge political conditions,' I hear. No, certainly not, and therefore I shall immediately return to my little notes on what I have experienced" (56).[33] In this situation, Jerichau-Baumann indirectly apologizes for her transgressive commentary by rendering herself as a babbling old lady, who must, of course, be excused for her excessive talking, and whose observations are trivialized as "little notes." Nonetheless, Elisabeth Jerichau-Baumann not only gets to say what she has to say, she also, in anticipating her presumably male readers' disapproval, gets to parody their objections. Ultimately, the strategy can be viewed as Pratt's "monarchic female voice that asserts its own kind of mastery even as it denies domination and parodies power" (213).[34]

As far as I am concerned, it is impossible to determine that one of Jerichau-Baumann's Orientalist discourses—the political *or* the erotic—is subordinated to the other. Theoretically, the narrator could, of course, be hiding her political attitudes behind her erotic, entertaining, and naive engagement, or she could be making up for her extreme eroticism by incorporating a discussion of women's rights into her text. A third possibility is that, in the spirit of the Modern Breakthrough, she sees the two as connected and therefore depicts women who are both politically and erotically aware (as they appear in both her verbal and visual renditions). And last but not least there is the possibility that Elisabeth Jerichau-Baumann—as the colorful and mixed person she is—assumes everybody's position. After all, the tension arising especially in women's travelogues stems not from their static but from their dynamic character. As Melman puts it, "What is so intriguing about the feminine discourse is not its 'separateness' but the dynamic interchange between it and the hegemonic orientalist culture" (10).

The Colorful Traveler

In the case of Jerichau-Baumann, I also, finally, want to call attention to her interchange between conventional and radical discourses of nationalism and Danishness. As indicated by the hyphen in her last name, Jerichau-Baumann represents the hybrid individual. "Jerichau" signals her attachment to her home—to her husband, her children, and the nation Denmark. "Baumann" signals the side of herself she refuses to give up as she marries: her ambitions as an artist, her connection to her native country (Poland) and the European continent, and her personal integrity. In a critique of loveless marriages Jerichau-Baumann comes across in both the Orient and in Denmark, she defines these as the woman's exchanging her name for that of the man without loving him (87)—a shameful act from which she distances herself by coordinating her husband's patronym with her own. The hyphen can be viewed as an emblem, not only of a joining together, but also of slippage—between different nationalities and gender roles.

First of all, it may be worthwhile noticing the absence of both the hyphen and Jerichau's own patronym (Baumann) on the travelogue's cover. As opposed to the travel narrative itself, the paratextual framing—including the cover, the dedication, and the epilogue—show intensified manifestations of Jerichau-Baumann's attachment to Denmark. The two pictures of the artist on the cover highlight her belonging to "Hjemme" (home) and "Præstegaarden" (the parsonage); the dedication to King Christian IX underscores her patriotism; and the epilogue constitutes a direct appeal for the reader to accept her as the mixed individual she is—based on the simple argument that others do:

> Here at home, many have gotten to like me despite the urge to travel that characterizes my erratic artist life; people have gotten used to the fact that I, without being a native Dane, love Denmark, that I, the mother of my Danish children, innocently and unintentionally differ from others here at home.[35]

Between these paratextual pages—in the travelogue itself—Elisabeth Jerichau-Baumann depicts herself as a cosmopolitan "Mor Danmark" (Mother Denmark). In her article "Moder Danmark blandt haremskvinder" (Mother Denmark among Harem Women, 2000), Anna Rebecca Kledal explains how Jerichau-Baumann, among Danish artists, belonged to a group referred to as "the Europeans" or "the Brunettes" as opposed to "the Nationals" or "the Blondes." Thus, Jerichau-Baumann belonged to the least influential group—those who took their inspiration from the international style of art.[36] In this context, Kledal considers Jerichau-Baumann's allegorical painting *Mor Danmark* (Mother Denmark, 1851)—an extremely popular national icon reproduced on innumerous objects[37]—as "an attempt to accommodate the expectations of the dominant national art institution" (Kledal, "Moder Danmark blandt Haremskvinder" 44). Kledal further explains that a woman is used to symbolize Denmark based on the romanticist view of women as bearers of the natural, the irrational, and the national (ibid.). These observations, I believe, are transferable to Jerichau-Baumann's text. Before returning to the paratext, I want to show how the combined cosmopolitan and national "I" is constructed in the travelogue.

The Cosmopolitan

Jerichau-Baumann puts herself forth as a magnificent cosmopolitan in two ways: by emphasizing the linguistic skills of her traveling "I" and by placing this narrating "I" outside the dichotomous categories of the foreign and the domestic. Her multilingualism is expressed at the level of plot as well as narration, that is, in the reconstruction of direct speech occurring abroad, and in the narrator's account aimed at the domestic reader. Sentences from the first category include this rather self-congratulatory statement (pronounced by Great Duchess Marie of Russia): "On peut parler de tout avec cette dame" (57). The quote shows that Jerichau-Baumann knows her foreign languages. In fact, she knows not only French (15) but also Polish, English (22), German, Danish, Italian (6), Arabic (8), and Turkish (9); according to her own count, she speaks eight living languages well (128). The statement furthermore illustrates Jerichau-Baumann's worldliness and her ability to discuss all topics. Fortunately she does not demand the same capacity of her readers, but she does expect them to know English, German, and French as she does not translate quotes in those languages and often intersperses her Danish narrative with phrases from these languages. This results in multilingual composites such as: "Stakkels Barn! Tout comme chez nous! Her gjaldt Heines Ord 'Es ist eine alte Geschichte, doch bleibt sie immer neu, und wem sie jüngst passiret, dem bricht das Herz entzwei.' Kun er der den Forskjel..." (Poor child! Tout comme chez nous! Here Heine's words were appropriate: "Es ist eine alte Geschichte, doch bleibt sie immer neu, und wem sie jüngst passiret, dem bricht das Herz entzwei." There is just the difference...) (87). Jerichau-Baumann, that is, switches between Danish, French, and German, and expects her reader to follow along, while she translates Italian, Arabic, and Turkish words and sentences.

Just as Jerichau-Baumann feels at home in world languages, she feels at home with various national characters. Throughout her travelogue she consistently balances her enthusiasm for the foreign with a similar enthusiasm for the Danish domestic. Her justification for embarking upon her journey is as follows: "Aside from making Oriental studies, the purpose of the journey was to return home with treasures; otherwise I would hardly, as a mother, have left my home for so long; *for there are plenty of interesting motifs in the North*" (42, emphasis added).[38]

In a similarly enthusiastic yet balanced way, Jerichau-Baumann compares the Northerner's natural traits with those of the Southerner in the spirit of Montesquieuian climate theory:

> In Italy as in the North, nature and its phenomena share everything with the people, and vice versa. In the North we have gray weather, fog, lasting storms, and cold... And thus the Northerner resembles the nature characterizing his home; the fog of melancholy covers the star of his eye... The condition is quite different for the Southerner and the South, this home of passion. Southerners are the children of passion...; here they are glowing, flaming, explosive, eruptive as thunder and lightning, and the showers are heavy, these floods of tears. (65)[39]

In Greece, the artist likewise compares Danish and Greek women through nature imagery:

> The woman of the North resembles violet and maiden blush, she resembles lily of the valley in the shade of the forest, she resembles the cornflower between

the spike of the rye, the sweet-smelling clover, she resembles the light forget-me-not..., the water lily...; but the Greek woman resembles the glowing pomegranate, the crimson rose, the lusterless white datura, the poisonous flower... the fantastic floral phenomena of the orchid.[40]

The comparisons are balanced in the sense that both types of people are described in positive terms. As a hyphenated woman, Jerichau-Baumann does not identify directly with the Northerner and does not feel confined by particularly Nordic traits. She seems able to evoke the positive characteristics of either ethnographic type in herself, and in opposition to other Nordic travelers, she does not regard the passion of the Southerner longingly. The Southerner does not represent a repressed side of her own being—something to which her passionately long sentences alone might testify.

The Dane

To assert herself as a *Danish* European, Jerichau-Baumann combines her cosmopolitanism with a thorough cultivation, maintenance, and confirmation of everything Danish. As the painting *Mor Danmark* also demonstrates, this author not only has insight into Danishness, she also actively supports the construction of a national image.[41] In Jerichau-Baumann's view, this role as guardian of the nation is feminine. In *Brogede Reisebilleder* she considers Russian ladies of nobility who refuse to speak a foreign language as heroines and develops this notion into one of relevance to all women as nation builders: "It is the women who advance at the front of the battle once they are fanaticized; it is the women who are the champions, who are the most dangerous propagandists of new ideas once they are seized by them" (58).[42]

In *Gendering Orientalism,* Reina Lewis illustrates how female artists, in accordance with Elisabeth Jerichau-Baumann's claims and praxis, often took on the role as guardian of the nation. In this context, she refers to *l'art féminin* as a female art "concerned with tradition and moral continuity which reflects woman's role as guardian of the nation" (Lewis, 61). In Jerichau-Baumann's verbal form of expression the travelogue—this female role emerges in passages in which she constructs her traveling "I" as overflowing with patriotism and national pride. In Greece, especially, she seizes upon the opportunity to display this side of herself.

Jerichau-Baumann exalts two aspects of Greece: the country's past days of glory and its king. The former admiration, that of Hellenism, she shares with most intellectual travelers of the nineteenth century, but her admiration for the king is specifically Danish. King George was born in Denmark, spoke Danish, and loved his native country: "The king then spoke Danish with me and spoke pleasantly of his native country, of his home. That good, young, Greek king! He has a great, loyal, Danish heart!" (31).[43] Besides loving King George's Danish side, Jerichau-Baumann also defines it. This she does according to the self-image the Danes created in the nineteenth century: King George, as opposed to his German predecessor King Otto, has *Parisian* taste:

> The castle built by King Otto is pompous and heavy in its proportions and décor and is marked by the German, heavy, contemplative spirit... In the queen's newly decorated rooms one is surprised to feel transported to Paris; this is a consequence of King George's exquisite taste. (30)[44]

Thus, as Jerichau-Baumann accentuates her patriotism and her close relation to the Danish royal family, she also confirms Danish national identity by stressing the Danes' natural affinity with the French—with Europe's cultural capital—in opposition to the Germans, Denmark's political and cultural archenemy at the time.[45]

In Athens Jerichau-Baumann seizes upon the opportunity to cultivate yet another Danish national representative—the frigate *Sjælland* (Sealand), which has represented "our dear homeland" at the opening of the Suez Canal (30). Here Jerichau-Baumann gives her all to act as Father Christmas *and* "Mor Danmark" (Mother Denmark) for the Danish sailors on Christmas Eve. She brings them Christmas cookies and other goodies, Christmas candles, a Christmas tree, and a self-composed Christmas poem. The most important aspect of all these items is that they are Danish. She has decorated the Christmas goodies with Danish flags and eaten her way through Athen's bakeries to find what might resemble Danish Christmas cakes (ironically, she ends up finding these at a German bakery). Her description of entertaining four hundred sailors on this Christmas Eve is full of pathos. The crew is described as "the bearded, sturdy, dear, Danish men, of whom so many have protected old Denmark during the difficult times of war" (35).[46] And the author describes herself as the great Danish mother. She has never felt greater joy celebrating Christmas—neither in church nor in the company of her own family: "I felt united with them as if they were my own children" (35).[47] The poem she wrote to the crew, included in the travelogue, once again equates Danishness with lightness: "det muntre, det danske Sind" (the cheerful, the Danish spirit) (ibid.). The charitable, patriotic project is so successful that later in Denmark, factory girls whose brothers were aboard the ship and have recounted their adventures with the famous painter, recognize and thank Jerichau-Baumann in public (36)—a fact the artist quite proudly makes sure to include in her travelogue in order, once again, to assert her role as guardian of the nation vis-à-vis her Danish reading audience.

Transculturation

While the foreign forms the point of reference in the main travelogue, the domestic forms the base in the introduction and the conclusion. These paratexts clearly take Danish nationalism and patriotism into consideration, illustrating what Pratt calls "transculturation." As mentioned in the introduction, transculturation refers to the way in which a subordinate group defines itself through the materials transmitted to it by a dominant culture—its modes of representation, its language, and its discourses (Pratt, 6). What Pratt wishes to highlight by using this term is the subordinate group's *active* selection and appropriation of the material. While this, for Pratt, pertains to Creole "self-fashioning," the term can also be applied to immigrants in general. The contrast between Jerichau-Baumann's dedication and her epilogue shows her—as a hyphenated Dane—as a subject employing patriotic discourses to her advantage while also maintaining a critical distance from them.

The travelogue opens with an unequivocal, patriotic dedication "Til Deres Majestæt Kong Christian den Niende af Danmark!" (To His Majesty King Christian IX of Denmark!). The dedication, written in verse, recounts that Jerichau-Baumann has traveled around the world to collect motifs, but that Denmark forms the very center of *Brogede Reisebilleder*. The fact that the author interchangeably insists on herself and on Denmark as the travelogue's center establishes a metonymic relationship between the two, and indirectly establishes her sense of national belonging. Linguistically the Danish point of origin is highlighted by referring to foreign places in terms that evoke their relationship to Denmark—Constantinople, for instance, is referred to as Myklegaard, accentuating a national golden age as well as the author's knowledge of national history. Concluding the dedication, Jerichau-Baumann once again emphasizes her national belonging:

> Then, faithfully, I bring it all back home where it is rooted,
> placing it with heartfelt praise at my king's foot![48]

The epilogue is far less submissive. Jerichau-Baumann seems certain that if she has not lost her reader during her travelogue's first 150 pages, she will probably maintain his or her attention over the concluding five pages—even if she pushes the boundaries a bit. The buildup of her return to Denmark is reminiscent of her dedication to the king in that it initially establishes her thorough knowledge of—and strong sense of belonging to—Denmark. First she assures her reader that "best of all is one's home" (149). She then describes this home with an encyclopedic list of Denmark's national natural icons: the beech, the rose, the sea, fields of grain, the south wind, the nightingale, and so on (ibid.). After once more demonstrating her knowledge of Denmark, she completes her discussion of her "dual call as a mother and an artist" (150), emphasizing that the kind of emancipation for which she is fighting is that of the individual—man and woman alike—and that she does not wish to be part of "those women who by cutting their hair short like men, and by wearing a hat, a frock, a walking cane, and pince-nez, seek equality with the stronger sex" (ibid.).[49] The discussion of what she calls "the ethical side of emancipation" (ibid.), combined with patriotism, constitutes the discursive field in which Jerichau-Baumann to a great extent is able to pick and choose from among the ideologies of her age in order to define herself as an individual.

As a hyphenated woman, Elisabeth Jerichau-Baumann usually positions herself *between* established dichotomies, asserting her right to slide in and out of the categories of the domestic and the foreign, the professional and the private, the masculine and the feminine. Instead of arguing for an essence, she takes advantage of the possibilities granted by her in-between status. Often this comes across as provocative, as when in 1866, she exhibited a painting resembling *Mor Danmark* in Berlin, but, on this particular occasion, had exchanged the title *Mor Danmark* with the title *Rule Britannia* (Kledal, "Moder Danmark blandt Haremskvinder," 44). In the same vein, it seems almost frivolous when Jerichau-Baumann finishes her epilogue—and thus her whole travelogue—by repeating that East or West, home is best, this time slipping into Swedish: "Øst och Vest, / Hemma bäst" (East and West, home is best) (153). Once again, she succeeds in expressing her Danishness with a distance that also harbors her cosmopolitanism.

Jerichau-Baumann's almost casual substitution of painting titles and national languages shows the degree to which she was aware of her time's ideologies and modes of representation. Thus her work provides the reader with insight into the nineteenth century's discourses of Orientalism, feminism, and nationalism. *Brogede Reisebilleder*—with its verbal and visual components—does not allow for an unequivocal interpretation of these discourses, but illustrates how they interact in a field of tension, which must at the very least be considered colorful and diverse. Yet, within this field emerge the contours of a woman artist whose life and work also shed light on *current* discourses. With its focus on intercultural encounters, postcolonial theory of the twentieth and twenty-first centuries brings new genres and people to academic attention. Feminist postcolonialism especially brings forth woman travelers and their travelogues, making it natural to reread texts such as *Brogede Reisebilleder*. In relation to postcolonialist discourses, though, the travelogue is relevant, serving not only as affirmation but also as negation. To a large extent it confirms theories of feminist Orientalism, but it also, as I hope to have shown, reveals their insufficiencies. In the case of Elisabeth Jerichau-Baumann, it is especially the assumptions and generalizations regarding national identities and belonging that prove problematic, since the theories tend to ignore the existence of the European hyphenated woman.

THREE

The Ironic Traveler
Danger and Identity in Knut Hamsun's Oriental Travelogues

IN TERMS OF LITERARY HISTORY, the travelogue has, as indicated in the introduction, been regarded as a precursor to the novel. Meanwhile in terms of the individual author's biography, traveling is often viewed as a precondition for his writing activity. In the case of Knut Hamsun, his novels—from *Sult* (*Hunger*, 1890) and onward—are tied to travel literature, both thematically by focusing on the traveler and generically by constantly crossing the boundaries between fact and fiction as the lives of the hero, the narrator, and the author slip into one another. The travelogue is, as we have seen, a genre always operating in a gray zone between fact and fiction, and through its basic epistemological uncertainty it is a genre that may appeal especially to the modern writer and reader. This indeterminacy, in any case, is what Hamsun so clearly emphasizes and plays upon in the title of his depiction of his journey to the Orient, *I Æventyrland: Oplevet og drømt i Kaukasien* (*In Wonderland: Experienced and Dreamt in the Caucasus*).

Traveling, however, is not just a matter of the author's opening himself to new impressions and experiences, but also of his exposing himself to a state of annihilation. Abroad, he risks losing his identity, and he may well find all his previous knowledge to be of no help in comprehending the foreign. While these moments of identity loss are rarely, if ever, experienced and expressed in earlier travel literature—such as that by Hans Christian Andersen and Elisabeth Jerichau-Baumann—they rather become the norm around the turn of the century, correlating with the rise of early modernism.[1] When Knut Hamsun undertakes a journey to the Orient in 1899, he also stresses what a courageous man he is:

Is it not pretty well done to plant one's foot in Turkey of all places? I continued thinking. Not everybody has shown this courage. The Turk does not eat people anymore, oh no. But does anyone dare claim he is toothless? Has any other Norwegian author dared come to this country? Goethe once traveled from Weimar to Italy; but did he visit Turkey?

To put it briefly, it is pretty well done.[2]

What the narrator's commentary reveals is an indirect wish that the Turk not be toothless. The reason is that once it becomes clear that the Orient does not constitute a *physical* threat, it begins to represent an *existential* threat to the European traveler. In terms of narrative strategies, Hamsun is able to work within the travel genre by turning the traditional battle scenes against external dangers into internal battles. The text turns into a psychological thriller in which the tension does not rely on the traveler's surviving concrete dangers in the Orient, but on his surviving an existential and textual identity crisis. The battle in the Orient turns into one between fantastic expectations versus reality; illusions versus disillusionment; and the traveler's construction of his own identity as a brave explorer versus his identity as a tourist walking in the footsteps of thousands of other tourists with his wife and his *Baedeker*. If we compare the turn from depicting external to internal dangers with the more famous case of Hamsun's contemporary Joseph Conrad, we may speculate that Conrad's serious mode reflects his direct involvement with a colonizing power—the British in Africa—while Hamsun, representing a peripheral nation with no direct colonizing involvement in the Orient, can view events at a greater distance, with more irony. As such, Hamsun is able to take on a satirical attitude toward traveling outside Europe that the writers representing the imperial powers cannot allow themselves, and Hamsun—as early as at the turn of the nineteenth century—ends up prefiguring a postmodern, parodic mode fully realized a century later, I would argue, in the writings of Erlend Loe (see chapter 8).

Less ironically, Hamsun's home audience also viewed his courage as exceptional; Vilhelm Krag, for instance, published his deep admiration—and perhaps encouragement—regarding his literary idol's travel plans. In *Fædrelandsvennen* (1890) he wrote:

> Hamsun is the new human being in Nordic literature... The newspaper tells me that he is strong as a lion and plans to go to Constantinople. A decision as

baroque as a Hamsunian sentence. To Constantinople... Might he be the one chosen by destiny to bring back some sunshine to our overcast literature,—If only we—after Jæger's sad days—got a bit of Oriental glowing colors.[3]

The expectations regarding Hamsun as a Constantinople traveler were great in terms of gender, nation, and aesthetics: as a man he is to live up to his image as a strong lion. As a Norwegian he is to contribute to Norwegian literature by counteracting—or at least counterbalancing—naturalism. And as a verbal artist he is to be baroque: subjective, imaginative, provocative, playful, and verbally conscious and innovative. That which is not expected, however, is a realistic depiction. "A bit of Oriental glowing colors" is to be added to Norwegian literature, rather than a realistic, sociopolitical portrait of a world Hamsun is about to explore in real life.

The attitude is hardly surprising. According to Edward Said, the Orientalizing attitude has been fundamental to the West's relationship to the East throughout the past two centuries. Previous Hamsun scholarship similarly agrees with Said by pointing out how Orientalist *I Æventyrland* fundamentally is. In *Luft, vind, ingenting* (Air, Wind, Nothing), Atle Kittang shows how the journey is driven by a desire to construct a myth of origins, structured antithetically around the Orient representing nature, and the Occident representing culture (132). Henning Wærp, too, has illustrated how Hamsun's travelogue—by polarizing the difference between East and West—concurs with a general European Orientalist discourse, as described by Said.[4] Finally, as a voice "writing back," Georgian literary scholar Kakhaber Loria, has pointed out how Georgians—ever since the travelogue was published in Russian in 1911—have disliked being depicted as Oriental Muslims, with Hamsun lumping together the Georgian, the Persian, and the Arabian, and completely disregarding the Georgians' Christian heritage.[5]

Hamsun's journey to Russia and the Middle East, however, resulted in *two* travelogues: *I Æventyrland* and "Under Halvmånen" (Under the Crescent Moon), both first published in 1903.[6] The more popular and debated depiction of the journey to the Caucasus Mountains is the more aesthetically successful of the two. In *I Æventyrland,* Hamsun's narrator masters his depiction of the Orient as a place where the experienced and the dreamed-of collide. Disillusionment is, after all, Hamsun's art, and he knows how to reemploy romanticist myths of the Orient in a modern way by depicting them ironically and subversively.

Yet, Hamsun chose not to incorporate his depiction in "Under Halvmånen" of Constantinople in *I Æventyrland*; as Wærp puts it, "Turkey, so to speak, is pushed out of Wonderland" (242). Why might that be, one may wonder. Because, I would argue, Hamsun's narrator does not master the encounter with the Other in Constantinople. The Other is not foreign enough in his eyes, and vice versa. In Constantinople the European traveler—by the end of the nineteenth century—emerges as a stereotypical tourist in the eyes of the Turks. This status calls forth a form of Occidentalism as the traveler is ignored and loses his individual identity.[7]

While earlier research has centered on *I Æventyrland*, I will read *I Æventyrland* and "Under Halvmånen" as one continuous travelogue in which the breaking point between the two proves symptomatic. As such, the travelogue illustrates that romanticist Orientalism can continue to exist in its ironic, neoromantic mode in the description of the remote Caucasus Mountains. Yet, as the protagonist travels westward, approaching Constantinople, the narrative is forced into a new regime. His gaze can no longer remain imperialistic, his mode no longer playful, and his drive toward a myth of origins turns into a utopian vision of the future, with Constantinople embodying a harmonious mixture of Muslim and Christian cultures. At this point his narrative is forced from a ludic to a serious mode prefiguring Said's critique as well as the political situation as it appears today, at the beginning of the twenty-first century.

Constantinople, in sum, brings about an existential and narrative crisis for three reasons: first, the city cannot be placed within a dualistic East-West epistemology. Second, in this city, the European traveler—viewed as a tourist—loses his identity as an individual, a European imperialist, a man, and as an author. And third, Constantinople ends up prompting utopian dreams of the future rather than nostalgic reveries of a romantic past.

Unplaceable Places

According to Said, the Orient situated most closely to Europe—culturally and geographically—is the most threatening to Christian Europeans. The Islamic Near Orient makes up "the 'bad' Orient" as opposed to "the 'good' Orient," located farther East (for instance, in India and in this case in the Caucasus).[8] This, claims Said, is because

[Islam] lay uneasily close to Christianity, geographically and culturally... The Islamic lands sit adjacent to and even on top of the Biblical lands; moreover, the heart of the Islamic domain has always been the region closest to Europe, what has been called the Near Orient or Near East. (74)

No Oriental city lies closer to Europe than Constantinople. This city even "ligger i to verdensdele" (is located on two continents), Hamsun's traveler remarks ("Under Halvmånen," 267)—in Europe and in the Orient simultaneously. To the traveler, however, Constantinople does not constitute a "bad" Orient because it is situated upon an earlier biblical landscape, but rather because it is situated beneath—and is regarded as being subordinated to—contemporary European representation. Like Andersen, Hamsun enters Constantinople from the seaside, but the view unfolding before his eyes does not contain the peeking minarets and Noah's ark of Andersen's depiction. Instead the minarets are hardly visible behind the modern European constructions now dominating the Constantinople skyline: "It starts with our seeing a couple of the great powers' legation hotels that dominate with their open location and appear hideous with their coarse size and their barracks style. Then we see the minarets" (Hamsun, "Under Halvmånen," 266–67).[9]

Constantinople has always been the city where Europe and the Orient met, and throughout most of the nineteenth century this mixture is considered "broget" and "malerisk" (colorful and picturesque). If we briefly turn back to Elisabeth Jerichau-Baumann, we find that only three decades previous to Hamsun's visit, Jerichau-Baumann expresses undivided enthusiasm at the European's presence in Constantinople. Arriving at the city, she cheers:

> After centuries [Constantinople] has once more become available to European culture. Once more Christian houses and churches are built on the extensive fire areas amphitheatrically extending from the shores of the Bosphorus. The flags of England, Russia, France and other nations are waving in the clear air against which the slim minarets by the thousands and a thousand times as many masts figure against the horizon.
> It is a lovely sight and all of these thoughts were whirling about in my brain, when Constantinople for the first time appeared before my gaze.[10]

The problem with the cityscape emerging in Hamsun's time, however, is one of proportions—the European is too domineering. Already in this initial depiction, the Oriental minarets form a stark opposition to the hideous, coarse, barracks-like legation hotels of the great European powers. The visual imbalance is converted into a verbal depiction of the European buildings taking up much more space than that of the Oriental ones. The European hotels attract all the modifying nouns and adjectives, while the minarets are mentioned without a single adjective. Thus, what Mary Louise Pratt refers to as semantic density can hardly be said to apply to this scenic depiction of the Oriental.[11] Later we are told that the minarets are white and stand against the sky. Perhaps there is simply no need to explain what they look like. They have, as we saw in chapter 1, been depicted many times before.

Considering that Hans Christian Andersen traveled to—and described— Constantinople a good half century before Hamsun, provides insight into Hamsun's dilemma with regards to previous European travelogues. Thus, the domineering legation hotels pointing to European representation in the Orient within a political and capitalist realm may also be viewed as referring to European representations in and of the Orient within an artistic realm. Despite Krag's joyful outburst that a Norwegian author is venturing to Constantinople, Hamsun is a belated traveler, and the city has already been thoroughly described and represented not least by artists embarking upon the *voyage en Orient* of romanticism.

Hamsun's narrator, in turn, seeks to forestall criticism of his belated journey by pointing out that the Turkey he sees does not at all coincide with that of previous European depictions. As the traveler arrives through the Bosporus, the narrator lets him marvel: "Everything we see is different from what we had imagined. Are we not in Turkey?" ("Under Halvmånen," 264).[12]

Just as Hamsun's traveler had imagined Turkey as a different place, he had also imagined something he calls "tyrkisk tid" (Turkish time) (261). Turkish time, on the one hand, turns out to be like European time: precisely measured and strictly governing daily activities. On the other hand, Turkish time is intriguingly ambivalent. On arriving at Constantinople, Hamsun's traveler asks a fellow traveler from Japan:

> What is Turkish time?
> Well, I will tell you at once, he answers and points to the fortress. You see the soldier there, the one walking toward the flagpole? Keep an eye on him.

> The soldier started standing by the flagpole.
> Suddenly a signal shot is heard; the soldier lowers the flag.
> It is six o'clock, says the Japanese. It is sunset.
> Just in front of our noses! Just as we had arrived at the fortress![13]

Turkish time is in complete harmony with nature, but it becomes indeterminable whether the sun governs Turkish time, or vice versa. There is something threatening and nearly castrating about the flag that—guillotine-like—drops at six o'clock sharp, thus arresting all activity and preventing the traveler from entering Constantinople on that day. This "Turkish time" stands in stark opposition to the timelessness depicted in *I Æventyrland*. In order to explain what I mean by these varying notions of time—Turkish and Oriental time—I will analyze a scene in *I Æventyrland*, which, like the flag scene, functions as a mise-en-abyme.

On his way to Vladicaucas, the traveler compares his European watch to a Jew's Oriental watch, admitting, finally, that the Oriental watch is more valuable—even though the European watch is made of gold while the Oriental watch is made of silver. The reason is that the Jew's silver watch contains an obscene picture. When wound up, it is not just "the watch that goes, the picture goes too, the picture is moving."[14] Thus, this is not a matter of a watch referring to mechanical time, but of one referring to bodily drives and rhythm. Or rather: it refers to both simultaneously—both the watch and the picture are in movement. Still, the traveler knows where to fasten his eye, and as the European's gaze is attracted by the obscene, his value system becomes undermined. Suddenly silver is worth more than gold, the natural overshadows the cultural, and bodily desires become more important than Western technology and progress.

The watch episode is also indicative of a general European notion of a timeless Orient, through which Hegelian world history has already passed. In the Caucasus, the narrator abandons himself to this eternal universe and literally experiences time standing still. His own gold watch stops and every day he reads the same old newspaper—paradoxically titled the *New Press*. Reaching a climactic moment, this timeless space inhabited by people with no urge to hurry or even sleep, turns into an ecstatic site: "[a world] of magical depths."[15] Narrative time, too, becomes expansive as events taking place in the outer world slip into depictions of dreams, fantasies, preconceptions, and memories. As Wærp, too, has noted, narrative time ends up reflecting much more than the journey's three weeks (Wærp, 256–57).

Time, theme, and perspective are all connected. If we consider the watch episode from a metapoetic point of view, it signals a temporal shift—from the measured to the expansive—as well as a thematic shift. This latter shift pertains not only to what the traveler sees but also to his way of seeing. Just as the trick watch is considered more valuable than a watch showing the correct time, the trickster travelogue—at the turn of the century—becomes more desirable than one meticulously registering the traveler's journey and empirical observations. Enlightenment's search for truth is thoroughly replaced by romanticism's sentimentality, and the fin-de-siècle travelogue further seeks out the erotic in a voyeuristic manner.[16]

In "Under Halvmånen," having arrived in Constantinople, Hamsun changes his narrative strategy. Read in continuation of one another, the two travelogues form a movement from past, to present and future. First Hamsun takes up the romantic-fantastic farthest East in the Caucasus, linking it to bygone days on a world historical as well as a personal level (often reminiscing about his childhood). He then turns to a modern presence in Constantinople, and finally, he lets his account culminate in a discussion about the future.

Structurally the difference between the two accounts comes across as the depiction of Constantinople, rather than being vague and expansive, is divided into sections carrying topographical titles: Bosporus, Coffee-house, Mosque, Graveyard, Bazaar, and so on. Compared to *I Æventyrland,* it appears that the topography of the capital city joined with the notion of strict Turkish time brings about a more regular form, while the journey along the railroad tracks and paths of the "timeless" Caucasus Mountains led to an imaginative, arabesque narrative.[17]

In Constantinople Hamsun's traveler regards the presence of the European great powers as domineering, unaesthetic, and coarse. This pertains not only to their hotels but also to their brash tourists from whom he and his wife do all they can to stand out. The "Yankee couples" and the British in their patent leather shoes eat together at the hotel while the Norwegian tourist couple roams around on their own and "want it Turkish style" ("Under Halvmånen," 275). Overall, Hamsun's traveler becomes ever more critical of the ability of the great powers to get into contact with, understand, and describe the Turks.

In an analysis that Foucault and Said could hardly have done better, the narrator throws himself into a critique of the one-sided media discourse of the West, in which the Oriental himself is never given a voice:

> Where the truth lies is hard to know—maybe because we have an almost unanimous European press telling us about it. One becomes a bit suspicious. The other side which also ought to be heard is mute...
> Only one side speaks, speaks nonstop and all over the world.[18]

Once again, this media critique makes "Under Halvmånen" significantly different from *I Æventyrland,* in which the traveler is more occupied with authenticity than with truth. As Hamsun's traveler's eyes are opened to a political reality in Constantinople, he also discovers a new dimension of Oriental silence. In *I Æventyrland,* Oriental silence and quiet are valued positively in opposition to Western noise, roar, prattle, and talk. In "Under Halvmånen," however, the traveler starts focusing on the potential backside of silence—as a sign of oppression and involuntary muteness.

European misrepresentation is a theme to which the narrator returns in his conclusive commentary on Turkey. Hence, the criticism of the media and their discourses ends up forming a frame tale in which the narrator creates a space for himself as a new type of political travel writer who introduces conflicting discourses in order to counter "the common judgments of the journalists" ("Under Halvmånen," 292). Yet, as Hamsun's narrator in "Under Halvmånen" vacillates between, on the one hand, still considering the Orient as located outside European time—in a space mirroring the timelessness of the imagination—and, on the other hand, depicting Constantinople in a political presence, his travelogue becomes fragmented and loses its overall aesthetic unity. The depiction turns into a mixture of baroque and naturalism, with the connection between the two being established simply, and only, by the chronology of the journey.

Places of Identity Loss

I mentioned earlier that Hamsun's traveler becomes a nobody in Constantinople, losing his identity not just as a literary writer but also as a

European imperialist, and as a man—or "lion." As to the issue of manliness, Constantinople had been, since the fall of the Ottoman Empire, depicted as an emasculating place where soft sultans were controlled by their mothers and wives. Virginia Woolf's *Orlando* may be viewed as a culmination point within this imagination with Orlando actually changing his sex in Constantinople. One morning he wakes up, places himself nude before the mirror, and "we have no choice left but confess—he was a woman" (137).

In Hamsun's case, the situation is not quite as severe, yet the issue of becoming emasculated is still relevant in connection with his visit to Constantinople. Within scholarship written on travelogues covering a journey to the Orient in general, there is a tendency to focus on the male traveler's relationship to his gender and sexuality in harem scene depictions. In *Haunted Journeys* (1991), covering French and English travel to the Orient, Dennis Porter, for instance, characterizes the harem as "the site of threat as well as of promise" (178). An ambivalent relationship to the harem occurs because the Westerner—in his fantasy—identifies both with the sultan (who has access to all the women), with the excluded men (who have access to none of the women), and last but not least, with the eunuchs (who serve the women, but are impotent) (ibid.). Hamsun explores this harem trope in both of his travelogues, but the third element—the eunuchs—is relegated entirely to "Under Halvmånen."

The most unforgettable episode in *I Æventyrland* must be the traveler's encounter with a Caucasian shepherd in Kobi. The narrator uses this account of the shepherd's alleged harem to mock common Orientalist discourses. This he does, not only in terms of romanticist and scientific Orientalism, but also in terms of feminist Orientalism—ironizing over the issue of women's liberation brought about during the Modern Breakthrough.

At first the traveler behaves like a voyeur on a par with a typical late-romanticist traveler, such as Gustave Flaubert.[19] While his wife lies sleeping, the protagonist steals a horse, rides into the mountains, arrives at a shepherd's house, and spots a couple of veiled women looking down at him from the attic of the house. Immediately the traveler starts fantasizing about the insatiable desire of the man of the harem: "The harem, I think to myself, the shepherd's harem! Oh, these Orientals—how awfully hard it must be for them to forbear!" (*In Wonderland*, 87).[20] As with

Andersen, the reader is left wondering whether the source of these projections is not located within the traveler himself. Yet, while Andersen's account is entirely earnest, Hamsun's narrator to a much greater extent reveals the narrator's thoughts as pure projections. This he does by showing how the narrator's notions of Oriental drama based on erotics and violence constantly turn out to be unfounded.

The traveler knows the topos of the harem well enough to realize that the ruler of the harem is a threatening figure. The narrator, accordingly, depicts him as dangerous, carrying "a splendid belt and both a dagger and a pistol by his side" (ibid., 84).[21] "And suppose that this man had wanted to murder me in my deep solitude and abandonment" (ibid., 85),[22] the narrator bursts out, after informing his reader that the puzzled shepherd has accepted his offer of a cigarette and clearly harbors no evil intentions. With regards to the reader, the stage is now set for exhibiting the traveler's pseudocourage through the use of the conditional. *If* the shepherd had wanted to kill him, the narrator continues, "I would have jumped him and clamped my paws around his throat. And when I'd nearly strangled him I would have paused for a moment and given him an opportunity to rue his life. Whereupon I would have finished him off" (ibid.).[23] And just in case the reader has not already understood how ludicrous the narrator's fantasies are, he adds, "I wouldn't much have minded if somebody at home had seen me in this terrible fight with a wild man."[24] Considering how inviting the narrator makes it for the reader to disclose the fact that in reality he is searching out moments of danger where there are none, this turns into a question of whether his desire may not rather be that his readers at home see right through his imaginary constructions of a heroic self in an Orient that does not live up to the stereotypes of earlier travelogues.

Like Andersen, the narrator constantly points to the representational level of his experiences. Yet, unlike Andersen he does so to emphasize the author's vanity and desperation rather than his poetic prowess. The narrator, for instance, often refers to his diary, as when he is visiting the shepherd, spots the two veiled women, and then conjures up a tale of Oriental love and passion that, as he points out, might furnish him with "another little gallant adventure in my diary" (*In Wonderland,* 89).[25] The narrator indulges in thoughts of how the two women make up the shepherd's harem with the favored wife being too good for the husband. This is the woman to whom the traveler wants to give his love, his money, and his liberating Western ideologies—all in exchange for his personal and professional satisfaction: i.e., the erotic relationship *and* the good story (ibid.). The protagonist plans to initiate both a women's liberation movement and an erotic adventure through his inflammatory writing:

> To begin with, I thought, I'd better write something for her. She would come to respect a man who could make such quaint shapes on paper. Then there was the content of what I would write, and precisely in this regard my superiority would win hands down. (Ibid.)[26]

As readers we are faced with a mirror in the text; we are like the women letting the traveler-narrator impress us with his writing skills. Whereas Andersen sought to impress us with his poetic vision, Hamsun's narrator plans on maintaining his superiority by means of the enigmatic. In the text, the traveler's new love object receives a paradoxical verse while we, as readers, are given a highly ambivalent travel account—the truth-value of which we can never be certain. On the one hand, the narrator claims that the Kobi incident is one he has experienced; on the other hand, he reports his wife's furtive reading of his diary and her subsequent accusations: "How can anybody lie so blatantly? . . . And I don't believe in your ride into the mountains from Kobi either" (ibid., 132).[27]

Yet, using Philippe Lejeune's terminology regarding autobiographical contracts, we might view this text as a "fantasmatic contract."[28] What matters here—in the spirit of neoromanticism—is not a realistic depiction of the Caucasus, but a depiction of human nature, revealed through an individual's fantasies. The story, in other words, is authentic, not true. And the sense of authenticity of this story is underscored by the information that the narrator records his dreams and experiences while traveling rather than inventing them upon his return to the West.

In *I Æventyrland* Hamsun has found a narratological solution to his belated journey to the Orient by writing a text that enters into a playful dialogue with the genre as it existed during romanticism. The themes are still danger, violence, and erotics, but they appear on an internal rather than an external level. Psychological (or "of the soul," to use the vocabulary of the time) conflicts play themselves out against each other in nerve-racking, self-exposing episodes. The travel writer's excitement, in turn, is passed on to the reader who is having to deal with a text that ironically points to itself as a literary construction, erasing the boundaries between fantasy and reality, fiction and fact.

I Æventyrland and "Under Halvmånen" differ in their narrative modes when it comes to harem depictions. As in Kobi, the traveler seeks out a harem adventure in the bazaars of Constantinople. Once again this encounter with beautiful oppressed women and dangerous Turks is to prove his male prowess—a need that has intensified as he experiences constantly being treated as a mere tourist as emasculating. It is one thing to steal a horse, escape one's wife, and seek adventure in the middle of the night in the Caucasus, and something entirely different being guided around on shopping sprees in Constantinople. Trotting beside his wife, having to follow another man's directions, forces Hamsun's traveler to insist that he is "the man of the house" and not just any man: "I am an exceptionally firm man" ("Under Halvmånen," 276).

From the morning, the traveler exhibits firm and active intentions: "I plan the route. For it is still I, after all, who has got a bit to say... But the Greek immediately veers off my route."[29] As the powerless male tourist progressively loses his role as the leader, he collapses "down onto a divan and stares himself blind." He turns "helpless," "gentle and lethargic," and cannot "defend himself" (ibid., 300). Losing his manly identity, he loses himself: "True enough, then I clicked" (ibid.). Desperately he tries to "resume his leading position" and regain his masculinity by seeking out harem women (ibid.). The feminine gaze is to reaffirm his role as the man he would like to be.

At first, the harem adventure the traveler runs off from his wife to explore is reminiscent of the episode in Kobi. Yet, while the women in Kobi allegedly return the traveler's gaze, the harem women in the bazaar do not deign to look at him. Instead he is confronted by one of their eunuchs:

> It was not the women who looked at me, it was the eunuchs... They are vicious toward men. They walk around with tough scourges... I approached a beauty and looked at her... Suddenly I hear an unpleasant sound, a rattle, and a huge eunuch stoops forward toward me. He looks stonily at me and starts chewing with his jaws. Here it is best to be careful, I think, and pull myself away.[30]

Here, one may say—referring to this chapter's introductory quote about the dangerous Turk—the Turk does show his teeth.

The traveler tries to approach yet another woman, but "a roar answered me and the eunuch struck his scourge on the counter with all his might."[31] Even this does not merit the attention of "the beauty": "She jumped a bit when the scourge fell, but continued looking at goods and chatting. Then I left her. When I meant nothing to her I had no more to do there."[32] For the traveler, gazes and meaning are inextricably linked, and once he is not seen, he means nothing and thus undergoes an identity crisis. In this case, the crisis pertains especially to his sense of masculinity, but as his visit continues, it also pertains to his identity as a European individual and imperialist.

The traveler does nothing to conceal his frustrated search for reciprocated glances in Constantinople. While the narrator of *I Æventyrland* seemingly masters everything he sees, the traveler in Turkey loses control of subject-and-object relations. This lack of control is thematized throughout the section on Constantinople: in the episodes about the bazaar, the coffee shops, and above all in the Aya Sophia mosque, the ultimate site of annihilating invisibility.

Throughout the history of Oriental travelogues, the Aya Sophia has served as a topos in depictions of Constantinople. The building's palimpsestic walls divulge its initial Christian status, provoking strong reactions among Christians as well as Muslims. In 1718, Lady Mary Wortley Montagu notes that the remains from Aya Sophia's Christian days are still visible in the mosaics, and that "the Turks are more delicate on the subject of this mosque than any of the others."[33] In 1841 Hans Christian Andersen similarly, as we have seen in chapter 1, depicts the angry eyes following him in the mosque: "It is strange walking in here, followed by armed people, regarded with angry eyes by those praying as if we were excommunicated spirits."[34] In the case of both Lady Montagu and Andersen, the Aya Sophia is highly charged, reflecting an intense religious conflict between East and West; it is a place in which the suspicious eyes of the Muslims follow the European visitors so that they do not for a moment forget who they are, and what they represent as Westerners.

Toward the twentieth century of disillusionment, Hamsun's travelers are confronted with neither the Muslims' suspicion nor their wrath; instead they are treated as nonexistent. Inside the Aya Sophia they are so thoroughly ignored that the traveler first assumes it must be a game. He and his wife stand watching some theology students reading the Koran ("Under Halvmånen," 273). Although their guide is talking loudly, the students do not look up. After returning to these theologians several times—only to be continually ignored—the traveler suspects that "they sat there posing and were absentminded in their studies of the Koran because they knew that there were strangers present."[35] The traveling couple subsequently engages in a fruitless game of hide-and-seek. They walk away, tiptoe back, secretly observe the students. "But everybody read. They read without stop."[36] While the two are watching an exceptionally beautiful young man, the latter suddenly raises his eyes,

> turns his gaze right at our faces, and continues reading with his lips...I will never forget it. This burning gaze came from far away and went far beyond us; when he looked down into his book again, he had hardly seen us. If we had been a royal couple in all of their finery he would have been indifferent to our presence.[37]

Finally, the traveler has to accept that he is invisible to the Muslim. His imperialistic gaze (to use Pratt's expression as well as the narrator's own reference to himself and his wife as a royal couple) is not returned, which suddenly renders him inferior in the power relationship between Occident and Orient, Christianity and Islam. Had this all been a matter of a game, the traveler could have sustained his hierarchical understanding of winners and losers. Yet, rather than thinking in terms of difference, he is forced to think in terms of equality.[38]

Hamsun's traveler is clearly shocked by the thought of cultural equality. Perhaps the Orientals are not interested in Western civilization. Perhaps they do not even consider the European civilized, but rather barbaric. As Constantinople increasingly emerges as a site of invisibility for the Western traveler, he loses his fate in the binary structures within which he thinks.

The annihilating experience is extreme in the Aya Sophia, but it occurs at regular intervals, for instance, in Constantinople's coffeehouses. In one of them, the traveler registers that "it is as if the guests agree not to gawk at us."[39] His interpretation of the situation is not the traditional one about the lethargic Oriental who enjoys coffee, tobacco, and opium—not to enter an *altered*, intoxicated state of mind, but to stimulate what for him is already a natural state of mind, as Henrik Ibsen for instance wrote in 1869.[40] On the contrary, the conclusion Hamsun's traveler reaches is that "the Oriental considers it beneath his dignity to show curiosity... We tourists... We Westerners, we barbarians, what are we to him?"[41]

Utopias

Forced out of his playful mood and ludic regime, the narrator concludes "Under Halvmånen" with a series of reflections on the relationship between East and West. In Constantinople, where the reformer Abdul Hamid II is modernizing his military powers and educational institutions, the narrator begins to doubt the validity of Western discourses portraying Turkey's "persistent decay and decline" (305). He does not see a monolithic country in which Abdul Hamid can be regarded as representing all Turks. To the contrary, he imagines a split kingdom in which "the orthodox Turk" does not understand "why his pasha mimics all these curiosities from European life" (306). And with the Christian powers' arrogant treatment of the East, the narrator becomes prophetic. He predicts that the Western nations are igniting a hatred that one day will burst into flames (310). Specifically, the narrator fears that Turkey, Persia, and Afghanistan might join forces and use European war strategies and weapons in the hands of Muslim soldiers against the West. According to the narrator, the European ideology of modernization envisions "the salvation of the world and future life simply in the construction of railroads and socialism and American roaring."[42] As an alternative to this misconception, the narrator finally envisions a place where "the civilizations of the West and the East could mix their sources and possibly bring forward a new culture, roaring in living streams."[43]

Hamsun's narrator characterizes this utopia as the culture of fools ("dårer"). He nevertheless experiences something in Constantinople that has him replace the nostalgic, Orientalist impulses of I Æventyrland with an anti-Orientalist vision of a future in which the differences between Muslims and Christians are suspended. The fool in this social context is modern man, who is created by, and capable of accommodating, ambivalence—in this case the ambivalence arising when Europeans and Orientals, Christians and Muslims, give up their separate identities. The thought describes a utopia, but this utopia is not based on the bygone Byzantium the fin-de-siècle artists otherwise loved to conjure up. It is rather based on the provocative, difficult-to-place contemporary city of Constantinople.

"Under Halvmånen" hardly lives up to Krag's call for the baroque. As Hamsun the traveler is ignored and loses his identity in the Oriental capital city, his introvert, subjective gaze is replaced by a more extrovert, objective look at the country's historical, political, and global conditions. The travelogue slips into the genre of a reportage, and the otherwise so central narrator places himself more humbly on the sideline; he does not go so far as to give the Oriental his own voice, but he opens for the possibility of and interest for such an utterance.

Dystopias

In the introduction to this chapter I mentioned that traveling served as a first step towards Hamsun's breakthrough as a writer. The destination of his first great journeys abroad was the United States (1882–84 and 1886–88), and according to Hamsun's son, Tore Hamsun, it was indeed "the stay in America that gave the young Knut Hamsun a final maturation and paved the path for his literary breakthrough."[44] One of the things constituting his breakthrough was his America lectures, which were later published collectively in *Fra det moderne Amerikas Aandsliv* (From the Spiritual Life of Modern America, 1889). I will conclude this chapter by presenting Hamsun's view on *the new era* and *the New World* because the American and the Persian persistently make up the main oppositional pair in Hamsun's East-West dichotomy—a dichotomy in which Hamsun clearly (as a Norwegian peasant) ends up identifying with the Persian.

Fra det moderne Amerikas Aandsliv constitutes a persistent attack on Americans' inanity, their lack of culture and intelligence, their superficiality, their greed and materialism, and last but not least, their chauvinism and their rejection of European cultural products. All the deficiencies Edward Said claims that the European ascribes to the Oriental in the nineteenth century, Hamsun assigns to the American and "the Americans' *Chinese sensibility*" at the onset of the twentieth century.[45]

A significant difference between Hamsun's experiences in the United States and in the Orient is that in the former his identity is never subjected to more harm than his being considered a Swede at best, and a Frenchman at worst. Regardless, he is being considered. In Constantinople where the Orientals seemingly agree not to stare, the Americans stare: "the good citizens of the big city could not justify not staring to their conscience."[46] In America's cities, Hamsun does not lose his identity by being overlooked, but rather he *becomes* someone by virtue of being gawked at. With his multibutton "Snesokker" (snow socks) he is anything but ignored: "Had I been a touring theater, I could not have created a greater sensation."[47] And this episode is far from singular—on the whole, Hamsun's narrator writes about the Americans' "rather uncivilized manner of gawking at strangers" (*Amerikas Aandsliv*, 122). Subjected to the "questioning" gazes of the Americans, Hamsun puffs himself up, finding himself and his voice in opposition to his surroundings.

Whereas Hamsun humbly thinks along the lines of a *utopia* based on the relinquishment of his own identity and of the Westerner's binary Orientalist way of thinking in Constantinople, he seizes on the idea of a *dystopia* in America. As opposed to his positive outlook on the hybrid culture of a utopia, his thoughts on an American dystopia are founded on condescending race theories. Not only was America built by European crooks, but they have also, since the Emancipation Proclamation in 1863, granted black people *white* privileges (*Amerikas Aandsliv*, 130). According to Hamsun's analysis, the subsequent nationwide miscegenation—brought on by American women's weakness for "barn Negroes" (118)—has resulted in the inane Americans—"the spiritual mulattoes," as he finally dubs them (131).

Hamsun's race theories and views of emigrated Europeans' misunderstood imitation of real (aristocratic) Europeans' way of life may be better analyzed through the postcolonial theories of Frantz Fanon and Homi Bhabha (with their focus on racial prejudice, creoles and *mimicry*) than through Said's Orientalism. Nonetheless, I will analyze Hamsun's reflections on America from an Orientalist point of view, since his understanding of the New and the Old World make up a basic dichotomy in Hamsun's worldview, which in turn ultimately captures the development of his own life toward stagnation and reservation.

In his elder years, Hamsun, who in his youth was so active and outgoing, becomes an ever greater adherent of slowness, quiet, and what he calls *poetic time*. In 1928, when the author sets out to give Americans a piece of good advice, he suggests—in his article "Festina lente"—that they make haste slowly and be grateful for what they have: "You Americans seem not to be content with just a little. You want to have the upper hand. You want abundance. The Oriental forms a contrast to this with his frugality, his innate ability to do without."[48] The Oriental Hamsun has in mind is the Persian. The Persian belongs to the Old World—the world Hamsun visited in the Caucasus where the natives, even when they had a watch, organized their lives according to the sun's passing across the sky. The Orientals' calm reflects their relationship to both time and space:

> The Orientals seem to me to possess a high degree of ethical wisdom. Since the olden days they were the fortunate possessors of satisfaction with life. They smiled at the Occidentals' restless squirming and lowered their heads with contemplative calm; they had enough of their own.[49]

As Hamsun turns into a spokesman for being satisfied with what one has—in his own case, according to the article, his plot of land—traveling becomes pointless. As a final insistence upon the futility of travel and attraction to the foreign, Hamsun recounts an episode of a Tuareg tribe's reaction to a plane crash in the Sahara Desert. The wrecked Europeans had expected to be met with the natives' interest, but instead they are ignored. The episode is reminiscent of the overlooked Hamsun couple in the Aya Sophia, but the conclusion differs. Instead of conjuring up images of what today might be called an ideal, multicultural society, Hamsun insists on local attachment and satisfaction. The leader of the Tuaregs is praised for rejecting the airplane and the entire notion of travel: "The sheikh, then, expressed his doubt that the invention, the journey, the whole idea was worth the sum of *human soul* going into the venture."[50]

Knut Hamsun, whose authorship was so inextricably linked to traveling and whose authorship revolves around the topic of the human soul—"the unconscious life of the soul"—paradoxically ends up placing traveling in an inverse relationship to the soul. If one draws the logical conclusion of this reasoning, one ends up without Hamsun's literature. If the younger Hamsun had listened to the older Hamsun's advice, he would never have left home. The cultural encounters would never have taken place, and the tension they brought about would never have been expressed in literary works of art.

It is precisely the encounter with the Other that provokes the ability of language to create order and meaning—whether this be expressed through the vision of a dystopia in which the foreign is expressed as the Other (in opposition to the well-functioning Self), or through the vision of a utopia in which the differences between the Self and the Other are dissolved. In *The Order of Things,* Michel Foucault explains how the coexistence of heterogeneous objects—heterotopias—breaks down our logic, our grammar, and our syntax. In the case of Hamsun, Constantinople emerges as a heterotopia, the disparate elements of which he cannot place within his traditional East-West way of thinking. The experience for him is one of either being misplaced or of not being placed at all—of being assigned the wrong identity (as a European tourist) or of being ignored and not being assigned any identity at all. In "Under Halvmånen," the heterotopia of Constantinople comes across first through the syntax breaking down on a generic level, and second through the coherence being regained in a utopia—in the nonplace of language where disparate elements can coexist after all. As Foucault rhetorically asks, "Where else could they be juxtaposed except in the non-place of language?" (xvi–xvii).

In the depiction of America, the logic and coherence are created through the notion of a dystopia—the nonfunctioning place that forms a contrast to a well-functioning Europe. In "Festina Lente," this modern dystopia is, in turn, viewed in opposition to the Persian's premodern Orient—while the disturbing in-between place, Constantinople, is left out of the Norwegian farmer's mythical and poetic ruminations. The world, once more, is divided into a modern America and a premodern Orient—a constellation in which the Orient may well figure as a source of inspiration for the Western, modern person, but in which the basic thought remains that the two places and their populations exist separately and shall never meet and unite. Thus, not only the Orient but the entire world is portrayed as an idyllic and poetic system—as one big Wonderland.

PART II

MODERN PRIMITIVE TRAVEL

Modern Primitive Travel

IN CONTRAST TO THE nondeveloping subject of the late-romanticist travelogues, the postromanticist, modern twentieth-century literary travelogues portray a subject in search of self-understanding. His journey is structured as a quest in the sense that it focuses on one particular object rather than an accumulation of impressions. The ultimate aim is greater insight into human nature in general and into one's Self in particular. The cultural Other no longer serves merely as exoticist material to stimulate curiosity and wonder at home, but as a source to understanding human evolution, the world, and the European's place within it. As the travelers seek out the primitive, their travel destinations change. The Orient is replaced with Africa and the Far East as these sites become available through modern technological and political development. Colonialism facilitates traveling or settling outside Europe—also in the case of Danes and Norwegians who travel to the colonies of other European nations. Darwinism and a new critical view of European modernization—what Freud calls "Das Unbehagen in der Kultur" (civilization and its discontents)—lead to an interest in premodern stages of humanity, with modern primitivism largely replacing romantic Orientalism.

The travelogues discussed in Part II are increasingly structured as linear narratives in order to represent Africa and the Far East as offering an outer *and* inner journey towards the primitive Other as well as the primitive Self. In the romanticist travelogues of Part I, the physical progression over a landscape in time provided sufficient narrative continuity. In the modern travelogues of Part II, this narrative is supplemented by a linear tale of the traveling hero's mental development and maturation. As the subject position changes so does the genre, with the travelogue increasingly resembling the novel. According to Percy Adams's study of travel literature and novels, the travelogues are no longer "just a set of notes jotted down each day or whenever the traveler has time... Far, far more often the account has been reworked..., polished, edited... In fact, nearly every *récit de voyage* published in the author's lifetime is not a pristine journal or set of notes, a fact that for the twentieth century is perhaps even more true."[1]

The Travelogue versus the Novel

The fact that the travelogue, at the turn of the twentieth century, is increasingly presented as a novel—thus blurring the boundaries between fact and fiction—leads us to consider the nature of the novel. In "Epic and Novel," Mikhail Bakhtin defines the novel as the critical genre par excellence. Constantly relativizing, problematizing, and "novelizing" its own and all other genres, it points outside itself, raising epistemological rather than ontological questions: "When the novel becomes the dominant genre, epistemology becomes the dominant discipline."[2] At this point, the author loses his authoritative position vis-à-vis the presented material, and rather treats it dialogically. One might also turn the situation around and say that once a modern person enters into an epistemological crisis, the novel is the available form that allows him or her to depict this uncertainty. If we look back at the travelogues in Part I, we see that Hans Christian Andersen, Elisabeth Jerichau-Baumann, and Knut Hamsun tend to represent identity—their own as well as that of foreigners—as static, ontological facts. Admittedly, Andersen does so to a greater extent than Hamsun. The travelers of the twentieth century, on the other hand, increasingly tend to describe their own dialogic involvement with the cultural Other as they admit to uncertainty, confusion, and revised points of view.

What Bakhtin notes is that genres depicting events occurring within our own lifetime are dialogical and inconclusive. Their inner openness, however, is accompanied by a stricter plot: "The absence of internal conclusiveness and exhaustiveness creates a sharp increase in demands for an *external* and *formal* completedness and exhaustiveness, especially in regard to plot-line. The problems of a beginning, an end, and 'fullness' of plot are posed anew" (31). Thus, in a period when other genres—in our case the travelogue—are novelized, we may expect that a strict plotline is superimposed upon the experiences gathered during travel as a form of compensation for the inconclusiveness one finds at the level of content. Inwardly, meanwhile, the travelogue is open, incorporating several dialogical voices. These dialogical voices pertain to the traveler and the foreigner, but also to those between the protagonist-traveler, the narrator, and the implied author whose different positions become an object of increasing interest in the twentieth-century travelogues. The travelogue's "I," in other words, becomes an ever more complex entity.[3] As we have seen, beginning with Hamsun, irony begins to play a bigger role in the travelogue, a trait accompanying that of the novel. According to Bakhtin:

> What are the salient features of this novelization of other genres...? They become more free and flexible, their language renews itself by incorporating extraliterary heteroglossia and the "novelistic" layers of literary language, they become dialogized, permeated with laughter, irony, humor, elements of self-parody and finally—this is the most important thing—the novel inserts into these other genres an indeterminacy, a certain semantic openendedness, a living contact with unfinished, still-evolving contemporary reality. (6–7)

Treating the novel as the main character of his study, Bakhtin tends to regard all other genres as subordinate to and halting after the novel. As the title "Epic and the Novel" suggests, Bakhtin analyzes the novel in relation to the epic and other "high" genres (4). Using the epic as his main source of contrast, it makes sense for Bakhtin to write that a long, complex, and tortuous battle of novelization has dragged other genres "into a zone of contact with reality" (39). Travel writing and other autobiographical genres have, however, always dealt with contemporary reality, and it seems more natural to regard the travelogue and the novel from a standpoint of mutual influence than from one of pure "novelization." In all fairness, Bakhtin also points out that the novel, as part of its critical enterprise, often incorporates nonfiction and extraliterary genres—"genres of everyday life" (33)—one of which, we may assume, is the travelogue.

In sum, we may say that through novelization, the exotic travelogue ends up reflecting a shift in contact zone—from a spatial contact zone, as the one described by Pratt, to a temporal contact zone as described by

Bakhtin. This "novelistic zone" (32), as Bakhtin also calls it, often makes the author him- or herself the central object of study.[4] Yet, both types of contact zones continue to coexist, and according to how you view it, the shift in emphasis to connect with one's own reality may be regarded as yet another example of Pratt's "anti-conquest."

The Travelogue versus the Anthropological Report

While the novel serves as the travelogue's generic Other on the fictional side, the scientific account serves as its generic Other on the factual side. Especially relevant for the early-twentieth-century travelogue is the anthropological or ethnographic field report.[5] The rise of anthropology as a separate field occurring in the beginning of the twentieth century also put pressure on the travelogue, forcing it toward a state of novelization. According to historian of consciousness James Clifford, disciplinary borders are under constant negotiation, with those between literary travel and anthropological fieldwork having undergone three main stages. Until Bronislaw Malinowski published his fieldwork-based ethnographic studies in the 1920s, ethnography was but one aspect of literary travel writing:

> Before the separation of genres associated with the emergence of modern fieldwork, travel and travel writing covered a broad spectrum. In eighteenth-century Europe, a *récit de voyage* or "travel book" might include exploration, adventure, natural science, espionage, commercial prospecting, evangelism, cosmology, philosophy, and ethnography.[6]

As anthropology came into existence as a separate discipline based on its own method of long-term live-in participant observation, the genres of anthropology reports and literary travel were separated (ibid.). A third stage of convergence between the two genres arose with postcolonialism when the

> growing awareness of the poetical and political contingency of fieldwork—an awareness forced on anthropologists by postwar anticolonial challenges to Euro-American centrality—is reflected in a more concrete textual sense of the enthnographer's location. Elements of the "literary" travel narrative that were excluded from ethnographies... now appear more prominently. (67)[7]

The focus of the next three chapters is on the transitional period between Clifford's first and second stage.

While Clifford's focus in describing the second stage of development—during which the genre of the ethnographic report came into being—is on the effect this had on the ethnographic report, we may focus, in turn, on the effect it had on the travel books. Their turn toward literariness and aesthetics—with the 1920s as a turning point—converges with literary modernism and aesthetic autonomy.

The three texts chosen to represent the modern Nordic travelogue progress on a scale from the factual to the fictional. Johannes V. Jensen's *Skovene* (1904) is published as a travelogue, with the traveler pursuing a scientific goal, that of gaining greater insight into human evolution. As a poet-anthropologist, Jensen insists on exploring the most primitive and modern societies on his world travel—presenting his observations as truthful—while he fictionalizes his traveling "I," presenting him with ironic distance, and using his inner world and dreams to create dramatic tension. In this sense, his technique resembles that of Hamsun—with Hamsun's late-romanticist Orientalism being replaced by Darwinism, modern anthropology, and primitivism.

Isak Dinesen (the English pen name of Karen Blixen) is both an anthropologist and a myth maker. *Den afrikanske Farm (Out of Africa)* is a nostalgic myth of a paradise lost. Unlike Hamsun and Johannes V. Jensen before her, and Axel Jensen after her, Dinesen, however, does not rely on dream imagery to create dramatic suspense in her story. The difference may be viewed as pertaining to time and experience. Living seventeen years in Africa, Dinesen is more than a traveler looking for a few adventures before returning home and writing a travelogue. In addition, writing her memoirs, Dinesen is older than the other writers, and she looks back at a main part of her life, reflecting more philosophically on what occurred. As we shall see, her anthropological endeavors include substantial reflections not only on what it means to be African but also on what it means to be Danish and Nordic—a perspective Dinesen has gained by living outside Europe for so long.

In *Ikaros: Ung mann i Sahara (Icarus: A Young Man in the Sahara)*, Axel Jensen creates more of a literary than a nostalgic myth. As his title suggests, he anchors his traveler's quest in classical Greek mythology. The effect is one of placing greater focus on the protagonist's development, with the people encountered in the "third world" functioning as props.

His gaze is much less anthropological than those of Jensen and Dinesen. Rather than exploring people in a historical context and generalizing about them, Jensen sets out to find eternal truths that may restore his faith in humanity after World War II. Thus, the contact zone of Axel Jensen's study is more of a contact zone in the Bakhtinian sense than in Pratt's sense of the word.

FOUR

Savage Science
Johannes V. Jensen in the Malay Jungle

JOHANNES V. JENSEN IS GENERALLY CONSIDERED Denmark's foremost author from the first half of the twentieth century.[1] This status was confirmed in 1944 when he received the Nobel Prize in literature and once again at the end of the century, when *Kongens Fald* (The Fall of the King, written in 1900–1901) was voted the Danish novel of the twentieth century by the readers of *Politiken*. Yet, like Knut Hamsun, Jensen is a problematic national hero whose racist and imperialist views can at best be excused as products of their time.[2]

When Jensen set out in 1902 on what would turn into a world tour, his quest was of a dual nature. As a writer he wanted to renew Danish literature through what might be considered a modern, expressionist aesthetic, and as a Darwinist he considered himself "a traveler of anthropology" seeking to understand all stages of human development—not least his own.[3] As opposed to the nineteenth-century travel writer, he turned his back on the Old World, heading instead for the New World and especially the United States. According to the author, traveling formed the core of his modern—and to a large extent modernist—authorship. When Jensen was asked for a brief autobiography for the Nobel Committee in 1945, he wrote:

> After extensive travels in the East, Malacca, China, and frequent visits in America I implemented a change of direction within Danish literature and media as I imported impulses from the American, Anglo-Saxon, spirit as a replacement for the hitherto domineering Gallicist, decadent taste.[4]

Jensen was, in many ways, of the same mindset as Hamsun. Both founded their literary careers on travel—traveling for inspiration and writing about modern humankind as permanently homeless. Also, both authors ended their careers writing regional literature, idolizing their own native soil. Yet, while Hamsun was reactionary, despising what he perceived as Anglo-Saxon "Mammonism" and seeking refuge from modernization in the Orient, Jensen worshipped the New World, superimposing the old upon the new, and vice versa, seeing, for instance, the jungle in the city and the city in the jungle. And while Hamsun fantasized about a premodern resting place, Jensen constantly moved between the primitive and the modern.

According to Marianna Torgovnick, the movement between the primitive and the modern characterizes not only modernity but also postmodernity. In *Gone Primitive,* she writes about the modern and postmodern human being: "We conceive of ourselves as at a crossroads between the civilized and the savage; we are formed by our conceptions of both those terms, conceived dialectically" (23). And in her sequel, *Primitive Passions,* Torgovnick claims that during the first decades of the twentieth century, every man feeling "anxious about his manhood or health, or maladjusted to the modern world" was given the following advice if he could afford it: "Go to Africa or the South Pacific...or to some other exotic site identified with 'the primitive'" (23).

Hence, in a broad Western context, Jensen's interests and patterns of movement are far from unique. By 1902 he had already seen much of Europe and the New World. He had traveled in the United States, Germany, Spain, England, and France, and he had begun developing his theories about the Gothic race—theories that he eventually published in *Den gotiske Renæssance* (The Gothic Renaissance, 1904). Subsequently, on his journey to the East, Jensen wanted to go to Further India to study the origins of the Gothic-Germanic race (Nedergaard, 220).[5]

Jensen's ambitions were part poetic, part scientific. He wanted to study primitivism, but he also wanted to explore his own. In this endeavor he did not hold back like his predecessors. While Hans Christian Andersen and Knut Hamsun kept at a decent distance from the Oriental (if not primitive) peoples they visited, Jensen could not get close enough. Instead of constantly being on the move, he settled down among people. And living with them, he did not sit at an observer's distance, as would the eventual father of anthropology, Bronislaw Malinowski. Nor did Jensen's vision suffice to satisfy his curiosity—he was not just one of Mary Louise Pratt's androgynous "seeing-men."[6] While earlier travelers had been content to look and subsequently feed their impressions to their imagination, and while future anthropologists would do almost the same, feeding their visual impressions to reason rather than fantasy, Jensen preferred getting close, dressing like the native people, sniffing and breathing them, drinking and partying, kissing and copulating with them. For Jensen, the contact zone is one of *intimate* contact. His travelogues are part science, part savagery. On the one hand, they contain anthropological observations and existential considerations; on the other hand, they are full of sensual experiences and poetic extravagances. Jensen, in other words, is a poet-anthropologist.

Yet, Jensen is a poet-anthropologist of a highly ironic kind. His text has been characterized as several types of parody. In *Litterære rejser,* Lars Handesten reads it as a parody on a sentimental journey;[7] in "Ironiske skraveringer" Ole Egeberg reads it as pure "Taskenspilleri" (verbal tricks);[8] and in a reflection on *Skovene* (The Forests) from 1932, Jensen himself characterizes it as "Parodien paa en Opdagelsesrejse" (the parody on a voyage of discovery).[9] In the following analysis, I will view *Skovene* (1904) as a parody on both the sentimental journey and the scientific exploration. As discussed in the introduction, these are the two types of journeys that emerged around 1735, setting the current generic pattern for the travelogue. According to Pratt, they resulted in "anti-conquest" narratives portraying the "seeing-man" who was not out to conquer the world through outward violence, but rather through knowledge of, and mutual engagement with, the cultural Other. What may ultimately be termed Jensen's anti-"anti-conquest" narrative has to be understood within a historical framework, taking into account modern aestheticism as well as the twentieth-century development and interconnectedness of literary travelogues and ethnographic accounts.

Previous Scholarship

In her introduction to *Imperial Eyes,* Pratt maintains that recent (in her case, prior to 1990) literary analysis of travelogues has fallen into the category of either aestheticism or existentialism: "More recently, an estheticist or literary vein of scholarship has developed, in which travel accounts, usually by famous literary figures, are studied in the artistic and intellectual dimensions and with reference to European existential dilemmas" (Pratt, 10). This tendency may also be said to hold true for scholarship on Jensen's *Skovene*. In terms of artistic or literary dimensions, *Skovene* has been read within the context of the author's overall oeuvre,[10] from a classical philological point of view tracing textual influences,[11] and more recently from a poststructuralist standpoint, seeing the text as an example of Roland Barthes's concept of the literary.[12]

As to *intellectual dimensions with reference to European existential dilemmas,* the travelogue has been read from a psychoanalytical as well as an intellectual historical point of view.[13] Lars Handesten's analysis of *Skovene* may be seen as this latter type of study. In *Litterære rejser,* Handesten reads Jensen's travelogues as indicative of a modern, European consciousness, focusing on the main symptoms of a modern civilization crisis, including constant movement and homelessness, loss of identity and loneliness, eternal longing, and fear of death (9). The aforementioned cultural-consciousness studies inevitably touch on Jensen's imperial consciousness, yet with a particular focus on this aspect, Bent Haugaard Jeppesen explores Jensen's imperialistic and racist consciousness in *Jensen og den hvide mands byrde* (Jensen and the White Man's Burden). Here, Jeppesen situates *Skovene* in a context allowing him to explore Jensen's political-ideological attitudes toward imperialism as they emerge in his public writing between 1900 and 1920 (9).[14] Yet, as his book was published in 1984, Jeppesen—like the other scholars—does not hold *Skovene* up against postcolonial theory. Thus, while the aesthetic line of scholarship tends to ignore a referential reality outside the text, the history-of-consciousness line tends to disregard the text's formal aspects as well as its political implication in an extra-European world.

Focusing on the parodic discursive strands in this chapter, I want to investigate how experiences (or projections, for that matter) are integrated and represented in a space of fiction. As a *parody* on sentimental travelogues, the text complicates postcolonial readings—from Torgovnick's critical approach to nineteenth-century primitivist male travelers, to Pratt's negative stance toward "anti-conquest" narrative strategies. For the author himself, the literary parody ultimately functions as a means through which Johannes V. Jensen, as a split subject, is able to make sense of the world. The coherent literary narrative illustrates the atheist's reliance on aestheticism to create meaning in an otherwise meaningless world, while the parodic mode captures his resentment that this can be achieved only through lies and exaggeration—that is, through fiction.

Narrative Structure

Skovene consists of twenty-two chapters, most of which form a linear narrative progression—or what Egeberg calls "a temporally displaced diary" (90).[15] Basically the narrative follows a journey in and out of the forests. The first chapter describes the overall setting: the kingdom, Birubunga. Subsequent chapters describe the city (two chapters), the river (four chapters), the forests (eleven chapters), the return to the river (two chapters), and the city (one chapter). A couple of chapters break up the chronological plot by containing either flashbacks (chapter 13), surrealistic fantasy images (chapter 16) or metapoetic reflections and allegories (chapters 19 and 20). The final chapter forms a narrative frame and consists of a dedication to Denmark—chanted from New York. As the journey is not over, Jensen replaces the return to the homeland, usually comprising the travelogue's natural end point, with a gaze directed toward his native soil, promising to return soon. This dedication is usually read as a parody of Viking heroic poems (Egeberg, 91).[16]

Although time mainly progresses linearly in *Skovene,* it also borders on the mythical. In Hamsun's *I Æventyrland* we saw how time turned mythical once the traveler entered the Caucasus Mountains. Similarly, Jensen situates *Skovene* mythically—"udenfor tiden" (outside time), as he has later referred to it—rendering it difficult, if not impossible, for the reader to know that the text reflects a five-week rather than a five-month stay.

Primitive Space as Poetic Space

In *Skovene* primitive and poetic space coincide. The travelogue opens with a depiction of the kingdom called Birubunga. As the name suggests, this is a land of longing. Jensen coined the fictitious place-name by combining the Malay words for "blue" and "flower" (Jensen, "Udenfor Tiden," 173). Birubunga, then, is symbolic, referring to a point of intersection between reality's geographically and historically situated Tringganu (in

Further India) and a subjective perception, influenced by the modern traveler's longings and fantasies, ultimately represented in a poetic format. The artistic result is similar to that of the romanticist, sentimental traveler, such as we have seen in Andersen's and Hamsun's texts in which land- and cityscapes are used to inspire Andersen's imagination or Hamsun's dreams. By comparison, Jensen's mental reactions are of an unprecedented, profane intensity, driven by bile rather than divine inspiration. As the narrator puts it, "I eat into my gall."[17] The *impressionism* of the romanticist, sentimental travelogues is thus replaced by what may be considered the *expressionism* of the modernist parody.

In the landscape of "Das Ding für Mich," a mythical place emerges where time and space dimensions are suspended: "Time and space are unknown there, the country has no history and is not a surveyed area but an eternity, a forest that is deep and barbarically lovely like the Old Testament."[18] Birubunga, one may say, is reminiscent of Sophus Claussen's "Ekbàtana" (1896), the Danish canonical symbolist poem depicting the moment of inspiration when "the world turned deep and Assyrian and wise." Like Ekbàtana, Birubunga refers to a transcendental moment when three times merge: that of a distant past, that of the recent past, and that of the poem's present. Yet, whereas Claussen's lyrical "I" experiences Ekbàtana in modern Paris, Jensen's traveler experiences Birubunga in premodern Further India, where the ideal state of mind, rather than being triggered by Platonic asceticism, is triggered by primitivist ecstasy. And while Claussen's poem circles around the climactic moment experienced, the travelogue rather depicts the process of seeking that moment—the path toward and away from it, as well as the vague determination that the moment has actually occurred. Here the persistent "I have lived a day in Ekbàtana" of Claussen's lyrical "I" is replaced by the poet-anthropologist's intellectual understanding of how such a moment may be said to have occurred on the primitivist journey.[19]

Primitive Religion and Modern Aesthetics

The infinite land, Birubunga, is a site of boundlessness and ecstasy, not only for the traveler, but also for the natives. The latter, according to Jensen, comprise a "Mohammedan" principality, the sultan of which is more preoccupied with eroticism than war: "As an innocent Malay, he thinks only of making love and sets a grand example for his people" (102).[20] The Prophet, the traveler claims, demands "jungle picnics" so that the sultan will recall what it means to be a human being (103). In the wilderness, the sultan sheds his clothes, eats, plays, hoots, sings, and screams—all while surrendering to his death instincts and abandoning himself "in howling delight" (104). In the native language, the feast of excess and abandonment is called a *makan besar,* and this type of feast and jungle picnic becomes the traveler's own goal so that he, too, may recall what it means to be human. Thus by the early twentieth century, Mohammedanism is considered an antidote to modern atheism—on par with any other "primitive" religion—rather than a threat to, or an alternative to, Western Christianity. The Muslim geographic realm, that is, turns into a symbol of, as well as a means to, a primitivist human mental condition.

According to Torgovnick it is precisely primitivism as ecstasy that is sought out by the men of the early twentieth century: "These men... ascribed to 'primitive' places the power of possibility, of renewal and revitalization" (*Primitive Passions,* 24). They associate the primitive with the feminine, the oceanic, the ecstatic, and the collective (14, 24, 41), but their quest always follows the same surprising pattern. At the moment when the possibility for an oceanic merging with the universe arises, they recoil in fear of letting go of their European, male identity (24). Torgovnick's argument is that a gender-based underlying assumption—based on myths, fictions, intuitions, neuroses, and speculation—renders the ecstasy and the merging with the primitive impossible for the European man. Ultimately he associates the experience not only with a momentary loss of his own identity but with the end of modern civilization. The ultimate reserve and timidity of Jensen's traveler fit into the psychological and philosophical mindset Torgovnick lays out. Yet, Jensen operates at a level of consciousness that Torgovnick does not take into account in her discussion of André Gide and Carl Jung as her exemplary travelers. Aware of, and quite explicit about, his urge to overcome his own feminine side by merging with it, Jensen mocks his own endeavors and his associating the feminine with the reigning female animal of the jungle, the tiger. Jensen's reserve ultimately reveals the self-reflective aestheticist's and anthropologist's understanding of how desire functions.

Not attaining one's goals can be a strategy of prolonged pleasure. Søren Kierkegaard depicts the intellectual aesthetic par excellence through the figure of Johannes in *Forførerens Dagbog* (The Diary of a Seducer, 1843). As a split subject, Jensen's traveler is quite reminiscent of Johannes, yet his perspective on seduction, erotics, joy, and ecstasy is couched in anthropological terms that in many ways evoke the language Georges Bataille uses in *Erotism*. Thus, I view Jensen and his understanding of desire as situated halfway between the philosophers Kierkegaard and Bataille—not too surprisingly, perhaps, as he wrote half a century after the former and half a century before the latter.

In *Erotism*, Bataille describes the conditions of erotics from a social-anthropological point of view. His main thesis is that all people long to escape the discontinuity into which they are born. They yearn for an original state of continuity, one that also becomes our final continuity. That is, continuity—or ecstasy—is experienced in death and in sexuality. Eroticism, in turn, constitutes the human (vs. animal) aspect of the act of sexual reproduction. When eroticism is governed by religious rules in which people blithely believe, transgressing the rules leads to an *outer* experience. As Bataille conversely puts it, "Whether we are discussing eroticism or religion in general a clear inner experience would have been out of the question at a time when the equilibrium between prohibitions and transgressions, regulating the play of both, did not stand out clearly defined and understood" (35).

Turning to *Skovene,* we may say that Birubunga's Mohammedan sultan experiences the transgression of everyday prohibitions during the religiously ordained jungle feast on an outer level without having grasped the religious system as a philosopher-anthropologist. As an intellectual atheist, however, Jensen's only option is to enjoy ecstasy as an inner experience. This type of inner experience, in turn, can only be kept alive through suspension. Yet, religion and eroticism also demand a final transgressive act—an act provoking real fear: "Anguish is what makes humankind, it seems; not anguish alone, but anguish transcended and the act of transcending it" (Bataille, 86). What Bataille subsequently refers to as "the greatest anguish, the anguish in the face of death" (87) can only be overcome in death. Yet, as a human being, one may overcome a lesser fear—fright and horror—through confrontation. This is Bataille's point: "I do not think that man has much chance of throwing light on the things that terrify him before he has dominated them. Not that he should hope for a world in which there would be no cause for fear... But man can surmount the things that frighten him and face them squarely" (7).

Bataille's understanding largely mirrors that of Jensen's traveler. This traveler seems to have accepted that he cannot experience ecstasy on an immediate level. As an anthropologist he somewhat condescendingly describes the Malays and the religious system that allows them moments of transgression. The Malay "gains consciousness in a system of strict paragraphs and commands that grow with him" (Jensen, *Skovene*, 102).[21] The narrator then lists all these laws, from rules about washing and praying, to rules about reading the Koran and not eating pork. Through ironic interjections, the narrator mocks Western pragmatic explanations of these rules, such as washing being good for the skin, pork rotting in the tropics, and there being plenty of fish in the local rivers and ocean. A better explanation views religion in relation to human desire. The Prophet, after all, also commands the occasional transgression of his commands: "Then, you know, the Prophet in all his wisdom allows or rather sternly commands occasional jungle picnics" (103).[22] The narrator's voice remains ironic, yet it seems that he understands the primitives in terms of the joy their naive understanding of the Koran brings them. As a civilized man, the traveler, on the other hand, has to rely on the *inner* experience of transgression and fulfilled desire.

Playing with Narrative Desire

Jensen's narrator ultimately turns his understanding of inner desire on the reader and *his* desire, namely, his narrative desire. In this process, games of suspension and substitution play a major role. Jensen's traveler is cunning and evasive, allowing himself constantly to redefine his quest. From the beginning of the journey he has expressed his goals in the vein of the adventurer. As the first European, he insists, he wants to climb "the world mountain" Bukit Alam, and then he wants to kill a tiger (108–9). The goals, however, are to be understood in terms of parody. Like Hamsun's narrator in *I Æventyrland,* Jensen's narrator maintains an ironic distance to his dramatic, neurotic, attention-craving antihero. This traveler is depicted as entering the ranks of British explorers by exuberantly announcing the aim of his expedition in the Singapore branch of the English Royal Geographic Society. And while he is at it, why announce a wish to shoot a tiger when he might as well employ the present participle and portray the event as a constant reflex: "I intended to explore and mount Bukit alam, shooting tigers right and left on my way" (109)?[23] Subsequently, the narrator shows his antihero filling his boat with weapons and provisions—including twelve bottles of whiskey—only to regret the absence of reporters:

> Unfortunately I could not be photographed at the departure, as I stood there fully equipped in my khaki suit straight from the tailor in Singapore—without a crease—my patent tropical hat and my cartridge belts crosswise on my chest. But I promised myself to leave hair and beard alone in the forest for the benefit of the interviewers when I came back with the tiger skin and the record from Bukit alam. (113)[24]

In a perfect Hamsunian way, the narrator succeeds in deriding not only his antihero but also the Western media hype surrounding the "explorer."

The parodic mode of the travelogue further includes a metacognitive, psychological understanding of the quest and its symbolic value. Jensen's traveler—distinct from all the other European tiger hunters described in *Skovene*'s fifth chapter—emerges as an intellectual, self-conscious, poetically inclined tiger hunter. The traveler is able to verbalize that to him, the tiger is not just an animal but a symbol: "The tiger is the essence of the great nature, it is the soul of the forests, it is the incarnation of the *female*. I want to measure up to it!" (121).[25] Several Jensen scholars have focused on this statement and read it into a greater psychoanalytical context regarding the mother-fixated, sexually frightened author.[26] Yet, *Skovene* is an ironic text in which the point of view often—as here—is impossible to determine. On the one hand, big-game hunters—a group of people to whom Jensen's traveler turns out not to belong—are ridiculed as the hunt for trophies is linked to a macho symbolism exposed by Jensen's traveler. On the other hand, the extensive tiger reflections also turn on the traveling "I" and his need to come across as an intellectual *Übermensch* in comparison to other tiger hunters. This self-ridicule emerges through hyperbole and a series of pathetic apostrophes, introduced by moaning interjections: "Oh, my snobs and monomaniacs, I thought, as I sat in Ali's boat and the afternoon heat and the fever and speed of the journey had made my head big. Oh, oh, my small souls, here comes another type of tiger hunter!" (121).[27] Through his desire to assert his superior intellectual difference, the hero, of course, reveals himself precisely as a snob and a monomaniac. The only thing that does not appear foolish in such an inner monologue, though, is the art of narration. The traveler, seeing himself as "a dazzling bundle of rays from a hot power of imagination" (ibid.), is usurped by the narrator in order to create a point of view resulting in an intense, subjective expression. Hence, the text ends up coming across more as a cleverly connected series of prose poems than as the exact representation of a traveler's sights and thoughts.

The narrator's ultimate aestheticization of the journey demands a climax and an assertion that the goals of the quest have been attained. Pushing on the boundaries of his genre—and of the readers' genre expectations of the travelogue—the narrator determines the climax as a combination of an intoxicating *makan besar* and a surreal fever dream that the traveler allegedly has the following night thanks to a terrible hangover; only here does the protagonist meet and struggle with a tiger. The poet's strategy reminds us of Hamsun's *I Æventyrland,* in which dream imagery is also used to create one of the most memorable episodes of the travelogue (i.e., the encounter with the shepherd in Kobi discussed in chapter 3). Dreams, then, become a strategy through which the travel writer may create narrative drama, climax, and peripeteia. The dream is not pure fiction; it may be regarded as an authentic and integral part of the travelogue as it is experienced during the course of the journey. Yet, while Hamsun uses the dream to establish uncertainty, depicting an episode that *could* have taken place in reality, Jensen uses its surreal potential to indicate modern humankind's subconscious primitivist associations. As readers we are never in doubt that this could not have happened in reality.

In his intoxicated nightmare, jungle and city, tiger and woman, nature and cabaret merge. *He* shoots, stabs, and slices her up; *she* sucks, licks, and sinks her teeth into him. In the end everything is drenched in blood, and the two suddenly receive a standing ovation from an excited audience. Serving as a climax, the dream points to the exhibitionist's need to display his erotic drives, and the angry bohemian artist figure's urge to expose his readers' voyeurism.

In the end, the reader is left reflecting upon his own narrative desire, his genre expectations, and the extent to which fiction may substitute for fact in a travelogue. As fiction, the text generally satisfies our demands for a beginning, a middle, and an end. As a travelogue, it satisfies our demand for an exploration. Finally, as a bildungsroman, it satisfies our demand for personal development—the development that will allow the traveler to return home, from a primitive to a modern realm. The traveler has gone primitive, and he has faced his fears—at least in the jungle of his subconscious transmitted to us through a poetic rendition of dream imagery. The modern reader, then, has to accept that the quest object of the traditional adventurer is first parodically downgraded and then surrealistically internalized. Together, the writing traveler and his reading audience operate on the level of the *inner* experience of transgression.

Anthropological Account and Poetic Travelogue

In order to investigate the more realistically depicted moment of ecstasy—the *makan besar* (jungle feast) during which the traveler does not confront his great fear, but rather faces minor fears that he is pretty sure of mastering—I want to return to the traveler's method, that is, the way he travels and enters into relations with the primitive and its inhabitants. As discussed in the introduction to Part II, James Clifford has traced the relationship between travel literature and anthropological fieldwork in the course of the twentieth century. A quick summary indicates that until Malinowski published his ethnographic observations based on fieldwork in the 1920s, ethnography was a natural part of any travelogue. Yet, once anthropology was established as an academic field in its own right, it became incumbent upon its methods and publications to distance themselves from common travel literature.

Clifford explains in more detail how the lines were eventually drawn between the scientific, stationary anthropologist and the romantic, literary traveler. While the anthropologist suppresses his emotions, the literary traveler first and foremost expresses them ("vents" might be a better verb in Jensen's case). Whereas the anthropologist marks his distance to the observed object by dressing European, the literary traveler goes "native" or "primitive"—also in his clothing (Clifford, 72–74). And while the anthropologist never surrenders to sexual relations, these—whether they be heterosexual or homosexual—become not just common but "quasi-obligatory" for many of the literary travelers (72). At the beginning of the 1900s, Jensen's traveler, however, can be categorized as the uninhibited poet-anthropologist who—before anthropology was institutionalized as a science—could move freely and fluidly in a discursive field, the boundaries of which were not set until about twenty years later.

When it comes to cross-dressing, the traveler in *Skovene* eventually sheds his khaki outfit and tropical hat, donning instead a sarong (203). Clifford calls this "cultural cross-dressing" (73), and Torgovnick sees it as part of the process leading to the moment of merging: "a symbolic expression of sharing, temporarily, in matters culturally coded as sexually other" (*Gone Primitive*, 172). For Torgovnick it is the feminizing aspect of dressing like the natives that is to expand the male traveler's consciousness. But in Jensen's case it is not clear whether the skirt is primarily tied to femininity. At the end of the journey, as he is leaving Birubunga, the traveler runs into two European engineers and exclaims:

> Here I had gone so far that I had thrown off my pants and donned the sarong like the other skirt people around me, professing Islam! I felt ashamed before the two white men, ashamed as a Christian dog over my Oriental costume. (203)[28]

The traveler, who throughout his stay in Birubunga has let himself get excited about and flirt with the Malay version of Islam, with its mandatory offenses and jungle picnics, suddenly sees himself through the eyes of a Christian European. At this point, his reaction turns more on nineteenth-century Orientalism than twentieth-century gender issues. The dichotomy constituting the traveler's understanding of religion has, as we have seen, not been Orientalist. Instead of viewing the world as divided into Christians and Mohammedans, the traveler has, as a postromantic European atheist, regarded the cultural Other as *religious*—in opposition to himself as irreligious, or ungodly.[29] The fact that he suddenly sees himself as "a Christian dog" must be a consequence of his counting the Englishmen as Christians—maybe based not so much on their nationality as their profession. The Bohemian suddenly sees himself through the eyes of the established bourgeoisie, and despite the great distance from the bourgeoisie he has left behind, he cannot avoid feelings of shame and guilt. It is also possible to read the ambivalent text so that the traveler's sense of shame as he appears in a feminine skirt vis-à-vis the masculine engineers is so great that instead of addressing it openly, he covers himself behind a nineteenth-century Orientalist discourse.

When it comes to sexual and emotional outbursts, Jensen's traveler can hardly be characterized as Clifford's anthropologist favoring "an understanding rapport and measured affection" (Clifford, 69). He fits rather into the category of the romantic traveler, who shouts out "expressions of overt enthusiasm and love" (ibid.) and for whom racial difference, rather than being downplayed, is highlighted as an arousing aspect of sexual interrelations (ibid., 70–71). Jensen's traveler's experiences culminate in the *makan besar*—a "Dionysian feast" (173)—when the traveler and his local guide, Matti, return from a hunt and find their two prostitute Malay girlfriends enormously intoxicated.[30] It turns out they have found and drunk the traveler's coffee. First the traveler wants to give the women an antidote, but it then occurs to him that the caffeine high of the primitives combined with his and Matti's alcoholic intoxication could even out their cultural differences:

> The whiskey stimulated Matti and me so that we sank to the lower level on which Aoaaoa and Lidih were located, and the coffee raised them up to us; we met in an atmosphere belonging to neither one of us, respectively, and thus was fresh to both parts. In a way we swapped gender, and that was really good. (173)[31]

Since ecstasy requires differences to be evened out in order to establish the oceanic and boundless, this is where the traveler's identity ends up at stake. And here it becomes clear that for him it is a matter of giving up not just what he considers his cultural superiority but also the supremacy granted by his gender. Primitivism and feminism are once again equated, as are civilization and masculinity.

The feast culminates in shouting, squealing, banging on a copper drum, and finally swinging (i.e., trading partners). The traveler who had first initiated a relationship with the younger Aoaaoa now desires the older Lidih, and the evening ends up with the *traveler* getting her—while the *narrator* launches into long lyrical passages, relating the traveler's desire toward the women and their names. In these prose poems, Aoaaoa and Lidih are placed antithetically, with Aoaaoa representing the warmth of the South; the valley and the jungle; youth, summer, and colors. Lidih, on the other hand, represents the cold of the North; the mountains; old age, fall, and grayness. The oscillation of desire between the two extremes is expressed through an inner monologue characterized by apostrophes, by repetition, by antitheses and by the very sound of their names. The focus on the names—Aoaaoa and Lidih—is symbolist and modernist with its insistence on the sheer sound and resonance of the names as aural imagery. If we compare the two names Aoaaoa and Lidih, we see the antitheses of repetition versus termination of syllables, vocal versus consonant driven sounds, deep back vocals versus light front vocals. All in all, Aoaaoa suggests primitive roaring, or as Henrik Wivel has put it, the name in and of itself is an orgasmic roar (75). Transcending the border between *signifié* and *signifiant* (between Aoaaoa and Lidih as women, and Aoaaoa and Lidih as sounds) thus becomes an important element of the ecstatic moment, which can ultimately be characterized as not only erotic but also poetic.

The Anthropologist Position as Inspiration

As the poetic trumps the erotic and scientific in *Skovene,* the traveler's anthropological depictions tend to stand out for a short moment and are then subsumed by the poet's urge to fuel his own inspiration. Even the more "scientific" observations are colored by the poet's fascination with the powerful side of primitivism. Jensen is never out to find its serene side. Thus, he seems quite satisfied to expound upon a personal theory on the Malay's body and temperament:

> The Malay has a tendency to go amok in all matters... I think this tendency to go amok is caused by an excitement of the muscles; it is a kind of flesh intoxication, an overheating of the muscles. The Malays are the fleshiest people in the world, they are solid as bulldogs, their flesh presses against their bodies. Therefore their sense of life is practically determined by the impression of power they get of themselves; their muscles are capable of depriving them of their power. (114-15)[32]

Read out of context, the observation could come across as scientifically distanced. Yet, as it appears in *Skovene,* it implies the traveler's subjective identification with the frustrated Malay.[33] What makes him the poet he is, is that he gets equally intoxicated and overwhelmed, and that his "sense of life," too, is determined by the "impression of power" he has of himself. In the preceding equation, one only has to replace the notion of flesh and muscles with that of nerves. For the poet, the excitement and overheating of the nerves lead to going amok in writing—either as he depicts his own rage directly, or as he uses it indirectly as a source of inspiration for subjective expressionism.

An example of the former, a direct depiction of rage, occurs when the traveler becomes the object of the natives' interest. Evening upon evening the traveler is confronted by "thirty insatiable, staring Malays," whose curiosity makes him "shake thin-skinnedly from a sense of loneliness, from rage and pain" (138).[34] Instead of enjoying the attention or emphasizing the reciprocal nature of the investigation, as Pratt would have it, the traveler inverts the relationship of his anthropological studies and turns himself into a schizophrenic scientist. This is a scientist who, in the encounter with the cultural Other, observes himself as much as the Other.[35] Suddenly the traveler's rage becomes the object of his inquiry into "the human states of mind" (139). The account turns into a parody on an anthropological account with Jensen the traveler—who really sees himself as representing the world's most superior race and culture—ultimately finding his own primitivism more interesting than that of the primitives.

In those of the narrator's expressionist depictions in which the traveler's subjective presence is less directly stated, the movement is once more one of making a concrete "scientific" observation and then turning it into a subjective, strongly emotional picture. An often commented upon ekphrastic moment occurs in the narrator's portrait of Aoaaoa. We have seen how he uses her name for an aural portrait, but he is also able to use her appearance for an expansive visual-verbal portrait. The traveler starts out acknowledging that his object is but a common Malay girl who is not particularly beautiful. He then renders her "picture":

> Her traits are not in her favor, her nose is brackish and spread into a couple of large coves with open smelling holes, and her mouth is a chap without a personal form. But this face of low type is practically made of colors in dark and mysterious hues.
> The basic color is glowing brown like pure copper, which in the shadows of her nose and around her eyelids fades into bronze and pewter, and her big lips

are lightly slate-colored. Her teeth inside are red like the fire of betel. From these colors that are perfect in their purity and light, emerges Aoaaoa's gaze from her black-brown eyes with whites that, in their freshness, are almost as blue as the sky. And behind her violet ears and around her full brick-colored neck flows her thick pit coal black hair. She sits on her one loin with her feet pulled up under her, hard and dry walking feet, upon one of which she wears a silver ring with a green stone on her brown toe. Her sarong, enveloping her long wonderful hips and fitting tightly across her narrow stomach, is a simple green flowery calico, and her upper body with her hardy chest is covered by a sulfur-yellow scarf. (166–67)[36]

The portrait is flattering as well as offensive. It is typically expressionist in its reliance on the primitive, ethnographic, racial, and sexual—all elements that ultimately combine into an explosive expression of longing. Partly, it builds on a modernist aesthetic of the abject—especially known from Jensen's oeuvre in his depiction of a horse slaughter in *Kongens Fald* (32–33).

With the gaze of a scientist, the traveler categorizes Aoaaoa as being "of low type" and deprives her of her voice and subjectivity by depicting her mouth as "a chap without a personal form" (166). Having thus subjugated her, the aesthete can surrender himself to his vibrant painting. The verbal depiction is amplified through semantic density—in this case through color associations pointing to natural, not cultural, elements: from earthly plants and minerals to heavenly bodies. Further expanding this associative field, the narrator adds that when, by dusk, he will possess her, he will, "together with, and in her, get back the bygone times I had lamented, Egypt's sun-red daughters, the Bible's brass-colored virgins, the blue girls from Palmyra" (167).[37] Like Birubunga, Aoaaoa turns into a means to an end as well as the end itself. As a primitive, she is to bring him into connection with times and places of the past on a historic as well as a personal level, her scent evoking his "childhood's lost paradise" (167). As an individual, however, she carries no meaning. As Egeberg puts it, "The object has receded into the background in favor of the subjective experience in fetishlike worship."[38] Seeing Jensen's portrait in the light of Pratt's imperial stylistics, it once more becomes clear that the Victorian stylistics employing adjectives to link the foreign to the familiar on a cultural level are increasingly replaced by a semantic density distancing the foreign. In the case of primitivism, the cultural Other is situated as far away from a familiar, modern, Western Self as possible so that, ultimately, it is invested with all the Westerner's losses on a collective as well as a personal level.

The space of primitive ecstasy is experienced as an eternal space as all boundaries are suspended—yet, it can only be experienced momentarily. In *Skovene*, Johannes V. Jensen has allegedly experienced the primitive and the ecstatic in Birubunga. Birubunga, however, is represented as a kingdom under constant pressure from Western imperialism. Frenchmen as well as the British are ready to colonize and exploit Birubunga's tin mines. This impending threat is presented to the reader first in the introduction, then in the penultimate chapter in which we are told about the two white engineers invading the kingdom after finally having been granted a concession to the mines (202). Read metapoetically this suggests that in new, modern times dominated by capitalism and imperialism, romanticist writing focusing on the blue flower of longing (Birubunga) may be turning obsolete. Read more pragmatically in terms of Jensen's creating suspense and drama in his travelogue, it indicates that at the very last moment the traveler succeeded in exploring this part of the world as a primitive culture. Still, one may wonder why the narrator states this fact without any sense of nostalgia or melancholy. As opposed to a previous fin-de-siècle generation bemoaning lost authenticity—such as Hamsun's lamenting the American invasion of the Orient in *I Æventyrland*—Jensen's traveler seems only to look ahead, toward the next stop on his dialectic route across the globe. Having satisfied his primitivist longings in Birubunga, he now heads for the modernity of the New World. Jensen's traveler is a modern "been there, done that" explorer. His psychological, aesthetic, and anthropological insight makes it impossible for him to take the "an sich" aspect and authenticity of people and places seriously. What seems most important is that the merging conclusions of a personal journey and a primitive stage of civilization form a poetic whole.

Ultimately, in terms of the poet-anthropologist, we may conclude that in *Skovene*, Jensen's anthropologist endeavors are constantly subordinated to his poetic endeavors. Birubunga, that is, overtrumps Tringganu. While Tringganu may disappear forever, Birubunga—the poetic traveler's own perception of the land—is captured eternally in his writings. Not in an idyllic account, but rather in an ironic account. In this parodic "anti-conquest" narrative, the traveler both engages in *and* distances himself from anthropological exploration, macho imperialist endeavors, and sensual encounters in the "contact zone." Jensen is the quintessential example of the split subject whose psychological insight and human understanding constantly leave him passionate and dispassionate at once. He is a modern aesthete, skeptical not only of his own desire but also of that of his reader.

FIVE

Humor, Gender, and Nationality
Isak Dinesen's Encounter with Africa

> Your *Kabilla*—your tribe—do not get as angry as other Europeans, ... you laugh at people.
> —Karen Blixen, *Den afrikanske Farm*

ISAK DINESEN'S *Out of Africa* (1937) is exceptional. It is exceptionally popular and well known—thanks especially to Sydney Pollack's 1985 film adaptation starring Meryl Streep and Robert Redford; it is exceptionally commented on and fought over within academia—by feminists and postcolonialists in particular; it is exceptionally well written, and is the most aesthetically recognized classic of those discussed in this book. It furthermore forms a general *exception* within this study of Danish and Norwegian travelogues. Generically it is less of a travelogue than those of Andersen, Baumann, Hamsun, and Jensen, since Dinesen did not travel about, but rather remained in one place for a period of seventeen years. In terms of nationality, it is less decidedly Danish or Norwegian than the other works because Dinesen—bilingual after her extended stay in a British colony—initially wrote her memoirs partly in English, partly in Danish.[1] In 1937 she published her Danish version, *Den afrikanske Farm*, for a Nordic audience (under her name Karen Blixen), a bit earlier than she published her English version aimed at an Anglo-Saxon reading audience in both England and the United States (under the pseudonym of Isak Dinesen).[2]

Out of Africa is usually characterized as a hybrid text carrying elements of the autobiography, memoir, travelogue, pastoral, myth, ethnography, poetry, and novel. The main issue at stake in characterizing the text usually revolves around its truth claim. As in travel literature in general, it is impossible to draw a straight line between fact and fiction. Traditionally this question has been aimed at the text's autobiographical content,[3] but with the advent of postcolonial studies, the question is more often aimed at its ethnographic content. In other words, the interest in Dinesen's depiction of her Self is replaced with an interest in her depiction of the Other.

In her article "Poesi, etnografi og sandhed" (Poetry, ethnography and truth, 1992), Nina Johnsen places *Out of Africa* in the context of what she defines as Dinesen's twenty-year-long project of depicting the Masai. Tracing Dinesen's efforts from an initial poem, "Ex Africa," published in 1925, to ethnographic sketches and more prosaic letters written home between 1914 and 1931, to Dinesen's monumental oeuvre written in 1936, Johnsen takes seriously Dinesen's search for a genre that will allow her to render the most truthful ethnographic depiction possible of the Masai.[4] Johnsen concludes on a positive note, finding Dinesen's subjective point of view scientifically unpretentious and truthful: "*Out of Africa*'s picture of the Masai as intangible but inevitable victims of the development [is] a very precise and truthful representation of a contemporaneous unsentimental realpolitik on the one hand, and of a contemporaneous poetic understanding of the individual, sensual level on the other" (87). Johnsen, publishing her article in an anthropological journal, may be viewed as representing what James Clifford has referred to as the third phase of anthropology—a humble stance taken in a postwar anticolonial era when the so-called scientific field of anthropology begins to question the objectivity of the participant observer, and the notion of the nonliterary ethnographic report.[5]

While anthropologists may look at *Out of Africa* as a cross between poetry and ethnography, postcolonialists tend to view Dinesen's book as a confluence of aesthetic and ideological discourses. Within literary postcolonial studies, the question posed is whether Dinesen and her text constitute an exception to Western imperialist and colonialist discourse. Are Dinesen's actions and attitude different from those of other European colonialists in British Kenya? No, says African author Ngũgĩ wa Thiong'o, characterizing *Out of Africa* as "one of the most dangerous books ever written about Africa," and its author as embodying "the great racist myth at the heart of the Western bourgeois civilization."[6]

Abdul JanMohamed, on the other hand, opts for glorification rather than condemnation. In *Manichean Aesthetics*, he casts Dinesen as a heroic, open-minded person, shedding her European identity and embracing the African landscape. To him Dinesen *is* an exception. Her aesthetic work is based on a structure of metonymy (rather than metaphor) that distinguishes her writing from that of other European colonizers and settlers (77). This structure of metonymy is, according to JanMohamed, based on a mythic consciousness that Dinesen learns and absorbs in Africa (71). Yet, one is left wondering what would make Dinesen more open to an African way of thinking than other settlers. In answering this question, JanMohamed lists "her greater strength of character and keener insights" (53), her "strong sense of obligation and her genuine affection for Africans" (57), and her "unusual understanding" (ibid.), which rather than being based on (humane) ideology is based on "trust and affection" (58). The one time JanMohamed attributes these qualities to categories outside Dinesen's individuality, he does so by following up on Dinesen's own claim about her national heritage. In *Out of Africa*, Dinesen describes *Scandinavians* as malleable and open to possibilities rising out of interaction with Africans. JanMohamed, operating with the logic that attitudes are determined partly by individuality and partly by ideology based on sociopolitical circumstances, then proceeds to surmise that Dinesen may identify more with the oppressed Other, since Denmark was occupied by the Germans during the war.[7]

Whereas JanMohamed vaguely draws on the category of nationality, Marianna Torgovnick bases her understanding entirely on gender. Substituting terminology of the oceanic and ecstatic for that of JanMohamed's mythic consciousness, Torgovnick, in *Primitive Passions*, divides her discussion of a modernist quest for primitivism into two main parts: "Men" and "Women." As we have seen in chapter 4, Johannes V. Jensen falls under the first category exemplified by the writings of Gide and Jung. Dinesen, on the other hand, is discussed as a representative woman who goes all the way in her quest for the oceanic, even when it entails shedding her superior European identity. Citing a passage in *Out of Africa* in which Dinesen writes longingly about her dead body being laid out on, and merging with, the African landscape rather than being buried, Torgovnick draws the following conclusion:

> This oceanic view of the self in relation to nature turns up with enormous frequency in women's writing about Africa. It contrasts strongly with Gide's and Jung's experience of Africa as dangerous to a sense of self and a writer's art. Women writers typically saw Africa as an opportunity to escape the limitations of women's domestic lives at home and actively sought there a vocation and self-fulfillment... The women want to merge with the land, and perceive their identities in and through it. (62–63)

Thus, many scholars from various fields hail Dinesen's text as an exception—some based on a postmodern understanding of science, some on a belief in the exceptional individual, some relating it to national origins, and some to gender. The focus of this chapter, however, is that to which Dinesen herself related it, namely, a Nordic sense of humor. In the following I will analyze her memoirs as an ethnographic *and* autoethnographic text, depicting and defining a Nordic or Danish "tribal" trait that, according to Dinesen, facilitated a sense of understanding between African natives and Scandinavian settlers. I will compare Dinesen's use of the comic to that of male travelers, such as Johannes V. Jensen, distinguishing between irony and humor. Finally, I will consider Dinesen as an in-between figure, whose bilingualism allowed her to construct two different identities—Karen Blixen and Isak Dinesen—in two separate works: *Den afrikanske Farm* and *Out of Africa*.

The Structure of *Out of Africa*

Thematically, *Out of Africa* depicts Dinesen's life and loss in Africa as a Fall of Humankind. On a personal level, Dinesen loses, first, the love of her life, Denys Finch-Hatton, who dies in a plane crash, and, second, her coffee farm, which eventually goes bankrupt. At the end, she has to leave the country and move back to Denmark. Forming a backdrop to Dinesen's personal devastation is Africa's loss as the country is colonized and the natives lose their land and rituals. In terms of function, the text serves as compensation, turning a personal loss into a poetic gain. *Out of Africa* is often defined as a myth of a paradise lost,[8] and more specifically we may view it in the context of Dinesen's effort in vain to convert her land into a natural preserve. Although her project of capturing, freezing, and protecting a place and moment in time in Kenya failed on a *literal* level, it succeeds on a *literary* level.

In addition to serving as a myth,[9] *Out of Africa* was also intended to serve as a historical document,[10] and finally, psychologically, Dinesen works through her loss by staging a tragedy for a reading audience.

Structurally, the text is divided into five parts. The first part, "Kamante and Lullu," spans the chronology of her entire stay—from her arrival, beyond her departure, to her being resituated in Denmark and receiving letters from Kamante. The second part, "A Shooting Accident on the Farm," focuses more narrowly on a particular event, and while Dinesen, in the first part, plays the role of a doctor, she here plays that of a judge. In Part III, "Visitors to the Farm," Dinesen emphasizes her role as a hostess, and the text is divided into separate chapters depicting various visits by natives, colonizers, Scandinavian settlers, and other people inhabiting Africa, such as an Indian High Priest. The fourth part, "From an Immigrant's Notebook," is the most fragmentary, containing a series of touching and often humorous anecdotes. Finally, in the fifth part, "Farewell to the Farm," the narrator gathers the threads of her story by recapturing all the deaths and losses experienced during her seventeen years in Africa: the loss of the farm, the death of a Kikuyu chief, and Denys's fatal accident. At the end, the narrator takes on a new perspective—that of looking back, while nothing is revealed about her future life in Denmark.

Overall, a tight composition becomes looser and looser—falling apart, like the protagonist's own life and dreams, in Part IV—while the final part presents the recomposed story and protagonist. Much has been written about this unusually structured memoir. Johnsen points out how, as the title indicates, the text is arranged spatially rather than temporally (83), and Dinesen herself has referred to it as a five-act tragedy (287). The type of tragedy at stake, though, is the tragicomic rather than the serious kind. The narrator of *Out of Africa* is no doubt a great humorist of the romantic kind.

The Philosophy of Humor

It is no news that Dinesen found solace in humor. She chose the pseudonym Isak because of the name's Hebrew meaning: he who laughs.[11] In *Out of Africa* her philosophy of humor is most clearly expressed in the chapter titled "The Roads of Life."

In one night a man is faced with one accident after another. He is awakened by a terrible noise. In the dark he runs down to his pond, stumbles over a rock, and falls into three ditches. Thinking he has run in the wrong direction, he turns around twice, stumbling over another rock and falling into three more ditches. Finally he realizes his fish dam is leaking and spends the rest of the night plugging its hole. As he wakes up the next morning, he looks out his window, and sees that the pattern of his movements—viewed from above—forms the outline of a stork.

Of course, the man does not really see this, but the listener who has followed the tale, together with the storyteller's illustrative drawings on a piece of paper, sees it. The story was one Dinesen knew as a child and in which she finds comfort as she is about to lose control over her farm in Kenya. Just as her existence is about to lose all meaning, she cites the story, concluding:

> He must have thought "What ups and downs! What a run of bad luck!" He must have wondered what was the idea of all his trials, he could not know that it was a stork. But through them all he kept his purpose in view, nothing made him turn around and go home, he finished his course, he kept his faith. That man had his reward. In the morning he saw the stork. He must have laughed out loud then. (262–63)[12]

The anecdote sums up Dinesen's tragicomic, aesthetic belief bordering on the religious. Alleviating the pain of life is the bird's-eye view creating a story, the representation of which, through drawing or writing, induces laughter.[13]

In her dissertation *Kunst og erfaring* (Art and Experience), Tone Selboe similarly emphasizes the power of the aesthetic bird's-eye view—or gaze at a distance, as she calls it—to create perfection and unity.[14] The gaze, writes Selboe, creates an aesthetic whole: "In *Den afrikanske Farm*, the gaze is that which unites beginning and end, origin and return" (67). But it also creates a social whole: "The gaze establishes...a relationship between text and world, narrator and reader: The gaze turns into speech. The gaze is the connection between the self and the world, the I and the others" (68). Thus, the aesthetic and social go hand in hand because being able to look at one's life from a distance creates harmony on both levels. When Selboe talks of distance, it is a temporal and spatial distance, and the Other is the reader—the home audience whether Nordic or Anglophone. Dinesen describes viewing the African landscape from an airplane or from a distant train station, and she writes about her farm in Denmark six years after having left it.[15] Yet, what Dinesen herself refers to in the tale of the stork is her own ability to be in the middle of things—with no spatial or temporal distance—and still be able to consider her fate at an *imagined* distance.

Without believing in an orthodox, Christian God, Dinesen suggests we may believe in an eye—a point of view—located outside ourselves. Through this viewpoint, humor can provide narrative and collective coherence as well as a sense of human solidarity. Dinesen's sense of humor may be viewed as Kierkegaardian and romanticist. For the romantics of the nineteenth century, humor turned into a philosophical aesthetic stance.[16] Viewing the humorous in relation to God, Søren Kierkegaard determined that humor is the last intermediary stage before the religious: "Humor is the last stage in existence-inwardness before faith."[17] In the reconstructed extended version of Kierkegaard's three life stages—the aesthetic, the ethical, and the religious—the gap between each existence-sphere is considered a transitional stage, and the final religious stage is divided into an A and a B part, with A encompassing religion in general, and B being Christianity in particular—a religion Kierkegaard views as founded upon a basic paradox.[18] Of interest here is Kierkegaard's use of irony and humor as intermediary steps between the aesthetic and the ethical, and between the ethical and the religious, respectively. Humor, according to Kierkegaard, is the attitude of the person who has realized that he or she needs to believe in a being outside him- or herself: "Humor . . . moves not in human but in the anthropological categories; it finds rest not by making man man but by making man God-man."[19] The humorist, however, is unable to make the leap of faith toward the religious stage and in Kierkegaard's view tragically substitutes the comic for the religious.[20] Rather than looking forward, this type of person relies on looking backward, on his or her memories: "The humorist . . . is femininely infatuated with immanence, and recollection is his happy marriage and recollection his happy longing."[21] On the whole, Isak Dinesen's humorous memoirs can be read within the context of this Kierkegaardian stage approaching the religious.

Dinesen herself finishes "The Roads of Life" by suggesting that the humorous creed substitute for the Christian one. At the end of her story, she rather abruptly introduces the Christian church's second article of faith: "That He was crucified, dead and buried, that He went down into Hell, and also did rise again the third day, that He ascended into Heaven, and from thence shall come again" (263).[22] Having cited this, she immediately presents the tales of the two men's fate as being equivalent: "What ups and downs, as terrible as those of the man in the story. What is to come out of all this?—The second article of the Creed of half the world" (ibid.).[23] The juxtaposition is jarring in its inversion. What is really the rhetorical function, one may ask, of concluding that the ups and downs of someone being buried, crucified, and resurrected are *as terrible as* those of a man who one night stumbles over some stones and falls into a series of ditches? How serious is Dinesen when she likens Christ to a fictional character known from childhood storytelling? On the one hand, Dinesen boldly establishes her own creed of laughter and humor as a substitute for half the world's Christian creed. On the other, she indirectly suggests that replacing the religious with the comic might be a somewhat unfulfilling— and in Kierkegaard's view tragic—substitute. Her stance toward her own creed seems to be ambivalent, yet obviously it is the best she can do, and she remains a humorist throughout her narrative.[24]

What I want to examine in the following is how humor and comedy are applied to the native people Dinesen encounters. The tale of the stork establishes a philosophy of humor based on a fictitious man's troublesome night. Throughout *Out of Africa,* though, Dinesen applies her sense of humor to people she has encountered in real life. On the one hand, the narrator thus depicts herself as a Nordic settler who uses humor inclusively to create, and feel part of, a human community composed of blacks and whites alike. On the other hand, the narrator—aiming her text at a Western audience—clearly depicts many of the natives as clownlike figures that she and her audience may find comic. Prompting its readers' laughter, the text ends up establishing a sense of community between the narrator and her readers. But rather than including the community of African natives in this post-African reading community, the new community of laughers ends up substituting for it.

The Social Aspect of Humor

While humor is philosophical, laughter is social. Focusing on the social aspect of comedy, humor and laughter, we may turn to the French philosopher Henri Bergson. In *Laughter: An Essay on the Meaning of the Comic,* Bergson sets out to pinpoint what exactly makes various episodes comic. Based on Bergson's study, Dinesen's humorous viewpoint expressed through the stork tale, for instance, can be characterized as a "dancing-jack" point of view. Bergson explains the "dancing-jack" as a character portrayed as speaking and acting freely "whereas viewed from a certain standpoint, he appears as a mere toy in the hands of another who is playing with him" (73). He subsequently equates the dancing-jack with a metaphor more common to Dinesen's oeuvre and to poets in general, namely the marionette. Much in line with Kierkegaardian existentialism, Bergson claims that "all that is serious in life comes from our freedom" and that our lives are often marked by "a dramatic and grave aspect" (74). What transforms this into comedy is "merely to fancy that our seeming freedom conceals the strings of a dancing-jack, and that we are, as the poet says,/ . . . humble marionettes/The wires of which are pulled by Fate" (74–75).[25] This type of comedy can, of course, be presented in two different ways—with or without dramatic irony, with or without the character involved seeing what the audience sees. What distinguishes Dinesen's humor, as it is expressed in the tale of the man and the stork, is her inclusive stance. Insisting that the man stumbling around in the dark must have laughed aloud himself, she laughs *with* and not *at* him. Humor is inclusive and conciliatory.[26]

Irony, conversely, establishes or builds on a hierarchical distance between human beings. While the distant view of humor places the narrating "I" in a site of subordination together with her fellow human beings, the distant view of irony places the narrating "I" in a position of superiority vis-à-vis other human beings. Thus, when Selboe, for instance, characterizes the tone and view in *Out of Africa* as wavering between nostalgia and irony—"a decidedly humorous-ironic gaze" (*Kunst og erfaring,* 38)—it becomes important to determine when and toward whom it is nostalgic and humorous, and when and toward whom it is ironic. With regards to the latter question, Selboe delivers a clear answer:

Although the irony in the text is aimed mainly at the white settlers, and the whites' presence in Africa is made the object of careful criticism, the racial and colonial relations are naturalized through the fact that the role as head of the farm, *memsahib*, is never critically examined. That which escapes irony is the I, not because it is never subjected to a humorous point of view, but because its role as *center* for the surroundings is never problematized. (46)

It is true that Dinesen is critical and ironic toward other European settlers—especially the British, with the great exception of Denys Finch-Hatton and Berkeley Cole. But it is not just herself but also various African tribes whom she depicts with humor rather than irony.

Landscape of Comedy and Tragedy

In *Out of Africa* humor and irony are not applied evenly to all tribes, races, and individuals. While most European settlers tend to become objects of irony, the Kikuyu are prime objects of humor, while the Masai remain tragic figures. In this landscape between the comic and the tragic, Dinesen uses the Kikuyu and the Masai as her main foils at different stages of her life. In discrete episodes, the Kikuyu mirror Dinesen the settler's comical efforts and sense of humor while she is still in Africa, holding on to her farm. But on the whole, Dinesen the writer, represented only through her strong narrating voice, stands forth as a proud, wise, and tragic figure. Life has taught her a lesson, removed her from a state of initial innocence, and turned her into a resigned, Masai-like figure. Like the Masai who maintain a strong yet barely described presence throughout the book as they loom in the distance on the other side of the river, Dinesen the writer also appears as a strong but disembodied voice in the distance.

In the first part of the book, Dinesen introduces her cast—that is, the various peoples she will be describing—through a topographic depiction. She briefly characterizes each people based on where they live in relation to her farm and to Nairobi. In Part II, she returns to this ethnographic overview, further delineating the historical background of each group of inhabitants (153–57). Five ethnic groups are mentioned: the Kikuyu, the Swaheli, the Somalis, the Indians, and the Masai. The Swaheli play but a minor role and are depicted mainly in negative terms as promiscuous

(12), lascivious (301), and in possession of a slave mentality (155). The Indians who are merchants and tradespeople play a slightly greater role, especially Pooran Singh, who serves as the farm's blacksmith. Once she gets to the Somalis, Dinesen introduces a sense of humor as a characteristic. Like her servant, Farah, the Somalis are scrupulous Muslims. Dinesen psychologizes that as a mixed race (part African, part Arab), they suffer an inferiority complex vis-à-vis pure Arabs, and that their strict adherence to Muslim rules serves as compensation (155). Somali men are in possession of what Dinesen calls "Somali mockery" (121),[27] a type of humor founded on arrogance and a strong sense of dignity. The women, on the other hand, like to laugh, especially at comical love stories in the vein of *A Thousand and One Nights* (188). Yet, unlike the Kikuyu women, who laugh raunchily at dirty stories, the refined Somali women's laughter rings out like silver bells (13, 188).[28]

The fourth group, the Masai, never laugh. They are nomads living on a reservation. They are great lovers and warriors, we are told (117); they are beyond all prudishness, both physical and sexual; and they are intelligent and live in accordance with nature, both their own inner nature and the landscape surrounding them (155–56). When referring to the bodies of the Masai, Dinesen emphasizes their nonhuman aspects. The Masai men are like statues or mosaics: "Their faces, with the high cheek-bones and boldly swung jaw-bones, are sleek, without a line or groove in them, swollen; the dim unseeing eyes lie therein like two dark stones tightly fitted into a mosaic" (142).[29] In addition, their shoulders are delightfully broad, their waists and hips slim, their limbs long and sinewy, and all their movements are supple and graceful (ibid.).

Finally, in strong contrast to the Masai are the comical, misshapen Kikuyu. The Kikuyu—far from embodying grace and impenetrable statuelike perfection—are wrinkled and crooked, and rather than walking gracefully, they "hobble and crawl."[30] *Out of Africa*'s first comic element appears through the initial introduction of the Kikuyu, presented bottom-up, so to speak. After having described the landscape surrounding her farm, Dinesen narrows in on the coffee farm itself, depicting first the coffee plants, and then her squatters. Among these we meet the Kikuyu: "Whenever you walk amidst the Kikuyu shambas, the first thing that will catch your eye is the hind part of a little old woman raking her soil, like a picture of an ostrich which buries her head in the sand" (10).[31]

Laughter

The scene now is set for the Kikuyu to furnish the comic element necessary for Dinesen's overall humorous tone. While Dinesen, in her role as narrator, provides the reader with humor, she, in her role as protagonist, also enters into humorous relations with the Kikuyu. A great and ambiguous moment of laughter occurring in *Out of Africa* is when the old Kikuyu women arrive in vain on a Sunday morning to receive the portions of snuff Dinesen usually has Farah hand out to them. The situation provokes so much mirth that Dinesen—still in bed—calls in Farah to find out what is going on. Farah explains that he has forgotten to buy tobacco, "so that to-day the old women had come a long way, as they themselves say, boori,—for nothing" (35–36).[32] Dinesen herself relates the fact that the women laugh to their overall understanding of the irony of destiny and their ability to view themselves from an outside point of view: "the old Native women ... have mixed blood with Fate, and recognize her irony, wherever they meet it, with sympathy, as if it were that of a sister" (35).[33] Subsequently Dinesen characterizes it as typical for Negroes to enjoy their own accidents with schadenfreude, as if they occurred to someone else. Bergson, on the other hand, sees it as typical for human laughter in general. According to Bergson, efforts made in vain are funny, and he cites Kant for claiming that "laughter is the result of an expectation, which, of a sudden, ends in nothing" (80). Yet, not all such episodes produce laughter, adds Bergson—they are humorous only if they disclose "a particular mechanical arrangement," a "rigid mechanism" and "a kind of *absentmindedness* on the part of life" (81). Dinesen and the old women have established a routine, the structure of which suddenly becomes apparent when an effort, instead of being rewarded, comes across as futile, absurd, and meaningless.

Yet, not only are the Kikuyu women able to laugh what Bergson would call a "corrective laughter" when their behavior comes across as ridiculous and purely mechanical, they also subsequently pull Dinesen into their laughter, which then takes on yet another level of social meaning:

> This happening was later on a source of amusement to the old Kikuyu women. Sometimes, when I met one of them on a path of the maizefield, she would stand still in front of me, poke a crooked bony finger at me, and, with her old dark face dissolving into laughter, so that all the wrinkles of it were drawn and folded together as by one single secret string being pulled, she would remind me of the Sunday when she and her sisters in the snuff, had walked and walked up to my house, only to find that I had forgotten to get it, and that there was not a grain there,—Ha ha Msabu! (36)[34]

Dinesen seems somewhat baffled by the situation—and understandably so as Farah's having forgotten to buy tobacco turns into *her* having forgotten. Furthermore, the women apparently laugh with her, as if they are in on a joke together. Perhaps Dinesen had planned the event to shed a ridiculous light on their behavior—or perhaps the absentmindedness is viewed as pertaining to all the women: the Kikuyu and Dinesen—who forgot. A social aspect of laughter is its inclusion. As Bergson writes, "However spontaneous it seems, laughter always implies a kind of secret freemasonry, or even complicity, with other laughers, real or imaginary" (12). In this situation Dinesen is presented with a situation in which she may be invited—or forced—to laugh along. If she laughs, it will imply complicity, and she will, in a way, have admitted either to having forgotten to buy tobacco or to having "forgotten" to buy it.

Body Humor

The comic requires a body. According to Bergsson, comedy is based on a lack of flexibility; thus the rigid body, and the body drawing attention away from a supple mind, is laughable. In their agility, the Masai possess a noncomic, ideal physiognomy: "The living body ought to be the perfection of suppleness, the ever alert activity of a principle always at work" (Bergson, 49). Conversely, we have the far-from-ideal, comic physiognomy of the Kikuyu. After having been introduced to the Kikuyu upside down, we are more thoroughly presented with the Kikuyu title figure of the first part: Kamante. Kamante is depicted as a dwarf, a cripple, a gargoyle, and a ridiculous and demonic figure (33). His head is big, his body is small and skinny, his elbows and knees "stood out like knots on a stick" (23),[35] and his hands are dark and crooked (38). Not all disfigurements are comic, but Kamante's body enters into a relationship with his soul that is bound to evoke laughter: he is a proud and arrogant loner. As such, Kamante illustrates the split person, and his body becomes an example of the body that "is no more in our eyes than a heavy and cumbersome vesture, a kind of irksome ballast which holds down to earth a soul eager to rise aloft" (Bergson, 49).

Kamante is a clever and contemptuous genius, possessing demonic, witch-like skills in the kitchen, reminiscent of those of Babette in "Babette's Feast" (1952): "In the kitchen, in the culinary world, Kamante had all the attributes of genius, even to that doom of genius" (38).[36] Yet, Kamante knows he is exceptional and in conceit he looks down on everyone around him: "He had a little mocking laughter, of which he made use in all circumstances, but chiefly towards any self-confidence or grandiloquence in other people" (35).[37] Kamante laughs not only at the strong, but also the weak: "[He] kept a little scornful laughter of contempt, and of knowing better, for the tears of the other sick children" (27).[38] As Kamante laughs at other people, pointing out their imperfections, he attempts to build himself up. His laughter is corrective in the sense that it is used to remind others that they ought not look down on him. Yet, his haughty strategy does not work. As Bergson explains, placing oneself above others constitutes a type of asociability, prompting in others the fundamental lack of sympathy required to laugh at a person: "Unsociability in the performer and insensibility in the spectator—such, in a word, are the two essential conditions" (131). Thus, alienating himself from others, Kamante has laid the conditions for becoming a laughingstock as soon as his body betrays him—which it often does.

A particularly mean, involuntary, and rather persistent case of parody concerning Kamante arises as a stork befriends him. With a broken wing, the stork dwells for a while at the farm, and evidently, it feels a connection with Kamante and starts following him around. This scene turns into pure parody for those watching:

> It was impossible not to believe that he was deliberately imitating Kamante's stiff measured walk. Their legs were about the same thickness. The little Native boys had an eye for caricature and shouted with joy when they saw the pair pass. Kamante understood the joke, but he never paid much attention to what other people thought of him. (66)[39]

According to Bergson, "*A deformity that may become comic is a deformity that a normally built person could successfully imitate*" (26). Yet, in this case, a "normally built person" does not even have to imitate Kamante as the stork takes on this role instead. As such, the scene contains a complex series of comic elements in which the laughter induced ends up being aimed not only at Kamante and the stork but also at the onlookers.

On the one hand, Kamante's stiffness is accidentally revealed—a classic trait of comedy; yet, on the other hand, the onlookers are also caught attributing human intelligence and intention to an animal, whose movements are as unreflected as Kamante's. Who, then, is ultimately staging this parody, in which Kamante, the stork, Dinesen, *and* the native boys become comic? We might answer that the parody is purely incidental. Yet, in Dinesen's mythical universe, nothing is. From the humorist's point of view, the incident is ultimately comic because it is as if some transcendental figure—be it fate, destiny, or a god—were pulling the strings to create this comedy. As in the story of the man whose running trajectory creates the outline of a stork when seen from above, what tickles the onlooker and reader in this situation is the scene at hand to which he is an observer *combined with* the thought of a higher power turning him into a participant, using all of us in the greater comedy that is life. Thus, once more, laughter is ambivalent, aimed both at another person and at oneself. From Bergson's point of view, the ambivalence brought on by this situation stems from the laugher's indirect malice: "In laughter we always find an unavowed intention to humiliate, and consequently to correct our neighbor" (123). But from the humorist's point of view, the equivocal nature of this particular situation has less to do with a sense of shame at being malicious than with a sense of being a comic object oneself. To the humorist, this "parody" is inclusive, establishing a community in which everybody, at some level, recognizes that he or she is a puppetlike figure, manipulated by something or someone outside his or her own realm of control.

Memory and Laughter

Bergson analyzes laughter on a strictly nonmetaphysical level. To him, laughter serves as a social means of correction. What sociability demands is flexibility, and the prime enemy of sociability is rigidity: "Laughter is, above all, a corrective... By laughter, society avenges itself for the liberties taken with it" (176). As we have already seen, this is a recurrent situation in *Out of Africa*. The Kikuyu women laugh at Dinesen for not having bought tobacco—either as a sign of wanting to correct *her* behavior if she has indeed forgotten to buy it, or as a sign of wanting to correct their *own* habitual behavior if it turns out she has "forgotten" it. Similarly, Kamante laughs to correct other people's sense of confidence.

Yet, in *Out of Africa*, laughter, as in the case of the Kikuyu women, does not arise only once in a given situation, but is often called forth over and again through remembering. People hold on to a memory and reintroduce the comic episode, both to master it in a Freudian sense (through compulsive repetition), we may surmise, but also to reinforce social relations. In addition to the example of the Kikuyu women and their subsequent encounters with Dinesen, another episode with Kamante will serve to illustrate this type of memory laughter.

Kamante has converted to Christianity, but in a moment of distress Dinesen forgets this. Kamante and Dinesen have just found Dinesen's Danish friend Knudsen lying dead on a path near Dinesen's house. Dinesen needs help carrying Knudsen, but realizes that no Kikuyu will touch a dead body. Asking Kamante to get Farah to help her, she complains: "'You Kikuyus are fools, you are afraid to carry a dead man.'... Kamante set up his little mocking noiseless laughter. 'You again forget, Msabu,' he said, 'that I am a Christian.'" (64).[40] Kamante, laughing silently, clearly corrects Dinesen, with his verbal explanation supporting the function of his laughter. But subsequently the episode is brought up over and over again:

> A long time afterwards Kamante had great satisfaction out of the thought of this instance of my ignorance. He would work with me in the kitchen, filled with a secret pleasure, and suddenly break out laughing. "Do you remember, Msabu," he said, "the time when you had forgotten that I was a Christian, and thought that I should be afraid to help you carry the *Msungu Msei?*"—the old white man. (64–65)[41]

Overtly, Dinesen interprets the subsequent episodes of laughter as a case of native malice, with Kamante delighting in the notion of Dinesen's ignorance. Yet, much more seems to be at stake. The recurrent laughter can be viewed as a persistent reproach, serving to draw Dinesen into a social realm that includes Kamante. In Bergson's words, society demands that "each member must be ever attentive of his social surroundings;... he must avoid shutting himself up in his own peculiar character as a philosopher in his ivory tower" (122). Dinesen, thus, is reproached for her general inattentiveness. She must remember not only that Kamante has converted to Christianity but also that she and Kamante—even more so by virtue of his having converted—are members of the same household, religion, and general community. The fact that Dinesen does not discuss this possible interpretation of the situation does not mean that she is not aware of it. She mentions enough of these recurring laughing situations to suggest that they are important. As they indicate the eagerness of the Kikuyu to establish a sense of community that includes her, they are, in and of themselves, flattering to the settler.[42]

Mimicry and Mockery

Viewed in light of postcolonial theory, the aforementioned episodes may also be regarded as examples of mimicry. In an article on *Out of Africa*, Kirsten Thisted notes that Dinesen depicts the natives as repeatedly behaving incomprehensibly, deeming it to Dinesen's credit that rather than judging the natives, she simply reports their behavior, thus leaving open the possibility that they may indeed be mocking the European settler. In line with Homi Bhabha's notion of mimicry, the natives, according to Thisted, subvert the colonizer's power through acts of pretense. Dinesen, in turn, may be viewed as picking up their trick and using it not only against them but also against the reader. In Thisted's words, the narrator "has learned the natives' art of dissimulation so effectively that she interweaves it into her writing, which itself turns into mimicry."[43]

Thisted talks of mimicry just as JanMohamed talks of a mythical conscious with both arguments of acceptance hinging on the idea that Dinesen has been open to, learned, and absorbed an African way of thinking while living in Kenya. Whether the before-and-after theory is true, I do not know. Dinesen's pretense could also simply be a case of Socratic irony—a pedagogical method used to force her reader to think more deeply about, and learn from, the depicted scenes. In either case the irony or mimicry expressed in these situations underscores Dinesen's overall humorous view of the situation. She and the natives think alike and are all objects in the hand of a higher destiny. As the Danish philosopher Harald Høffding puts it in his study of humor (based on Kierkegaard's philosophy), "The type of irony characterized by a positive acceptance of others' premises, is close to humor. There is a subterranean connection between the humorist and his object" (69–70).[44]

Irony versus Humor

Humor and irony can be difficult to keep apart. They may slide into one another, and they may also serve one another. As a rule of thumb, we may say that in irony, the humorous lurks underneath the serious, while in humor, the serious lurks underneath the humorous (Høffding, 70). A comparison of Dinesen's depictions of the Kikuyu in *Out of Africa* with Johannes V. Jensen's depiction of the Malaysians in *Skovene* shows how one author uses mimicry, parody, and the comic in a predominantly ironic way while the other uses it in a primarily humorous way. Both Dinesen and Jensen create comedy by objectifying people. Dinesen, for instance, turns a native into a marionette (as in the depiction of the Kikuyu woman's wrinkled face being drawn into a smile by invisible strings), and Johannes V. Jensen describes an old Malay as having an ash-filled grid chest and a dried-out rubber-ball stomach.[45] As Bergson would say, these depictions are comic because "we laugh every time a person gives us the impression of being a thing" (56). Objectified people can be funny, and in Dinesen's humorous description we may even note a bit of racism as her portrait involves an accentuation of the woman's black finger and dark face. As late as 1900, in any case, Bergson "philosophizes" that clowns and Negroes alike make us laugh because they look like white men in disguise—with the Negro in particular looking like he is hiding behind dirt, soot, or ink (Bergson, 41–42).

Still, there is a difference of degree between Johannes V. Jensen's and Dinesen's irony and humor. While Jensen is mainly ironic, establishing a condescending distance between himself and the cultural Other, Dinesen is mainly humorous, pointing to how the natives wish to include her in their community.

For Jensen the relationship between European and native people is always presented as strained, antagonistic, and hierarchical. Jensen, too, imagines that the natives may be playing games with, tricking, and mocking him (and that they may be doing so in accordance with a higher power), but he never presents this as a situation that might potentially evoke common laughter based on a common understanding. Realizing that the natives—pretending to take him on a dangerous tiger hunt—have only led him in circles in the flatland, Jensen reacts:

> Had the two Malays, then, led me in a circle and not, as I assumed all along, straight ahead? Had Ali, Holy Ali, inspired in them this piece of advice as the best for both them and me? I scrutinized their expressions; they looked pious but could only meet my gaze with a certain lack of expression.
>
> Very well. There, then, it seemed, I had walked for several hours—for me an entire generation—with my life in my hands as free entertainment for two Malaysians superior to me when it came to the art of pretense... I felt as if higher powers had put me in their mouth and spit me back out again.[46]

By referring to the natives' "art of pretense," Jensen also points to mimicry in Bhabha's sense of the word. Yet, where Dinesen is open to the possibility of solidarity between European and African vis-à-vis an instance of a higher order—they are all puppets on a string—Jensen presents but antagonism and paranoia. As he refers to higher powers—a point of view outside himself—he does not suggest that it be a viewpoint providing unity and harmony through humor. Nobody in this scene is laughing; Jensen and his macho aesthetics do not allow for mirth and merriment, only misery and resentment.

What Jensen the narrator exhibits for his Danish reading audience is Jensen the traveler as a Kierkegaardian ironic:

> The ironist thinks he has realized the hollowness of the aesthetic stage, but he does not believe that ethical seriousness can solve the problem. With biting contempt and intellectual sharpness he can thus criticize (and ironize over) everything and everybody—including himself. He possesses a good mood—but no humor.[47]

Like the natives, Jensen's impervious protagonist is *also* one engaging in the art of pretense, clowning around for the reader, without necessarily having learned this from the natives themselves. Because he displays himself as so rigidly paranoid and ironic, he ultimately turns *Skovene* into a comedy with himself playing the comic lead. As Bergson points out, character comedies are based on inflexible types who are unable to adjust to changing situations. They are a social threat as society "insists on a constant striving after reciprocal adaptation" (23). The comedy thus serves a social function as "rigidity is the comic, and laughter is its corrective" (24).

Jensen's rigidity lies in the fact that he lacks suppleness of mind and has only one mode of interpretation upon which to fall back, whenever events turn out different than he expected. This mode is a self-deprecating form of paranoia. On the plot level, Jensen the traveler concludes that the natives are out to make a fool of him. On a narrative level, however, Jensen the writer usurps the imagined position of the natives, as *he* makes a fool of the traveler for his reading audience at home. The presentation of paranoia thus really serves the twofold function of a comedy: it criticizes social rigidity while creating a community of laughter in which Jensen plays a double role. While Jensen the traveler is *ex*cluded as the object of ridicule, Jensen the writer is *in*cluded as a split subject who is willing to aestheticize and poke fun at his own vices. Considering the process of autobiographical writing, one can interpret Jensen as having learned from his mistakes. As a reflective writer he is a wiser man, able to exhibit his previous foolishness. In this process, the natives play but a secondary role, and *Skovene* is ultimately a text centered on the traveler himself, aimed at a fellow community of Danes. *Out of Africa,* on the other hand, forms a much more complex net of shifting communal relationships. Comparing the two episodes just discussed, this comes across even textually, as Dinesen's final gesture in the tobacco episode is letting a Kikuyu woman get the last word: "Ha ha Msabu!"

Male Irony and Female Humor

Of course five weeks in Malaysia are not directly comparable to seventeen years in Kenya, as the person living with another people over an extended period of time is more likely to establish a sense of mutual understanding with these people. In addition, the amount of time elapsed between the occurrence of an event and its being written down makes a difference. Jensen, writing and publishing while still traveling, leaves his writing more susceptible to the immediate, the self-centered, and the paranoid, while Dinesen, allowing six years to pass between leaving Africa and writing her memoirs, has time to cool down. As Aiken notes, "by contrast to the *Letters from Africa,* with their poignant, emotionally mercurial account of Karen Blixen's seventeen-year sojourn," *Out of Africa* appears smoothed out: "in writing the book she carefully composed herself, in both senses" (212).

Still, gender may also be a determining factor. In *Imperial Eyes,* Mary Louise Pratt observes humor and irony playing themselves out differently in travelogues written by men and women, claiming that women may forfeit the need for certainty and control that texts written by males demand. Using Mary Kingsley's *Travels in West Africa* (1897) as her example, Pratt illustrates how Kingsley, as a woman, allows herself to reject "the textual mechanisms that created value in the discourse of her male predecessors: fantasies of dominance and possession."[48] Instead, Kingsley "foregrounds the workings of her (European and female) subjectivity" (ibid). Kingsley's male predecessors are, of course, not Hamsun and Johannes V. Jensen, but rather the earnest male explorers of the first half of the nineteenth century. As we have seen, Hamsun and Johannes V. Jensen also develop narrative strategies relating to earlier explorer travelogues based on irony and inversion. Yet, what they construct is a macho antihero surrounded by potential antagonists as opposed to Kingsley's endearing woman surrounded by just as endearing fellow humans. As Pratt puts it, "The bumbling, comic innocence of everyone in her writings, including herself, proposes a particular way of being a European in Africa" (215). The narrative positions available to men and women thus come across as different. Available to men is the ironic macho position; available to women is the humorous female position.

Like Kingsley, Dinesen proposes a particular way of being European in Africa based on her living similarly to, and in concordance with, those around her. On the narrative level, though, Dinesen opts for a strategy located between the typically male and female nineteenth-century discourses. Her protagonist is humored, but is not depicted with "masterful comic irreverence" (Pratt, 215) the way Kingsley—and Jerichau-Baumann for that matter—depicts herself. Dinesen uses comic irreverence solely in her depictions of the Kikuyu. In addition, Dinesen does not stick to domains untouched by her male counterparts, such as swampy exteriors or domestic interiors. She is just as fond of mountaintops, promontories, and overviews as are male travelers. As Selboe points out, Dinesen favors the bird's-eye view (*Kunst og erfaring,* 38) and turns this view into "a perfect narration" (ibid.). And finally, in comparison to her female predecessors, Dinesen seems beyond using ironic reversals to depict women as oppressed by European men. Pratt uses Anna Maria Falconbridge's *Narrative of Two Voyages to the River Sierra Leone* (1802) as an example of this rhetoric of inversion, and, as we have seen in chapter 3, Jerichau-Baumann employs feminist orientalism to assert women's rights. Dinesen, on the contrary—backed by her colonial status, farm ownership, and a greater level of women's rights, including female suffrage—opts mainly for what Pratt considers male discursive strategies without overtly problematizing gender differences. Indirectly, they are, however, as Aiken points out, constantly problematized through destabilization. According to Aiken, "The European or American reader who takes up this book is likely to be struck by the sense of having experienced at once a shaped, coherent, and fulfilling whole and, simultaneously, a kind of bricolage—fragmentary, heterogeneous, almost random" (229). Like Pratt and Foucault before her, Aiken aligns the project of creating order through writing with that of Western imperialism:

> If on one level both the inscription and the reading of *Out of Africa* repeat the colonizing gesture, seeking to capture "Africa" in language, on other levels the text is most powerful precisely in the way it reveals Africa—and itself as "Africa" in words—to be always slipping from the grasp, always existing as/in *excess* of what finite human schemes, both colonial and critical, can contain. (232)

Whether Dinesen's fragmentary text is masterful, creating a unified whole, remains a matter of interpretation. But if one looks at Dinesen the protagonist and Dinesen the narrator separately, one may conclude that as a main character, she is typically female in the sense that she depicts herself as having a sense of humor. As a narrator, though, she is masculine and remains an example of Pratt's "monarch of all I survey" trope (201).

Vice and Virtue: The Fool of Comedy

When Dinesen depicts herself as a comic figure—as one of Pratt's self-deprecating women—she does so in an ultimately self-aggrandizing and ingratiating way. While Jensen portrays himself as a hopelessly rigid male, dependent on alcohol to *go primitive,* Dinesen depicts herself and her own potential character flaw as that of possessing—if anything—an excessively flexible mind. The greatest social virtues of all—flexibility, elasticity, and, consequently, empathy—can, if exaggerated, come across as comic vices, but only as slight and very endearing ones.

Part of what makes Dinesen's writing so enjoyable to read is that she presents life as endlessly intriguing, as something that can be interpreted and understood in an infinite number of ways. In *Out of Africa* she often depicts a situation from several perspectives and suggests various interpretations in rapid succession, employing dizzying strategies of inversion, particularization, and universalization. As we have seen, she regards the people around her as squatters on her land, but conversely considers that they may be regarding *her* as a squatter on *their* land (10). At other times she considers herself the only sensible person among the insane, only to turn this around and suggest that she would have had exactly the same feeling had she been the only insane person among the sane (343). A typical Dinesen introduction is the ever-intriguing "It might also be that..."[49]

The anecdote "The Swaheli Numeral System" epitomizes the protagonist's attraction to unpredictable situations serving to stimulate her fantasy and prompting thoughts of hitherto unknown systems of logic. Using Bergson's terminology we might say that the episode illustrates her *tension* and *elasticity* to a fault (22). Dinesen has lived only a couple of months in Africa when a young Swede teaches her how to count in Swahili. As the number nine resembles a Scandinavian word for peeing/penis, the Swede decides to skip it, insisting that the Swaheli number system does not include nine—or any compound including that number, such as nineteen, ninety, and nine hundred.[50] Jensen's protagonist would most likely have reacted with rigidity, anger, and frustration in a similar situation. Dinesen's protagonist, on the other hand, welcomes the strange and unforeseen. As she puts it, "The idea of this system for a long time gave me much to think of, and for some reason a great pleasure. Here, I thought, was a people who have got originality of mind, and courage to break with the pedantry of the numeral series" (284).[51]

In Dinesen's mind, the newly acquired "fact" triggers a series of reinterpretations and new ways to make sense of the world in general, and of her African surroundings in particular. The number nine, she reasons, may in fact be illusory, and it might also explain why one of her servants is missing a finger. Dinesen's disappointment, then, is great when she discovers that the number nine does indeed exist in Swahili. Yet, she keeps her disappointment at bay by allowing herself to hold on to her fictitious explanations: "Yet I have still got the feeling that there exists a Native system of numeral characters without the number of nine in it, which to them works well and by which you can find out many things" (285).[52]

Up until the point when she is informed of the wrong premise for her theories, Dinesen has demonstrated an outstanding openness to what might be a matter of cultural relativity. At this point, however, she becomes comically rigid, as she holds on to her new theories. Her interpretation mania risks getting the upper hand. Consequently, as a social hero she comes across as *close* to ideal, with the limit to her flexibility and power of mental readjustment being only endearing. As a character flaw her slight stubbornness makes her human. As an eccentricity, though, it also makes her an artist. The episode thus also serves a metapoetic function, pointing out to the reader that Dinesen will sacrifice pedantic truth claims for the purpose of a higher truth located in the fantastical.[53]

Nationality and Humor

In *Out of Africa,* Dinesen proposes a particular *humorous* way of being a European in Africa. In doing so, she comes closer to JanMohamed's vague notion of the nationally determined than to Pratt's and Torgovnick's gender-based views. According to Dinesen, she relates well to Africans because of a specifically Nordic sense of humor. Kikuyu and Somalis alike recognize this particular trait. As indicated in the epigraph, Dinesen, one day, is approached by Kamante, who upon having discovered that a certain Mr. Nepken is Danish, concludes, "Your *Kabilla*—your tribe—do not get as angry as other Europeans, . . . you laugh at people."[54] Dinesen seems to agree with this perception, explaining its cultural roots: "'Yes, we dare nothing else,' I said. 'We have an old Bwana who has taught us that and who keeps us in order. There he is, on the shelf.'"[55] Dinesen then points to the comedies of Holberg.

Ludvig Holberg, Denmark and Norway's comic talent par excellence, who—in the 1720s—wrote character comedies in the vein of Molière, constantly portraying the fool on stage and inducing social order through corrective laughter in the audience, is one of Dinesen's role models. Not only does she end up writing in a comedic and humorous vein like Holberg, but she has also been brought up to look at the world through his plays. Holberg, as she would have it, has installed in her and the rest of the nation a tendency to look at oneself from a comic distance—and to alleviate the pain of being ridiculously human through laughter.[56]

Kamante is not the only one commenting on Dinesen's Danish-Norwegian humor; the Somali Ismail, too, is cited as having noticed the same trait in Dinesen's dog Dusk: "He once said to me: 'I know now that the Dusk is of the same tribe as you yourself. He laughs at the people.'"(74)[57] Being of a tribe that laughs instead of getting angry is of paramount importance in a colonial situation where power is distributed unevenly. The counterexample to laughter—illustrating how terrifying the outcome of anger can be—is "Kitosch's Story." Here Dinesen recounts how a British settler beats a native to death ostensibly because the native, Kitosch, rode the settler's horse when he had been told not to, and indirectly because the settler could not control his temper. Dinesen tells the story to criticize the European court of law, not to point out a difference in national backgrounds between Northern Europeans. Yet, viewed in connection with her insistence on Scandinavian laughter and the natives' appreciation thereof, the fatal incident serves as a contrast, illustrating a point often made in Dinesen's oeuvre—namely, that the ability to laugh is a matter of life and death.

As a Dane in British-colonized Kenya, Dinesen was not a direct representative of the colonial power; neither was she exempt from imperialistic exploitation. Dinesen clearly benefited from an imperialistic world order. She associated with the British among whom she found her best friend and lover; yet she also identified strongly with the natives as a *non*-British person.[58] As this chapter's epigraph illustrates, Dinesen insists on her exceptionally benign European presence in Kenya with her native Kamante's recognizing her "tribal" difference. Kamante's use of the word "tribe" suggests a reciprocal status between Dinesen and the natives, and Dinesen's use of the word further suggests that the Danish reader look at him- or herself through (auto)ethnographic eyes. When Dinesen, in turn, sets out to explain the Danish tribe, she relates its peculiarities to both genetic and cultural factors.

Interracial Understanding

In a literary tradition running from at least Adam Oehlenschläger in the early 1800s to Johannes V. Jensen in the early 1900s, Dinesen develops race theories explaining the attraction and compatibility between people of the North and of the South.[59] Like Jensen, she views Mediterranean races as decadent, while the Nordic as well as the African races are pure. According to Dinesen, opposites attract: "There is a susceptibility to the Southern countries and races that is a Nordic quality" (17).[60] Northern people grow patient and loving regarding the South—first the Southern Europe of the eighteenth-century's educational journey, then Africa. Dinesen writes that tough, domineering, easily enraged Nordic men (summed up in the American version as "hasty red-haired Northern people," [17]) "would stand no nonsense from their own country or their own relations, but they took the drought of the African Highlands, and a case of sunstroke, the Rinderpest on their cattle, and the incompetency of their Native servants, with humility and resignation" (18).[61] While Torgovnick argues that *women* possess the ability to let go, Dinesen argues that *Northerners* are willing to forgo their individuality for an experience of the oceanic:

> Their sense of individuality itself was lost in the sense of the possibilities that lie in interaction between those who can be made one by reason of their incongruity. The people of Southern Europe and the people of mixed blood have not got this quality. (18)[62]

Dinesen's Danish-English In-betweenness

Dinesen's use of the word "Nordic" tends to be nebulous, and we are often left uncertain as to whether the British are included in this term. Yet, writing and publishing for the Anglo-Saxon part of the world, Dinesen regarded herself as part of the British-American community as well. As Aiken notes, "Dinesen seems always, textually, in flight. Neither truly English nor simply Danish, neither 'oral' nor yet fully written, neither 'man' nor 'woman,' she dissolves both selves and texts into a continual play of transformations" (xxi). Living in Kenya for so long, Dinesen became a multilingual cosmopolitan who looked upon Africa *and* the Anglo-Saxon world as second homes. Hence, in some respects Isak Dinesen may be considered another in-between female figure, similar to Elisabeth Jerichau-Baumann.

Living abroad, neither Jerichau-Baumann nor Dinesen was a tourist; both went abroad to work. Both wrote memoirs, focusing on the ethnographic Other and creating a sense of aesthetic unity based on their own strong subjective textual presence. Jerichau-Baumann's and Dinesen's in-betweenness allows both of them a certain amount of flexibility, as they are able to regard Denmark from an insider as well as an outsider position. Yet, the emigrant versus immigrant positions also differ. As an *immigrant,* Jerichau-Baumann, as we have seen in chapter 3, represents her Danishness in an autoethnographic text partly bearing the symptoms of an inferiority complex. At times her encyclopedic and historic knowledge of things considered Danish comes across as compensatory—even in a nineteenth-century cultural context in which the preoccupation with defining a Danish national identity was commonplace. Dinesen's references to things Danish, on the other hand, come across as less ingratiating. While Danes were wary of Dinesen, whom they considered too aristocratic and snobbish, Dinesen's national identity was not a point of contention.

A fairer comparison between autoethnographic gestures in Jerichau-Baumann's and Dinesen's texts will, in fact, entail a study of how Dinesen constructs *Dinesen* as opposed to *Blixen.* For her Anglo-Saxon audience, Dinesen does indeed tone down her Danishness. Further complicating this comparison, however, is that Dinesen wrote two separate texts for two separate projects.

Out of Africa versus *Den afrikanske Farm*

Feeling better understood by Americans, Dinesen embarked upon her literary career writing in English and publishing her works in the United States. Her debut was *Seven Gothic Tales* (1934), a collection that she translated (and in some cases rewrote) into Danish and published in Denmark the following year. *Out of Africa* and *Den afrikanske Farm* follow a more complex pattern. First, she sat in Denmark and wrote parts in English and other parts in Danish.[63] She then published the books almost simultaneously in Denmark, England, and the United States. Thus, while Jerichau-Baumann's dual voice pertains mainly to gender as she addresses her male and female readers distinctly in passages existing side by side in one work, Dinesen develops two voices directed at different national audiences in two separate texts.

Several scholars have analyzed the differences between Dinesen's texts. In a translation study of *Seven Gothic Tales* from 1982, Knud Sørensen points out that Dinesen adapted *Seven Gothic Tales* to a Danish audience through three types of omissions that served to avoid (1) insulting Danish readers, (2) explanations that were unnecessary in a Danish context, and (3) having to insert explanations with regards to things that would be unknown in a Danish context (Sørensen, 293–94). More interestingly, when it comes to additions, Dinesen added a "particular Danish coloring" (294)[64] and changed pronouns to include herself among the Danes. An impersonal "you" would reappear as a communal "we." As Sørensen points out, "Here Karen Blixen takes her Danish readers by the hand and says: we are in this together" (ibid.).

In *Den afrikanske Farm,* Dinesen[65] similarly emphasizes her sense of belonging to a Danish national culture. She relates, for instance, how happy she is when old Knudsen visits her and they can talk their own language: "It was a joy to both him and me to speak Danish, so we exchanged many observations about happenings on the farm, just so we could express ourselves in our own language" (49).[66] In *Out of Africa,* the emphasis on speaking a native language is toned down: "It was a pleasure to both him and me to speak Danish, so we exchanged many remarks over insignificant happenings on the farm, just for the joy of talking" (60). In this latter sentence, Dinesen mainly likes to talk, and Danish could be any language; it is not emphasized as her native language. It seems fair to assume that Dinesen chose not to tell her Anglo audience that she felt most at home in the Danish language in order not to alienate herself *and* her text from them.

In *Den afrikanske Farm,* Dinesen also describes being homesick: "For some time I had in the house a stork with a broken wing. I became homesick when I looked at it, for it looked as if it belonged in Denmark."[67] In *Out of Africa,* Dinesen simply omits the second sentence (66). Finally, for an Anglo audience Denmark tends to be presented more generally as the North, in which case it could also include England. Hence, "It was like a rainy day in Denmark"[68] appears in *Out of Africa* as "The day was like a rainy day in a Northern country" (366).

Most important for this analysis, many of Dinesen's Danish autoethnographic depictions are absent from *Out of Africa*. Dinesen, for instance, entirely omits the section about Kamante's wondering why her *Kabilla* laughs at people, and Dinesen's answering through a reference to Holberg. From a practical standpoint, Dinesen avoids explaining who Holberg is, and from a social standpoint she once again avoids alienating herself from non-Danes (or non-Norwegians).

Sørensen concludes that Dinesen was close to bilingual, but not quite (295).[69] One indication of her having a greater command of the Danish language is that she replaces English words with more nuanced Danish ones: "A colorless English verb is replaced by a verb semantically congruous with the adverb" (290). The depiction of the laughing Kikuyu women provides a good example of more colorful verbs replacing neutral ones (even when not related to adverbs) in *Out of Africa*. In the Danish version we are told that the old women "had hobbled and crawled the long way to the house,"[70] while in the English version they "had come a long way" (35–36).

In order to understand Dinesen as an in-between woman, the consensus seems to be that one must read her in both languages. In his translation study of *Out of Africa*, Sørensen concludes: "It seems difficult to get around that the full understanding of her works is attainable only through a meticulous comparison between the Danish and the English language" (307). Even Aiken writes: "We should read 'Karen Blixen' and 'Isak Dinesen' as different though intricately intertextual authors—both children of a single but by no means single-minded literary mother" (xxiv). Part of what the two different texts show us is Dinesen's ability to ingratiate herself with different national groups—and when it comes to a Danish reading audience, she especially builds upon a national self-perception of possessing a great sense of humor.

The Big Farewell Laugh

So far we have looked at laughter first in an episode of fiction within the fiction—the stork tale—in which Dinesen lays out her philosophical humorous stance. We have then looked at concrete episodes—fact within the fiction—in which the Kikuyu laugh. The last type of laughing episode I want to examine comes closer to the former, as Dinesen in her characteristic romanticist manner personifies the African landscape, projecting her own philosophical stance onto the entire continent.

When Dinesen, toward the end of her stay in Africa, suffers from feelings of uncertainty and incomprehension, she demands "a sign" (380).[71] She subsequently witnesses a ten-second battle between a chameleon and a cock. The former is the natural underdog, but shows courage, lashing its tongue at the cock. The cock, in turn, "stood for a second as if taken aback, then swiftly and determinately he struck down his beak like a hammer and plucked out the Chameleon's tongue" (381).[72] Dinesen is horrified and stones the chameleon. Without her having explained the sign, it is clear that she interprets the episode allegorically, seeing herself in the image of the chameleon that has lost its means of subsistence, and is best served by being killed.[73] Dinesen, in other words, is best served by giving up her role as coffee farmer and moving back to Denmark.

Ultimately Dinesen finds solace in the fact that she was given the sign she asked for. She continues to think mythically, in terms of humor and laughter, and concludes: "Great powers had laughed to me, with an echo from the hills to follow the laughter, they had said among the trumpets, among the cocks and Chameleons, Ha ha!" (382).[74] This final episode recalls that of the Kikuyu women. Africa's inhabitants and landscape get the last word—in the form of (the echo of) ambiguous laughter. In the English version Dinesen uses the preposition "to," and it is difficult to determine whether the laughter is inclusive, that is, whether the powers laugh *with* or *at* her. In the Danish version this ambiguity is made explicit, as Dinesen uses both prepositions. *At, to,* or *with*? The answer to that question is a matter of power relations.

Laughter of Contempt—Laughter of Love

Bergson operates with a rather categorical notion of laughter and ultimately links laughter to egotism, arrogance, and bitterness (178–79). Høffding, on the other hand, operates with a more nuanced view of laughter.[75] In *Den store Humor,* Høffding claims that we laugh scornfully at an object who arrogantly assumes he or she can work against us: "The object, in this case, signifies an opposition assuming superiority, but which is overcome and falls to the ground" (52).[76] This type of laughter is based on antipathy and does not contain humor. It is the corrective type of laughter about which Bergson writes. Elaborating on the power relationship implied in this situation, Høffding explains that oppressed, the laugher depends on, and cannot ignore, the object of his laughter at whom he feels compelled to laugh over and over again: "Contempt is antipathetically concerned with its object and carries with it the urge to preoccupy oneself with it over and over again in order to emphasize and specify its [the object's] powerlessness, its stupidity or its meanness" (60). This *could* explain the aforementioned examples of memory laughter, were it not for the fact that Dinesen herself presents the laughter of the Kikuyu, like that of Africa, as a sympathetic type of laughter.

When a power relationship is clearly uneven, Høffding claims that scornful laughter turns compassionate: "Real superiority rests in itself, and its self-esteem does not come across as contempt for other things or others" (53). In Dinesen's case, she indirectly depicts herself as a helpless chameleon having no chance of surviving against the superior cock. As this source of comparison is given to her by a higher power laughing at her, it becomes a sign of the highest degree of humor.

Høffding lists several degrees of humorous (vs. scornful) laughter, from that founded on feelings of mild sympathy to that founded on love and wit. At the lowest level, sympathy replaces antipathy. The stronger subject acknowledges his or her dependence on an inferior object, and without necessarily experiencing a very positive type of sympathy toward the object of laughter, he or she respects the other's peculiarities. These peculiarities can produce a sympathetic smile or laughter, and a bridge can be built between the two of them (Høffding, 53). This type of humor more accurately captures Dinesen's relationship to the Kikuyu (upon whom she acknowledges over and over that she depends), as well as the inverse: the relationship of the Kikuyu to Dinesen the settler. In fact, the relationship between Dinesen and the Kikuyu may even be regarded as one in which the laughing subject—whether it be Dinesen or the Kikuyu—feels superior to the degree that he or she not only understands the object of laughter but also feels at one with it, and tries to protect it: "There is an inner bond, not just an outer bridge between subject and object" (ibid.). This is the type of reciprocal sense of superiority vis-à-vis the Other—"the mutual illusion," Dinesen calls it[77]—upon which she reflects in "Of the Two Races."

In extension of humor based on sympathy and understanding, is humor based on nostalgia and longing. This type of humor, I would argue, captures the relationship between Dinesen the writer and Dinesen the settler as well as that between Dinesen and Africa. Not only does Africa care enough about Dinesen to warn and protect her through the sign of the chameleon, but the landscape is also represented as sympathizing with Dinesen as both of them are suffering the loss of a Golden Age. The basic tone of *Out of Africa* is one of nostalgic humor, a tone reflecting the writer's relationship to her past, as well as the final relationship between Africa and Dinesen. As Høffding expresses it, "Through the expansion of the feeling... the individual's own mood may end up assuming responsibility for the others' interest and striving, especially when these others themselves are consigned to the world of memory or hope" (53). Given that the narrator has structured her account so that her own tragedy parallels that of Africa, the reader understands that Africa may be interested in Dinesen's sufferings as the country itself is relegated to a world of hope and memories.

This type of humorous nostalgic or hopeful laughter is further elevated when it takes place against an existential backdrop:

> A human being with extensive experience, using his reflection, will naturally arrive at the conviction that there is a great order of things on which all events depend, even those that most affect people's welfare. And this conviction will cast off a background, a horizon, against which that which preoccupies human interest may appear as insignificant and vanishing. (54)

At this level we find the existential laughter Dinesen consistently evokes and in which she believes.

The ultimate level of humorous laughter is founded not on sympathy based on understanding, but on understanding based on sympathy. It is based on a synthesis of love and wit; "such a bond exists... wherever love of mankind and appreciation of a human spirituality reigns" (ibid.). This type of great humor, according to Høffding, is not without its costs as it requires life experience, reflection, and a journey through Purgatory—"a purgatory in which life's contradictions and the battling forces of existence have exercised their influence on the innermost core of spiritual life" (56). Everything has left its mark on the great humorist: "The great and the small, the noble and the mean, the light and the dark, everything has left its mark, and reflection has taken into consideration the universal laws of life" (ibid.). In the end, this is the level of humor upon which Dinesen's text builds. As a thorough account of Dinesen's humanity and spirituality, *Out of Africa* functions as a declaration of love, and as such, it implies that this love is reciprocated—both by higher powers and by Africa, its inhabitants and its landscape. While Kierkegaard characterizes this stage as simply building on a feminized sense of nostalgia, Høffding—in overall agreement with Kierkegaard—nevertheless elevates the importance of the humorist in a way that may coincide better with Dinesen's own understanding of the humorist.

Depicting Africa as echoing a benign laughter, Dinesen thus elevates Africa and Africans to a paramount position. The gesture, nonetheless, works two ways and is also self-aggrandizing, as a person's ability to laugh (back) with humor reveals that person's own strength. As Høffding puts it, "In the great humor there is a double movement. It expresses the type of self-importance that builds on self-understanding" (57). Dinesen, together with the higher powers and Africa, is aware of her own limitations, and of how insignificant her existence is in the overall scheme of things. The humorist, says Høffding,

> measures himself as well as others against the great background life has confronted him with, and his relationship to this background determines both the place he assigns himself and that which he assigns others. Everywhere he seeks the core behind the peels... The great humor is connected with eternal searching and opposes all dogmatic wisdom, whether this appears in the name of plain common sense, science or religion. (58)

Dinesen possesses the great humor that allows her to think in terms of equality between herself and the Africans rather than in terms of inferiority and superiority. This great humor, according to Dinesen, characterizes people of her own nationality who have been brought up with the great comedian Holberg. Dinesen, on the other hand, does not mention this in *Out of Africa*, which may be why Abdul JanMohamed ascribes her openness to her particular individuality and why Marianna Torgovnick ascribes it to her gender. On this count, *Out of Africa* and *Den afrikanske Farm* do not tell the same story, and it may be of interest to note that so many interpreters—including myself—attribute the protagonist's difference to a category that does not exclude the reader. JanMohamed, too, can possess individual qualities, Torgovnick is both an individual and a woman, and I am an individual, a woman, and a Dane. As admiring readers, we all, perhaps, judge Dinesen's attitude toward the colonized from a point of view implying that we, ourselves, are beyond racism, colonization, and imperialism. It is a particular relief if we can assess someone as unprejudiced and know that we possess the same qualities. Thus, Dinesen's two different discourses, aimed at Danes and non-Danes, respectively, once again underscore the author's great understanding of human beings and their need to feel included. With *Den afrikanske Farm* and *Out of Africa* she convinces all of us that we—together with her and the natives—may be great humorists.

As a tragicomedy, *Out of Africa* expresses a split worldview, and Dinesen herself appears as a split person in the text. As a settler-protagonist she is oftentimes comic, while as a wise, reflective, disembodied narrator, she comes across mainly as tragic. As a tragic figure, she relates to other Scandinavians and to the Masai. She emphasizes their common worldview in a passage depicting the Swedish actor-immigrant Emmanuelson, who seeks momentary refuge among the Masai:

> The true aristocracy and the true proletariat of the world are both in understanding with tragedy. To them it is the fundamental principle of God, and the key,—the minor key,—to existence. They differ in this way from the bourgeoisie of all classes, who deny tragedy, who will not tolerate it, and to whom the word of tragedy means in itself unpleasantness. Many misunderstandings between the white middle-class immigrant settlers and the Natives arise from this fact. The sulky Masai are both aristocracy and proletariat. (213)[78]

As tragic figures the Scandinavians and the Masai, as opposed to the (other) white settlers, have something in common: both groups live in harmony with their destinies. Yet there is also a big difference between the two groups, namely, that the Scandinavians are split, modern individuals, while the Masai are nonreflectively tragic heroes. The Masai, in other words, are considered pure primitives, living in harmony with their inner and outer nature, with bodies that do not distract from their nobility of mind. Dinesen and her fellow Scandinavians, on the other hand, are painfully aware of needing to cast themselves as tragic figures. To them, life is not a natural state of affairs, as it is to the Masai, but is rather a reflected and theatrical project in need of an audience. Thus, they become actors and philosophers.[79] The truly tragic, as Høffding argues, lies beyond the humorist, and the humorist grants it "the highest place" (104). And the truly tragic hero, such as the Masai, is someone who does not reflect upon these matters; he is, as Dinesen puts it, *sulky*—or as Høffding argues: "The highest degree of pathos makes one silent, or at least taciturn" (ibid.). Dinesen, on the other hand, can hardly be accused of being uncommunicative. Through her memoir, she comes across as a wise, philosophical humorist, who may even—paradoxically—have understood that she, far less noble than the Masai, makes for a better poetic tragic hero. As Aristotle points out in his *Poetics,* good men suffering a change from prosperity to misfortune do not evoke fear or pity, but shock. The audience of a tragedy rather needs a hero—or heroine—with whom they can identify: "We feel pity for a man who does not deserve his misfortune; we fear for someone like ourselves."[80]

Being a heroine to whom the audience can relate requires faults and imperfections. By finally revealing her laughable sides, Dinesen at least gains a sense of inclusion, both as a settler among the Kikuyu and as a narrator vis-à-vis her reading audience. As the outcome of tragedy is exclusion while that of comedy is inclusion, we may note that while the Masai are objects of great admiration, they do not include Dinesen in their Africa. The Kikuyu, on the other hand, draw her in through laughter and humor, appreciating Dinesen as a humorist. Yet being caught in the tragicomic—between tragedy and comedy, exclusion and inclusion—is an ambivalent position. It reflects the ambivalence Dinesen feels toward herself, and the split person as whom we, her readers, experience Dinesen. The same ambivalence, finally, is expressed in Dinesen's last depiction of the Kikuyu women. In an ultimate gesture capturing the ambivalence, Dinesen momentarily emphasizes a tragic aspect of her comic figures par excellence: the Kikuyu.

Toward the very end of her memoir, the old Kikuyu women's faces are used almost as the happy and sad masks framing a Danish theater stage with the motto: "Ei blot til lyst" (Not just for amusement). The old women arrive at the farm on account of Dinesen's imminent departure. First we see their laughing faces as Dinesen writes: "A joke, or a cup of tembu, would make their wrinkled toothless faces dissolve in laughter" (396).[81] As opposed to the first depiction of the Kikuyu women's laughing faces, the invisible strings have been removed, and Dinesen no longer calls forth the comic in their appearances through a dancing-jack point of view. Instead she concludes that the women's "strength, and love of life . . . to me seemed not only highly respectable, but glorious and bewitching. . . . The old women of the farm and I had always been friends" (396).[82] Moments later we are told of a Kikuyu woman's face having imprinted itself in Dinesen's memory during her final days at the farm. Dinesen does not know her well, but as they suddenly stand face-to-face, the woman begins to cry, "tears streaming over her face" (397).[83] We have moved from laughter to tears, but still, in the very next sentence, Dinesen maintains that "[she stood] like a cow that makes the water on the plain before you" (ibid.).[84] The simile suggests the impulsive, immediate, and natural aspect of the Kikuyu's behavior, but comparing a human being to an animal—especially to a cow—also relegates it to the realm of the comic, and thus the Kikuyus—especially the Kikuyu women—remain consigned to the realm of the comic throughout *Out of Africa*. The description would come across as entirely contemptuous were it not for Dinesen's sense of identification with the woman. We are told that the Kikuyu woman, too, is on her way to build a new home for herself—just as Dinesen is on her way back to Denmark to build a new home and life for herself there.

Still, Dinesen never exposes her own body, its drives and its natural functions, to her reader. Rather than being *in* her body, she is above it—always maintaining a bird's-eye perspective of herself and her surroundings. She remains what Pratt—in connection with the humorous Mary Kingsley—calls a female version of "the monarch of all I survey." What stands forth as one has finished reading *Out of Africa,* is a person who is able to establish a humorous connection with whomever constitutes her community at a particular place in time. Her sense of identification with the chameleon is apt. Dinesen possesses the gift of social adaptability and uses humor to fit in with her surroundings. In Africa she laughs with the Africans, and in Europe she laughs with the Europeans—at the Africans.

A more sympathetic gesture might have been that of self-deprecation—of directing a common laughter at her own potentially comic inadequacies. Instead, Dinesen depicts her former friends as physically awkward clowns, while she herself maintains her dignity as an entirely disembodied voice. The result is haunting in its beauty, its wisdom, and its humor. But one is also left with the disturbing image of the chameleon's death. Attempting to fit into one environment at the expense of no longer fitting into another is risky. One may misjudge the situation, one may get caught, and as a human being with a consciousness, one may end up feeling split, guilty, and at a loss of voice, life, and identity.

SIX

The Traveler and the Tourist
Axel Jensen's Desperate Frolic in the Sahara

AXEL JENSEN (1932-2003) traveled extensively and spent about half his life living abroad.[1] He took on jobs ranging from sausage making to coordinating poetry festivals. In his youth, he experimented with LSD cures and swapped girlfriends with Leonard Cohen (Cohen's "Goodbye Marianne" is about the couples' interrelationships). Eventually, Jensen converted to Hinduism and married the Indian woman Pratibha with whom he shared the rest of his life, living for years on a houseboat in Stockholm harbor.[2] In his older age, he ended up surviving a surprising number of years paralyzed by amyotrophic lateral sclerosis, yet he continued to write experimentally and fight for freedom of expression. He was especially engaged in protesting the fatwa against Salman Rushdie and won International PEN's first Carl von Ossietzky Award in 1994.

Jensen made his debut in 1957 with *Ikaros: Ung mann i Sahara (Icarus: A Young Man in the Sahara)*. The book is based on the author's own travels in Africa, where he ended up spending a year in the Sahara Desert. Jensen first went from Italy to North Africa in 1952. After having been to Tunis and Algiers, he was hired aboard a ship sailing to Kuwait and Iraq and then to Scotland and Great Britain. Tiring of living a bohemian existence in London, Jensen subsequently went to Paris, where he was given a ticket back to Norway by the Norwegian consulate. A couple of months later, Jensen traveled to Algiers with a Norwegian friend. There they took the train as far as they could to the Algerian city of Touggourt, which is built around an oasis, and then continued into the Sahara Desert. In Tamanrasset, Axel's friend Per started missing a girl back home and left Axel by himself: "'So the whole journey in 'Ikaros,' where there is only one man, was really the journey of two people. But things like that were too complicated to describe. Per had to go."[3] Axel Jensen ended up spending a year in the desert (Mollestad, 42).

Icarus is existential in its kind as it combines the depictions of an inner and an outer journey. According to Jensen, he wrote the travelogue in only three weeks while working as a warehouse assistant in 1956. Once the inspiration was in place, his narrative flowed easily. As Jensen has put it in an interview, "In 'Ikaros' it is just me telling and rambling between truth and fantasy" (Mollestad, 58).[4] Combining truth and fantasy indiscriminately, Jensen writes himself into a Norwegian tradition harking back to Knut Hamsun's "experienced and dreamt."[5] As the title signals, though, Jensen—as opposed to Hamsun—prioritizes the general above the particular. *Icarus* is not to be understood solely as one individual's explorations of his personal dreams and experiences, but rather as the depiction of the mental life of a general type. This type may be viewed as a universal young man, but given the text's plot and setting, he is more precisely defined as the young, post–World War II, Western male seeking to comprehend the European culture to which he belongs, from its initial rise to what is perceived as its present-day fall.

In terms of literary history, the book may be viewed as influenced by the late symbolist literature arising after the war. In this age of despair, artists reacted against the atrocities of the war—especially the extermination of Jews in concentration camps and the dropping of the atomic bomb on Hiroshima[6]—by reviving ancient symbols and appealing to a new faith in humanity through these common symbols. The artistic project was formulated in the Danish journal *Heretica*: "The belief of a new era grows forth from the core of the belief that is dying, from its primitive symbols. Granting these symbols new power of actuality is the true mission of artists today."[7] Jensen stands forth as such a visionary artist, claiming, too, that "the Greek myths are just as relevant and strong a source of power today as they were back when they were created."[8] As opposed to the sincerity of the Danish *Heretica* group, though, Jensen, as we shall see, reemploys these symbols with an ironic distance. In his authorship, Jensen has repeatedly used form (here the Greek myth) as a source of irony (Mollestad, 119). Jensen is half a generation younger than the members of the *Heretica* group, and *Icarus* may be read as a young poet's attempt to follow the literary and ideological doctrines of his postwar predecessors. The attempt, however, turns into a halfhearted affair, with the protagonist eventually giving up life's greatest questions to return home and surrender to the joys and trivialities of everyday life.

Previous scholarship has focused on the themes and sources of ideological inspiration in *Icarus*. In "En norsk femtitallsroman," Audun Tvinnereim has outlined the text's main thematic oppositional pairs as civilization versus simplicity, the North versus the East/South, individual versus society, and body versus soul. Tom Eide has written most extensively about Axel Jensen in his dissertation on the early part of Jensen's authorship, *Outsiderens posisjoner* (The Positions of the Outsider). Here he lists Axel Jensen's main foreign sources of inspiration, emphasizing Jensen's interest in Jungian psychology.[9] Eide's own approach to Axel Jensen and his authorship is psychoanalytical with a particular focus on object relations.[10]

Eide's analysis is convincing from a structural and psychoanalytical point of view. Yet, the psychobiographical analysis leaves out greater sociohistorical perspectives on the one side, and the sociopsychological function of humor on the other. From an individual psychoanalytical perspective, *Icarus* may contain what is but a pseudohappy end in which psychological conflicts are not resolved.[11] *Icarus*, however, is ironic, parodic, and humorous, and as we saw in chapter 5, humor may serve a social integrating and reconciling role. Hence, viewed from a psychosocial point of view, what is not attained on the level of psychological individuation may still be attained on the level of a general life philosophy. The hero realizes he belongs to the Norway he left behind and ultimately writes a self-deprecating book reingratiating himself with this community.

In this chapter I will focus on the theme of the traveler versus the tourist as it applies not only to the protagonist but also to the narrator and the implied author. On the plot level, the protagonist overtly sets out to distinguish himself from the common tourist. Being a traveler corresponds to being an outsider, an individualist, and one of a select few. Being a tourist, on the other hand, corresponds to being bourgeois, being one of the masses, and not possessing any particular intellectual or artistic vantage point. Hence, the protagonist's ultimate downfall and humiliation are marked by the fact that he has to regard himself as a tourist—or as "normal." As Jensen puts it, "The ghastly thing about my craziness is that it gives me such a horror of being normal. The word 'normal' makes me feel that I am suffocating."[12] The quote clearly reveals the traveler's insight that his angst and aversion are unhealthy, and that he needs to find a more nuanced position between the ordinary and the extraordinary.

On the level of the narrator and the implied author, the traveler-versus-tourist theme is to be understood metaphorically as related to literary ambitions. Traveling, in this sense, is a matter of intertextual traveling as the narrator establishes overt and covert connections with literary forerunners on the level of content as well as form. In this case, too, the narrator has to renounce his initial lofty ambitions of writing the apocalypse of the twentieth century and ultimately find a balanced form, allowing him to appeal to the ordinary as well as the sophisticated reader. Highlighting the development of the traveler-writer from an extremist to a more moderate attitude toward life, the novel eventually follows the home-out-home pattern of a standard quest or bildungsroman. It does so dripping with self-deprecation and humor—not with the great humor that Dinesen can allow herself after seventeen years in Africa, but with what we may call the small humor a twenty-five-year old can allow himself after having been abroad for one year.

The Icarus Plot

Icarus is divided into three main parts that, in turn, are divided into chapters. In Part I, we meet the unnamed protagonist who has fled from Western civilization, leaving Norway for the North African coastal city Algiers. Sickened by the big city's crowds, traffic, the smell of asphalt, and the entire human race (32/37), he begins his process of going native, exchanging his suit for a djellaba, leaving his books and other belongings behind at the Norwegian consulate, and catching a ride with two Arab smugglers going farther into the desert, to the French colonial town El Golea. By entering ever deeper into the African landscape, the protagonist hopes to gain a sense of spiritual enlightenment—or "the Philosopher's Stone" and "the miraculous, the crazy, the impossible" (43), as he calls it. After a short stop in El Golea, during which one of the Arabs tries to rape him, the protagonist gives up his ride and walks the last part into the desert.

In Part II, the traveler hangs out with French military personnel, including the army doctor Bobo, in Tamanrasset. The place, however, does not live up to the protagonist's associations and childhood fantasies:

> I had imagined Tamanrasset as a grim, medieval knight's castle perched up on the side of a mountain. The streets were to be narrow... I was to come across black-garbed Tuaregs everywhere. They would slip past me like beings from another world. Well over six feet. (79)[13]

As in the case of Hamsun, the Tuaregs evoke dreams of the premodern, noble savage, arrogantly rejecting Western civilization. As such they serve the same function as Dinesen's Masai. They are "barbaric giants with fair hair and blue eyes" (38). Yet, the Tuaregs have left Tamanrasset after it has been colonized, and the old Tuareg capital turns out not to be located on the expected mountain shelf; ultimately it feels more like a French provincial town than a place located two thousand kilometers inside the Sahara desert (79/80).

In Part III, the protagonist leaves Tamanrasset on donkeyback, going even more native as he penetrates farther into the desert—to Thaza—assuming the Arabic name Mustafa. Thaza becomes the journey's final destination. Here the protagonist fully explores his primitive, aesthetic, and spiritual sides. He settles among a group of Tuareg nomads, and enters into a sexual relationship with Tehi, based purely on primitive, idealized animal instincts. Already at their first encounter, "Mustafa" notes that "she devours me with primitive avidity in her eyes" (124).[14] Eventually the protagonist builds a stone hut and settles down as a farmer cum author, composing what is to become an apocalyptic masterpiece. In addition, he regularly seeks out a French mystic, Nerval, who lives in a nearby cave. In Thaza, "Mustafa" attains his desert dreams—a moment of ecstasy, or what he calls the oceanic (39/44): "At my feet ran the boundary to empty space. And the empty space ravished me and I have never been closer to the miraculous" (119).[15] Reflecting upon this moment a few months later, he still recalls the fear-inspiring aspect of the ecstatic moment: "And when I stood by the chasm and looked out over the desert, my consciousness had been flooded by something great and mighty that was more than I myself and that frightened me" (141).[16]

As we saw in the chapter on Johannes V. Jensen, Marianna Torgovnick traces this urge to go through a liminal, oceanic state of mind and experience a sense of rebirth—to "go primitive"—back to the early twentieth century.[17] As Torgovnick points out, the impetus behind going primitive is the disgust the traveler experiences for Western civilization. Using Jung as one of her primary examples, she also accuses the Western male of never daring to go through with his project. Axel Jensen, who had read Jung's African travelogues, was similarly disappointed that Jung did not succeed:

> The weakness I sensed with Jung was that when he writes about his encounter with foreign cultures, for instance, when he was in Africa, then he is constantly wearing his pith helmet, if you know what I mean? . . . It is as if he did not manage to shake off his Eurocentric winter coat.[18]

As for Jensen's protagonist, the outcome of his project of going primitive is ambivalent. On the one hand, he describes the great existential "rape" and the experience of the desert cleansing his soul and reinvigorating his deadened senses (178/175). Yet, eventually, the snake, so to speak, enters paradise in the shape of the German silver digger Joseph Schlumberlaum. Materialism replaces spiritualism, and in an episode entitled "Døden" (Death), the narrator enters a feverish state of mind, walking up a mountaintop, barefoot and overexposed to the sun.

As opposed to the mythical Icarus, though, the narrator's getting too close to the sun does not lead to his drowning. Rather than dying, the hero—who at this point turns into an antihero—is saved by Bobo, who cures him and brings him back to civilization. The wax that finally starts melting is the protagonist's spiritual dreams. These lofty ideals are replaced with homesickness. The protagonist misses Norway, his friends back home, the sound of civilization, a bit of materialism, his roots, and his own generation. The final state of enlightenment—the wisdom of "the Philosopher's Stone"—turns out to be the opposite of what he set out to find on his quest. Rather than denouncing materialism, civilization, and humanity in general, the protagonist gains new faith in humanity. As Bobo tells him, it is inhuman to denounce one's animal instincts, not to drink, and not to have sex. Being human means being social. When the protagonist asks Bobo what kind of humanity he is talking about, the doctor puts him in his place:

> The humanity that makes it possible for us to sit here talking together. Or to be blunt: the humanity that makes me travel through the desert for several days and nights in order to patch up a fellow who wanted to find the Philosopher's Stone. (184)[19]

The protagonist appreciates the reprimand: "I had nothing to put up against that. I just sat there and accepted it. It hurt a bit, but right inside I liked it" (184).[20]

Although Jensen, in contrast to Jung, has managed to surrender to the oceanic at least momentarily, he does not manage to doff his Norwegian winter coat in the long run. The conclusion the traveler reaches is one of fundamental cultural relativity:

> Even if you feel a glow and a sense of solidarity with the Tuaregs, even when you touched the live nerve, joined in the mating cry and felt your throat quiver with strange ecstasy, even then there was a continent between you ... We each had our line of destiny—one white and one black ... my destiny and the nomad's destiny. (172)[21]

The civilized European may feel at home with the primitive nomads, but nevertheless their lives are governed by impenetrable cultural codes:

> I felt so free and easy when associating with these simple, primitive people. Because of that I was surprised each time I discovered that they were not so simple after all. Thus even among the Tuareg in Thaza I was the foreigner with the foreigner's lack of sensitiveness to the finesses of behaviour that have stratified in people's minds through the ages. (146)[22]

As is often the case in modern travel books, *Icarus* depicts what ends up being a "displaced" myth.[23] What starts out as "the archetypal monomyth of heroic adventure" is "lowered [and] brought down to earth" (ibid.). On the level of the journey this is made clear as the traveler sets out to go to Tibet, but cannot gain a visa and has to replace his first-choice destination with the Sahara (22/28). On the level of the travelogue, the bringing down to earth of the initial project is reflected in the lowering of the protagonist-writer's overall literary ambitions. Whereas the traveling protagonist sets out to write the apocalypse of the twentieth century (112/112), he ends up writing *Icarus*. Hence, in the end, the myth of Icarus applies not only to the rise and fall of the main character and of Western civilization in general, but also to that of Jensen's travel book itself. Flying represents writing, and in its literary, intertextual, and prophetic ambitions, *Icarus* risks getting too close to the sun.[24] By playing on the contrast between the symbolist writing of the late 1940s and the eventually more naive, life-embracing writing produced a decade later, *Icarus* punctures its own symbolist loftiness, and the story is ultimately pulled down to earth and saved from drowning. Parodic contrasts, in other words, function as the literary work's Bobo—its voice of humanity, its savior, its doctor, and its cure.

Tourism and Traveling

Turning to the text's overt tourist-versus-traveler theme, we see that the protagonist's ultimate development from desiring a critical and prophetic outsider position to longing for being part of his home community is captured in the vulgar figure of the tourist. It is no coincidence that post–World War II travel literature thematizes the difference between the tourist and the traveler. As we saw in Part I, tourism is commonly dated back to 1840 due to, among other advances, the development of steam travel. A good century later, charter tourism created an entirely new form of mass tourism as hordes of tourists were brought to sunny, exotic destinations, first by bus, then by airplane.[25] In El Golea, the protagonist spots a group of charter tourists, viewing them as condescendingly, as he claims the locals do:

> The tourists came by air. Direct from the civilization. They like to stay a couple of days at Hotel dal Piaz. They ate a five-course dinner. Relaxed in the lush garden in front of the hotel. Dozed in deck-chairs. Drank Pernod and became merry. Drank cognac. Became sleepy. Drank ice-water. And in the end became ill. (49)[26]

Tourists lack originality, curiosity, and energy. Unlike the protagonist, who has *gone Arab,* they wear bright white clothes and bright white pith helmets, and view the Sahara through sunglasses and cameras that prevent them from having an authentic experience of the place (45/50).

Initially the protagonist insists on being regarded as anything but a tourist. Having arrived in Algiers, he becomes furious when the owner of a whorehouse might be regarding him as such: "She thought perhaps it was just a randy little devil of a tourist she was talking with. She did not see there was anything extra about me, anything magical, that I lived a symbolic life" (28).[27]

The protagonist aspires to the role of the romantic traveler, whose main characteristics, according to John Urry, are "solitude, privacy and a semi-spiritual relationship with the object of the gaze."[28] In *The Tourist Gaze* (2002), Urry discusses "the mass character of the gaze of tourists" as opposed to "the individual character of 'travel'" (3). As the single quotation marks suggest, Urry is wary of the travel concept and tends to view everybody as a tourist. He subsequently divides the tourist into two types: the tourist possessing a romantic gaze (what we might also think of as the traveler), and the tourist possessing the collective gaze (what we think of as the typical tourist). As the earlier quotation indicates, Jensen's protagonist is also only believable as a traveler in quotation marks—as a pseudo traveler. His infantile means of argumentation leaves the reader to suspect—through dramatic irony—that he is, indeed, a randy little devil of a tourist.

Strengthening this suspicion is the protagonist's reason for continuing from Algiers to Tamanrasset as it is also inspired by tourism—this time the tourist poster. The protagonist may well refer to "Thomas Cook's turistanstalt," using the pejorative term "anstalt" (32),[29] and subsequently justify his choice of Tamanrasset poetically, by claiming that it was the sound of the word that attracted him (34/39).[30] The fact remains, however, that it is a glossy poster featuring a stereotypical Tuareg that prompts his desire for this destination: "a Thargi warrior with lance and sword and shield, enveloped in black, mysterious garments, sitting astride a milk-white camel and gazing at mountains that would not let go of the sunset" (37).[31] As Roland Barthes points out in *Mythologies* (also published in 1957), this form of stereotypification is the standard sign of bourgeois tourism. In his reading of *The Blue Guide,* Barthes finds that the inhabitants of various countries exist only as types: "We find again here this disease of thinking in essences, which is at the bottom of every bourgeois mythology of man" (75). Although Jensen's traveler is able to maintain an intellectually critical distance from the tourist poster, describing it as "mendacious and enticing," he nevertheless succumbs to it on an emotional level, continually caught between intellectual haughtiness and emotional submissiveness—between the positions of the traveler and the tourist (32/37).

Toward the end of the journey, the protagonist finally gains this insight himself. When Bobo, in Part III, says, "you tourists cause us a hellish lot of trouble" (181), the protagonist, as we have seen, meekly submits to this classification. Thus, the reader's initial suspicion is confirmed. The protagonist is youthfully overambitious, does protest too much, and the expectation that the tragedy will ultimately emerge as a comedy is met. As Eide has put it in *Outsiderens posisjoner,* Axel Jensen interprets the tragic myth of Icarus in a way that "excludes precisely the tragic" (134). Yet, as it turns out, succumbing to the role of the tourist is a sign of being human. When the protagonist furthermore manages to inhabit the role of part traveler, part tourist, he ends up in the nuanced, all-encompassing situation that makes him a heroic figure nonetheless.

The Whorehouse Tourist

In the twentieth-century travelogue, the vulgar tourist and the noble traveler constitute opposite ends of a spectrum, lending themselves to comedy and tragedy, respectively. Refusing this dichotomy, Axel Jensen's unnamed hero is situated between these classic Aristotelian figures as a semivulgar subject—a tourist-traveler—written about in a noble style. Jensen's protagonist thus lends himself to the mock-heroic parody, while comic and tragic figures conjured up in the plot serve as his one-dimensional foils. As the plot progresses toward its conclusion, the tragic figure is in focus, both through direct references to Nerval and, as I will show, through indirect references to the protagonists of Paul Bowles's *The Sheltering Sky.* Yet, in the beginning of the plot, it is the comic figures who receive most attention, not least in the shape of the Norwegian sailor, a man who is "inferior but not altogether vicious," as Aristotle would say.[32]

The narrator employs two strategies to indicate the sailor's inferior status: vulgar language and what Urry dubs the tourist gaze. As the sailor and the protagonist walk the streets of Algiers, the sailor accosts three Arab women, all of whom reject him. The sailor, in turn, explodes in a racist barrage revealing his unrefined means of expression:

"What women!" he said. "Standing there wanting to hook some poor Arab devil. Shocking! All veil and white lace. Can that make you het *[sic]* up?"

No, damn it all, he went on, the girls in the Sphinx were a darned sight better! He had been there, yes, sir! No veils and tricks about them. They came from France, they did. Proper white whores. They knew all about it. That was what you wanted. (21)[33]

The protagonist, on the other hand, lives a philosophical life, quoting T. S. Eliot and insisting that "my world was far removed from the sailor's world" (21). The protagonist has set out to renounce his animalistic side, and when he finally does give into prostitution—which he does over and over again—he imagines that his whore is completely different from the rest. To conjure up this illusion of distinction, the protagonist relies on his romantic gaze, emphasizing solitude, privacy, and spirituality.

The romantic scene is set up as a contrast to the vulgar scene connected with the sailor. The sailor, who enters the whorehouse first, walks into a room described by the protagonist as loud and crowded. Glasses are clinking, voices are buzzing, and a whore is not only laughing but shrieking with laughter (17/23). Further emphasizing the sensuality and corporeality of this scene, the whore is depicted as fat and yellow-skinned as she pulls up her skirt, mounts, and rides a soldier while smearing lipstick all over his forehead. The gaze pertaining to this scene is that to which Urry refers as the collective gaze. This gaze "necessitates the presence of large numbers of people . . . [who] give atmosphere or a sense of carnival to a place" (Urry, 43).

In contrast to this scene, the narrator manages to portray his subsequent encounter with a whore through a sublimating, romantic gaze. Rather than laughing in a crowded room, she stands leaning against a pillar, pensively smoking a cigarette (18/23). She is sophisticated, elegant, and ethereal, the last attribute of which is also captured in her name, Angelina. The moment of intercourse is supposed to be sexual as well as spiritual—or "semi-spiritual" as Urry calls it. The protagonist, however, does not live up to his own sexual ambitions. His experience turns out to be much less unique, private, and intimate than he had hoped. Angelina does not take off all her clothes—she leaves on her bra—and it turns out the sailor had had sex with her just before the protagonist arrived.

While the protagonist's project fails, that of the narrator succeeds. On the level of the plot, the protagonist's youthful innocence is once more revealed in a forgivable way. Not only is the protagonist hopelessly romantic, he also ejaculates prematurely. Again, this contrasts with the experience of the sailor: "I fucking thought I'd fuck my dick out of joint."[34] The encounter with a prostitute thus serves as yet another aspect of the protagonist's frustrated ambitions. He is not the romantic he wishes he were, neither as a traveler, as a writer, nor as a lover. And over and over again, it is his age—connected with immaturity and a lack of experience on the one hand, and with vitality, curiosity, and passion on the other—that gets in the way of the ideal.

Literary Tourism and Traveling

Used metaphorically to designate the clichéd versus the sophisticated, the theme of the tourist versus the traveler pertains to the protagonist not only on the level of his outer and inner journeys but also on the level of his literary project. *Icarus,* as mentioned in this chapter's introduction, can be viewed as the result of a complex intertextual journey establishing connections with a series of literary forerunners. The work is related to Jung's depictions of Africa; to Hamsun's travelogues; to Axel Jensen's main source of inspiration, Colin Wilson's *The Outsider;* to Scandinavian late-symbolist writing; to Paul Bowles's *The Sheltering Sky;* and not least to Greek mythology. The travelogue, in addition, is sprinkled with references to the Old Testament, to classical Roman literature, and to canonized Norwegian literature—such as Ibsen's *Peer Gynt*—as well as to the books the traveler brings along on his journey, works by Nietzsche, T. S. Eliot, James G. Frazer, and Ouspensky. *Icarus,* in other words, marks itself as highly intertextual, concentrating as much on Western literature as it does on African landscapes.

In terms of intertextual traveling, *Icarus*'s relationship to its Greek namesake is one of intertextual "tourism"—the connection is obvious. On the other hand, the travel novel establishes a less overt relationship of intertextual "travel" with other literary forerunners. Thus, while the myth of Icarus serves as an explicit intertext, Paul Bowles's *The Sheltering Sky* can be read as an implicit intertext, highlighting the inversion of the tourist-traveler theme on the plot level, while establishing a more sophisticated tourist *and* traveler relationship on the formal level. Using Gérard Genette's terminology, we may say that the myth of Icarus serves as an explicit hypotext, with the relationship between the travel novel and the myth being one of playful transformation—one of parody. Axel Jensen does not imitate the style of the myth but extracts "a pattern of actions and relationships, which he treats altogether in a different style" (Genette, 5). *The Sheltering Sky,* on the other hand, serves as an implicit hypotext. *Icarus* eventually inverts all its themes, turning the tragic into the comic and the misanthropic into a confirmation of humanity.

Bowles's work is never commented upon in the text, and, as Genette points out, "the less massive and explicit the hypertextuality of a given work, the more does its analysis depend on constitutive judgment: that is, on the reader's interpretive action" (9). Still, two things lead me to interpret *The Sheltering Sky* as a textual prototype. As Arne Melberg points out in *Å reise og skrive*—while also viewing *Icarus* in light of *The Sheltering Sky*—Paul Bowles's travel novel is generally "the novel that constitutes the model for literary desert journeys with metaphysical dimensions" (Melberg, 217). If we turn to the themes and literary structure of the two texts, the similarities between them further suggest an intertextual relationship.[35] Thematically, they revolve around the same subject. Bowles's two American protagonists, Kit and Port, are also fleeing Western civilization in the aftermath of World War II, and they, too, are questioning the notion of humanity. Port's view of humanity is entirely misanthropic: " 'Humanity?' cried Port. 'What's that? Who is humanity? I'll tell you. Humanity is everyone but one's self. So of what interest can it possibly be to anybody?' " (Bowles, 74). Formally, the texts are based on the same structure, beginning with a dedication to a woman, followed by a disclaimer, and then three main parts each of which is introduced by an epitaph. Finally, when it comes to the titles, both allude to the motif of the sky—one through a reference to Greek mythology, and the other through what turns out to be an existential theme of the sky providing us humans with false hope as we look up expecting a vantage point that might give meaning to our lives. In reality, according to *The Sheltering Sky,* the sky that we see only shelters us from the void that really surrounds us.

Thus, while the myth of Icarus is transformed, *The Sheltering Sky* is imitated in an act vacillating between pastiche and parody. Ultimately, imitation demonstrates generic mastery. It is a more complex form of transformation as it operates not only on a thematic but also on a formal level. According to Genette, the author of the hypertext draws "inspiration from the generic—i.e., at once formal and thematic—model" established by the writer of the hypotext (6). Thus, through its explicit and implicit intertextuality, *Icarus* emerges as a literary travel novel appealing to what we may call the "tourist" reader—who is interested in seeing what others see—as well as to the "travel" reader, interested in establishing his or her own connections between the obvious and the less obvious underlying structures.

The Tragic Traveler

When it comes to the differing plots of *Icarus* and *The Sheltering Sky*, we see that the main characters of *The Sheltering Sky* are tragic figures who reach a point of no return. They follow their destiny to its only possible conclusion and are never reintegrated into the society from which they fled. As such, they remain true travelers. Port's reflections on being a traveler rather than a tourist suggest the book's tragic aspect. It does so in two ways: (1) through a total lack of irony between the narrator and the characters—the attitude of the third-person narrator agrees with that of the protagonists[36]—and (2) through Port's laconically living up to his own definition of the traveler:

> He did not think of himself as a tourist; he was a traveller. The difference is partly one of time, he would explain. Whereas the tourist generally hurries back home at the end of a few weeks or months, the traveller, belonging no more to one place than to the next, moves slowly, over periods of years, from one part of the earth to another. Indeed, he would have found it difficult to tell, among the many places he had lived, precisely where it was he had felt most at home.... Another important difference between tourist and traveller is that the former accepts his own civilization without question; not so the traveller, who compares it with the others, and rejects those elements he finds not to his liking. (Bowles, 10–11)

As a traveler by his own definition, Port lives in a constant state of homelessness. Rejecting elements of a civilization means not fully accepting any civilization. While *Icarus*'s main character cannot be said to accept his own civilization "without question," he does realize that he ultimately feels more at home in his native country than anywhere else. Thus, while Jensen's protagonist ends up being no true traveler—neither by his own nor by Port's definition—Port and Kit are indeed presented as serious travelers who never return home.

Port dies, and Kit ends up escaping into the desert, where she is raped by Arabs and marries one that she likes in particular, becoming his fourth wife. When she eventually has had enough of being an Arab wife, she once more runs away and is found by Europeans who take her back to the Casbah. There she could have let her fellow Westerners take her back to the consulate—just as *Icarus*'s protagonist returns to the Norwegian consulate in Algiers, where he retrieves the Norwegian identity he had left behind. Kit, instead, runs off once again and has reached a point of no return—in all senses of the word. She will not go back "home"; she has gone mad, and all we are left knowing is that she remains on an overcrowded streetcar, riding it to "the end of the line" (Bowles, 256). With these words *The Sheltering Sky* reaches its conclusion, and we are left with an overall grim, brutal, and realistic novel, centering on the themes of death, loneliness, and insanity. This is a far cry from *Icarus*, which transforms the story of *The Sheltering Sky* into a parody, replacing a serious topic with a lighter and more playful one. Instead of main characters dying and going insane, *Icarus*'s protagonist simply has to learn a little lesson of humility, after which he can return to a presumably happy life in Norway. The bleak is replaced with the hopeful, the grim with the humorous, and thoughts of existential loneliness are replaced with a belief in love and human sociability.

The Narrative Layers of *Icarus*

Comparing *Icarus* to *The Sheltering Sky* reveals three ways in which Axel Jensen creates comedy: (1) through the ironic use of form (applying the myth of Icarus to the adventures of a contemporary young man); (2) through narrative layers representing different value systems and fictional levels; and (3) through what I call "small" humor. As indicated earlier, there is no narrative distance in attitude between the implied author, the narrator, and the main characters in *The Sheltering Sky*. All three come across as disparaging misanthropes. In *Icarus*, on the other hand, the layers of irony and parody are complex, leaving readers in a constant state of tension, uncertain what to think, but given the opportunity to release their tension through laughter. When, for instance, the narrator discusses himself—his protagonist—as an immature twenty-year old, the reader is led to believe that the narrator has gained a certain amount of self-knowledge since the journey took place five years before. Yet, the reader also understands that the protagonist has not gained enough insight to realize he might still be quite immature. Toward the end of the novel, the narrator sums up his adventures, explaining the title of his work:

> The Tuareg called me Mustafa. But since then, for it was some years before I had the courage to write about it, I have liked to think of myself in terms of the Greek mythology and I call myself Icarus, he who flew up so high towards the light that the wax in his wings melted and he fell back to earth.
> I flew towards the horizon so that I should be filled by the horizon. But it was all so different to what I had thought. (191)[37]

As this passage indicates, the narrator comes across as pompous and pathetic. At the still tender age of twenty-five, he claims to have matured immensely, gaining the courage and insight to compare himself with one of the greatest heroes of Greek mythology. The mode is one of irony and exaggeration, prompting the reader to laugh. Yet at whom is the reader laughing?

What distinguishes *Icarus* from the previous travelogues we have looked at in terms of narrative strategies is the level at which its irony is played out. While Hamsun and Johannes V. Jensen base the parodic mode of their travelogues on an ironic distance between the traveler and the narrator, Axel Jensen bases his on an ironic distance between the narrator and the implied author. Thus, Axel Jensen does not ridicule his traveler as much as he ridicules his narrator and, read autobiographically, his very own literary ambitions.

Icarus appears as an autobiographical novel framed by multiple layers of paratextual commentary, making it difficult to know where the factual comments end and the fictionalized travelogue begins. On the cover, *Icarus* is characterized as a novel. Then follows a dedication to Marianne, as well as a disclaimer that really serves as a marker of authenticity. While Bowles uses the straight disclaimer, "The characters and events in this story are entirely fictitious," Jensen writes: "In order to avoid too close an identification of the people the author met during his stay in the Sahara in 1953, most of the book's names have been changed."[38] The book, in other words, *is* based on real-life people, many of whom Axel Jensen names in subsequent interviews and already had named in the three travel letters he published in *Aftenposten* before further fictionalizing them in *Icarus*.[39]

As a final lead-up to the travelogue, we are presented with a letter signed "Your friend the Author" in 1957. This letter constitutes yet another pseudoconscientious disclaimer and is addressed to Bobo, the person who turns out to be the travelogue's true hero. Bobo is warned that the author has written about what happened in the desert five years before. He realizes that others may think he is too young to write an autobiography, but insists on doing so anyway—hoping only that the contents of his book will not hurt any of the protagonists "in our little drama." Considering that the final paragraph points out that Bobo may never get the opportunity to read this letter, since the author has not had it translated into French, we are left with the impression that it is really aimed at us, the readers, more than at the factual or fictional Bobo. The letter, that is, serves as a simultaneous flashback and flash-forward. It summarizes what has happened in the five years that have passed since the author was in the desert; it introduces the reader to the main characters and events of the travelogue; and—most important—it paints a picture of a somewhat deceptive, young, and precocious narrator. The word "author" may well appear in the signature, but because the letter is so clearly written by a young, overdramatic, and pseudosensitive person—one who concludes his letter with the sentence: "Here in the great chaotic world things are all so difficult"[40]—the reader understands that the implied author is actually constructing a somewhat preposterous, unreliable narrator. Paratextuality, in the end, creates mystery rather than clarification, or as Genette has put it, "Paratextuality... is first and foremost a treasure trove of questions without answers" (4).

In terms of tourism and traveling, the narrator may then be viewed as a superficial traveler who has not gained much substantial self-knowledge. He is but a tourist in the landscape of his own psyche. In *Outsiderens posisjoner,* Eide views Axel Jensen in general as having been inspired by

Carl Jung's psychology in an excessively selective way. Jensen allegedly has not grasped Jung's theory of individuation in its entirety, and he has overlooked Jung's warnings against an overzealous identification with symbolic or magical figures. To prove his point, Eide quotes Jung's words of warning:

> One cannot be too cautious in these matters, for what with the imitative urge and a positively morbid avidity to possess themselves of outlandish feathers and deck themselves out in this exotic plumage, far too many people are misled into snatching at such "magical ideas" and applying them externally, like an ointment. People will do anything, no matter how absurd, in order to avoid facing their own souls. (57)[41]

Eide concludes from this passage that Jensen inadvertently becomes a spokesman for that against which Jung admonishes his reader. In the case of *Icarus,* however, I would propose that we have to distinguish between the narrator and the implied author who uses Jung's warning as a source of comedy. When the narrator, at the age of twenty-five, looks back and understands himself in terms of Icarus, he almost literally possesses himself of outlandish feathers and decks himself out in not only exotic but also classic plumage. His comparison is superficial and absurd, and he clearly has not entirely faced his own soul and come to terms with who he is. Hence, the narrator remains a comical figure whose condescending attitude toward himself as a twenty-year-old traveler emerges as more amusing than convincing. This, however, is not to say that the implied author also remains a comical figure who lacks insight and understanding. Rather than figuring as a comical figure, the implied author ultimately comes across as a humorist. Through the self-irony expressed at the very moment of writing his travelogue, *Icarus* ends up a particular example of Bakhtin's inconclusive, novelistic zone. As the implied author presents himself as an immature writer, Bakhtin's "living contact with unfinished, still-evolving contemporary reality" ends up reflecting not so much on the represented world as on the author himself.[42]

Viewed historically, the author's self-ironic stance has to be regarded in the context of the Scandinavian welfare state that emerged in the 1950s. Unlike his literary predecessors from the 1940s, *Icarus*'s protagonist has grown up just in time to be spoiled rotten by a paternalistic welfare society in which everybody is constantly taken care of—unlike the Sahara, which Nerval informs the protagonist is no welfare state, so that he should be happy that someone nevertheless has saved him and he is alive (170/167). Axel Jensen's *Icarus*, we might say, prefigures Erlend Loe's *L* with both sets of authors and protagonists being "victims" of the Scandinavian welfare state—one at its earliest and one at its latest stage.

In *Icarus* we see the protagonist ranting against every ideology the West has to offer: "Anarchy is mere immaturity. Socialism a swindle. Communism a fraud. Capitalism is a growth on the world's rump and as such loathsome. The welfare state is a ridiculous mistake and all religion blasphemy" (34).[43] Speaking in the protagonist's own vocabulary, it is tempting to point out that the welfare state—regarded as a ridiculous mistake—and the Western political situation in general are what save his "rump." The protagonist is exposed as someone who can use the world as his playground for travel because whenever things go wrong, there is a European consulate to save him. We have seen how the French army doctor, Bobo, has to drag the protagonist out of the desert, and we have seen how the Norwegian consul in Algiers lets him deposit his Norwegian identity markers at the consulate, while he plays at "going native." In interviews, Axel Jensen has indicated that these episodes represent reality. In "real life," Jensen could always rely on consulates—also on his trips preceding the journey to the Sahara. In Algiers, Jensen had previously shown up at a consul Stenersen's, half-naked and sick with dysentery. Stenersen gave him medicine and offered him a job painting his house while Jensen gathered strength and money to travel on (Mollestad, 34). Having made it back to Paris, Jensen, meanwhile, went to the embassy there, too, to convince a general consul Werring to lend him money so that he could return to Italy to fetch the books he had left behind. Werring was not quite as compliant as Stenersen, but gave him money for a ticket home: "Oh well, we are after all talking about Norwegian tax money" (Mollestad, 36–37). What emerges is the unchallenged citizen who is good at playing but cannot take anything seriously. Yet, the protagonist's problem at the outset is that he tries too hard to take things seriously. Realizing that he is but a member of a community in which people take care of each other—a fact that may not be so bad after all—becomes part of his learning process.

Real, Fictional, and Psychological Figures

In Thaza the final drama plays itself out among rather one-dimensional characters: the Tuareg nomadic family consisting of Mukazzem, Tehi, and Haddah; the French mystic, Nerval; the German materialist, Schlumberlaum; and finally the humanist, Bobo. In *Outsiderens posisjoner*, Eide views these characters as elements of the protagonist's psyche appearing with escalating intensity. Thus, Tehi is the final woman in a series of three (Angelina, the dancer Khadija, Tehi) representing a mother figure—this time a mother figure who fulfills his desire for a preoedipal, oceanic state of being. Tehi's husband, Mukazzem, and Nerval represent opposite father figures—Mukazzem the prohibiting father[44] and Nerval the good and almighty father (125). Schlumberlaum is the final man in a series of three (the Norwegian sailor, the Arabian rapist Fedallah, Schlumberlaum) representing the protagonist's inner demons—this time a shadow figure that does not leave the protagonist's side (130). Overall, the surrounding landscape, Thaza, becomes the final place in a series of three (Tibet, Tamanrasset, Thaza), also representing the protagonist's longing for a preoedipal stage (125). Like Tehi, Thaza also fulfills this role, at least for a while.

Viewed from a psychoanalytical standpoint, the final apocalyptic storm, according to Eide, represents yet another inner demon (132), Nerval's snake becomes a symbol of sexual and spiritual potency (135), Mukazzem's killing of Nerval's snake represents a castration fantasy (127), and the apocalyptic vision brought on by Mukazzem's wrath, Schlumberlaum's greed and dishonesty, and the storm's vengeful dimensions represents an ultimate avoidance of psychic conflict resolution (133). Eide's interpretation succeeds in explaining the novel in its entirety, placing the narrative elements from each of the text's three parts in an intensifying relationship to one another. Viewing the events from a psychological perspective furthermore makes sense given Axel Jensen's own documented interest in psychology.

From a postcolonial perspective, however, it is necessary not merely to subsume difference pertaining to geographical, ethnic, racial, and national difference under the category of inner psychology, but to look at how psychic patterns of demonizing and idealizing are mapped onto various real-life groups of people. Frantz Fanon has shown how black and white function in a psychologically dichotomous relationship related to racial perception, and Edward Said has shown how a similar psychological dichotomy is projected onto East and West, with the inhabitants of the Arab world in particular serving as the Europeans' Other.[45]

Given the postwar political circumstances of the 1950s, Jensen's allegory reveals a rather typical geopolitical mind-set, not only with respect to black-white, East-West, and Arab-European, but also with respect to nations located within Europe. The fact that the mystic who has suffered internment in Sachsenhausen during the war is French points to the stereotype of French spirituality. The fact that the most loathsome person of them all is German points to the real-life vengeful demonizing of Germans following World War II.[46] If we look at the series of three men whose vileness intensifies, we see that the least loathsome is the Norwegian sailor, the more loathsome is the Arabian rapist-smuggler, while the vilest of all is Joseph Schlumberlaum. Whereas the other Europeans seek spiritual or at least aesthetic inspiration in the desert, Schlumberlaum is hunting for material wealth. He stinks, has bad breath, and boasts of his stay in Norway during the German occupation. In addition, he is a thief who steals the protagonist's shoes. He represents the worst humankind has to offer while Nerval represents its victim.

The protagonist seeks insight into the extreme suffering that has propelled Nerval into the position of the ascetic: "It was just the past that I wanted to fathom. I wanted to see the real reasons for his breaking with civilization" (137).[47] Nerval eventually shares his background with him, telling him how he was tortured during the war by being made to walk on a floor covered with soap and broken glass. This form of torture he describes as typically German:

> It's so simple. Only a German could think of anything so simple... The simplest and cheapest method you can imagine... the whole floor covered with soft soap—all they do is to smash some beer bottles—bits of glass everywhere... You are in there naked. (139)[48]

Lending meaning to the happenings of his own life by turning them into symbolic events, the protagonist subsequently views his own desert trek during which his feet are scorched as a process of identification with the suffering of Nerval—and as if that were not grand enough, he throws in additional figures of identification such as Nebuchadnezzar.[49] Again, the discrepancy between the tourist's going on a small hike up "a little peak" (160), and people's experiencing the pain of a true via dolorosa, creates an ironic and humorous situation that illustrates the protagonist's haughty ambitions coupled with the young man's lack of experience.

From an intertextual point of view, however, the dramatic climax also becomes humorous as a parody both on travelogues and on the symbolist literature of the late 1940s. First, in the vein of Hamsun's and Johannes V. Jensen's playing with this genre by inventing a turning point through dream imagery, Axel Jensen, too, uses feverish dreams to replace real-life drama. Like Johannes V. Jensen, Axel Jensen fantasizes about the ultimate hunt—not for a tiger, but for the German, and "in the end I hit the German full and square in the chest" (160).[50] Axel Jensen's protagonist, however, is much less of a hunter and not nearly as macho as Johannes V. Jensen's. As a sensitive antihero, his initial ambition is to climb a small mountain rather than "verdensbjerget," and he cannot shoot a gun. While Johannes V. Jensen's hero shoots at and hits various small animals, including birds, Axel Jensen's hero misses both the vultures at which he finally aims.

Second, if we return to the late symbolist writing of the *Heretica* group, for instance, we find writers who are reacting against the war and Western civilization by carrying out a project very similar to that of Axel Jensen's protagonist. They turn their backs on civilization, idealize a primitive lifestyle, and view the poet as the visionary outsider who can put people and civilization back on the right track. Their hopes for a better future are based on the individual's taking the world's destruction—the end of civilization—upon himself as a personal matter. As Peter Madsen points out in *Dansk litteraturhistorie,* this notion of compassion and identification is based on Christian mythology—on Christ's crucifixion and resurrection—and on the overall idea that change will come about through a process in which the individual withdraws into ascetic meditation in both physical and spiritual terms, living and reflecting only on what is most essential. This exercise will culminate in an intense consciousness of death that will finally enable the individual to return to this world and its reality.[51] This is the method the protagonist of *Icarus* seeks out. On the level of the plot, he retreats to a state of primitivism and he seeks to familiarize and identify himself with the vulnerable, suffering, Christlike victim and survivor of the concentration camps.[52] On the level of art, his ambition is that of the symbolist visionary, yet on both accounts his project fails. The failure is attributed mainly to the protagonist's naïveté, youth, and vitality. Like many members of the generation following the *Heretica* group, the protagonist simply realizes that the way of his predecessors is not for him. It is a role that does not fit his own life situation; his political engagement is not grounded in sincerity, and he is really just an individual who is more thrilled than scared by life. The attitude toward an earlier generation's ideological art and lifestyle may be one of admiration, yet this art and lifestyle are deemed invalid for a new generation whose futile attempts to imitate the sincerity of their predecessors turn unnatural and preposterous.

In the end, the protagonist is saved by Nerval and Mukazzem—Eide's two father figures who, together, also represent a combination of (European) spirituality and (African) animal behavior; one of Mukazzem's distinguishing features is his animal likeness—his animal or tiger strides (147, 183/145, 179). Having faced death, the protagonist is finally able to exist in the Kierkegaardian sense of the word. As Nerval tells him, "Consciousness begins with fear of dying" (166).[53] The hero has been through a rebirth, and in a final apocalyptic vision, Thaza is destroyed by a storm, and all the Europeans eventually characterized as tourists—Nerval, Schlumberlaum (dead by the end of the journey), and the protagonist—are brought back to civilization, to Tamanrasset, by Bobo upon whom Mukazzem has called to help. Notably even Nerval is characterized as a tourist. Like Kit and Port in *The Sheltering Sky*, he has occupied a tragic role, if not that of the traveler, then that of the exiled. Yet, Axel Jensen insists that the African desert force all its European visitors to leave. Sending Nerval back to a European civilization may be viewed as a final response to the critical attitude toward civilization following the war. Jensen's ultimate solution is that everybody must return to a normal life with other people:

> Nerval had seen the Light. And in the concentration camp he had also seen into the blackest darkness. The span of his mind was too giddy for me to grasp . . .
> But why could one not find the same light down on earth? In the company of animals and people? Yes, just with people! (191)[54]

In this educational project, Thaza has played a typical Orientalist role as a site of idyll, violence, and inversion. Mukazzem is the cultural Other upon whom the narrator projects African primitiveness as well as the Old Testament violence also associated with the Orient. His premodern features are timeless, linking him to the eternal. As he crushes Nerval's snake against a rock and decapitates seven goats, the narrator traces his lineage back to the Old Testament: "Mukazzem... takes his heavy, sharp Tuareg sword. His inheritance from his father. His father's inheritance from Cain" (179).[55]

As the female primitive, Tehi has acted the animalistic, soulless, natural, and uncomplicated lover. During intercourse she uninhibitedly bites and screams, never denying "her body relief, if it asked her for it" (144). In terms of a Norwegian literary imagination, the scenes constitute but a rawer and more explicit version of the North Africa depicted by Henrik Ibsen nearly a century earlier in *Peer Gynt* (1867). Tehi has been to "Mustafa" what Anitra was to "the prophet," and climbing a small mountain, nearly losing his sanity, has been the equivalent of Peer Gynt's entering the Egyptian madhouse. Further establishing this intertextual connection is Jensen's protagonist's use of *Peer Gynt*'s onion metaphor (after Ibsen, no Norwegian can talk of identity without talking of onions): "How idiotic! I thought. The greatest banality of the century: to find oneself!... To peel the skins off the onion of one's soul till one was left sitting there with tears in one's eyes and a vacuum between one's hands" (182).[56] While Peer Gynt's identity project is made available through Ibsen's Orientalist imagination, that of Jensen's protagonist is made available to the author through French colonialism. Like Dinesen, Axel Jensen is not the colonizer in a direct way, but he benefits from being European, being carried in and out of the Sahara desert by a French colonial settler.

Peer Gynt eventually returns to his Solveig, but what about Axel Jensen's unnamed hero? Figuring in a dichotomous relationship to Jensen's Africa is Norway, the welfare state with its innocent, temperate inhabitants: "a country a long way away... a country where autumn is long and summer short and where the women have fair hair and very blue eyes and Norwegian faces and slight bird-like voices" (182).[57] As opposed to the African women encountered by the protagonist—Angelina with the provocative split in her dress, Kadijah with her bovine expression and orgasmic dancing, and Tehi with her primitive fierceness and warm animal mouth—the Norwegian girls are depicted as being blond, blue-eyed, and having "norske fjes" (Norwegian faces). Norwegian faces are not bovine or animal-like, and whereas African women scream out in ecstasy and orgasm, Norwegian girls have "spinkle fugleaktige stemmer" (slight bird-like voices).[58] The girl the protagonist misses in particular is one he loves, one whose face he longs to hold between his hands, into whose eyes he longs to gaze, and with whom he wants to exchange the words "I love you," words never exchanged, or needing to be exchanged, with Tehi. Further emphasizing the innocence and purity of Norwegian girls, the protagonist describes them as lying naked in the sun, heading home around midnight, kissing good-night at the door, and simply making plans for the following day. Nice, bourgeois girls date, but they do not sleep with their boyfriends. Within this worldview, the Norwegian constitutes innocence, purity, and idealism.

Small Humor

The book ends on an ambivalent note. Looking forward to going home, the protagonist feels "one doubt and one hope, one bewilderment and one triumph," and he finally concludes, "I have come to the end of the road" (192).[59] The travelogue's last sentence is indicative of the text's slippery fictional levels. Who, we may wonder, is the final "I," and to which journey does he refer—the inner psychological journey, the outer geographical journey, or the literary, intertextual journey constituting the travelogue itself? In terms of the inner journey, the traveler-protagonist may be arriving at the conclusion that he will always be split between the two emotions of hope and despair; he will always be drawn to the primitive as well as the civilized; and he will always be an outsider as well as a member of his bourgeois welfare state nation, Norway.

On the level of the outer journey, the closing line simply suggests that the protagonist is about to leave Africa and head back to his homeland. And finally, in terms of the travelogue, the statement "I have come to the end of the road" refers to the autobiographical narrator having finished writing; this is where his novel ends. The indeterminate stance once more leaves the reader hesitant, not sure how to interpret the text's irony and unclear position on a scale extending from fact to fiction. Yet, as the narrator indicated in his preface (in the form of his letter to Bobo), the travelogue is determined by its writer's young age. Rather than avoiding the in-between stage of youth, the implied author embraces it. In terms of his life journey, the young man—expecting to live a long life—may be in no position to evaluate the outcome of his life. He may turn out to be a life traveler, but he leaves open the possibility that he intermittently will act the role of a life tourist.

Hence, *Icarus* is an expression of humor—not of the great kind we came across in *Out of Africa*, but of a small kind. As indicated in chapter 5, great humor requires life experience, reflection, and a journey through purgatory. While Dinesen's seventeen years of trying to survive in Kenya may be convincing as a mental purgatory where, as Harald Høffding puts it, "life's contradictions and the battling forces of existence have exercised their influence on the innermost core of spiritual life," Jensen's small trek through Africa—at the age of twenty—still leaves us, as well as him, uncertain as to the innermost core of his spiritual life.[60] Consequently, *Icarus* can only demonstrate the insight that within the autobiographical genre, an author cannot qualify as deep and wise as long as he is young. This may produce an inner conflict in a young man's ambitious mind, but the autobiographical writer ultimately knows how to use it to his advantage, through novelization, self-deprecation, and open-endedness. What we are left with is the image of a young man with good intentions, one who aspires to be a great humorist, but who does not have the life experience yet to be one. Irony *has* to replace nostalgic humor and ends up serving as a form of anti-conquest, not just from a postcolonial but also from a philosophical point of view.

Finally, when it comes to the tourist-traveler dichotomy, Jensen has presented himself as going through a humbling process, facing the fact that he is but a tourist in life—a tourist-traveler. Yet, as Roland Barthes points out in his chapter on the writer on holiday in *Mythologies*, this may be the most aggrandizing gesture of all. Represented as both banal and wise, the author figure ends up coming across as an *Übermensch*. He is both like you and me and something more. He is a tourist *and* a traveler, banal *and* wise, animal *and* spirit, an insider *and* an outsider. According to Barthes, the banal and quotidian mystifies to an even greater extent: "To endow the writer publicly with a good fleshly body... is to make even more miraculous for me, and of a more divine essence, the products of his art"

(31). Not only do writers demonstrate their humanness as tourists, they also, through their so-called logorrhea (30), "manifest themselves as universal conscience" (31). The reader is invited to assume this position of awe throughout the text, as when the Tuareg are said to become morally confused when "Mustafa" turns out to be a regular at the local whorehouse *and* a hermit in the desert—body and spirit all in one mysterious, Nordic figure (136–37/134). In interviews, Axel Jensen himself had no qualms about this point of view, explaining that the poet's supernatural status made his métier attractive: "Becoming a poet was something great and alluring. Almost superhuman."[61] When Barthes treats this topic, he writes about authors whose quotidian image is rendered not through their fiction but paratextually, through magazine reports and interviews, for example. Yet, his viewpoint lends itself particularly well to the modern travel novel in which the paratextual information about the author's traveling is an integral part of the fictionalized text. Within this autobiographical genre, the author stands forth not just as an artist but as an artist of life *(livskunstner)*. As *Icarus*'s protagonist puts it when he throws his apocalypse away, rejecting modern art—and the doctrine of art for art's sake: "The artist's art is to make art superfluous and let life itself become an art" (173).[62] What better way for an artist to accomplish this fusion of life and art than in the fictionalized memoir—as in the travel novel.

PART III

LATE AND POSTMODERN TRAVEL

Late and Postmodern Travel

IN *Imperial Eyes,* Mary Louise Pratt analyzes travel writing from 1750 to 1980, with the early cutoff excluding the topic of this last part: travelogues written since the early 1980s. Pratt finishes her narrative trajectory with Joan Didion's *Salvador* (1983), the brevity of which alone "suggests a dead end to all of this" (Pratt, 225). Thus, Pratt leaves her reader with the impression that travel writing, like her own book, has arrived at a logical end point: a dismantling of the genre. It then remains Pratt's last tentative hope that the dominated and *resistant* historical subject will finally claim authority and speak for him- or herself, while the Westerner abdicates, having realized that he or she cannot comprehend and assume the voice of the Other (227).

Travel literature—together with other (auto)biographical writing—has, however, gained in strength and popularity during the past three decades. Peter Hulme writes about a British breakthrough of travel literature since the late 1970s.[1] Yet, both postcolonialism and globalization have left noticeable marks on recent travelogues. Increasingly, themes of epistemology, politics, and representation are incorporated into the texts. As I mentioned in the introduction to Part II, postmodern anthropological accounts and literary travel narratives merge, with both genres emphasizing an awareness of the poetical and political contingency of fieldwork forced upon the observer.[2] The result is that the two types of discourses have renegotiated their key relations: "Signs of the time include a trend toward use of the first-person singular pronouns in accounts of fieldwork, presented as stories rather than as observations and interpretations" (Clifford, 68). At the same time, the novel and the literary travelogue cross paths, with both genres problematizing the divide between fact and fiction. Often a work's paratext and content contradict each other, leaving readers in a state of tension, not sure whether they should read a text as a novel (fiction) or as an autobiographical account (fact). The strategy is not entirely new, as we have seen in previous chapters, but it becomes ever more aggressive and boundary breaking.

Globalization has also challenged the genre from a more pragmatic point of view. The prevailing sense that there are no white spots left on the map and that the travel writer's home audience has access to the entire world—if not through travel, then at least through television and other media—leaves travel writers wondering not only *how* to write but also about *what* to write. Problems seem to provoke answers, and new strategies have emerged to tackle the problem of the post- or late-modern travelogue.

In his analysis of English travel literature written between 1940 and 2000, Peter Hulme divides travelogues written since 1975 into "five broad and overlapping strands" (93): the comic, the analytical, the wilderness, the spiritual, and the experimental. These categories may also be applied to Scandinavian travelogues, with Erlend Loe representing the comic and Carsten Jensen representing the analytical and the wilderness.[3]

In this part of the book I will first turn to Carsten Jensen's enormously successful eleven-hundred-page, two-volume travelogue that decisively put this genre on the literary map in Denmark. *Jeg har set verden begynde* (1996) and *Jeg har hørt et stjerneskud* (1997) cover a nine-month journey around the world, with Jensen employing a twofold narrative strategy. On the one hand, Jensen's traveler may be viewed as what the Norwegian historian Terje Tvedt calls the *narcissistic cosmopolitan* of the 1990s (as opposed to the romanticist of the 1970s and the humanitarian of the 1980s).[4] Jensen's protagonist travels where people have gone before him, but the important thing is that the journey is new and existentially significant to him as an individual. Like the sentimental traveler of the eighteenth and nineteenth centuries, he needs not uncover new territory as long as he describes the old in a new and personally engaged way. On the other hand, Jensen—outside of his travelogue—is known as a highly politically informed and well-read journalist, war reporter, and essayist. Thus, in addition to recounting a personal developmental journey, Jensen the reporter provides a thorough historical and political commentary on the countries through which he travels.[5] *Jeg har set verden begynde* and

Jeg har hørt et stjerneskud, published collectively as *Jorden rundt* (2003), are but two of many travelogues Jensen has published. In his recent works, he has also collaborated with photographers to provide illustrated texts in which photographs serve a documentary function. I will draw on these texts in the conclusion of my chapter on Carsten Jensen.

Finally, I will turn to Erlend Loe's parody *L* (1999) to illustrate another way in which the travelogue is still going strong in a new millennium. Loe's spoof on Norwegian national hero Thor Heyerdahl raises questions of postmodernism, postcolonialism, and postnationalism—all wrapped into a lot of humor. In *L,* photographs are used mainly as a source of contradiction. While Jensen uses pictures to illustrate a third-world reality (in his travelogues published after *Jeg har set verden begynde* and *Jeg har hørt et stjerneskud*), Loe uses them to provoke and confuse his readers. On the one hand, the pictures form a parodic intertextual contrast to Thor Heyerdahl's travelogue in which photographs are used to illustrate the participants' brave deeds and warm encounters with the cultural Other. In *L,* the pictures mainly point to the participants' boredom. On the other hand, the photographs contradict the labeling of the text as a novel as opposed to an autobiographical travelogue. Showing Erlend and his friends around the world, the photographs force readers to reconsider the reading contract established through the paratext. What is truth? What is fiction? What is a travelogue? And how do we know?

L also raises questions about the relationship between different cultures in a globalized world. Do current media make it less interesting to travel abroad? And if so, is that because state-of-the-art technology brings the unknown so close to home, or is it because it dulls our minds and quenches our curiosity? Finally, both Carsten Jensen's and Erlend Loe's works raise questions about the status of the peripheral nation in today's world. While Erlend Loe focuses on the national and Norwegian, Carsten Jensen maintains a global perspective. Referring to literature and events from all over the world, Jensen writes himself into an international context, believing in the universality of education and experiences. Yet, when his own work was translated into English and made available to the entire Anglophone world, it became clear that a Nordic best seller—despite the fact that it in no way emphasizes a particular Scandinavian perspective— cannot be assumed to arouse interest on the world market.

SEVEN

From the Personal to the Universal—and Back
Carsten Jensen around the World

CARSTEN JENSEN IS A MASTER at combining the particular with the universal. When he found himself divorced in the mid-1990s, he turned his quest for a new personal identity into a global quest. In nine months he "did" the world, returned home, and wrote *Jeg har set verden begynde* (*I Have Seen the World Begin*, 1996/2000), sharing with his readers his newfound understanding of himself and the world in which he lived. *Jeg har set verden begynde* covers Jensen's journey from Russia to the Far East. It was quickly followed by a second volume covering his travels through the Pacific Islands and South America and returning back to Denmark over Paris. *Jeg har hørt et stjerneskud* (I Have Heard a Shooting Star, 1997) also turned into a commercial and literary success, and Jensen by now is one of very few Danish writers who has gained literary status based mainly on his travelogues.[1]

As the first-person singular pronouns and sensory verbs of Jensen's titles suggest, the travelogues are subjective, personal, and existential. Jensen the traveler wants to absorb the entire world and cosmos through his senses. He starts out a distant observer, seeing and hearing the world, but the farther he travels, the more intimate and tactile his investigations become. Along the journey, traveling from West to East in *Jeg har set verden begynde,* Jensen moves from a masculinized, intellectual, lonesome sphere— represented by Russia in particular—to a feminized, bodily, communal world. In Vietnam, this world of liminality culminates with Jensen's entering into an intimate relationship with Tam. Feeding each other, sleeping together, and touring together, the two are represented as giving in to natural, essential drives—reminiscent of those depicted by Axel Jensen in the protagonist's meeting with Tehi. Yet, just as Axel Jensen's traveler also experiences the dangerous and painful sides of bodily experiences—through sunburn, cut-up feet, and fatigue, on the one hand, and the threat of a homosexual rape, on the other—Carsten Jensen too experiences sickness and perversity. In Hong Kong he undergoes a hernia operation (not knowing what he is being operated on for) and in Tahiti he falls for Karinna—only to discover *she* is a *he*. Jensen discovers the human body—not least his own—in all its pleasure and vulnerability.

While both Axel Jensen's and Carsten Jensen's journeys are made up of sensual and existential explorations, the narrative form given to their experiences differs. Whereas Axel Jensen opts for a classical myth rendered in the genre of a novel, Carsten Jensen chooses the first-person narrative of a bildungsroman rendered in the travelogue genre. Both strategies can be viewed as signs of their times; the postwar search for common symbols uniting people and their life experiences is replaced in the 1990s by the postmodern search for an autobiographical narrative providing the individual with what Anthony Giddens calls "self-identity."

In *Modernity and Self-Identity,* Giddens presents the quest for new "narratives of the self" as characteristic of what he calls high modernity, or the late-modern age. As in the texts of Jensen and other (male) travelers,[2] though, Giddens's point of departure is the trauma of divorce. Citing a study on the impact of marriage breakup, Giddens writes that divorce "is a crisis in individuals' personal lives, which presents dangers to their security and sense of well-being, yet also offers fresh opportunities for their self-development and future happiness" (10). In Jensen's case his breakup prompts a journey around the world, the result of which is an affirmation of, and return to, the person he already was: "There was someone I had left before I set out. In this lay the start of my journey. That someone was also the one I loved. In this lay the discovery of my journey."[3] After a nine-month separation, Jensen returns home to his former wife and they start a family. Thus the title "I Have Seen the World Begin" takes on added meaning. In a brief prologue describing the birth of his daughter, Jensen humbly acknowledges that "all I know about the history of the world is what I have learned from witnessing the birth of a child" (1).[4] Jensen thus has also seen the world begin for a newborn child.

While Jensen states that he knows so very little about world history and that his book is not a book about politics and history, this is exactly what makes up the other narrative strand of his travelogue. The well-read Jensen fills page upon page with information about politics, history, social science, and literary studies—bits that no doubt have contributed greatly to the popularity of his travelogues. Known as a sharp and intellectual journalist, essayist, and war correspondent, Jensen is able to combine the small story with the greater one. As Paul Fussell has noted in his study of British travelogues, this is a prerequisite for literary success:

> Successful travel books effect a triumphant mediation between two dimensions: the dimension of individual physical things, on the one hand, and the dimension of universal significance, on the other... The travel book authenticates itself by the sanction of actualities... At the same time it reaches in the opposite direction, most often to the generic convention that the traveling must be represented as something more than traveling, that it shall assume a meaning either metaphysical, psychological, artistic, religious, or political, but always ethical. A travel book is like a poem in giving universal significance to a local texture.[5]

Carsten Jensen's ability to turn a particular event into a universal symbol permeates his travelogues on all levels. Not only is the main quest both individual and global, but observations made along the journey also turn into prose poems "giving universal significance to a local texture." A Chinese woman's scream, for instance, turns into the expression of the repressed anger of a whole nation:

> The screaming woman did not appear to be in the grip of any one particular neurosis. It was more as if she raged with a collective tension. Her fit of anger stemmed from the inner pressure that builds up wherever too many people live cooped up too close together. Her screams were the inward screams of everyone. (43)[6]

As this example indicates, the interpretive gesture turns problematic in an ethical context. While Jensen is generally widely applauded for his universalizing, symbolizing, and aestheticizing capabilities, critics have also attacked him based on a more negative, postcolonial understanding of stereotyping and essentializing. Danish literary scholar Frits Andersen, for instance, ends up wishing that Jensen's texts were simply labeled as fiction—as novels—and not as fact-based travelogues.[7] Jensen, on the other hand, explicitly maintains that they must be read as travelogues in which everything represented has been seen and experienced and is thus authentic. The only invention, claims Jensen, is the person called "I."

As in previous chapters, I will distinguish among Jensen as the (implied) author, the narrator, and the protagonist traveler. The distance between these three figures, it turns out, is quite small. First, we may note that Philippe Lejeune's autobiographical contract is explicitly intact. Quoting a Vietnamese man's reflections on the traveler's name, the narrator writes: "Take your name for example. Your surname is Jensen . . . Now I won't ever forget your name. Jensen" (335).[8] Second, the temporal distance between travel and narration is small. Fragments are published along the way as travel correspondence in Scandinavian newspapers, and the travelogue is written down shortly upon the traveling author's return to Denmark.[9] Third, the lack of temporal distance is not replaced by an emotional distance — neither parodic, ironic, nor nostalgic. When it comes to the relationship between the (implied) author and the narrator, Carsten Jensen is no Axel Jensen, mocking a precocious author. Nor is he, when it comes to the relationship between the narrator and the traveler, a Hamsun or Johannes V. Jensen. Rather than portraying a ridiculously rigid and macho nonhero, Jensen the narrator depicts an open, honest, and sensitive traveler. As such, he comes closer to Dinesen than to the other twentieth-century male writers discussed in this book — with an important difference being that he establishes meaning and coherence by psychologizing rather than mythologizing.

The aim of this chapter is to further investigate Jensen's interweaving of a personal identity quest that may be understood in light of Giddens's theories of modernity and self-identity with his representations of the Other. While outside voices accuse Jensen of universalizing and Orientalizing the Other, Jensen's own narrator also raises questions about the possibility and ethics of representation. The last part of this chapter will focus on Jensen's own perception of moral dilemmas related to interaction with, and representation of, people living in cultures different from his own. In *Jeg har set verden begynde* and *Jeg har hørt et stjerneskud*, the question of literary genres related to representation is particularly relevant. As Jensen has also copublished several travelogues with photographers, I will eventually draw on additional examples from these to further relate the ethical question of representation in the late-modern travelogue to visual media.

The Late-Modern Self

When Jensen at the age of forty sets out on a worldwide journey, he situates his self-exploration as a midlife project, between that of the young and the old traveler. An eighteen-hour bus ride from Kunming to Lijiang in China provides plenty of time for reflection on what a man his age may and may not achieve by traveling: "Hence the necessity of travelling when young... Then the journey may become a formative experience" (85–86).[10] Thus, the protagonist is not out to discover himself for the first time or to shape a new Self.

Nor is Jensen on a nostalgic journey, looking back and trying to reconnect with his own youth: "I set out with no nostalgic illusion; I was not on a quest for my younger self and the limitless potential of youth" (248).[11] Jensen depicts himself as being neither a pubescent Axel Jensen forming himself abroad, nor a nostalgic Hamsun retrieving the northern Norway of his childhood in the Orient. Instead the traveler sets out to find and describe a balance between the impermeable and the liquid Self—and to ultimately rewrite this Self.[12] Unchallenged by others, Jensen easily becomes too much himself. In Kunming, for instance, he retires to read and write in his hotel room and then finds out "I had become too absorbed in myself and was no longer taking things in" (85).[13] Attaining too solid a sense of Self risks leaving the protagonist impervious to the sensual and concrete. Conversely, leaving himself too open to new experiences may result in a lost Self. Arriving in Hong Kong, a sense of ecstasy seizes Jensen but immediately turns into fear:

> It was a moment of unexpected ecstasy, leaving me strangely bewildered, with a feeling that this journey was far too insurmountably big for me, and that it would soon eat me up so that everything I had gotten used to calling my self would merely remain as a leftover.[14]

As the Self has to be so carefully managed, a question of primary importance becomes: What exactly is this Self? The travel narrator provides an explicit answer. As we have seen, it is something he has gotten used to *calling* himself. Rather than being ontological, it is epistemological: "your so-called character [is] a fiction that can only be reinforced by familiar surroundings" (85).[15] Thus, the traveler's understanding of his identity coincides with that of Giddens to the extent that it involves an autobiographical project—the creation of a fiction—as well as social surroundings confirming this fiction by believing in it. As Giddens puts it, "The reflexive project of the self... consists in the sustaining of coherent, yet continuously revised, biographical narratives" (5). Giddens explains that the autobiographical project is to be understood in a broad sense "whether written down or not" (76). Jensen's project, however, operates on two levels: through the stories he tells himself along the way, and through the autobiographical travelogue he writes and publishes once he is home. Thus, he also attains the social confirmation comprising the second part of his own equation, not least in a public realm. The first editions of the travelogues especially link Carsten Jensen's personal identity to the autobiographical narrative by carrying rather startling, black-and-white close-ups of Carsten Jensen's face on the cover.

Jensen the traveler, however, is on a quest for confirmation on a more intimate level, which may also be seen as characteristic of our age. According to Giddens, the late-modern person has become increasingly dependent upon "pure relationships," that is, social relationships that are "internally referential," depending fundamentally "on satisfactions or rewards generic to that relation itself" (244).[16] In a global or late-modern world, larger social institutions no longer provide ontological security as they have become uprooted. In this light, too, we may understand the crisis of the divorced man. Once he has lost his lover and most reliable guarantee of selfhood, he needs to replace her. Thus, while modern travelers such as those of Johannes V. and Axel Jensen hook up with prostitutes and "primitive" natives to explore their own raw sexuality, a late-modern traveler such as Carsten Jensen's protagonist insists on the trust, reciprocity, and mutual sharing of life stories involved in the intimate encounter. At the same time, it is important to insist that they do not share enough of their life stories and personal secrets to enter into a more permanent relationship. The traveler needs a reason to go back home, and at this point, the travelogue turns into a bildungsroman. On his journey out, in his encounters with the Other, the traveler has to get to know himself and develop into a complete and stable person who can convincingly return home and fulfill a public and private social role. Considering that this is an autobiographical story written in the 1990s, part of what makes it a rhetorical masterpiece is the narrator's ability to frame his quest for female encounters as one that has the requisite happy ending as he returns to his ex and establishes a family with her—after having flirted and slept his way through large parts of Asia and South America. The trick, in part, lies in employing a late-twentieth-century psychological vocabulary of vulnerability.

Geographics of Gender

Vietnam is Jensen's prime site of femininity, eroticism, and sexual exploration. The travelogue's two relatively short opening chapters on Russia provide a stark contrast to the Far East. Russia is linked to emotional and physical coldness. It is a world so brutal, totalitarian, militarized, monotonous, and masculinized that even women trying to dress femininely come across as drag queens:

> The women of the Soviet society... had had to transform into men. You could still see it. Now, when under the influence of the West or of an irresistible inner pressure, they attempted to recapture their femininity, they ended up looking like hookers or transvestites.[17]

The farther east Jensen travels, the more feminine the women become. Mongolians turn out to be childishly cute with ruddy cheeks, black braids, shapeless bodies, and big, accommodating smiles (60). Next stop is China, where the women are pretty, gracious, and fashionable, and even those employed in customs end up looking like runway models (67). After Cambodia, where women are hardly discussed, there is Vietnam.[18] Jensen builds up his story of an Oriental love affair, using a series of rhetorical strategies involving what Mary Louise Pratt calls "imperial stylistics" and "mystique of reciprocity."[19]

Pratt in particular stresses the rhetoric of arrival scenes, "a convention of almost every variety of travel writing [serving] as particularly potent sites for framing relations of contact and setting the terms of its representation" (79–80). The scenes tend to be depicted as panoramic scenes and are aestheticized in a subjective manner, allowing the traveler to project his own personal and cultural associations onto a land- or cityscape. In chapter 1 we saw how Hans Christian Andersen Orientalized Constantinople while establishing a sense of mutual interest and hospitality between himself and the Turks. Through simile, Andersen let the mosques' roofs evoke images of Noah's ark, and through anthropomorphization, he suggested that the trees were peeking back at him, eager to meet him. Arriving in Saigon, we may say that Carsten Jensen naturalizes the big city, turning culture into something organic:

> The suburbs of Saigon were like all suburbs in the Third World: a chaotic jumble of buildings; additional floors, some finished, some only half-finished; painted or bare concrete, enamel signs and small shops, piled higgledy-piggledy one on top of the other. (203)[20]

The description, stressing the organic through words like "sprouting up naturally" and "budding," further touches upon a link between the organic, bodily, and sexual by introducing the notion of nakedness and lying tumultuously on top of each other.[21] The depiction is a far cry from what Pratt views as a standard contemporary inversion of romanticist aesthetics. While the romanticists looked out on natural landscapes, praising beauty, symmetry, order, and the sublime, contemporary male writers, she claims, look out on third-world cities, lamenting their "ugliness, incongruity, disorder and triviality" (217). Using Alberto Moravia's *Which Tribe Do You Belong To?* (1972) and Paul Theroux's *The Old Patagonian Express* (1978) as her examples, Pratt concludes that "the impulse of these postcolonial metropolitan writers is to condemn what they see, trivialize it, and dissociate themselves utterly from it" (217). While this may be true for travel accounts written in the 1970s, it hardly captures Jensen's account from the 1990s, which may be regarded as more gleefully postmodern in the way it embraces hybrid cultures. Time and again, Jensen stresses that he neither expects nor wishes to come across "pure" cultures. Instead, he finds humor and beauty in Westernized non-Western places.

Jensen's eye for seeing the cultural as natural and further feminizing the big Asian city is moreover expressed through his depiction of women riding scooters downtown:

> There were a few cars on the roads leading into Saigon, but zig-zagging in and out between them were, it seemed, thousands of little Honda scooters. The closer we came to the centre, the more of them there were, many of them ridden

by young women in long trousers and white silk tunics slit up the side. Their delicate faces were framed by glossy, blue-black hair that hung down to their narrow waists. A good number of scooters carried two women, one on the pillion elegantly side-saddle, an arm round the waist of the driver who carried a primrose parasol to ward off the sun. The young women wove in and out of traffic like motorized flowers and I forgot the architecture and abandoned myself to the sight of them. (203)[22]

Saigon is brimming with slim-waisted, beautiful women who, summed up as "motorized flowers," constitute a perfect mix between the modern and the natural. They are not Jensen's cultural Others—as are the other two Jensen travelers' primitive women—but are rather likeminded equals who may be able to pull him out of his own overmechanized world. Perched on scooters rather than trapped inside cars, they show off their bodies, wrap their arms around each other, some keeping their legs tightly together, others keeping them apart. With their parasols, they evoke imagery of flowers—related to the natural in general, and to reproductive activity in particular. Flowers need bees, and as the traveler later puts it, "I do not think I am exaggerating if I say that nowhere has my confidence in my own masculinity been stimulated as much as it was in Vietnam" (302).[23]

The motorized flowers, then, represent a contemporary Orient. Clarifying what constitutes the imaginative Orient of today, Jensen, while still in China, has explained that the Westerner's traditional associations of the Orient with the enigmatic have been replaced first by associations with poverty, then political homogeneity, and finally with economic growth and technological advancement: "The mystery of the Orient had been replaced by that of the robots; the enigma of the East by that of efficiency" (31).[24]

While China may to some extent have represented Oriental robots and efficiency, Vietnam still turns into a classical Orient characterized mainly by enigmatic eroticism, sexuality, and perversion. The traveler realizes this himself:

> Nonetheless, Vietnam revealed itself to me as a land of parallel universes, continually presenting me with new ways of being, other identities, a whole string of possible selves. I was struck not by the delirious freedom of youth but by something quite different and more powerful: by a sense of my own thoroughly plastic malleability. I could be a murderer, a thief, a corrupter of minors, this country offered me the lot and in my anonymity... I was conscious of my own response. I was beguiled and enticed... Vietnam was a land where I could become lost inside myself, a land of inner opportunity. (248)[25]

After this introduction, the stage is set for the readers' high expectations to be met with depictions of criminal and perverse behavior—an Oriental trope typical of late-nineteenth-century French travelogues.[26] Jensen's protagonist can show off his normally suppressed wicked and lecherous sides and the reader can hardly blame him—it is the country's own fault, we are led to believe, for being so tempting. In fact, the imagery linking Vietnam to a great, moist seductress is intensified throughout the Vietnam section, as when, for instance, the traveler arrives in Hue, where the entire town, allegedly, is populated by scantily clad women. Here Jensen hardly senses his own walking around—it all just feels like afterplay:

> You [felt] more as if you were lying next to the city after happy lovemaking. The hot, humid air; the fine rain falling as intimately as sweat on your skin; voices; glances—all blending into one generous caress; an all-embracing erotic experience in which an entire culture converged on you in a single loving touch. (261)[27]

Through narrative depictions like this, one is left wondering who is seducing whom. Is Vietnam seducing the traveler, or is the narrator seducing the reader? Together with the traveler, the readers are bombarded with erotic vistas leading them to let down their guard and accept criminal and sexual behavior they, too, may otherwise have condemned.[28]

Vietnam seduces the traveler by gently calling forward his trust. As Giddens points out, the late-modern person especially experiences a sense of ontological insecurity based on not being able to trust the people and abstract systems that make up his surroundings (3). While Giddens describes a general state of affairs, this issue of anxiety, we may assume, only becomes more critical as one travels to foreign places. Jensen, in any case, is acutely aware of his own need for defense mechanisms, and he explains how these are broken down in Vietnam. Using the onion metaphor known from *Peer Gynt* (1867), it becomes clear that for the late-twentieth-century man, identity is linked to trust:

> I have always made one rule when travelling: no physical contact with strangers. But in Vietnam, strangers constantly made physical contact without my feeling threatened... With every touch another layer of the onion fell away and I drew closer to the surrender inherent in the acceptance of one's own anonymity. It did not matter that they touched me. They were welcome to do so, because I trusted them, or rather my trust grew out of these caresses. (248)[29]

Evoking the imagery from *Peer Gynt* is apt as Peer, too, loses and finds himself in the Orient—in his case Morocco and Egypt. Yet, while Peer peels through the layers of the onion to discover that modern humankind has no core identity, Carsten Jensen's narrator emphasizes the materiality of the onion. Identity, for the late-modern man, is linked to issues of trust related to the body. This, too, is characteristic of our age. According to Giddens, "The flesh that is the corporeal self has to be chronically guarded and succoured" (126). In earlier modern days psychologists thought of children as discovering first the boundaries of their bodies and then a stable comfort zone allowing them to interact trustingly with their environment. Giddens, however, insists that while this model fittingly describes an "uneventful" modern world, it does not account for the situation of the reflexive, risk-focused person of a late modernity whose "protective cocoon" or "mantle of trust" is never to be taken for granted.[30] Thus, it makes sense that Peer in the late 1800s uses the onion metaphor existentially to answer a question about a precarious spiritual Self, while Jensen's traveler, a century later, transfers it to a physical realm to reflect upon a precarious corporeal Self.

Vietnamese women of all ages caress, kiss, flatter, flirt, and play with the traveler and his body, so he can finally shed his protective layers and develop the trust needed to be a complete person. Where, one may wonder, are the Vietnamese men in all this? The general avoidance between the traveler and the Vietnamese men—who are summed up as uninteresting and withdrawn (492/314)—is depicted as being mutual. In addition, Jensen insists on an image of the country and culture at large as feminine, or at least nonmacho. Holding up the Vietnamese to the Russians, he concludes that even in the case of warfare, the Vietnamese identify with the physically weak David rather than the great Goliath. The guerrilla warfare tunnels in Cu Chi, for instance, illustrate that while Communist Russia has cultivated machine power, armor, and muscular manliness—or, in short, "kraftberuset brølende maskulin idioti" (352) ("power-drunk, bellowing, male lunacy") (218)—the Vietnamese war hero "var alt det modsatte" (352), ("quite the opposite") (218). Finally, the Vietnamese men whom Jensen does meet and like tend to be of a feminized kind—from the male housewife whose wife tells him: "You may look like a man. But you're not a real man. You're a woman" (256),[31] to dead and buried eunuchs who, while alive, wore embroidered flowers on their coats, symbolizing their lack of gender (448/279).[32]

In this nonthreatening, feminine world, Jensen can build up his identity through his ability to trust. Unlike earlier male travelers whose sexual encounters with women underscore their virility, Jensen's encounters ultimately underscore his openness and sensitivity—and his ability, finally, to enter into Giddens's late-modern "pure" relationships.

Equality across Cultural Boundaries

In his article on *Jeg har set verden begynde* and *Jeg har hørt et stjerneskud*, Frits Andersen views Jensen's travelogues as Orientalist in the vein of eighteenth-century sentimental travel: "Carsten Jensen's recycling of notions from the overheated melting furnace of Orientalism is blindly carried on" (10). With regard to Jensen's Oriental love affairs, Andersen points out that, when it comes down to it, Jensen's protagonist basically socializes with semiprostituted women, or women who—longing to leave Vietnam and try out their luck elsewhere—throw themselves at the affluent European traveler. The narrator, however, refuses to acknowledge this, insisting, as Andersen puts it, on an extreme naïveté:

> In innocent play or in the enjoyment attained by playing the role of a child while actually occupying the dominant position, Carsten Jensen in reality repeats Orientalism's register of sentimental stereotypes about lovely, Asian women and the erotic mystery of interracial love. (Andersen, 8)

The fact that Jensen comes across as a classical Orientalist or postcolonial traveler who, as Pratt would say, employs infantilizing "anti-conquest" strategies raises the question of what distinguishes a late-modern "neo-Orientalist" traveler of the 1990s from his nineteenth-century Orientalist counterpart. Jensen's text, after all, does reflect an awareness of postcolonialism and political correctness, and what characterizes the travelogues in opposition to those of nineteenth-century and earlier-twentieth-century travelers is once again the reflexivity of the project—the amount of effort put into justifying the traveler's dubious actions.

In the early part of the century, Johannes V. Jensen's macho traveler unscrupulously has intercourse with the two prostitutes, Aoaaoa and Lidih. In the mid-1900s, Axel Jensen's more sensitive traveler has sex with urban prostitutes, despising his irrepressible animal side, and then proceeds to have what he considers pure, unadulterated sex with the primitive Tehi. Carsten Jensen's traveler, finally, sets out to establish a physical relationship with an in-between type of available woman. Tam is not to be understood as a vulgar prostitute like those sitting "astride little Honda scooters" on the Dong Du street (229). Nor is she a primitive—in fact, it becomes incumbent upon Jensen to view and depict her as a sophisticated, Westernized equal—a woman with whom he shares life stories (365/227), and a woman who, like him, is already tied to someone else (380–1/240).[33] Still, as readers we are also led to realize that Tam basically gets what she deserves when the traveler leaves her, seeing that she is demanding, tiring, unstable, unable to love, and ultimately unlovable: "I did not love her and she was too preoccupied with her own fate to be capable of loving anyone else" (245).[34] As Pratt argues, an important outcome of the interracial "erotic drama" is that "no hearts get broken" (89).

The narrator employs three main strategies to convince his reader that the meeting is one between the Western man and the Oriental, yet equal, Other. The strategies are first structural, then argumentative, and finally generic. In terms of structure, the narrator benefits from presenting the story in nonchronological order. By beginning with the end, he establishes an overview and an interpretative framework guiding his readers' reactions.[35] Not only are the readers presented with his claim that Tam will always remain an enigma (suggested by the fact that the traveler never found out the meaning of her name), but they are also presented with excerpts from her diary, revealing how she, too, understands relationships between men and women as being based purely on natural, essential, irrational, and uncontrollable drives. Thus, Tam's own voice (quoting English texts) disavows the geopolitical and historical power relations governing the relationship, insisting instead on pure biology. With Tam's consent, the relationship is to be understood, as the narrator later puts it, as "some invisible history of encounters quite unrelated to the dictates of topography or the long shadows cast by violent occurrences" (237).[36]

In terms of argumentation, the narrator employs a version of postmodern political correctness, insisting on seeing similarities between people by using concrete differences metaphorically. Through universalizing speculation, the narrator succeeds in relativizing prostitution, noting how we are all, at some level, prostitutes. "Unhappy people will sometimes behave like prostitutes, giving themselves away in return for the small change of a little attention. I ought to have known. There have been times in my life when I have done the same" (232).[37] Thus, entering an intimate relationship with someone who may at some level be a prostitute, yearning perhaps just as much for your cultural as your financial capital, is acceptable since prostitution can be viewed as a matter of degree. Existential philosophical and psychological speculation establishes universality and equality across cultural borders through the rhetoric of metaphor. The example is one of how postmodern writing "may erase difference, implying that all stories are really about one experience: the decentering and fragmentation that is currently the experience of Western white males."[38] As Mascia-Lees, Sharpe and Cohen caution, "Such readings ignore or obscure exploitation and power differentials and, therefore, offer no ground to fight oppression and effect change" (29).

Jensen's third narrative strategy pertains to the traveler's generic status. As the hero of a travelogue founded upon the structure of a bildungsroman, the reader expects and roots for his return home, where he will become reintegrated, reproducing the bourgeois family structure of which the reader has been informed in the prologue.[39] A potential vice is thus turned into a virtue as the narrator proclaims that he could not possibly love Tam, since he is still in love with the woman he has left behind. He is haunted by a *skyggekærlighed* (shadow love) to which he remains emotionally faithful. "My shadow love became the sum total of my inner reality, the only stable point in this journey's shifting sands of places and people" (229).[40] Hence, the story about the traveler and Tam is to be read not only as a tale of interracial love but also as a declaration of love for the woman back home. It is by opening himself up to encounters in Vietnam that the traveler learns to trust again, that he is able to return home as a complete man and reunite with his prime object of love and stability. Again it is tempting to point out the similarities with *Peer Gynt*. Ibsen's modern hero also has his shadow love—his one and only stable point in an unstable world. The difference, however, is that while the stable Solveig located on the Norwegian mountainside in 1867 might be somewhat believable, the stable shadow love of Jensen's protagonist is not. In the 1990s, I suspect, we can no longer imagine the urban, Scandinavian woman's blind faith and patience at home. Women, too, have become part of a modern, even late-modern world that constantly threatens with—and offers—new beginnings.

Moral Dilemmas

While Jensen's narrator's rhetoric may be viewed as colonialist, totalizing and stereotypical, as Andersen puts it (10), it is, in all fairness, also marked by self-doubt and self-reflection as far as ethics of viewing and representation are concerned. Unlike his nineteenth-century Orientalist counterpart, Hans Christian Andersen, Jensen does not exclaim "Do not cover up... we would not... hurt them with evil eyes!" Rather he reflects upon issues of *disponibilité* (availability) and truth—with regards not only to the tourist but also to the anthropologist, the journalist, and the travel writer. This type of reflection can also be viewed in light of Giddens's theory of late-modern reflexive persons, who not only may not take any of their roles for granted, but also see themselves as connected to the rest of the world in an age of globalization where the previously stable boundaries of modernity are crumbling away—or where the institutions of modernity become increasingly "disembedded," as Giddens phrases it. Thus, the late modern person's projects of self-actualization are not viewed as existing separately from that of other human beings, and what one desires, according to Giddens, is "the creation of morally justifiable forms of life that will promote self-actualisation in the context of global interdependence" (215). Moral and existential issues come to the fore, and as one ponders one's own existence, one tries to figure out what it means to be a human being at all (224).

Jensen's second travelogue, *Jeg har hørt et stjerneskud,* begs a discussion of the traveler's understanding of the interconnectedness between himself and the ethnographic Other, between early and late stages of modernity, and between the first and the third world in general. First I will analyze Jensen the anthropologist in the Pacific. I will place this part of the text in relation to other contemporary travel literature covering the same zone, while also comparing it to that of Johannes V. Jensen to point out differences between the early- and late-modern traveler-anthropologist. I will then turn to Jensen the journalist as he emerges during the second part of his journey in the second volume of the travelogue, namely, on his tour of South America where he visits Chile, Bolivia, and Peru. Here I will compare Jensen's reflections upon the Westerner's portrayal of third-world poverty with Hans Christian Andersen's "Turkish Sketch" (analyzed in chapter 1). What emerge are not only romanticist-versus-modern differences but also striking similarities.

What then, one may wonder, about the erotic encounters? In *Jeg har hørt et stjerneskud* they take up less space. In Peru the traveler establishes yet another sexual relationship with a sophisticated woman whose final word of departure captures the alleged essentials of their encounter. "Hombre," she says, whereupon he answers, "Mujer" ("man" and "woman").[41] As in *Jeg har set verden begynde*, though, the women encountered in the first region are uninteresting. Like Russian women, the women of Papua New Guinea are unfeminine: "Both men and women looked as if they were suffering from a scary surplus of male hormones."[42]

Postmodern Ethnography

The fact that Jensen *goes anthropologist* rather than *primitive* in the South Pacific is characteristic of contemporary travelogues. According to Patrick Holland and Graham Huggan's *Tourist with Typewriters*, "Contemporary travel writing about the Pacific inevitably supplements its testimonies of experience and contact with a variety of other discourses, particularly those of ethnography, for whose development the region has been so instrumental" (91). The first half of *Jeg har hørt et stjerneskud*—approximately two hundred out of five hundred pages—covers the traveler's one-month stay in Papua New Guinea and constitutes a history of anthropology as well as depictions of contemporary encounters. Jensen's point of departure is Bronislaw Malinowski and Margaret Mead, and as he arrives on Easter Island he includes Thor Heyerdahl—obviously a Nordic kinsman who, like Jensen himself, masters the art of creating universal, synthesizing accounts by subjecting the carefully observed detail to a lively imagination. Yet, long before arriving on Easter Island, Jensen discusses Malinowski and especially Mead to mark himself as one of James Clifford's third-stage anthropologists—one who is aware of the impossibility of representing the Other without to a greater extent representing the

Self.⁴³ Indirectly Jensen warns his reader that anthropological accounts actually say as much about our own dreams as they do about the Others' culture: "Anthropology is just as much a catalogue of our dreams as it is a catalogue of the diversity of humanity."⁴⁴ Jensen then recounts Mead's books to explain how anthropologists are easily misinformed by natives who are either eager to please, or who simply like to jest. At the same time, Mead's titillating accounts of Papuan and Samoan gender and sexuality end up forming a backdrop to Jensen's own encounters, and become rather believable as Jensen himself is pampered by gentle male natives. The creation of this ambivalence is, however, also typical of late-modern travelogues: "The travel writer's irony hollows out time-worn illusions but also holds them in suspension—as if there might be something to them after all" (Holland and Huggan, 94).

In terms of Jensen's depictions of his own present-day encounters, we are often left in suspense as to whether the narrator could possibly be serious. His ethnographic descriptions come across as a mixture between cartoonish stereotypes and sincere accounts surprisingly reminiscent of those of early-modern travelers. An instance is when the narrator develops a hypothesis about the natives' pent-up energy—not very different from Johannes V. Jensen's "kødrus" theory (see chapter 4). Upon his arrival in Papua New Guinea, Carsten Jensen provides a thorough account of the odd-looking race he sees: "Both genders were very muscular, and although we found ourselves in the middle of some kind of city, it was obvious that it was association with nature that had made their hard, angular bodies."⁴⁵ A reference to their flattened feet that could not possibly fit into any commercially made shoes ensues, then a description of their faces:

> Even more striking were their gnarled faces. They had deep lines down their cheeks and around their mouths and wrinkles in their forehead, folding in layers and down their hooked noses. Their gloomy expressions were reinforced by blue tattoos and ornamental scars that many of them, both men and women, carried in different parts of their faces. Most of the men had a frizzy full beard, and the women a big wild head of hair that made it look as if they had just gotten a sturdy electrical shock.⁴⁶

Cartoonish moments abound. Not only do women look as if they are electrified, some men also resemble cannibals. The first Papuan driver with whom the traveler gets a ride supposedly "looked like...a real cannibal, hungrily sticking his head out to search for lunch."[47] On the one hand, the caricatures might hark back to earlier times with a mixed sense of irony and nostalgia. On the other hand, they seem genuine—as if the traveler really is surprised to meet people who look like this. While you might suspect the traveler living in a postmodern world of global media flow to be inundated with verbal and visual images arriving from the remotest corners of the world and thus to be quite aware of a variety of races, he may also be a victim of too much information. As Susan Sontag has argued, the circulation of photographs makes events more real, but "after repeated exposure, it also becomes less real."[48] Thus, seeing a real Papuan may actually be as surprising to the late-modern traveler as it is to the early modern traveler, evoking as many racist reflections. The Papuans have unhappy eyes, and it was as if

> they were brooding over their fate of having been provided with more power than they could release. There was something lost about them, as if they were isolated from practicing a natural function, like birds in a cage prevented from stretching their wings, or predators whose hunting instinct is replaced by restless wandering while they are waiting for their feeding signal. It could not be Port Moresby... that made them behave as if they were in captivity. It was something inside themselves that had gotten stuck and was prevented from getting release.[49]

Papuans in anything but natural surroundings appear unnatural to the Western traveler. Like various animals—birds and beasts of prey—they seem to need to be out hunting in a premodern world. While Johannes V. Jensen's fleshy Malays are still able to go berserk in the jungle, Carsten Jensen's Papuans appear to the traveler to have become resigned—except when they smile at him.

Just in the Nick of Time

The early- and late-modern Jensens not only resemble each other when it comes to their (pseudo-) anthropological reflections, they also build up suspense in their travelogues by using three similar strategies. The first pertains to timing, the second to a personal crisis, and the third to inaccessible areas. First, both Jensens create drama by framing their narratives as last-minute accounts. While Johannes V. Jensen's traveler, on his way out of Birubunga, runs into two British engineers arriving to turn the jungle into tin mines, Carsten Jensen, on his way out of Papua New Guinea, suddenly sees a freeway under construction. The sight leads to an apocalyptic vision: "There was something emphatic and pompous about the road building, as if progress that had been on its way for so long would compensate for its slowness and announce its arrival with a roar of thunder."[50] Thus, both Jensens present us with visions of a decisive industrial and technological before and after. The difference, however, remains that Johannes V. Jensen has managed to visit a *pure* and *primitive* culture. Carsten Jensen, on the other hand, has witnessed a culture influenced by its modern surroundings, a culture, as he puts it, perched between the stone age and the arrival of white people in the 1960s.[51] The striking aspect of the account is the aggrandizement of this particular moment of hybridity. Arriving after the freeway has been built obviously will not be as satisfying as having arrived at the very end of an era beginning in the 1960s and ending around the turn of the twenty-first century.

The strategy is one of many contemporary anti-imperialist narratives, celebrating the hybrid cultures arising from what Pratt would call transculturation.[52] In these cases, the natives use the traveler's hunger for exotic Otherness to their own advantage. On New Ireland, for instance, Jensen's traveler's native guide informs him that he is concerned about his village's losing its traditional customs. In an effort of self-preservation he has called upon anthropologists to study his customs and language: "I did it because I know that big changes are on their way and that the customs of our village might soon be history."[53] The attitude, then, has turned from pleasing Western anthropologists by telling them what they want to hear, to telling them what one wants to be documented for prosperity—not just for the rest of the world to read, but for one's own future generations. Suddenly it is not so clear who is serving whom. In addition, the natives have come to view their storytelling as a commodity: "I realized it was a transaction I was involved in. They gave me their stories and I had to give them something in return. Gauze and aspirin were my currency."[54]

One instance of transculturation Carsten Jensen's narrator especially applauds is the natives' ability to take advantage of tourism. Catering to cruise tourists' eagerness to encounter a "so-called primitive culture," the natives have turned a traditional house of spirits into a department store. Or rather, it is a mixture of the two, signaling intercultural exchange. The house of spirits represents:

> Something authentically old and something entirely new. It was a house of spirits. But it was also a department store and it would be wrong to look at this commercialization of these activities that previously had served only their rituals, as a loss of culture and authenticity, as a sale that was also a spiritual self-rendering.[55]

The traveler seemingly experiences no longing for bygone, precapitalist days, but understands that the nonisolationist exchange with the surrounding world is healthy and beneficial, as it contributes to renewing the natives' culture while also earning money to maintain it: "They stepped into the global circulation of money, but not to subject themselves and let their uniqueness be eradicated. There was no talk of a battle between old and new, but of a meeting between them, a synthesis, allowing their world to develop and expand."[56] The viewpoint is refreshingly nonpurist, but also professes a humanist ideology based on global capitalism and consumerism. It is an attitude Simon During has called "the global popular":

> The global popular... produces a mood in which exoticism, normality and transworld sharedness combine, and in which consumption warmly glows. The global popular's humanism cannot be dismissed, precisely because it is so openly commercial. Its "general magic" relies on the trick by which global markets, technologies and information flows fuse into a humanism transcending national boundaries at the same time as, in its clear dependence on marketing, it leaves in tatters the idealism and naïve appeal to human nature so integral to older humanisms.[57]

Thus, what ties people together across cultural boundaries is their ability to market themselves so that in satisfying other people's desires, they are able to satisfy their own. This marketing strategy likewise captures that of the travel writer himself. He, too, is able to present another culture as sufficiently exotic—if not in a pure, then in a hybrid form—to warrant the consumption of travelogues depicting it, especially as he has arrived to depict it at a most interesting in-between moment, at the very last moment.

Danger and Identity in Late Modernity

Having created a sense of breathlessness with regards to the big story—capturing a special moment in time—both Johannes V. and Carsten Jensen create a parallel dramatic climax for their personal stories. Apocalyptic cultural and personal identity crises, in other words, go hand in hand. Yet, while Johannes V. Jensen's traveler's identity crisis is of a physical kind, the contemporary Jensen's traveler's is of a mental kind. As we have seen, the early-modern traveler sets out to test his bodily strength, his drives, and reactions—whether this be done in a rush of adrenaline face-to-face with a tiger, or in a rush of alcohol face-to-face with a native woman. The late-modern traveler's frailty, on the other hand, remains a matter of verbal exchanges.

As the identity of a late-modern person is a matter of reflexively maintaining a coherent autobiographical account, turning anthropologist constitutes a verbal danger. In principle Jensen's traveler wants to collect stories—as Holland and Huggan put it, "One of the minimum requirements of the travel writer is that he or she be a good listener" (13).[58] Yet, input and output of stories have to be delicately balanced, and the scale gets tipped in the wrong direction at the height of the traveler's anthropological involvement:

> So far I had lived a double-life on my journey. I sat at night, alone in a hotel room with my books and my diary. It was a loneliness that both terrified me and wore me out, but it was also in this, that I pulled myself together and rediscovered myself.[59]

The double life on the journey pertains to what Giddens sees as normal for all human beings who "in all cultures, preserve a division between their self-identities and the 'performances' they put on in specific social contexts" (58). While Giddens discusses the strained situation in light of what may appear to be a "false self" (59), Carsten Jensen's case lends itself better to an analysis of a vanishing Self. In reading and writing, the traveler maintains his (Western) self-identity. In his performance as an anthropologist, however, he is overwhelmed by the Others' stories and by the effort he has to make to bridge the gap between his own and the lives of the Others:

> I spent my evenings surrounded by people who constantly awaited my initiatives, and between us there was a gap pertaining to experience and lifestyle that

was so deep that bridging it demanded my utmost attention and concentration. I missed a familiar face, most of all my own.[60]

According to Holland and Huggan, contemporary travel writers often depict efforts "to bridge gaps between the observing subject and its 'other'" (97). Aside from being unscientific, the anthropological endeavors, however, often fail, and the travel accounts "may also attest to the trials (or defeats) of interpretation, pointing in some cases to a measure of resistance to the traveler's apparent cultural mastery" (98). In Jensen's case, though, the lack of cultural mastery is presented as secondary to the lack of personal mastery. The crisis arises not because Jensen cannot know the Other, but as he stops knowing himself. Writing in his diaries and reading European classics, the traveler tries to maintain his identity, but the natives disturb him by looking at him: "My only moments alone were the hours when I slept or when I snuck in some time to write in my diary or read a couple of pages of *Don Quixote*, always surrounded by curious eyes and questions that—although the natural right of the innocent—disturbed my peace."[61] The scene is indicative of what Pratt calls "reciprocal vision" or "mutual appropriation" (Pratt, 80). The traveler is not only curious about the natives—they are curious about him, too. On the one hand, this establishes an ideal of reciprocity; on the other, it is an ideal the traveler has trouble accepting. Like Johannes V. Jensen's traveler, Carsten Jensen's nevertheless maintains the upper hand in this battle for the observer's role by turning his attention toward himself. While the early-modern traveler focuses on his own rage and irritability—the bile that constitutes the fuel of his writing—the late modern traveler focuses on his vulnerability; that constitutes the impetus behind *his* writing.

Not Wanting to Know

As mentioned earlier, Jensen's late-modern travelogue is less about the lack of cultural mastery vis-à-vis the Other than it is about the lack of personal identity mastery vis-à-vis the Self. In fact, Carsten Jensen prefers that the natives, at times, reject his inquisitiveness. Thus, as the two Jensen narrators exhibit vastly different attitudes toward the issue of *disponibilité*, a third common narrative strategy is that of thematizing the traveler's reactions to off-limit sites. The reflections ultimately constitute a means of lodging a mystery in the readers' minds, leaving them with the sense that there are still sites out there to explore—or sites that might better be left unexplored.

Both Jensens experience being led around in circles, and not gaining access to the mountaintop they allegedly want to climb. The accounts of these moments, though, vary vastly in the narrative positions the two travelers inhabit. While Johannes V. Jensen assumes the position of a hostile, arrogant traveler, Carsten Jensen assumes the position of a humble, sensitive, and sympathetic visitor. Like his predecessor, Carsten Jensen hires guides and carriers for a mountain-climbing expedition. And just like Johannes V.'s traveler, Carsten's traveler is led in circles—the way the reader is ultimately led in narrative circles around something mysterious and unspeakable. If we look at the details of the two accounts, we see how the former's expressionist rage is replaced by the latter's introverted reflections and gratefulness that the natives are proud enough to resist him. The late-modern traveler, that is, approves of the natives' reluctance to make everything he wants to explore accessible to him.

Johannes V. Jensen's Ali in this scenario is replaced by Sebastian—whose old age and skinniness also become an object of scrutiny: "He had grizzled hair and a wrinkled face. His stomach muscles had turned weak with age, but his skin was smooth and shiny as that of a young man, and the contours of his muscles could be traced beneath his skin."[62] Where Johannes V. sees a rubber ball and an ash-filled grid, Carsten Jensen more respectfully sees soft skin and muscles. Carsten Jensen is just as humble toward the old man when he discovers he is being purposely misled: "I realized he was there to lead us around and around in circles and keep me away from those sites that, in his opinion, were none of my business."[63] And: "I realized that it was not the old man's intention that I should reach the top of the mountain."[64] Where Johannes V. Jensen's parody of an explorer starts raging—while he is most likely quite relieved that he will not have to confront a real tiger after all—Carsten Jensen's traveler obligingly acknowledges that he has no business satisfying his own restless curiosity in a foreign culture: "I could not help but agree with the old man. I had no business on the mountain, and if its top, to them, was an area surrounded by mystery that they did not want disturbed by the transgression of a stranger, then I had no right to insist."⁶⁵ The attitude is humble, respectful, and romantic, insisting that there actually is an area surrounded by mystery. For all we know, this may apply more to Jensen's narrative than to the cultural site itself.

Jensen the narrator admits to his tendency to romanticize and thematizes it as a weakness. Although professing to value hybrid cultures, it is largely the aspect still mysterious and untouched by modernization that he is happy to find in Papua New Guinea. Speaking to a group of schoolchildren, the traveler finds himself saying, "When the world comes to you, you will realize . . . that you have lost something essential."⁶⁶ Immediately he corrects himself for the reader: "I immediately regretted what I had said. I had no right to be romantic on their behalf."⁶⁷ Telling us what he said as well as why he should not have said it, the narrator reveals his dual consciousness. On the one hand he is a romanticizing, nostalgic traveler, longing for the cultural and primitive Other—thinking in sharp Eurocentric Self-Other categories (the world vs. them). On the other hand, he knows better as the late-modern traveler, who realizes that what Giddens would call his own self-realization project cannot morally be at the expense of, but has to harmonize with, other people's self-realization projects.

Regarding Poverty

Having compared the two Jensens as representing the early- and late-modern anthropologist-traveler, I will finally turn to one of Jensen's most interesting discussions of the traveler's right to observe. A comparison of Jensen's portrayal of poverty with that of Hans Christian Andersen shows the turn from beautifying romanticism to uglifying modern realism. Yet, Jensen's example also illustrates how, in recent years, the media once again include beauty in their depictions of the "real." Wanting to stir indignation and admiration simultaneously, late-modern depictions have become reminiscent of the poetic realism we saw in Hans Christian Andersen's "Turkish Sketch."

In the Bolivian mining town of Potosí, Jensen wants to document the living conditions of the poor. As the subtitle of this chapter suggests,

"Fattigdommen i forhør" (Poverty Interrogated), Jensen is not able to carry out the project without feeling guilty. The sense of guilt he describes serves as an overall introduction to and frame for the chapter:

> Suddenly I realized that this was not sightseeing and that the sentence "I would like to see how a mining family lives" was no sufficient reason for what I was about to do. I had spent the entire day as a spectator to these people's tragedy. Should I now also force my way into their home to witness their misery? By what right did I ask them to humble themselves before my eyes? That of the author, the journalist? Because I was here not on account of my own private curiosity but as a witness—on account of the world—to provide them [the rest of the world] with a view of, and make them part of, Potosí's drama that has lasted for four hundred years and still had not come to an end? Was this not just a self-righteous explanation covering up a voyeurism that imagined itself as politically and morally legitimized just because it was not directed at other people's sex life, but at their misery?[68]

Jensen suspects he may be a mere consumer of others' poverty and that journalists are but curious visitors on par with all other tourists.

The reporter's dilemma has become an issue of increased debate and attention in recent years. In *Regarding the Pain of Others,* Susan Sontag revisits the themes she first debated in *On Photography.* While her main focus is on modern media's portrayal of war—and the effect this has on the viewer—her arguments also apply to other types of accounts of misery, such as the witnessing of poverty. Like Jensen, she questions the role of the journalist: "Being a spectator of calamities taking place in another country is a quintessential modern experience, the cumulative offering by more than a century and a half's worth of those professional, specialized tourists known as journalists" (*Regarding the Pain of Others,* 18). And like Jensen, Sontag questions the effect the journalist's report may have on the viewers (or readers) back home: "Information about what is happening elsewhere, called 'news,' features conflict and violence . . . to which the response is compassion, or indignation, or titillation, or approval, as each misery heaves into view" (ibid.). While there are no easy answers to how one may best stir particular reactions, Sontag historicizes representation, referring to a "classic" operation of "beautifying" and a "modern" operation of "uglifying." While beautifying provokes no moral response, uglifying and showing something at its worst "is a more modern function: didactic, it invites an active response" (81).

Like Hans Christian Andersen, Jensen does both, opting for the dual imprint of the ugly and the beautiful on the reader's retina. First he goes through with his initial project, delivering the fact-filled report, originally intended to be a journalistic article. We are given an inventory of the Villa family's possessions and told the ages of the adults and their children, the parents' respective incomes, their rent, their disabilities, and their plans for the future. This material captures what Jensen regards as their "misery," while leaving out their "humanity" (357). At the end of the chapter, however, Jensen leaves us with a depiction of the latter—of the family's humanity. By accident he sees them heading for church on a Sunday morning. This time he remains incognito and is able to see what they look like when not interrogated by "the rich world" (355). Jensen then leaves us with an image of sunshine, tinkling church bells, and festively clad Indians. The Villa family's oppressiveness of the previous evening, we are told, is replaced by free and natural movements (358). It is then up to the reader to reflect upon the two images and maintain a nuanced view of the poor—as both miserable and dignified.

In both Andersen's and Jensen's depictions, the narrator's reflective voice tying the two images together has a strong presence, serving a rather self-congratulatory function. While Andersen proudly emphasizes his poetic capabilities, Jensen emphasizes his moral capabilities. In the late twentieth century, romantic poetics is thus replaced by late-modern ethics, and Jensen's narrator indicates that the travelogue is the reflective genre par excellence, allowing for misery and humanity, objective depiction and subjective reflection. Having rendered the picture of the churchgoing family, he ultimately elevates the episode with the following epiphany: "It was at this moment that I decided not to write an article about them. The world is already full of journalism which—pleading to improve people's living conditions—deprive them of their dignity."[69] Journalism, as we know it, is out. It oversimplifies and leaves too unequivocal an impression. The travelogue, on the other hand, allows for multiple layers of depiction and reflection, capturing the ambivalence and contradictions of a complex life.

After having written *Jeg har set verden begynde* and *Jeg har hørt et stjerneskud,* Carsten Jensen has collaborated with Danish and Norwegian photographers, publishing various illustrated travelogues. In *Træet i ørkenen* (The Tree in the Desert, 2003), depicting Niger—the world's second-poorest country—Jensen and photographer Tine Harden have opted for the beautifying strategy. Harden's colorful photographs show a dynamic, proud, hardworking, and often cheerful people whose future lies not in charity, but in being drawn into a capitalistic world market. As in *Jeg har set verden begynde* and *Jeg har hørt et stjerneskud,* Jensen represents a potentially "global popular" attitude, holding up the example of a man from Niger who has succeeded as a great capitalist transculturator, selling Africa's colorful landscape and textiles as high fashion on the world market.[70]

While *Træet i ørkenen* seems rather uncontroversial, the use of photographs in *Det glemte folk* (The Forgotten People, 2004) has been much more controversial. The travelogue is an account of the Karens' fight for liberty in Burma. In this context Elmer Laahne's photographs have been looked upon as unethical in their aestheticizing endeavors. The book has been reviewed as "Tragedies in Technicolor" and "Guerrilla Tourism," and it hardly helps that the book has the look and format of a coffee-table book.[71] Depicting war may be a much more sensitive issue than documenting poverty, but in either case, the travelogues illustrate a move toward aestheticization—indicative of what has become known as a postmodern callousness and regard of even misery as spectacle and entertainment. Or, it may indicate a "de-Othering" strategy according to which the will to react is aroused, not through the imagery of grim naturalism—to which Westerners can hardly relate, perhaps—but rather through the imagery of oppressed peoples whose lives are not entirely different from our own, in that they also contain moments of joy, pride, and enthusiasm.

On his last stop on the way back to Denmark, Jensen's protagonist-traveler's identity is questioned by passport control at Charles de Gaulle Airport in Paris. On the last leg of his journey from Paris to Copenhagen, the identity questions keep reverberating in his mind, taking on greater and greater existential dimensions, and the reader is finally left with a question and a promise: "Who was I? I would find out" (513). The answer lies in the travelogue the reader has just finished reading—a travelogue that ultimately stresses its dimension as an inner journey while downplaying its role as an outer journey. The initial launching of the travelogues further stresses the autobiographical rather than anthropological endeavor. A colorful picture of the exotic Other *could* have graced the book's cover. Instead it features a striking black-and-white ultra close-up of Carsten Jensen. Jensen's eyes are prominent and his gaze intensive. But how are they to be understood? Are they appropriating, imperial eyes? Are they inquisitive eyes? Or are they vulnerable eyes? The same tactic is used on the cover of *Det glemte folk*. Jensen, surrounded by weapon-carrying Karens, gazes off into the distance. Are we to interpret his gaze as self-assured? Or as worried? Are these the eyes of a macho traveler, a sensitive traveler, a reporter, or a voyeur? Is the focus on the Other, or is it on the Self?

Aside from being understood as a type of commercial branding, Jensen's face, I would argue, must be read as a Janus face. Like Janus of Roman mythology, Jensen is the guardian of portals whose doors open both ways. And like Janus, Jensen's narrator is deceptive. As readers we can never be quite sure which way the door is opened. What at first glance appears as portrayals of the outside world—of the Other—may turn out to be pure projections of inner emotions and preestablished knowledge. And this is exactly what makes Jensen's travelogues so successful. Wishing they were marketed as novels instead of as travelogues (as Frits Andersen does) is not just a matter of disliking Jensen's deceptive strategies, but of disliking an entire, and perhaps the most successful, branch of the twentieth-century travelogue. As the modernist novel shies away from the coherent narrative structure of the nineteenth-century bildungsroman, the twentieth-century travelogue keeps the genre alive, combining the individual and the universal, the inner and outer quest, and placing a personal story alongside world history. As Holland and Huggan put it with regards to contemporary travelogues, "The subjectivity of travel writing might be seen, in this sense, as a form of wilful interference: it is not that travel writers try to veil their personal interpretation but, on the contrary, that they impose it on their putative reportage" (11). As in Hans Christian Andersen's poetic realism, the responsibility, then, becomes that of the reader. Unlike the reader of journalistic writing, the reader of a travelogue must be able to hold two opposing images in mind simultaneously. And, the reader of a travelogue must know the genre well enough to expect that not everything recounted is true.

EIGHT

Futile Journeys
Parody, Postmodernism, and Postnationalism in Erlend Loe's *Traveling*

ERLEND LOE, who was born in 1969, is probably Norway's most popular contemporary author. He debuted with *Tatt av kvinnen* (1993), which was followed by *Naiv: Super* (1996). With his second novel, Loe was written into Norwegian literary history as the voice of a new generation, employing neonaivism not only as a literary strategy but also as a late-modern survival strategy.[1] Loe's third novel, *L* (1999), is an explicit parody on Thor Heyerdahl's *Kon-Tiki ekspedisjonen* (1948).[2] It depicts the autobiographical protagonist, Erlend, as he sets out to put Norway on the map. First he develops a theory about how the Polynesian Islands may have been populated—not just by people arriving on balsa rafts, as Heyerdahl claims, but also by "a daring autochthonous population in South America" who skated across the Pacific Ocean during a previous ice age.[3] Then, like Heyerdahl, Erlend sets out to prove his theory, seeks sponsorship for his expedition, gathers a crew, and eventually flies to the island of Manuae in the South Pacific. Here Erlend and his six friends dig for skates and carry out other pseudoscientific tasks for about a month. Most of the time, though, they do nothing and are bored. Unlike the typical modern traveler who wants to "go primitive" or "go native," Erlend and his friends just want to go home.

Back in Norway, Erlend subsequently writes about his expedition, structuring his travel novel like that of his heroic predecessor. As such *L* functions as a postmodern travelogue. In typical postmodern fashion, it draws on previously established literary and historical discourses while also absorbing a mixture of high and low contemporary cultural discourses. These discourses range from commercial jingles, movie titles, pop music, proverbs, and clichés to an abundance of specifically Norwegian nation-forming discourses—from the literary classics of Henrik Ibsen and Knut Hamsun to the more popular travelogues of Norwegian folk heroes like Thor Heyerdahl, Roald Amundsen, and Fridtjof Nansen. Last but not least, they include postmodern, metafictional theory itself.

"You say that the grand narrative is dead? . . . You want small narratives? . . . Damn it, that you're going to get."[4] The reference of this opening declaration in *L* is clearly to Jean-François Lyotard's depiction of the postmodern condition in the 1979 book by that title. The introduction may be read as a response to Lyotard's call for a war against totality. Yet, the very key phrase is not Lyotard's theory, but rather the initial "Dere sier" (you say). Erlend Loe and his generation are sick of being told how things are, what they mean, and how they are interconnected. As *L* makes clear, they were born into a world in which everything has already been said and done. It is a ready-made and fully explored world. As the protagonist points out, "In my world there are no more white spots on the map" (9).[5] His generation is "we who did not build Norway" (24), and Erlend concludes, "I seem to have been born relatively late in the evolution of humans, too late to influence social structures in any significant way, too late to discover land or central phenomena" (30–31).[6] Likening the world to a home, he complains, "It is a bit as if the world were finished when we were born into it. It is not ours. We have not built it. The only thing left is maintenance and repair. We were born into a fixer-upper. How tantalizing is that?" (362–63).[7] As the opening reference to Lyotard shows, Erlend is born too late, even, to theorize this world—his is the posttheory generation for whom the only thing left to do is to problematize—through irony and parody—and, conversely, to insist upon not being interpreted at all. For 450 pages *L* thoroughly challenges everything "dere sier." Erlend questions postmodernism, postnationalism, and postcolonialism, delivering so-called small stories, yet tying them together through the autobiographical genre of the travelogue in which the narrating "I" maintains a strong and cohesive presence. Concluding his tale, Erlend returns to the issue of interpretation, insisting that his generation be given space to act without hordes of interpreters pinning down the meaning of their behavior:

> And just before we head home, Egil wants to have the floor and say that he is sorry he was a bit grumpy the last days on the island, and now that we are gathered, he wants to tell us that he loves us. All of us. Each and every one.

> And he ends up saying it in a tone of voice and with a barely discernible smile that create a distance. A distance that shines through ambiguously, but clearly enough. Maybe we can call it irony. But in that case it is no straightforward type of irony. It is not like most ironies. It is subtle and does not mean the opposite of what he is saying. In a way he is telling us he loves us, but he opens up for it also meaning other things. Totally different things. Things that are not located in the words and that nobody can tell where they come from. The utterance carries nuances way beyond what's normal. It makes me smile and feel warm and I hardly care what it is really about.[8]

The irony of what is often called "the ironic generation" opens up to an ambiguity of words and actions whose meaning Erlend refuses to limit.[9] What it is "really" about is uninteresting, and the *im*possibility of determining this meaning is liberating and lends a particular identity to Erlend's generation, setting them off against their theorizing predecessors. Erlend snidely continues: "I feel certain that future sociologists, psychologists, literary scholars and what have you, will map these things in thorough ways. We can just take it easy."[10]

L was received with its share of disappointment. Most critics found amusing and quoteworthy episodes in the book, but formally, they tended to agree it was too long, and thematically, the seemingly disengaged, melancholic, ironic generation Loe depicts proved tiresome at best and loathsome at worst. In fact, the formal and thematic faults were connected; only a generation as narcissistic as Loe's could go on dwelling on everyday nonevents for that long—and expect readers to enjoy it.

As Linda Hutcheon has pointed out, postmodern literature typically contests narrative centering, situating itself "between a unified biographically structured plot, and a decentered narration, with its wandering point of view and extensive digressions."[11] Loe's *L* is full of digressions and is characteristically postmodern in that it problematizes distinctions among literary genres, between fiction and nonfiction, between art and criticism, and between art and life (Hutcheon, *A Poetics of Postmodernism*, 7, 9, 10). It operates from a "both-and" position, acknowledging that there are no totalizing grand narratives while illustrating that we constantly construct such narratives nevertheless.[12]

Overall, *L* occupies a postmodern position between two stages of postmodernism: between a first phase of self-reflexive postmodernism and a second phase of posttheoretical postmodernism. Loe's aggressive way of quoting Lyotardian theory as well as his closing statement about a generation's fondness for one another through irony indicate this ambiguous "post-postmodern" position. The postmodern split has, however, also fallen prey to postmodern theory, as in the writings of Linda Hutcheon. What is new and post-postmodern about Loe's *L,* then, may also be viewed as falling within the postmodern paradigm once this is redefined.

In *A Poetics of Postmodernism,* Linda Hutcheon attains this goal by going back on earlier equations of the postmodern with the purely metafictional. While the metafictional novels (which in a Norwegian context especially characterized the 1980s) were first considered postmodern, Hutcheon reclassifies them as examples of late-modernist extremism (*A Poetics of Postmodernism,* 52), reserving the term postmodern instead for literature that—like postmodern architecture—incorporates and reflects upon the historical past in the present. Thus, the determining factor in postmodernism is not merely self-reflexivity but "a grounding in the historical, social and political world" (ix). Two things in particular distinguish the postmodern in opposition to the modern(ist): a nonautonomous contact with the world as text and intertext (125), and a constant process of viewing the world from an "ex-centric" point of view.

The practitioners of postmodernism, according to Hutcheon, are the "ex-centric," those "marginalized by a dominant ideology" (*A Poetics of Postmodernism,* 35); their privileged mode of expression is the parody (ibid.); and their goal is critically to confront the past with the present (39), to question institutions (9) and conventions of discourse (xiii), and to reevaluate the individual's response to society (41). Writing in the 1980s, Hutcheon defines ex-centrics as those who are excluded from the center, who are off-center and decentered, by virtue of race, gender, sexual preference, ethnicity, native status, and class (61). Ever since the 1960s these minorities, she explains, have worked to reformulate "the dominant white, male, middle-class, heterosexual, Eurocentric culture" (130). What Hutcheon might not have predicted, though, is that some of those included in the depiction of her centered and dominant group would, in the 1990s, become ex-centrics themselves—not necessarily because previously marginalized groups have taken over the center, but because of a previously disregarded factor of distinction—that of generational difference. Erlend Loe's generation is ex-centric; they are Generation X, who have been so firmly established in the center that they have nothing to live for, nothing to fight for, nothing to prove, and nothing to defend.[13] As *Norwegian* Generation Xers, Erlend Loe and his age cohort are furthermore doubly decentered, a fact that becomes apparent in the dual nature of Erlend's project. Not only does he want to put himself on the map—"I want to do something for Norway" (27)—he also wishes to put Norway on the world map (32).

Juxtaposing Norwegian nation-building discourses with transnational discourses of global consumerism, *L* is also thoroughly postnational. On the one hand, it questions the institutions of the nation and the welfare state in a specifically Norwegian turn-of-the-twenty-first-century context. As such it may be compared to Axel Jensen's *Ikaros* with these two travelogues reacting to what may be the beginning and the end of the Norwegian welfare state.[14] On the other hand, it questions ideologies of globalization, mass culture, and world citizenship. This, too, is characteristic of the postmodern parody in which "the local and regional are stressed in the face of mass culture" (Hutcheon, *A Poetics of Postmodernism,* 12).

In this discussion of *L,* I will focus on three aspects of postmodernism and postnationalism: (1) postmodern intertextuality and parody in general, (2) the postmodern travelogue in particular, and, finally, (3) postcolonial encounters defined as the meeting between the cultural Self and the Other. Whereas all the travelogues up to this point have shown an interest in the cultural Other, *L* is permeated by a sense of sameness and indifference with its travelers coming across as shockingly, though somewhat cordially, blasé. Rather than figuring as interesting objects of study, as they have for previous generations, the natives of the Pacific Islands—in the minds of Generation X—figure as yet another example of objects whose meaning has already been established by previous generations. If anything, they are considered as supervisors—or even babysitters. Thus we are far from the epistemological power hierarchy established by Western science and imperialism and, as always, the Gen Xers just want to be left alone.

The Postmodern Travelogue

In an article on the postmodernization of the travelogue, Manfred Pfister lists its defining thematic and structural characteristics.[15] Pfister's test case is Bruce Chatwin's *In Patagonia* (1977), yet another travelogue written during the decade to which Mary Louise Pratt attaches the label "The White Man's Lament."[16] While Pratt, as discussed in the chapter on Carsten Jensen, emphasizes an inversion of romanticist aesthetics in these travelogues, Pfister argues this point on the level of the plot. What he looks at is the overall postmodernization of a genre that he argues lends itself particularly well to a "postmodern turn" (264).[17] As we shall see, Pfister's defining characteristics largely apply to Erlend Loe's *L*—yet, as in Hutcheon's case, they do not quite account for the extreme position of a Norwegian Generation X.

If we start out looking at the similarities, we find that in terms of content, the classical travelogue is structured around the master narrative of a quest, with the postmodernized travelogue downgrading this quest through irony, anticlimax, parody, and carnivalization. The lowering of the value of the quest object becomes a recurring process throughout the journey. In Loe's case, he starts out wanting to find the ice skates on which a South American tribe may have arrived in the Polynesian islands. Yet, long before leaving Norway, the downgrading of the mission begins. Just in case the main project does not work out, Erlend encourages his friends to bring miniprojects of their own. Thus, a main quest is replaced with subquests. Even, for instance, sets out to discover whether it is possible to sleep more than seventeen hours a day (79), and Martin sets out to complete his master's dissertation—a periodic table of women (85). Of course, none of these experiments ends up completed either, and in the end, the quest object—or the trophy of the journey—is downgraded to the most banal of all motives for a Norwegian to travel to a sunny country: getting a tan (407).

As the initial quest object is not found, the traveler in a postmodernized travelogue does not experience any epiphany, illumination, or other type of sublime moment (Pfister, 256). In fact, the climax is deliberately turned into an anticlimax, often through carnivalization and references to unsightly body functions. To prove this point Pfister notes that Chatwin's traveler, instead of finding the skin of a giant sloth (already downgraded from the goal of finding a Golden Fleece and then to that of finding the skin of a brontosaurus), ends up with the giant sloths' turds—or just "a load of shit" (256). Chatwin's depiction of this moment builds on parody and inversion as his narrator then describes the chanting of nuns arising to accompany this nonmoment of apotheosis. This parodic humor is reminiscent of the strategies Pratt describes as typical of travelogues written in the 1970s. The sublime is replaced with the trivial, and the beautiful with the ugly. Yet, *L* differs from its 1970s counterparts in that the anticlimactic moments are further deflated through deadpan cynicism. Whereas the travelers of the 1970s are disappointed or at least act disappointed, having hoped for something greater from the outset, Loe's protagonist-narrator never even expects moments of clarity and unity—he is just a detached and unimpressionable observer to whom it would not even occur to use straightforward or inverted tropes of romanticism. This disillusioned, stunted, and matter-of-fact attitude may be seen as one of the major characteristics of a new Generation X.

A quick comparison of Carsten Jensen's and Erlend Loe's travelogues—published only a couple of years apart—shows the generational gap between these two writers—the late modern and the postmodern—with Loe's *L* being driven by a particularly antiromantic impulse. Like a classical traveler, Jensen experiences one epiphany after another; he is, as discussed in the previous chapter, a master of spotting a particular detail and turning it into a universal symbol. The two travelers' encounters with hermit crabs illustrate the difference, with hermit crabs, according to *Webster's New World Dictionary of the American Language* (1984), being crabs that "have asymmetrical, soft abdomens and live in the empty shells of certain mollusks."

In Carsten Jensen's travelogue, the sight of hermit crabs inspires a universalizing, symbolist interpretation of human existence—of every human being's drive toward the impossible. Jensen spots hermit crabs on the beach of New Ireland—all carrying houses of different sizes, shapes, and colors as they try to mount the walls of a split coconut: "There were green conical shells, there were red snail shells, there were blue and black shields, and hauling this colorful housing, the crabs crawled to mount the steep inner side of the coconut."[18] As a romantic traveler, Jensen is absorbed and enthralled, noticing every detail in this scenery. And as a romantic writer, he subsequently renders what he has seen in a poetic depiction, rich both in visual and verbal artistry. Alliteration, for instance, abounds ("brogede beboelse," "kriblede og krablede krebsene"), and in a final epiphany,

Jensen identifies entirely with the destiny of these crabs. In fact, we are all hermit crabs engaged in a never-ending, Sisyphean task of climbing up, wishing to transcend the laws of gravity, yet always falling down again: "like the hermit crab up, up, and then down again" (513). The image of the symbolic hermit crabs ends up concluding Jensen's eleven-hundred-page travelogue and stands as the final answer to the protagonist's question of who he is: "The hermit crabs on New Ireland had given me a kind of answer. Perhaps it was not the most lucid answer, but it was what I brought back from my journey and I could not think of anything better" (ibid.).[19] Thus, in this last sentence of his travelogue, Carsten Jensen leaves his reader with an enigmatic symbol capturing the drives, passions, futilities, hopes, disappointments, and incurable optimism of human existence.

Not so with Erlend Loe. Rather than inspiring a poetic vision of wholeness and meaning, the sight of hermit crabs in *L* prompts disgust. Loe's protagonist is appalled by the crabs' aggressiveness, greed, and appearance. Far from being individuals searching for the impossible, Loe's hermit crabs are relentless, starving herds hunting for anything to eat, throwing themselves at human remnants and at each other:

> We are so to speak surrounded by hermit crabs. The smallest of them are about the size of a little Swedish meatball, but most of them are big as fists and totally red. There are hundreds, perhaps thousands of them. The sound of a thousand is unpleasant and terrifying. They scramble and look for something edible. They eat anything, totally uncritically. They eat shit, if they have to. (257)[20]

Completely estranged from, and rather frightened by natural elements, Erlend and his fellow travelers spend the rest of their days on the island trying to get rid of the crabs, throwing them into the fire (260), throwing rocks at them (346), and trying to drown them (300). Whereas Jensen leaves his reader with a vision of hermit crabs on a romantic quest for the impossible, Loe leaves us with a vision of them having oral sex. Included among his photographic illustrations as "bevis 2" (proof 2) is a picture of two hermit crabs that, according to Egil, are engaged in mutual oral stimulation, "the 69-position, in other words" (359). Through the carnevalesque, Erlend Loe does what he can to deflate potentially romanticized imagery. Gone are epiphanies, feelings of the oceanic, and moments of the sublime. No single moment captures wholeness, meaning, and totalizing worldviews that call for being rendered verbally through poetic symbols.

Instead of alliteration and carefully wrought sentences, we are left with syntactically simple sentences, relating the traveler's experiences through references to the concrete, the tangible, and the disparate: meatballs, fists, and dung in the preceding example. Once again, Loe marks himself as a member of the "after theory" generation for whom objects from this world do not turn into interpretable signs.

A final comparison to Heyerdahl's encounter with hermit crabs is in place. Neither a sensitive romantic nor an estranged, half-frightened/half-disgusted city dweller, Heyerdahl knows what to do. He just eats them. Arriving on his uninhabited paradise island, he acknowledges that "the most important inhabitants of the island were large blood-red hermit crabs which lumbered along in every direction with stolen snail shells as large as eggs adhering to their soft hinder parts."[21] Heyerdahl does not offer them another thought until it is dinnertime. Then one of his crew members lights a fire, "and soon we had crab and coconut milk with coffee for dessert" (215). Thus, unlike his postcolonial, late- and postmodern followers, Heyerdahl treats his surroundings pragmatically and is action-oriented in the vein of European imperialism. The world is out there to be mastered and used, to be taken in and digested in all senses of this word. For both Jensen and Loe, however, the natural world is out there not to interact with but mainly to observe—either as a source of self-projection or as a source of alienation.[22]

Postmodern Digressions

As the preceding example shows, content and form are closely related, and in the case of *L,* it is difficult to discuss the deflated and emptied-out topoi of questing without considering the connection between this and the stripped-down language through which the topoi are recounted. While Loe's narrator's linguistic style indicates a lack—a lack of emotion, of exuberance, of faith, and of expectations—on the sentence level, the size of the book with its many digressions suggests excess—not least excess of information in a flat, postmodern world without hierarchies of meaning that might separate the trivial from the nontrivial.

When it comes to the structure of the postmodern travelogue, Pfister finds that its two main modes of expanding are through concatenation (i.e., the linear linking together of stories) and through embedding (i.e., the linking together of stories in a hierarchical manner creating mise-en-abymes and room for reflection through similarity and contrast) (Pfister, 257). Yet, while Pfister finds that Chatwin's linked-together and embedded stories are all tales of disillusionment, reflecting back on the melancholy of the main narrative, Erlend's stories are simply trivial. Erlend, for instance, launches into a vast digression about the Fox brand of caramel of his childhood. Once more in the carnivalesque (or childish) manner centering on body functions, Erlend dwells on how the Fox caramel dissolved in a way that produced two colors of saliva simultaneously. He is in the middle of telling a story about running into his friend Roar, but having mentioned that he had just come out of a store where he had bought Fox caramels, he loses track of his main story and spends the next fourteen sentences discussing the Fox-produced saliva, the chemicals used in Fox caramels, the reasons why we uncritically consume such chemicals, how he thought they had gone off the market, but evidently have returned. After concluding that Fox is just as good today as it was then, he returns to his story: "So, I had bought a Fox and came out from the store where, as I have already mentioned, Roar and this other guy were standing, summing up the weekend" (105).[23] The next story, then, is also of the embedded kind, as the protagonist-narrator relates the two guys' summing up the weekend. Again, the story involves body fluids. Roar has been to a party at which the guys initiated a masturbation contest. The goal of the contest was to ejaculate the most into a glass, and the winner, it turns out, filled a milk glass. Typical of Erlend's reaction is the dwelling on odd details, like how big a milk glass might actually be:

> When you say milk glass you are not talking about a small glass. When you drink milk you don't sip. You eat a couple of slices of bread and then chug glass upon glass with milk. Big glasses. A milk glass is not a small glass. That is for sure. And this party participant filled it up. (106)[24]

After having dwelled on details and verbal expressions, the protagonist typically turns this into a discouraging story about how everybody else has already done something so great that he will never be able to compare—we are back to the curse of Generation X:

He was hardly aware of it himself, but he had contributed to up the ante quite a bit for the rest of us. If it was the milk glass you had to reach for, you would feel rather like a failure for many years to come. I recall the sense of powerlessness that day outside the store. It felt impossible, and it still does. (Ibid.)[25]

As this childishness suggests, Generation X never grows up. Erlend admits: "No. I never grew up" (89), and Yngve reflects: "I feel like an adult boy and not like a man" (133).[26] Consequently, the Generation X postmodern travelogue does not quite comply with Pfister's depiction of postmodern questing into an idealized, personal past. While Chatwin uses his travels abroad to regress and reexplore his childhood dreams of adventure, Loe has never been out of childhood. Childhood becomes a matter of continuation rather than regression, as Erlend for instance even at the age of twenty-nine plays with a dinner roll handed to him on the plane to New York: "I quickly become attached to this roll. We become friends. I pretend the roll is a living being. Afterward I let it sit on my shoulder and look through the window" (198–99).[27] The difference between the adult men of the 1970s and the in-betweens of Generation X is not only a childhood and a childishness that have never been abandoned, but also a childhood and a childishness that were never passionate. With Erlend, one gets the notion that he has always been cynical. Thus, while Chatwin turns his geographical quest into a parallel exploration of childhood dreams, passions, and fantasies, the dispassionate Erlend does not indicate having felt anything but mild admiration and wonder for Heyerdahl and his exotic explorations. This difference between modern enthusiasm, postmodern disillusionment, and a new generation's total lack of disillusionment also comes forth in the depictions of arrival scenes.

Postmodern Arrivals

Not too surprisingly, the arrival of Heyerdahl's men on the Pacific Islands is one of sheer enthusiasm and physical involvement. Heyerdahl writes about being overwhelmed at the sight and touch of the real and authentic: "we should never see a more genuine South Sea island" (188). What they arrive at is "a little bit of concentrated paradise" (210), and what they long to do is touch real palm trees (41). The postmodern travelogue, on the other hand, relies on intertextuality to illustrate an awareness that encounters with the so-called authentic are determined by, and have been premediated through, existing discourses. This may in itself be a source of interest. In the case of Chatwin's *In Patagonia,* Pfister notes:

> These "pretexts" do not just enrich Chatwin's perceptions of Patagonia with further information, they are themselves part of the object perceived. *In Patagonia* is at least as much about the fantasies about Patagonia as it is about Patagonia itself. Or, to go one step further, it claims and demonstrates that Patagonia as a *Ding an sich* does not exist. The wide, empty spaces of Chatwin's Patagonia are not a *tabula rasa*, but written over with layers and layers of text, inscribed with the traces of the most diverse cultures. (259)

By using intertextuality as a source of embarrassment rather than enrichment, Erlend goes one step further in the process of postmodernizing the travelogue. Rather than being "inscribed with the traces of the most diverse cultures," Erlend's Pacific island is but a commonplace: "In front of us is the cliché of a Pacific Island. It is like a part of all of our collective unconscious. Enigmatic smiles are the only sensible reaction" (223).[28] As they disembark and wade through the water toward Manuae, the island nonetheless impresses the group: "We are spellbound by the sight awaiting us. By the island. It is incredibly beautiful" (227).[29] Yet while Heyerdahl expresses his excitement through emphatic adjectives like "green-green"— writing about "the bright, green palm forest" (188) and "the bright green roof of a rolling, billowy jungle"—Erlend keeps his depiction at a minimum without falling prey to Pratt's adjectival modifiers creating "density of meaning."[30] Nothing extraneous is used to emphasize beauty, colors, or the picturesque:

> The beach is about twenty meters wide and consists of a mixture of sand and crushed coral. It slopes down toward the lagoon lying there, alternately blue and green, with scattered collections of coral above and beneath the water. A couple of hundred meters from the beach is the reef. We can see the waves crashing against it so that the water rises high up in the air. (227)[31]

Gone are the adjectival modifiers of imperial stylistics; Loe's travelogue breaks entirely with Pratt's description of such stylistics. Loe's narrator is sober and precise, and does not relate what he sees to objects back home. Characteristic of Generation X, he furthermore dwells as much on the *signifié* as on the *signifiant*. Referring to the greenery, he gets stuck on the word "jungle": "Behind us is the forest, or the jungle. I am not quite sure what it takes for something to be a jungle. There are, at least, a lot of trees here" (227).[32] As Hans Ulrich Gumbrecht has pointed out in *Production of Presence,* the current trend is for artists and literary scholars to regard the sign not just as a Saussurian conveyer of meaning but as an Aristotelian sign whose material side cannot be discarded.[33] Gumbrecht's emphasis is on the aesthetic experience of the material sign while Erlend Loe's narrator dwells more pragmatically on the literal meaning of words and expressions. Both may, however, be regarded as proponents of a post-theory movement in which one hesitates before signs—before employing them and before assigning meaning to them.[34]

Thus, as we have seen in the foregoing examples, *L* is a postmodernized travelogue as it presents a downgraded quest and a traveling antihero who gains no insights. Structurally it is characterized by interruptions, digressions, and intertextuality, yet compared to the postmodernized travelogue of the late 1970s, these sideplots serve a function of sameness rather than of difference. Instead of acting as foils capturing other people's tales of disillusionment, the childhood fantasies of bygone days, or interwoven discourses rich in cultural diversity, *L*'s sideplots work monotonously to capture likeness. Erlend registers no contrasts in his life—not even when he goes abroad. Whereas the blasé city dweller of the twentieth century could recapture a sense of distinction abroad, the blasé world dweller of what is almost the twenty-first century is stuck with what was previously considered an urbane—not a global—attitude. Nothing stands out.[35] Erlend does not once feel differently, his friends do not feel differently, other people are of no interest, and whereas Pfister describes the subject of the postmodern travelogue as receding into the background, as opposed to the romantic or postromantic travelogue placing the traveling Self at the center, Erlend never leaves the center.[36] He may be a somewhat humble man in the center, but he never relinquishes this predominant position. It is in this difference one finds the main mark of the Generation X version of the postmodernized travelogue. As a narrator, the traveling subject is extremely present, but he does not experience anything, he avoids the potential contact of the contact zone, and he uses his mental energy for self-reflection. Unlike Carsten Jensen, he is not out to construct a new Self through narrative, but rather to tear down all discourses comprising his world, not least those constituting his nation.

L as a Parody of *Kon-Tiki*

As Gérard Genette points out, hypertextuality is "most often revealed by means of a paratextual sign that has contractual force."[37] In *L,* however, the connection to Thor Heyerdahl's *Kon-Tiki* is signaled first and foremost in the text itself. With all its references to Heyerdahl, *L* leaves us with little doubt as to its "massive... and more or less officially stated" hypertextual relationship to its hypotext (Genette, 9). In terms of paratextual clues, these are limited to the photographic material inserted in the middle of the book. Beginning with the cover and the title, we receive none of the clues contained, for instance, in Axel Jensen's *Ikaros.* The cover looks more like brand-name packaging than a visual and verbal indication of what might be inside the book. On what comes across as a green rectangular package (the book), concentric dark green and white circles surround a red spot with a white L inside. Underneath the circle, the author has put his somewhat naïve-looking signature, drawn in a thin black line, all in capital letters.

The cover has been interpreted as a learning sign similar to the homemade learner's permits Norwegians put on their cars while learning how to drive. Consequently the title is read as an indication that Erlend is of a generation that will remain learners and never grow up, or who refuse to learn social rules by heart without questioning them first.[38] *L* has also been interpreted as a reference to Erlend Loe—put together his initials and you get EL, the sound for the letter L, or simply use the initial of his last name.[39] Reminiscent of an aim, however, the cover may also allude to the opening image of *Robinson-ekspeditionen* (Survivor), the first successful Scandinavian reality show, portraying everyday Scandinavians who are placed on a tropical desert island and given various tasks and challenges. This interpretation is backed up by the second part of the book's being divided into bonfire sections reminiscent of the bonfire episodes in *Robinson,* during which the members voted each other out. Considered from a postmodernist perspective, the bull's-eye cover suggests an effort to establish a center—a center that may pertain to Loe and his ex-centric generation as well as to the notion of creating a coherent story. And finally, considered from the perspective of globalization, the cover appears as an international logo rather than a national title. As Naomi Klein points out in her book *No Logo*, logos "have become the closest thing we have to an international language."[40] The comparison is pertinent as it points to the persistent postnational questioning of Loe's book. On the one hand, Loe is aware of living in a globalized world, in which logos communicate better than any particular language—including English. On the other hand, he is unmistakably Norwegian, tied to Norwegian language and culture. As Erlend puts it in the book: he could move abroad, to Denmark, for instance, but he likes Norway better (26–27). And as Loe puts it in real life: he has lived in France and had the opportunity to settle down with a career in Copenhagen, "but there is something about the language. To me it is enriching to be in a country where I master codes and nuances."[41] Thus, Loe in a typical late-modern or postmodern manner ends up suspended between a local national and a global consciousness.

Viewed as a logo, the book's cover also serves as an ironic commentary on contemporary cultural production, namely, parody. Tied to branding the prefabricated rather than producing something new, the logo suggests that *L* as a parody is a matter of branding something that already exists rather than producing something original. Repackaged and carrying the brand *L,* Heyerdahl's book *Kon-Tiki,* through clever marketing skills, turns into a Loe product. And at the same time, the reference to contemporary mass culture is also one of critique—turned not only against Loe's own project and its relation to contemporary mass culture but also against the general notion of origins and uniqueness. Reenacting and rewriting *Kon-Tiki* is not a matter of replicating an original. Heyerdahl himself based his expedition on reenactment and copying a previous historical event. Heyerdahl writes about his raft, "the whole construction was a faithful copy" (64). Repackaging Heyerdahl is rather a matter of passing on cultural heritage from one generation to another. The narrator explains that he is concerned he may not yet have passed on all that is necessary from previous generations: "One has passed on knowledge. Through generations. I taught you this, then you use it for fifty or sixty years and pass it on to your children. And if you happen to think of something new along the way, then that won't hurt" (19–20).[42] The *Kon-Tiki* expedition took place in 1947, and it is time to pass its legacy on to a new generation, preferably with a few original modifications.[43]

L is based on Heyerdahl's *Kon-Tiki* on the level of content as well as form. Every aspect of Erlend's project, including the development of a theory, the gathering of a crew, the raising of capital, carrying through in the leadership role, being in contact with the media, and finally writing a best-seller travelogue is based on Heyerdahl. Erlend's brother Even is far from wrong when he concludes, "In other words, we are very much basing our trip on Heyerdahl's" (19–20).[44] And it is specified in the contract for staying on Manuae that "this is a follow-up of Thor Heyerdahl's expeditions in the South West Pacific" (179). The connection is coincidental as well as necessary. The coincidental background is that one Christmas Erlend gets a pair of ice skates as well as a copy of Heyerdahl's *Kon-Tiki ekspedisjonen*. During the days following Christmas he finds himself skating on a lake with the wind at his back. This reminds him of what Heyerdahl wrote about the passat winds and their influence upon the currents in the Pacific Ocean. Before long, Erlend decides that the South Americans could also have skated across the ocean, helped by the same wind at their backs, if the Pacific Ocean, that is, had only been covered by ice. One way of proving that this could have happened would be to go looking for the skates. The skates might of course have disintegrated, but not if they were made of gold. And, as Heyerdahl has also taught him, one might also look for other types of evidence, in native art, for instance. Perhaps one may discover that the native Polynesians have incorporated the sound of golden skates cutting across the ice in their folk music: "I feel certain that to this day, this sound of skating is reflected in the music from Polynesia" (37).[45] That, too, would prove Erlend right. At least it would not prove him wrong.

Still, the text also lets us know that building on Heyerdahl's legacy is a matter not only of coincidence but also of necessity. Granted his status as a national icon, Heyerdahl becomes inevitable. At the time *L* was written, he was the most famous Norwegian alive (35). As Erlend marvels, he had just been elected "the Norwegian of the twentieth century" (ibid.). While preparing for the journey, one of Erlend's friends and crew members, Egil, impresses Erlend by talking about "the great puzzle of migration in the Pacific" (122). Erlend thinks, "Egil is one hell of a guy taking this so seriously" (ibid.). But then Egil smiles and admits he just quoted Heyerdahl:

Egil, then, has not drawn on his own inspiration, but, he says, we must consider that those days are over. Today, very little can be drawn from one's own inspiration. It is not possible anymore. People have thought the thoughts before. Our project will be to refine them. (Ibid.)[46]

Thus sounds Egil's and the book's postmodern credo. As Umberto Eco has put it, "We cannot ignore the discourses that precede and contextualize everything we say and do."[47] Nothing is original, but it may perhaps be refined by being told in new ways—perhaps, if we follow this story, by being seen in light of the present. Hutcheon maintains that the postmodern novel articulates the present "in terms of the 'presentness' of the past" (*Poetics of Postmodernism*, 34); it both enshrines and questions the past (126); and in the end it shows "both its critical awareness and its love of history by giving new meaning to old forms, though often not without irony" (31).

Whether the ensuing ironic parody is to be regarded as a denigration or commendation of Heyerdahl and his scientific and literary endeavors is also a matter of paradox. As Hutcheon insists, postmodern parody is a fundamentally contradictory enterprise that uses and abuses the tradition at once. Erlend himself lays the grounds for a "both-and" attitude when he decides that developing a new theory is a matter of complementing rather than invalidating that of Heyerdahl:

> After all, it does not mean that Heyerdahl's theory is any worse off. On the contrary. These are two sides of the same thesis. Heyerdahl followed his idea. I have to follow mine. Others could, of course, have crossed the ocean on balsa rafts later on, when the ice disappeared. Nothing would prevent that. Then they even had someone to visit. This seems quite coherent. (36–37)[48]

Thus, the "post" in the term "postmodern" marks both a difference from and a connection with the past (Hutcheon, *A Poetics of Postmodernism*, 125). The overall desire—which nevertheless is deemed impossible—is for wholeness and unity ("dette ser ut til å henge godt sammen"). This, as we have seen also in Carsten Jensen's travelogues, is what Heyerdahl represents: the commonsense ability to synthesize. Carsten Jensen says that Heyerdahl's method is "the mixture of unimpressed matter-of-factness and fantasy," culminating in "a synthesis-seeking mode of thinking that considers all the great world cultures as internally connected in reciprocal, fruitful influence" (Jensen, *Jeg har hørt et stjerneskud*, 259–60). Yet, whereas Heyerdahl ends up serving as a figure of identification for Jensen, who also uses his own knowledge, common sense, and fantasy to create universal theories, symbolic images, and cross-cultural, human understanding, Erlend in *L* can admit only to desiring such unity: "Specializing is not very attractive. I would rather know something about everything. Renaissance man. The universal genius. Drawing connections here and there. Seeing the whole. That is how I would prefer to be seen" (31).[49] As the slippage of subjectivity in this passage shows—with Erlend shifting from being the active subject to being the passive object—Erlend does not really believe in the possibility of this task, that is, in the task of humanist and scientific endeavor. Hutcheon speculates that "the ironic distance of modern parody might well come from a loss of that earlier humanist faith in cultural continuity and stability."[50] In the end, Erlend can only relate to Heyerdahl through a thick layer of irony.

Textually and structurally, *L* parodies Heyerdahl's book on the level of composition, through direct and indirect citation, and through the incorporation and recirculation of photographic documentation. Because of the autobiographical nature of both works, and because Heyerdahl was still alive and interacted with Erlend, applying Genette's structural categories of hypertextuality becomes rather complex. The relationship between the two works is not just one of hypertextuality but also of metatextuality and intertextuality. When Axel Jensen, as we have seen in chapter 6, bases the hypertextuality of *Ikaros* mainly on the Greek classical myth and on *The Sheltering Sky*, this becomes a somewhat clear-cut literary experiment in the sense that one text bases itself on another, and we can explore the relationship from the perspective of literary hypertextuality only. What complicates the straightforward comparison, though, is that the textual comparison also interferes on the level of the plot, with Axel Jensen's main character trying too hard to live a symbolic life, identifying with literary and mythical figures. This type of interference may be viewed as a first step toward the even more complex interference between the fictional and factual in Loe's novel. Not only is one text an imitation and a transformation of another, and one protagonist's actions inspired by those of another, Loe also incorporates Heyerdahl through lengthy quotes (Genette's intertextuality and metafictionally),[51] through photodocumentary, recycling Heyerdahl's pictures and juxtaposing them with his own

(Genette's paratext), and, finally, through involving the real-life Heyerdahl in the media hype surrounding himself and his expedition. Erlend Loe organizes an interview with Heyerdahl on Norwegian national TV that, in turn, is incorporated into the book. Thus, while Genette's categories are helpful in discussing particular aspects of *L,* the overall project is better captured by Hutcheon's expanded definition of a postmodern poetic, as this definition is based on a nonautonomous, interart view of modern parody. Rather than speaking of imitation and transformation, Hutcheon discusses "trans-contextualization": "Parodic 'trans-contextualization' can take the form of a literal incorporation of reproductions into the new work or of a reworking of the formal elements" (*A Theory of Parody,* 8).

The Structure of *L*

Once Erlend gets into his story about the expedition to Manuae, he structures his narrative chronologically, using some of the same chapter headings that Heyerdahl uses. *L* is divided into Parts 1 and 2, with the first part covering the preparations and the second part covering the journey. Following Loe's first chapter "Vi som ikke bygde Norge" (We Who Did Not Build Norway) are two chapters whose titles are copied from Heyerdahl's two first chapters: "En teori" (A Theory) and "En ekspedisjon blir til" (An Expedition in the Making). The final chapter in Part 1 appears as an appendix with printouts of an e-mail correspondence between Magne, a Norwegian contact person on the Cook Islands, and Erlend, in which the contract to visit Manuae is agreed upon. Part 2 consists of yet another epitaph—this time on the importance of science—followed by another two chapters copying their titles from Heyerdahl's book: "Over Stillehavet" (Across the Pacific Ocean) and "Blant polynesere" (Among Polynesians). Then Loe resorts to the episodic titles of contemporary TV reality shows, such as *Robinson.* The final chapter is entitled "32 bål" (32 Bonfires) and is divided into sections meticulously called "1. dag" (1. day) and "1. bål" (1. bonfire), "2. dag" (2. day) and "2. bål" (2. bonfire).[52]

L, then, is structured partly like *Kon-Tiki ekspedisjonen,* but as we saw in the case of *Ikaros,* hypertexts tend to include added layers of fictional introductions, wavering in status between that of paratext and text, fact and fiction. *L* includes three such extra paratextual elements at the beginning of the travelogue: the aforementioned Lyotardian epitaph, a prologue signed "Erlend (Marco Po) Loe... 1998," and a letter to the editor of a Swedish newspaper. The overall movement is one from a general theoretical viewpoint, to a world-historical global view, to a local reflection in the present. We have already discussed the epitaph, and if we turn to the prologue, we find Erlend comparing and contrasting himself to Marco Polo, acknowledging that his own travelogue will not expand Europeans' horizon more than that of his predecessor, Marco Polo. The author thus zooms in on European exploration, situating his own project parodically vis-à-vis the great European travelogues of exploration, and finally, in his last paratextual element, he grounds his project in the contemporary and local. The Swedish letter to the editor in *Dagens Nyheter* from 1998 is written by a reader concerned that today's children are too slow and will not grow up to be "useful citizens." The reader calls for more resources being given to research "so that we may discover why sluggishness is so widespread." Loe's book may be read both as an answer and as a challenge to this idea. One of the experiments carried out on the island, as mentioned previously, is not how we can be quicker and more productive, but rather how many hours it is actually possible to sleep per night. Even has reached a maximum of seventeen hours, and wishes to increase this. Overall, though, the three initial references to Lyotard, to Marco Polo, and to an anonymous reader of a daily newspaper situate Loe's project within a context establishing connections to texts of the past as well as those of the present, to theoretical as well as trivial discourses, to the academic as well as the popular, to the classical as well as the quotidian, and to global as well as to local voices.

The prologue signed by the author also establishes an autobiographical contract in which the author's name (aside from the inserted parenthesis) coincides with that of the narrator, which in turn coincides with that of the protagonist. Although he is usually referred to only as Erlend, the protagonist's full name shows up on reproduced official documents such as a check written to the Explorers' Club, a letter Erlend receives from the king's cabinet, and the island contract mentioned earlier (179). Still, Erlend and Erlend are not identical. *L*'s protagonist, for instance, has not written two novels that have made him, too, a national icon. Erlend the protagonist has constructed nothing of value for society (18), is no artist, and feels no need to provoke people unnecessarily (28). Were he not more of a good-for-nothing than Erlend the author, the parodic contrast between the great Norwegian Thor Heyerdahl and the small Norwegian Erlend Loe would not work nearly as well. A classic feature of parody—not just postmodern, but Aristotelian parody, as we saw in chapter 6—is to let a light and playful subject replace a serious subject, with light and playful action replacing serious action. Heyerdahl is, of course, on a more serious mission than Erlend and his friends, but it is not as clear that Erlend Loe, as a contemporary author and cultural commentator, is not also on a serious mission in trying to make a Norwegian Generation X and other fellow citizens understand their position in a postmodern, post-theoretical world. As Hutcheon has pointed out, in postmodern parody the line between the playful and the serious is not drawn so easily: "To include irony and play is *never* necessarily to exclude seriousness and purpose in postmodernist art" (*A Poetics of Postmodernism*, 27).

In the chapters on Knut Hamsun, Johannes V. Jensen and Axel Jensen we have seen how the irony of the travelogue plays itself out, first on the level of the traveler, and then, with Axel Jensen, on the level of the narrator revealed as a precocious young man with excessively lofty literary ambitions. As a Norwegian postmodern travelogue, however, *L*'s irony is directed toward a collective rather than an individual. Generation X is set up against Heyerdahl's post–World War II generation. On one level, the incongruity of this comparison shows brave and active men as opposed to overintellectual young men, used to living passively in hyperreality as they watch TV and movies, play computer games, and read books, but do not venture far beyond home. Where Heyerdahl's men are World War II heroes, Erlend's are military dissidents. Where Heyerdahl's men fight bears, Erlend's fight beavers. And where Heyerdahl's men have fought against the Germans in war, the riskiest thing Erlend and his friends have done against Germans is peeing on them through a train window once.

The Necessity of Small Talk and the Monomaniacal Voice

The comparison of the two generations, however, also shows a generation used to thinking of themselves as individuals as opposed to a generation that has been brought up and educated through a national, scientific, and liberal humanist ideology of the collective. The problem for Generation X is not just that the world is ready-made and presents them with no real dangers, but also that they have been forced into disregarding individual drive and difference. For Erlend the emblematic aspect of this upbringing is the group work in which he was forced to participate in school. Metonymically, group work in "O-fag"—short for *orienteringsfag* (environmental studies)—stands throughout the book for Norway and its relationship to the rest of the world, and for scientific exploration and its relationship to scientific progress. O-fag, as Erlend explains, was a flagship of a subject "where everything related to nature and society melted together in an elegant and educational way" (42). Erlend was good at it. He includes his report card from the fifth grade as photodocumentation, since it explains that Erlend works well, has a positive attitude, and engages in independent problem solving. He is also pleasant and polite.[53]

Yet, we also find a countervoice to this statement of congeniality. The narrator himself reveals that he hated group work. He has more or less succumbed to the ideology that thinking collectively is for the best, but the price paid for collective progress is the quenching of individual drive and difference, frustration and boredom, and way too much babble:

> The purpose of group work is that there are no shortcuts. You cannot get away in the same way that you can when you work alone. You have to listen to everybody's opinions. If you talk bull, someone will stop you. The system is secured that way. Talk. Talk. Evaluate. Sharpen your skills. Open yourself to others' suggestions. The stupid ones, too. They also belong to the group. Over time, the good suggestions will probably win out.
>
> Already in school, I hated group work. I was terrible at cooperating. I felt it went too slowly, that the others were fools, and that nothing got done if I did not do it myself. (30)[54]

Erlend's ambivalent attitude to group work and collective thinking is reflected in the makeup of the book, which reveals a provocatively compliant—bordering on the vengeful—narrator. What is most annoying about the book is essential when viewed from the group work upbringing forced upon its narrator. Reviewers have, for instance, said that the book contains too much small talk (Opset, 62). Yet, small talk and silly digressions—

talking "bull"—is obligatory for a generation that has been brought up to be open and tolerant toward "the stupid ones, too." Thus, viewed from the perspective of the book's inner logic, this seemingly negative quality contributes to the unity and consistency of the work.

Focusing on the authoritative rather than trivial aspect of *L*'s narration, Aage Borchgrevink, who is the same age as Erlend and his friends, has criticized its autistic point of view and monomaniacal voice.[55] Borchgrevink, that is, sees through Erlend's playfulness, pointing out the authoritativeness behind the humorous surface, the naivistic lurking behind the naive, and the aggressive individualism hiding behind the meek group participation. These strategies of power, however, all reflect back on Erlend's education and the social behavior for which he was rewarded from an early age. Since the fifth grade, Erlend has learned to suppress his individuality and to think and act in solidarity. At the same time, he is used to taking charge. Pleasant, but not entirely submissive, Erlend is the perfect expedition group leader. And viewed from a postnational perspective, he exemplifies the paradoxical heavy-handedness of the well-intentional welfare state.

The issue may furthermore be viewed as exemplary of postmodernism. As Hutcheon points out, "What is important in all these internalized challenges to humanism is the interrogating of the notion of consensus" (*A Poetics of Postmodernism,* 7). In this regard, *L* once more operates at the opposite end of the scale in relation to Axel Jensen's *Ikaros*. While *Ikaros* is a parody on *The Sheltering Sky,* inverting the themes of its hypotext as it turns the tragic into the comical and the misanthropic into a confirmation of humanity, *L* remains ambiguous. As indicated in the introduction, Erlend insists on having it this way. The members of his generation are fond of each other, but they cannot say they love each other without an ironic tone emerging in their voices.

Erlend's authoritativeness comes through in his monotonous, or, according to Borchgrevink, monomaniacal voice. One of the places in which this becomes most obvious is in Erlend's long narrative introductions of every crew member. While Heyerdahl briefly draws an impressive and pertinent sketch of every crew member in *Kon-Tiki,* Erlend writes repetitive depictions of his crew, each rendered in the same voice and made according to the same mold. In the end, each biography shows a young man who has studied at the university; lived a fairly sheltered life; is interested in the fictional world of film, literature, and computer games; and who, despite his own parents' divorce, still is surprisingly idealistic, believing, above all, in true love.

The uniformity of the depictions points in two directions. The members of Generation X may indeed all be alike, indoctrinated or even brainwashed by a homogeneous set of voices originating in a particular mix of a standard Norwegian upbringing and globalized popular culture. The other way of understanding this similarity, however, is by regarding Erlend, in his role as narrator, as a homogenizing force, turning an entire generation into mirror images of his own Self.

Encountering the Other

When it comes to meeting Pacific Islanders, Erlend relies on similar strategies of turning potential difference into sameness. The cultural Other becomes the cultural Same. As the cultural Other is de-exoticized, he also becomes uninteresting. The Pacific Islanders in *L* are represented by two natives, Mii and Tuaine, who accompany the seven Norwegians to their desert island. Erlend's and his friends' reaction to the natives' going with them is primarily one of frustration. Mii and Tuaine, they figure, will make them self-conscious and put a damper on their escapades. It will be like having babysitters around, and they might even have to wear swim trunks on the beach (217).

Thus, *L* breaks with the tradition of defining the European in opposition to the Oriental, primitive or exotic Other. Instead, the post–World War II generation continues to function as a source of contrast. Relentless parodic references to Heyerdahl's *Kon-Tiki ekspedisjonen* emphasize the difference between the two generations. When, for instance, *L*'s narrator matter-of-factly refers to Mii and Tuaine as "our brown friends" (228), one may read this as emblematic of Erlend's condescending attitude toward the natives. One may, however, also read it as part of his project to define his own generation in relation to that of Heyerdahl. What would currently be deemed a politically incorrect reference is a verbatim quote from *Kon-Tiki,* in which the narrator refers to the Polynesians as "brown figures" (224), "our brown friends" (226), and "our brown admirers" (239).

Turning to Heyerdahl's text, we find a classical encounter in the contact zone written in the name of engaged interaction. Having arrived at their destination on their raft, Heyerdahl and his crew are thrilled to meet the Polynesians. The narrator, in turn, pulls the reader into his excited account through humorous, exoticizing depictions of two Polynesian chiefs. First we are introduced to Teka: "Teka was a tall, slender Polynesian with uncommonly intelligent eyes. He was an important person, a descendant of the old royal line in Tahiti ... He had been to school in Tahiti, so that he spoke French and could both read and write" (225). Teka's cochief is Tupuhoe: "Tupuhoe was a pure child of nature and a sterling fellow, with a humor and a primitive force the like of which one meets but rarely. With his powerful body and kingly features he was exactly what one expects a Polynesian chief to be" (229). The depiction of Teka prompts more respect—for a man who is more like us—than that of the corpulent Tupuhoe, who is subsequently referred to as "stout Tupuhoe" (230) and "portly Tupuhoe" (239). Still, both depictions are imbued with adjectival modifiers purveying a sense of nobility. Teka is "important" and comes from an old "royal line," and while the depiction of Tupuhoe in part turns him into a comic figure, it also arouses the reader's respect through words underscoring his noble savageness and authenticity: "pure child of nature," "sterling fellow," "primitive force," "kingly."

Heyerdahl's subsequent story is one of mutual exchange and enrichment. When it comes to the research project, the Polynesians furnish Heyerdahl with useful evidence that their ancestors may have arrived from Peru by recounting old songs and legends. The Polynesians, in turn, are grateful that Heyerdahl believes in and confirms their otherwise disregarded tales of origin. Heyerdahl's crew also gives the Polynesians cigarettes and medicine and cures several sick children in the local village with penicillin. Finally, the two groups enrich each other through entertainment and amusement. They eat, drink, sing, dance, and party together. Illustrating how open he is to the rituals of foreign cultures, Heyerdahl accepts Tupuhoe's request that he lead the rest of them in one of the island's oldest ceremonies, the bird dance. A good sport, Heyerdahl enthusiastically gives in to the request. Then, as a narrator, he depicts the scene with as much zest as one expects him to have displayed in his dancing:

> As the dance leader's main task appeared to me to consist in uttering wild howls, hopping around on his haunches, wriggling his backside, and waving his hands over his head, I pulled the wreath of flowers well down over my head and marched out into the arena. While I was curving myself in the dance, I saw old Tupuhoe laughing till he nearly fell off his stool, and the music grew feeble because the singers and players followed Tupuhoe's example. (236)

Thus, what Pratt refers to as a Western ideology of reciprocity figures prominently in Heyerdahl's account. The Europeans and Polynesians reinforce each other's sense of knowledge, they help each other, they laugh together, and they end up crying together when Heyerdahl and his men are finally picked up by a French schooner that the governor of the French Pacific colonies has ordered to bring them to Tahiti. The following claim may well serve as the section's heading: "It was as much of an adventure to the natives as it was to us" (226). As a final sign of how integrated they have become with the Polynesians, the Polynesians also "adopt" them and give them Polynesian names (239).

While Heyerdahl's encounter is one of engagement, interaction, and reciprocity, that of Erlend and Mii and Tuaine is largely one of disengagement, avoidance, and overall indifference. Erlend and his friends first try to camp as far away from the two natives as possible, but quickly realize it is to their advantage to capitalize on their local expertise. Erlend is in no way curious about Mii and Tuaine, but when they nonetheless exhibit differences, this inspires only mild musing and embarrassment—not least because Erlend and his friends are painfully aware of what is clichéd and what is politically incorrect. Having been brought up to respect others, they cannot allow themselves immediate, unreflected reactions. Instead they cover up their hostility with feel-good phrases of tolerance. When, for instance, Mii and Tuaine say grace before eating, Erlend and his friends are shocked that they actually believe in God: "We cannot take it seriously. We try as hard as we can, but do not quite succeed. But, naturally, it is serious. Mii and Tuaine believe in God. We have to respect that. Every single day we learn something about ourselves and others" (233).[56] The last two sentences are highly ambivalent. Taken at face value, they reflect tolerance, yet, loaded with irony, they also reflect disrespect and unwillingness to gain new insight. As Borchgrevink points out, the ironic gaze turns all unknown impressions into known phenomena: "everything becomes alike" (16).

Still, it is a matter of whether this glossing over difference with clichéd statements of tolerance is not also an object of irony. In *Verdensbilder og selvbilder* (2002), Terje Tvedt, as mentioned in the introduction to Part III, characterizes the Norwegian of the 1990s as a narcissistic cosmopolitan. Politically, the country vowed to become a humanitarian great power, and the prime minister Gro Harlem Bruntland proclaimed that it was "typically Norwegian to be good."[57] In Tvedt's view this resulted in a nauseating, national "better-than-thou" self-image, with Norwegians lacking all sense of irony and self-deprecation. Using Jan Kjærstad's trilogy *Forføreren, Erobreren,* and *Oppdageren* (1993–99) as an exemplary discourse on Norwegian "cosmopolitan nationalism," Tvedt bemoans that "the work is completely devoid of irony and is not intended as satire" (96).[58] Loe's *L,* in contrast, may be read as relentless ironizing and critical of that same do-good attitude.

Caught between accusations of imperialism, narcissisism, and autism— between too much and not enough world engagement—*L* illustrates how difficult it is to write a travelogue or travel novel at the turn of the third millennium without falling into the pitfalls of postcolonialism, imperial stylistics, and Gen X self-sufficiency. As a postnational parody, *L* is an original type of postmodern, collective travelogue, functioning to define a new generation in relation to their national predecessors. Whereas Carsten Jensen, for instance, ends up focusing on individual identity, writing, "Who was I? I would find out" (513), Erlend Loe concludes with a focus on collective identity: "In a hundred years one will know all about this. Then one will know who we were."[59] "I" is replaced by "we," and the narrator does not expect the identity question to be answered within his own lifetime.

Several critics have suggested that the time-based sense of identity in *L* is new. Hadle Oftedal Andersen notes how Loe's protagonists think diachronically rather than synchronically. Instead of wondering why certain contemporaries differ from him, the protagonist wonders why his predecessors are different.[60] Elise Seip Tønnessen has pointed out that Loe's characters are members of a new generation who have no faith that time will provide them with a sense of meaning—they will not, like their parents and grandparents, one day look back on their lives and see how they ultimately fit into a larger historical narrative.[61] The overall implication is that for Generation X, time becomes pertinent only in an epochal sense. It marks their generation as distinct—as distinctly beyond, as posttheoretical, postmodern, postnational, and posthistorical.

As Generation X breaks with modern ideals of historical development and progression, its members end up disregarding previous categories of difference. They no longer operate with a notion of "postcolonial belatedness" as Homi Bhabha, for instance, has pointed out with regards to the marginalization of former colonies and the third world.[62] Feeling estranged from a European, humanist tradition, Generation X feels no need for the Oriental, exotic, colonial, or primitive Other. They could, one imagines, have related to the ex-centric positioning of the Other, but Erlend's generation is too paranoid to do so. Rather than regarding Mii and Tuaine through a lens of solidarity—as equally decentered—they place them in the position of their dominant, European parents—as yet another set of babysitters who will tell them what to do and how to behave. Using Freudian vocabulary we might say that the cultural Other is regarded not as a counterimage to the ego (as in the case of Orientalism), nor as an image of the id (as in the case of primitivism), but as an image of the superego.

Disregarding the Other as dominant rather than marginalized has implications for the travelogue. When the Westerner no longer travels to seek out the foreign, cultural Other, but rather uses traveling abroad as a source of intertextual comparison, we end up hearing very little about foreign cultures and are left instead with representations of the national, generational Self (in this case Heyerdahl and his crew) as strangely Other. The position of indifference toward the foreigner is nevertheless one of privilege. The members of a Norwegian Generation X have the means to travel the world and to use it as a backdrop for the exploration of a postnational Self. It is difficult to imagine Mii and Tuaine having the means to go to Norway on a similar quest.

A final issue with the generational travelogue is its implicit othering of fellow Norwegians who do not see the world as ready-made. Loe writes about seven people who end up representing a whole generation. Most critics have accepted this totalizing gesture, but Borchgrevink, as we have seen, objects to being inscribed into a generation depicted as postnational, postmodern, and posthistorical—or into what he terms "a national, social-democratic bubble cut off from intellectual and emotional engagement" (16). Compelled to protest, he labels Erlend and his friends as *homo scandinavicus ironicus,* condemning their irony and their lack of engagement (13) and insisting that they might have found a way of engaging with cultural Others that is neither a matter of traditional stereotyping nor a matter of wearing blinds and ignoring them. Yet, as pointed out, Erlend the narrator and Erlend the author are not the same person. A final paradox of this semiautobiographical travel novel, then, is that through Erlend the narrator's totalizing gesture and through his othering of fellow Norwegians, Erlend the author may still be able to provoke, engage, and prompt his contemporaries into pondering not only their relationship to their national heritage but also their relationship to those living beyond Europe.

Conclusion

The Status of the Literary Travelogue

IN 2004 HORACE ENGDAHL, secretary of the Swedish Academy, which awards the Nobel Prize for Literature, commented on the contemporary fascination with travel literature:

> A new type of text has emerged that is no longer fictional literature, but that employs a literary linguistic form. The enormously increased importance of travel literature in recent years—among others by authors like the postcolonialist Nobel Prize winner V. S. Naipaul—is an example of this. But one also finds the travelogue among a large variety of traveling journalistic authors.[1]

Travel literature is no longer just an object of popular reading but also an object of literary study. In a Scandinavian context, I have mentioned Lars Handesteen's, Arne Melberg's and Anka Ryall's monographs on the more literary exemplars of the genre. In addition, anthologies containing readings of individual travelogues as well as analyses of less literary travel reportages attest to the resurgence of the genre within and outside academia.[2]

At this point, then, one can hardly regard travel literature as one of the academy's ugly ducklings. Instead it has turned into a popular field in which new discoveries are constantly made. Attention is turned to the travel writing of canonized writers such as Hans Christian Andersen, Knut Hamsun, and Johannes V. Jensen; scholars discover previously unheard-of writers like Elisabeth Jerichau-Baumann; and the works are studied from the perspective of both literary aesthetics and cultural studies. It has been the ambition of this book to capture both strains of study, and to make sense of these in a historical context, with an eye to world history as well as literary history.

The Genre

In this book I have focused on the relationship between the literary travelogue and the novel during three phases: the romantic, the early modern, and the late modern or postmodern. As I showed in Part I, the romantic *voyage en Orient* tends to be represented as an outer journey with the traveler gathering disparate impressions along the way. The linear plot of the travelogue is provided by the chronology of the itinerary, and the travelogue is not yet novelized in the Bakhtinian sense of that word. Instead, the travelogue is structured around a series of subgenres with shorter episodes being presented as, for instance, fairy tales, prose poems, and sketches. The traveling subject possesses a stable core identity; he or she is not traveling to develop as an individual, but rather to collect impressions of an exotic Orient. Viewed from a postcolonialist point of view, we see that the attitude toward the Orient is imperialistic, with the traveler expecting the Orient to adapt a Western lifestyle. For Hans Christian Andersen this attitude is suggested by his expectation that the Christians will once more control Aya Sophia, and for Elisabeth Jerichau-Baumann it is suggested by her hopes for women's liberation and a Western aesthetic pertaining to art as well as fashion. The attitude, however, is not that of the colonizer who expects his or her own or other European nations directly to govern the Orient.

Once we approach the end of the nineteenth century, Knut Hamsun modernizes the Oriental travelogue. On the formal level, he does so through irony and novelization, relying on psychological imagery to create tension through, for instance, dream imagery and paranoia. Thematically, he turns his back on Western development and civilization, positing the Oriental and his lifestyle as preferable to that of the Westerner—especially the American.

As we arrive at the beginning of the twentieth century, the focus shifts from the Oriental to the primitive Other. Johannes V. Jensen exemplifies this turn by traveling to Further India, where he engages in Darwinistic, anthropological studies of the primitive, not least the primitive within himself. His main aim in writing a travelogue, however, remains poetic. Jensen may be said to further develop Hamsun's fictionalizing strategies.

In Jensen's case, irony once more plays a great role; in addition, dreams and psychological drives are used to conjure up images of a pseudoquest.

Isak Dinesen's elegiac tone differs entirely from that of Jensen, but she, too, operates with a great distance between the narrator and the traveler. In her case the distance is nostalgic rather than parodic. She bases her narrative on the genres of comedy and tragedy. As Dinesen views modern culture at large as a downfall, she considers the European colonization and modernization of Africa tragic. These movements nonetheless provide the circumstances for her own stay in Kenya.

Like Dinesen, Axel Jensen seeks out Africa to escape a modernized Europe, in his case the atrocities of World War II. Generically his is the most novelized of the travelogues analyzed in this study. It is highly intertextual and follows a strict composition in which the traveler—in a rather ironic manner—is portrayed as the hero of a bildungsroman. Axel Jensen's travelogue is also, of course, the first of the texts in this study carrying the label of novel.

Finally, in Part III, I turned to examples of the late-modern and the postmodern travelogue. Carsten Jensen illustrates how the late-modern individual constantly narrates his own biography with this text constituting his ever-developing identity. While the first part of his travelogue was written in a bildungsroman manner, the second part to a greater extent approached ethical issues faced by the late-modern anthropologist or journalist.

In the final chapter we saw how Erlend Loe exemplifies a postmodern Generation X, world-weary and preferring to stay home, where one may submerge oneself in the virtual realities of film and computer games. That, at least, is a world the Gen Xers may have to themselves—a world that has not already been explored, described, and theorized by their parents. Generically, *L*—labeled a novel—represents a postmodern stage of convergence in the development of the relationship between the travelogue and the novel. At this stage, the novel tends to challenge the perceived line of distinction between fact and fiction. Thus, during the romantic stage, the traditional novel and the travelogue operate mainly as two distinct genres. During the modern stage, the modernist novel veers away from the coherent bildungsroman structure, while the travelogue, in turn, adopts this structure, focusing on the development of the traveler in a more coherent, novelized form. Finally, during the postmodern stage, the novel problematizes its status as autonomous fiction by transgressing the boundary between factual genres such as the historical, the biographical, and the autobiographical—including the autobiographical travelogue. As Engdahl puts it in the quotation that began this conclusion, the surge of travelogues coincides with the end of literary modernism.

Looking at the travelogue's relationship to anthropological and ethnographic reportage, James Clifford's claims to a three-stage pattern seem to hold true with the travelogue, including ethnographic reportage until the 1920s. Johannes V. Jensen's *Skovene* was the best example of this. Then, until the postmodern era, the author of the literary travelogue tends to leave anthropological reports to those representing the newly established field of anthropology. In a postmodern era, however, the travelogue once more incorporates anthropological observations, and—as in the case of Carsten Jensen—this is carried out in the self-reflective manner the anthropological report has also come to adapt.

Postcolonialism and Intersecting Theories

While discussing the development of the genre, its protagonist, narrator, and implied author, its fictionalizing strategies, tone, and attitude, I have throughout viewed the travelogues in the light of postcolonialism. In this endeavor, I have wanted to investigate the role of the Other, both in the traveler's encounter with the Other, and in the writer's subsequent representation. Stereotypes are commonplace. As people and landscapes, the Other is to put the traveler in touch with a lost part of himself—even Hans Christian Andersen seems to discover an inner Turk. In the writing process, the Other tends to be cast to create a particular type of narrative—I have gone into most detail on this in my analysis of Isak Dinesen's use of various native tribes in creating her tragicomedy.

In my postcolonial analysis I have relied mainly on Mary Louise Pratt's *Imperial Eyes*, but I have also broadened the discussion to include other relevant theories as I have seen fit for each particular travelogue. In my first chapter, I drew most heavily on Pratt in order to establish her theories vis-à-vis Andersen's depiction of the Orient. In chapter 2, however, I turned to theories on feminist Orientalism, viewing these as apt in describing Elisabeth Jerichau-Baumann's verbal and visual works of art. My chapter on Hamsun drew a great deal on Edward Said's *Orientalism*, and Marianna Torgovnick's study of primitivism to a greater extent captured Johannes V. Jensen's quest. In Jensen's case, Georges Bataille's and James Clifford's theories on eroticism and the field of anthropology, respectively, shed light on the author's poetic-anthropological efforts. When it comes to Dinesen I have been particularly fascinated by her humor, and combined Henri Bergson's, Søren Kierkegaard's, and Harald Høffding's theories on laughter and humor to explicate the comic aspect of her tragedy as well as her overall life philosophy. Gérard Genette and John Urry were particularly useful in my chapter on Axel Jensen in which I wanted to discuss intertextuality and the notion of the traveler versus the tourist. In exploring Carsten Jensen's writings I found Anthony Giddens's work on late-modern self-identity helpful, as well as Susan Sontag's historical and ethical reflections on representing misery. Finally, Erlend Loe seemed an ideal candidate for the theories Linda Hutcheon has developed on postmodernism.

Nordic Autoethnography and Transculturation

While Pratt's postcolonialist stance forms the central theoretical backdrop of my readings, I also contend that the Scandinavian literary travelogues challenge the dichotomous West-and-the-Rest model of Pratt's study. They do this in ways that may be understood from Pratt's own notions of autoethnography and transculturation. Whereas Pratt applies this notion to the self-representative texts written by the non-Western Other, I find it applicable to the self-representative texts written by European nongreat colonial powers such as the Scandinavians. Hence, one particularly important strand of investigation has been the travel books' specific Danish and Norwegian acts of self-representation and transculturation.

From Andersen to Loe, the authors discussed here represent and define their own national identities in relation to the non-Western Other, as well as to dominating Western world powers such as England, France, and the United States. They do this on two levels: that of the traveler vis-à-vis the people he or she meets on the journey, and that of the narrator recounting his or her journey to a home audience.

During the romantic period, Hans Christian Andersen's and Elisabeth Jerichau-Baumann's depictions of the Danish seem a matter of ingratiating themselves with the reading audience to whom they have returned. Both are uncertain of their status in their home country—not least Jerichau-Baumann, who was not born Danish. On the journey itself, however, neither Andersen's nor Jerichau-Baumann's traveler appears eager to stress his or her Danishness. Instead, both regard and present themselves as European cosmopolitans abroad. The conflict between these two strategies becomes particularly obvious when Andersen tries to establish an affinity with other European artists through his dedications—an act for which Danish critics deride him.

The postromantic and modern travelogues written by Hamsun, Dinesen, and the three Jensens show the Scandinavian travelers insisting on being better able to relate to the Oriental, primitive, racial, or exotic Other than do Westerners arriving from major colonial powers. At the turn of the century, the national attitude displayed by the traveler abroad is most aggressive. Hamsun speaks Norwegian in countries where there is no reason to think his language will be understood. He and his wife want it "Turkish style" in contrast to the British and the American couples at their hotel. Johannes V. Jensen indirectly mocks the English Royal Geographic Society and depicts British engineers as his cultural Other. Like Hamsun, he rejects capitalist exploration and development, positing himself as a more engaged scientific and poetic traveler—as one of Pratt's "seeing-men."

Dinesen distinguishes herself from the British colonial power, claiming that Scandinavians, through their sense of humor, relate better to the native Africans. Her project is of a double nature, though, as she writes in both Danish and English. In *Den afrikanske Farm,* writing as Karen Blixen, she especially seeks to distinguish herself as a Scandinavian in opposition to her fellow British colonialists. In *Out of Africa,* however, the more internationally inclined Isak Dinesen writes in English and eliminates passages on particular Scandinavian traits from her work. Both positions serve to ingratiate the author with her different reading audiences.

On the plot level, Axel Jensen plays up German and French stereotypes, setting himself apart from both. Meanwhile, on a formal level, the narrator's intertextual references to *Icarus, The Sheltering Sky,* and the Old Testament signal a Western cosmopolitan disposition. The Western references are nonetheless counterbalanced by national references to Ibsen and by distinguishing depictions of Norwegian women, a Norwegian landscape, and a Norwegian lifestyle to which the hero ultimately wishes to return.

During the late-modern and postmodern period, the authors of this study display an increasingly postnational attitude. Carsten Jensen's travelogue picks up the strand that is traceable to Hamsun's writings depicting Americans—as opposed to the British and French—as the Scandinavian's cultural *Western* Other. This becomes particularly striking in the chapter on Hong Kong (omitted from the English translation). Here a woman by the name of Patsy figures as the typically naive, overzealous, materialistic American lacking the self-discipline and guarded manners that—according to her French friend—are necessary to land a high-paying job in finance. Yet, Carsten Jensen ultimately veers toward a mixture of a cosmopolitan and a postnational view of human traits. Of all the authors analyzed in this book, he is the least inclined to flatter his home audience with depictions of a particular Danish mentality. And when it comes to the United States—or "America"—Jensen explains the futility of using national categorization. According to Jensen, "Americanized" is a misnomer and one ought to consider what "this universally extended cultural form, called Americanizing, actually represents."[3] The "America" of "Americanized" is a state of mind rather than a particular continent, claims Jensen. It is the supranational dream of starting anew harbored by all emigrants, and when it appears that everybody has become Americanized it is not because America's influence has increased, but because there are ever more emigrants in the world (ibid.). Thus, Jensen shies away from explanatory categories based on national identity, opting instead for a universal view of humanity.

Loe's postnational point of view differs from Jensen's as it is expressed through parody. *L*'s postnationalism is based on the frustration that Norway's nation-building era is over. It is *national* in the sense that it focuses on Norway, and *post* in the way it problematizes Norwegianness. Loe's postnationalism also captures a notion of universal sameness, but this is based less on Jensen's universalizing understanding of humanity than on the protagonist's self-centered projections. These are projections that primarily capture the need of a generation to set themselves off from an older generation—and in this equation nationhood hardly matters. For Erlend there is *Generation-X-and-the-rest* and nobody is Orientalized, primitivized, or exoticized in a traditional manner.

In sum, one sees that until the postcolonial period, Danish and Norwegian writers hold on to a particular national identity when this allows them to claim a privileged relationship with non-European natives or to establish a common ground with their readers. At the same time, they harbor a strong wish to be regarded as cosmopolitan and to partake in a general European or Western discourse. During the Romantic period they attain this by downplaying their Norwegianness or Danishness as travelers abroad, and during the modern period they attain it by establishing intertextual links to the Western literary canon in their writing.

In the case of *L*, the novel's intertextuality is based on both literature and current media and pop culture transgressing national, European, and Western boundaries. Thus, while the modern writers discussed in this book assume their readers' narrative expectations to be formed by the novel, present-day travel writers may regard this as only one source among many, including film, computer games, music videos, and television shows. The modern travelogue's generic Other, then, is the traditional novel, while that of the postmodern travelogue is also reality TV and other global media genres.

Perspectives for Further Research

Notions of the postnational may be held up to Anthony Giddens's theory that the institutions of our globalized world have become "disembedded." Giddens defines the disembedding characterizing late modernity as "the lifting out of social relationships from local contexts and their recombination across indefinite time/space distances."[4] Yet, if we return to Carsten Jensen's cosmopolitan travelogues—in which Jensen hardly discusses Danishness—it appears that Giddens's theories pertain less to the national, language-based institutions supporting Jensen's writing than to its British counterparts. As mentioned in chapter 7, the translation of Jensen's travelogue into English did not result in an international breakthrough. Abroad the author is not known to his reading audience. The marketing of his travelogues in Denmark (and Scandinavia), by contrast, has been local as it has relied on the recognition of his name and face. Thus, in areas speaking less commonly spoken languages, social relations are still rather bounded.

I cautiously insert the adverb "rather" in the preceding sentence because the localized and bounded cannot be taken for granted either. A form of late-modern "disembedding" that *has* left its mark on Scandinavia is the fact that we can no longer assume we are the sole spectators of our own cultural institutions. In Norway, this became obvious when journalist Åsne Seierstad wrote *Bokhandleren i Kabul* (*The Book Seller of Kabul*, 2002/2003). The book was translated into English and the depicted bookseller read it. Suddenly Seierstad was brought face-to-face with her own main character as he had jumped on a plane and flown straight to Norway to confront her.

In Denmark, the "disembedding" of national institutions became even more painfully clear in the case of the Mohammed caricatures. Drawings from a Danish newspaper quickly circulated around the world by means of modern technology. These moments of crisis have further stimulated questions of national and Western identity and positions toward foreign cultures, and they have stimulated questions of *universal* human rights, such as freedom of speech. Interest in the world beyond Europe is growing, and as it does, the issues initially brought on by postcolonialism seem ever more relevant. In what is increasingly regarded as a postcolonial, postmodern, and postnational age of globalization, tracing the literary representations of various cultures allows us to gain a better understanding of present-day East-West relations. As well, working with literature produced on the European periphery allows us to nuance and deconstruct the monolithic paradigms upon which postcolonial theory tends to be based. The Scandinavian countries are often neglected by theorists who equate Europe with the great colonial powers, England and France. Yet, if we take Homi Bhabha's deconstructionist understanding of *peripheries, in-betweenness, hybridity,* and *third spaces* into consideration, we find that not only third-world colonies but also marginalized European countries such as Denmark and Norway can provide a vantage point from which hegemonic discourses may be revealed and deconstructed.

Notes

Unless otherwise indicated, all translations into English are my own.

Introduction

1. The travelogue is based on one of the world's first scientific expeditions. It was initiated by the Academy of Science at Göttingen University, financed by King Frederik V of Denmark, and consisted of six members: the philologist Christian von Haven, the physician Christian Carl Cramer, the botanist Peter Forsskål, the servant Berggren, the illustrator Baurenfeind, and the physicist and mathematician Niebuhr. The expedition left Copenhagen in 1761. Within a couple of years everybody had died except Niebuhr. Niebuhr returned to Copenhagen in 1767, and his travel depictions were published in three volumes in 1774, 1778, and 1837 (posthumously). They were written in German and translated into English, French, Dutch, and now also Danish. For more information on the journey and the travelogues, see Michael Harbsmeier's introduction to Carsten Niebuhr, *Rejsebeskrivelse fra Arabien og andre omkringliggende lande*, 9–32.

2. In his traveling practice and writing style, Carsten Niebuhr is recognized for his honesty and accuracy, both in his own times and today." Frits Andersen, "Felix Arabia." A year and a half later, when the second translated volume was published, Andersen repeats these points in his review, this time suggesting that the travelogue become part of the obligatory Danish literary canon in school. As a unique and ideal figure in the history of travel literature and ethnography, Niebuhr ought to "be included in the canon... assigned the same status as Hans Christian Andersen, whose travels were but excursions focusing on the author himself more than the world in which he lived." Andersen, "Ørkenspejlinger."

3. Bredal, "Hos araberne."

4. Bredal similarly insists that Niebuhr's travelogue may well be the best place to begin for those wishing to understand Islamic people and their culture. His review celebrates Niebuhr's Enlightenment spirit that led the scientist to write straightforwardly, without prejudice, and without generalizations. Ibid.

5. Pratt, *Imperial Eyes*, 4.

6. See, for instance, Billie Melman and Paul Fussell, who cover the periods leading up to and following World War I, respectively. Melman, *Women's Orients*, and Paul Fussell, *Abroad*.

7. Ryall, *Odyssevs i skjørt*, 17.

8. Like Pratt, Said views travelogues as reinforcing Europe's political power. According to him, imaginative and travel literature "strengthened the divisions established by

Orientalists between the various geographical, temporal, and racial departments of the Orient... For the Islamic Orient this literature is especially rich and makes a significant contribution to building the Orientalist discourse" (99).

9. See Bhabha, "The Commitment to Theory."

10. In this equation then, there are three elements: (1) Scandinavia as European periphery; (2) old empires, especially England and France, as European center and metropolis; and (3) non-European countries as the cultural Other. The relationship between the national Self and the non-European Other is thus not a direct relationship, but rather one that is, to a large extent, mediated through the European center. This is a model for which I also argue in *Nordic Orientalism*.

11. Eriksen, "Been There, Seen This."

12. Admittedly, my own study, written in English rather than a Scandinavian language, also constitutes an autoethnographic text. "The Modern Breakthrough" is the name given to the movement of naturalism and debate that replaced romanticism in nineteenth-century Scandinavian literature. Authors during the Modern Breakthrough rebelled against tradition, wrote socially and politically engaged literature, and expressed freer views regarding sexuality and religion as well as a greater interest in scientific developments such as Darwinism.

13. All are Western, except for Ma Jian's *Red Dust: A Path through China* (2002).

14. Cf. Hans Hauge's linking postcolonialism to postnationalism: "Postcolonialism... makes it possible for us to view the Nordic, literary tradition in a new, critical and different way, i.e., at least in a postnational way." Hauge, *Post-Danmark*, 161.

15. Adams, *Travel Literature and the Evolution of the Novel*, 283–84.

16. Carr, "Modernism and Travel (1880–1940)," 74.

17. While Bakhtin relates the birth of the novel to the classical high genres—the epic in particular—Percy G. Adams emphasizes its relation to travel literature. For instance, *Don Quixote*, which serves as Bakhtin's point of departure, may well be read as travel literature.

18. According to Horace Engdahl, publishers do not like hybrid forms: "Consequently, one often places the label novel on something that is not a novel so that it will sell." *Modernismen er død*, Feb. 20–24, 2004.

19. American sociologist Paul Fussell has made the claim that during the 1930s many essay collections were sold as travelogues (204).

20. Lejeune, "The Autobiographical Contract."

21. Pratt explains transculturation as a term ethnographers have used "to describe how subordinated or marginal groups select and invent from materials transmitted to them by a dominant or metropolitan culture" (6).

I. Romantic Journeys to the Orient

1. Hulme and Youngs, "Introduction," 2–3.

2. The Grand Tourist had usually just finished his studies at Oxford or Cambridge University and would leave home for one to five years to polish off his education at

the age of sixteen to twenty. James Buzard dates the Grand Tour as beginning in 1660 and ending in 1840—or more precisely as running "from the Restoration of the British monarchy in 1660 to the accession of Queen Victoria in 1837." Buzard, "The Grand Tour and After (1660–1840)," 38 and 41.

3. The heyday of picturesque travel and travelogues is 1780–1840; ibid., 38.

1. Discovering His Inner Turk

1. Kierkegaard's first book, *Af en endnu Levendes Papirer* (1838), was a review of Andersen's novel *Kun en Spillemand* (Only a Fiddler, 1837).

2. The count varies on this. Poul Houe, for instance, refers to Andersen's fifteen years abroad. Houe, *En anden Andersen–og andres*, 315.

3. "Systematik er ikke denne rejsendes anliggende." Baggesen, "En rendestensunges dannelse," 141.

4. On a more existential note, Lars Handesten notes that at times the buoyant travelogue is interrupted by passages hinting at Andersen's private miseries—caused by unrequited and belittled love, a lack of recognition of his artistic talent, and a great sense of homelessness. Handesten, *Litterære rejser*, 37.

5. Andersen, *En Digters Bazar*, 1:173.

6. "Man har faaet Reisebeskrivelser paa saa mange Maader, men som Dialog troer jeg endnu ikke." Ibid., 1:178.

7. As Helen Carr points out in her article on travel *writing* turning into travel *literature*, Ford Madox Ford has dated the beginning of increased mobility to the 1840s, "a decade in which railway trains were already reaching thirty-five miles per hour." Carr, "Modernism and Travel," 70. In Denmark, the first railroad, which stretched from Copenhagen to Roskilde, opened to the public in 1847.

8. E.g., Nielsen, "'Den menneskelige Kløgt,'" 116–17.

9. "Signalpiben... lyder ikke smukt, den har meget tilfælles med Svinets Svanesang i det Kniven trænger det igjennem Halsen." Andersen, *En Digters Bazar*, 1:42.

10. "I Poesiens Rige ere ikke Følelsen og Phantasien de eneste, der herske, de have en Broder, der er ligesaa mægtig, han kaldes Forstanden." Ibid., 1:44.

11. "Vor Tidsalder er ikke længer Phantasiens og Følelsens, den er Forstandens, den tekniske Færdighed i enhver Kunst og i enhver Haandtering er nu en almindelig Betingelse for deres Udøvelse... Alt Technisk, saavel det Materielle, som det Aandelige er i vor Tid i sin høieste Udvikling." Ibid., 1:36.

12. "Toner jeg ikke kjendte, Toner jeg ei har Ord for, tydede paa Orienten, Phantasiens Land, Digterens andet Fædreland!" Ibid., 1:38.

13. The journey also marks a transitional moment in terms of Andersen's personal history. He had already been on a more traditional Grand Tour educational journey when, in the early 1830s, he spent two years in Rome. Visiting Italy a second time on his way to the Orient tends to evoke a sense of melancholy and weariness. Leaving Italy, he reflects on his disappointment with Italy and his hopes for Greece and the Orient: "Nyhedens duft var borte!... En ny Reise, et nyt Liv maaskee, skulde begynde. Denne

sidste Time var Overgangs-Ledet" (The scent of novelty was gone! ... A new journey, a new life, perhaps, was about to begin. This last hour was the connecting link). Ibid., 1:198. As long as he is still connected to traditional travel itineraries, he struggles internally, seeking to free himself of the reins of duty and to give into his passions and delights instead. Approaching the Orient—on Malta—he depicts himself as feeling ever further transposed into the world of *A Thousand and One Nights* (1:211). The island is a composite of Italy, Africa, and Orient, and among these elements, Andersen longs ever more for the mysterious non-European while expressing his ennui concerning Italian churches and catacombs—the sight of which has "overmættet ham" (stuffed him). Andersen talks of the traveler's tiresome duty to visit those sites described in European books in opposition to his drive towards "de halv tilslørede Bønderqvinder, hvis Øine lynede bag Sløret" (the half-veiled peasant women whose eyes flashed behind their veils). Ibid., 2:216–17.

14. Topsøe-Jensen, "Efterskrift," 235.

15. Baggesen, "En Rendestensunges dannelse," 141.

16. Nonetheless, a look at Andersen's diaries reveals the rationalizing process he had to go through to appreciate the bazaar as a different, but still orderly, representation of the world in miniature. His first visit to the grand bazaar left him in a state of distress, so overwhelmed he had to flee: "Jeg aandede først ret igjen da jeg kom paa Havet" (I was not able to breathe again until I was at sea). Andersen, *Dagbøger*, 195. And Andersen, who was normally very prudent with his money, also found himself buying "Stads" (finery, frills, or simply junk) for a couple of piastres. Four days after his first visit, he returned to the bazaar. His diary then indicates that now that he felt better oriented, the bazaar did not oppress him like it did the first time (202). He was back to his careful spending habits and his meticulous accounting. This time he noted exactly what he bought (two pairs of shoes and a scarf) and how much he paid for it (203). By the time the market experience has been mulled over back in Copenhagen and turned into the Orient chapter's opening section, the narrator unabashedly claims that a stranger in Constantinople should first of all visit the bazaars. *En Digters Bazar*, 2:79.

17. "Thi Industrien og Poesien ere uensartede Størrelser, som ikke lader sig bringe under ens Benævnelse." Quoted in Topsøe-Jensen, "Efterskrift," 242.

18. Politically, travel to Constantinople was made possible by the Tanzimat (the reorganization), Sultan Abdülmecid's Ottoman reform that welcomed Westernization and modernization projects between 1839 and 1876. Military, educational, and governmental reforms were initiated by Mahmud II, but gained in strength when his son Sultan Abdülmecid came to power in 1839. For more about the various reforms, see Lewis, *The Emergence of Modern Turkey*, 80–106. The Tanzimat, in Lewis's words, "established equality of persons of all religions" (107). Not only were Western Christians safe in Constantinople (generally under the protectorate of European consuls), but they were also increasingly free to go sightseeing even in places forbidden to infidels, such as mosques. Melman, *Women's Orients*, 13.

19. "Under mit Ophold i Constantinopel, sluttedes Handelstractaten mellem Hans Majestæt af Danmark og den Ottomaniske Port." Andersen, *En Digters Bazar*, 2:109.

20. "Det var hele vor Conversation. Ingen af os vidste mere; men gode Venner vare vi!" Ibid., 1:236.

21. Earlier in the article, Jens Andersen delivers an equally positive outlook on Hans Christian Andersen's ability to face other cultures without prejudice: "H. C. Andersen was a tolerant traveler. It was formidably easy for him to cross boundaries, as well as religious beliefs and political systems, without any great fear of the foreign. Whereas Denmark and the Danes of our time often have approached Europe, and especially more foreign peoples and religions, signaling their reservations, Andersen repeatedly overstepped this moat between 'us' and 'them' in the 1800s." In his study of Danish travelogues, Lars Handesten passes similar judgment upon the traveler in *En Digters Bazar:* "Andersen is open and for the most part he encounters the modern world, foreign customs, and people quite without prejudice—only the excessively materialistic rituals of the Catholic Church receive some Protestant slaps." Handesten, *Litterære rejser,* 37–38.

22. In his introduction to the 1975 edition of *En Digters Bazar* (2:10), Kjeld Heltoft describes Andersen as "a visual talent—a distinct see-man."

23. "Paa Reisen maa jeg tumle mig fra Morgen til Aften, jeg maa see og atter see! man kan jo ikke bestille Andet end pakke hele Byer, Folkefærd, Bjerge og Have in i Tanken; altid tage, altid gjemme, der er ikke Tid til at synge en eneste Sang!" Andersen, *En Digters Bazar,* 2:158. This depiction does not stand uncontested. While Andersen thus presents his traveling "I" as an active seer in the travelogue, his traveling companion in Italy, H. P. Holst, wrote a letter home accusing Andersen of not observing anything at all: "God knows what he will do in Greece and Constantinople, for it would be difficult to spend time in a more ridiculous manner than he does. He sees nothing, he enjoys nothing, he rejoices at nothing—he does nothing but write." Quoted in Topsøe-Jensen, "Efterskrift," 232.

24. The notion of (European) cosmopolitanism forms the thematic backdrop of Poul Houe's review of Andersen's thirty journeys abroad; Houe, *En anden Andersen—og andres,* 305–63.

25. "Gjenboe kunde magelig ud af sit vindue tage en Priis af Gjenboens Daase." Andersen, *En Digters Bazar,* 2:64.

26. "En forslidt Koffert paa Stylter, hvortil der var heftet en blodig Svanehals." Ibid., 2:66.

27. "Det [digtningen] kommer nok, veed jeg! indeni syder og gjærer det, og naar jeg saa er i den gode Stad Kjøbenhavn og faaer aandelige og legemlige kolde Omslag, saa skyde Blomsterne frem!" Ibid., 2:158.

28. "Her var en lystighed, ganske forskjellig fra hvad jeg havde tænkt mig hos den gravitetiske Tyrk." Ibid., 2:72. That is not to say that the episode erases the notion of the solemn Turk from the traveler's mind. The last image he presents to the reader as he is about to sail away from Constantinople is once again of "den gravitetiske Tyrk, med korslagte Arme;—det var som et Drømmesyn! En scene i et Eventyr!" (the solemn Turk with his arms crossed;—it was like a vision! A scene in a fairy tale). Ibid., 2:114.

29. "Tyrkerne ere de meest godmodige, de ærligste Folk." Ibid., 2:77.

30. "Jeg giver Billedet, som jeg har seet det"; "Men findes her ingen Straale af Poesi i hele dette Uvæsen!"; "Jo, thi jeg husker de store Viinranker, der ved enkelte Huse strække deres tykke Stamme op ad Trævæggen, og brede sig som et Løvtag hen over Gaden til Naboens Huus, som den pynter med sit Grønt!" Ibid., 2:94–95.

31. "Jeg husker den veltilgittrede, høiere Etage, der omslutter Qvinderne og skjuler dem for den Fremmedes Blik! her er poesi!" Ibid., 2:94.

32. "Hvilke Tanker flyve gjennem hans Sjæl -! Ja det er en Tyrk!" Ibid., 2:98.

33. E.g., Folsach, *I Halvmånens Skær*, 81.

34. "Tilhyl ikke de smukke, hvide Qvinder, Du gamle hæslige Karl, dem ville vi just see, driv dem ikke ind i Buret, vi skulle ikke, som Du troer, skade dem med onde Øine!" Andersen, *En Digters Bazar*, 2:83.

35. For more on Andersen's *Mulatten*, see Oxfeldt, "'Han er jo næsten hvid.'"

36. "Han kunde give os en Skildring af Slavindemarkedet, som ikke vi kunde." Andersen, *En Digters Bazar*, 2:83.

37. "Her [ved Bosporus] beiler Orienten til Europa og drømmer sig at være Hersker." Ibid., 2:114.

38. "Danmark havde plantet sit hvide Christikors i Tyrkens Land." Ibid., 2:121.

39. See Folsach, *I Halvmånens Skær*, 80.

40. "Man bør følge Lands Skik eller Land flye." Andersen, *En Digters Bazar*, 2:89.

41. "See ei saa vred paa os, Du gamle Præst, din Gud er ogsaa vor Gud! Naturens Tempel er vort fælles Guds-Huus, Du knæler mod Mekka, vi mod Østen!" Ibid., 2:84–85.

42. "Kirken... drømmer om hiin Skrækkens Nat, da dens Porte bleve sprængte og de christne Altre vanhelligede... hiin Nat, da den forvandledes til en Moskee... Drømmer Du maaske ogsaa frem i Tiden, Aja Sophia! har en Anelse, beslægtet med den der rører sig hos Folket herinde; skulle de udkradsede, christne Kors paa Døren atter fornyes? Skal Altret flyttes fra Hjørnet mod Mekka og indtage igjen sin Plads mod Øst?... Gjennem Kirken runge de Christnes Hymner." Ibid., 2:84.

43. "Hvad kunde det ikke vorde med europæisk Cultur." Quoted in Folsach, *I Halvmånens Skær*, 80.

44. Only once does Andersen come across a situation that prompts him to intervene. On his way home along the Danube he meets a poor peasant boy who seems extraordinarily intelligent, innocent, and noble. Andersen wishes he were rich enough to pay for his education so that he might become an officer rather than a soldier. He ends this chapter with a direct plea to a possible wealthy, Hungarian female reader: "'tænk paa *Adam Marco* ved *Drencova* og hjælp din lille Landsmand frem'" (think of *Adam Marco* at *Drencova* and help your little compatriot advance). *En Digters Bazar*, 2:173.

45. Inge Lise Rasmussen has likewise pointed to the similarities between Andersen's verbal and visual renditions. In a chapter on Andersen's drawings from his first journey to Italy in 1833–34, she writes: "On the other hand, there is a perfect connection between Hans Christian Andersen's own line and verbal art, for instance the same

originality, the same suggestive rhythm and joy at everything visual." Rasmussen, *Øjets sekraft og billedets fødsels*, 130.

46. "Sorte Cypresser og lysegrønne Løvtræer, tittede arabeskartigt frem mellem dette Steen-Hav af mørkerøde Bygninger, hvor Moskeernes Kupler med gyldne Kugler og Halvmaane, hver hvilede som en Noahs Ark; og hvor i hundredeviis de høie, søileagtige Minareter med deres spidse Taarne skinnede mod den graa, skyfulde Luft." Andersen, *En Digters Bazar*, 2:75–76.

2. The Hyphenated Woman

1. The word *broget* translates as "colorful," "multicolored," "diverse," and "mixed." It is a more neutral word for "motley."
2. Jerichau-Baumann, *Brogede Reisebilleder*, 62.
3. In his encyclopedia of Danish painters, Sigurd Müller writes about Elisabeth Jerichau-Baumann that in her older days, she began to write, and that her main work was *Brogede Reisebilleder*. In this text, according to Müller, her narration is "light and sparkly as fireworks, yet consistently obliging, riveting, charming, and everywhere so individually and so artistically creative in the particulars that now, a thorough Danish literary history can hardly be written without Mrs. Jerichau's name being commemorated in it." That, however, is not how things have worked out so far. Müller, *Nyere dansk Malerkunst*, 168–77.
4. Melman concedes that Edward Said somewhat adjusted for his gender blindness in *Culture and Imperialism* (1994). Melman, *Women's Orients*, xxii.
5. "Det bliver altsaa meget brogede Billeder, jeg vil male, og jeg maa forlods bede den strænge Kritik om Forladelse, om Naade endog, ifald jeg hist og her træder lidt over Stregen; thi Ægyptere, Tyrkere, Grækere og Italienere ere alt for forskjellige Elementer, til at de kunne danne en Helhed, undtagen det da skulde lykkes mig at kunne forene dem ligesom Solstraalerne, der jo have samme Udgangspunkt, i ét og samme Brændpunkt, nemlig i kunstnerisk Enhed." Jerichau-Baumann, *Brogede Reisebilleder*, 2.
6. "Denne min Skildring bliver et Spejlbillede af mig selv, jeg er Centrum i det evigt vekslende Kaleidoskop og disse Fremtoninger, hvis Basis, hvis Aarsag og Opfattelse mit egentlige Jeg er: altsaa er det Hele aldeles subjektivt, individualiserende, men arabeskagtigt; det er stedse skiftende Billeder." Ibid., 62.
7. In her chapter "Professional Opportunities for Women in Art and Literature," Reina Lewis writes: "Women whose progressive endeavours might lead us to presume they were personally radical, often emphasized the allegiance to the ideology of the separate spheres—precisely because it deflected attention from their potentially de-sexing cultural activities" (62–63).
8. "Rejsens Maal var jo, foruden at gjøre orientalske Studier, at bringe Skatte til Hjemmet, ellers havde jeg som Moder næppe forladt det i saa lang Tid." Jerichau-Baumann, *Brogede Reisebilleder*, 42.

9. Lewis writes: "To publish for money transgressed all the codes of the separate spheres. Like careers in art or design, women frequently claimed that writing was undertaken in response to dire need, rather than out of personal ambition and often emphasized that writing did not compromise their 'normal' femininity and family responsibilities" (69).

10. With regard to Baumann's maternal role, Marie-Louise Svane has published an interesting article on the artist's sketches and drawings of mother-child motifs. According to Svane, these strongly represent the artist's desire, her autonomous sexuality, her drive to achieve, and her ability to enjoy. In these paintings, the national *stand-ins* (Danish and Roman peasantry) also function as alibis signifying more "natural" sensual feelings. Svane, "Moderkroppen tegner sig."

11. In her description of Danish Orientalism, Birgitte von Folsach, however, places Hans Christian Andersen's *En Digters Bazar* and Elisabeth Jerichau-Baumann's *Brogede Reisebilleder* in the same category: "reality seen through a romanticist-artistic temperament." This category is contrasted with "the romanticist and imaginative depiction." The categorization makes sense based on the notion that the romantic and imaginative depiction is not based on a witness account. The two travelogues, on the other hand, are rooted in an actual encounter with a foreign country. Still, the common categorization of the two downplays what remains vastly different ways of describing the Orient. Folsach, *I Halvmånens Skær.*

12. The only country of interest in this context, according to Dennis Porter, is Holland, where the artificial landscape to a certain extent attracts the aestheticist. Porter, "Modernism and the Dream of Travel."

13. "[Den orientalske kvindes] eneste Betydning er netop den sanselige Tilværelse." Jerichau-Baumann, *Brogede Reisebilleder,* 4.

14. "Det lade, indolente, orientalske Væsen"; ibid., 85. The quotation is taken from a passage in which Jerichau-Baumann discusses national costumes. The red and white colors of the Danish costume frame the Danish peasant girl's fresh complexion perfectly, while, we are told, the Oriental wide and comfortable costume fits the idle, indolent, Oriental being.

15. Evidently Jerichau-Baumann herself does not like blond Jewish girls, but despite her unflattering depiction of them, she is convinced that taste is culturally determined: "Hvad er smukt? Ja, det er relativt. Negerens Ideal er Sort med brede Læber, Kineserens har Griseøjne...Jeg finder, at en skjøn Jødinde bør have sorte Øjne, sorte Haar, blegbrunlig Teint og en Næse, der krummer sig kjækt. Men i Smyrna anses vandblaa Øjne, impertinent blondt Haar, om muligt kruset, og en rød og hvid Teint som Skjønhedsidealet...Mangler efter min mening...'Jeg maa male en Dame med sorte Øjne,' sagde jeg; 'i Europa vilde man ikke tro, at det var en rigtig Orientalerinde, naar jeg malede Dem, med Blondt Haar og lyseblaa Øjne.'" (What is beautiful? Well, that is relative. The ideal of the Negro is black with wide lips, that of the Chinese has pig-eyes...I find that a lovely Jewess ought to have black eyes, black hair, a pale brownish skin and a bold hooknose. But in Smyrna, water-blue eyes, impertinent blond hair—preferably kinky, and a red and white complexion is considered the ideal of beauty...

NOTES TO CHAPTER 2 251

Lacks according to my taste . . . " 'I must paint a lady with black eyes,' I said; 'in Europe one would not believe it was a real Oriental woman if I painted you with blond hair and light-blue eyes.' ") Ibid., 87.

16. Folsach also takes the painted subjects' direct gazes into consideration in her interpretations of Elisabeth Jerichau-Baumann's Egyptian pot sellers. However, her conclusion differs from mine as she sees *En ægyptisk Pottesælgerske ved Gizeh* (1876–78) as exuding innocence, purity, sweetness, and naive grace due to, among other things, her direct gaze. The subject of *Pottesælgerske* (1876), on the other hand, seems "extremely self-assured" (88–89). To me, they both seem extremely self-assured, but stage their exotic seductiveness in two different ways—one through a flirtatious pseudo-naively attentive gaze, the other through an experienced gaze of abandonment.

17. "Raa Latter, Kvindestemmer og Synet af flere Fruentimmer og Soldater." Jerichau-Baumann, *Brogede Reisebilleder*, 46.

18. "Den farligste Situation, jeg nogensinde har været i; vist er det, jeg gik ikke mere paa Menneskejagt i Cairo." Ibid.

19. "De ægte gammeldags, tyrkiske Hanummer, fulgt af sine hvide eller sorte Slavinder." Ibid., 19.

20. "Men Ve Den, der iagttager dem skarpt! Jeg havde nær faaet et Slag i Ansigtet af en af disse barbariske Husmødre." Ibid.

21. " 'Væk med Giauren!' 'Han slaar os ihjel!' " Ibid., 45.

22. "Den ene af Kvinderne lod et Øjeblik det sorte, klare Klædebon synke, fordi det var saa uhyre hedt; hun troede at være ubemærket, og hendes Legemes Skjønhedsfylde aabenbaredes for mig, endmere frembaaren ved det rige, nubiske, frynsede Bælte-Brudesmykke—det Eneste, som Manden, naar han forskyder sin Hustru, er pligtig at give hende." Ibid., 49.

23. "Hun var en mærkelig Blanding af orientalsk og evropæisk Indflydelse." Ibid., 22.

24. "Saaledes vare hendes Bevægelser afrundede, bløde, langsomme, elastiske, og dog tillige snigende og kraftige som en Panthers. Hendes aflange, mandelformede, sortfrynsede Øjne vare lyseblaa, languissante og vilde." Ibid.

25. "Om hun aldrig var bleven berørt af europæisk Kultur." Ibid., 24.

26. "Intetsteds mere end i Orienten neutraliseres . . . de forskjellige Nationaliteters Individualitet, sandsynligvis ved det slappende, til Nydelse indbydende Klima og ved Langsomheden af Forretningsgangen og Samkvemmet med de sløve, demoraliserende, tyrkiske Autoriteter og den sløvede, nedværdigede Befolkning." Ibid., 84.

27. "De [fire jødiske danserinder] drejede sig i Kredse, de omkredsede hinanden, det sænkede Øje flammede af Lidenskab, og om de end stode stille paa et Sted, bøjede og vendte de sig saaledes, at Barmen og hele Overkroppen dirrede. Skjønt Danserinderne havde Klæder paa, hvilket ikke er Tilfældet med de tyrkiske Almedanserinder, saa bare disse Bevægelser i den Grad Sanselighedens Præg, at jeg maatte vende mig bort." Ibid., 91.

28. "Her først følte jeg den østerlandske Kvindes Fornedrelse, der ved Fortid, ved Vane, ja endog ved Lov er bleven hendes anden Natur, hvilket saaledes vel tjener til hendes Undskyldning, men tillige bærer Orientens Demoralisation og Undergang i sit Skjød." Ibid.

252   NOTES TO CHAPTER 2

29. The chapter on Nazili Hanum also contains a personal address to a Madam Bunsen in London, reassuring her that the traveler has not just entertained the women in the harem in silly ways, but also kept in mind "den alvorlige Side" (the serious side) of her visits to the harem (28). Aside from that, I do not conclude that the author and person Jerichau-Baumann necessarily believes in her narrator's rigid, dichotomous notion that men possess one gaze and women another. Rather, these are conventions with which she plays, well aware that both male and female readers read the *entire* travelogue.

30. "Oh Nazili, at måtte vansmægte iblandt Barbarer! Du svulmende Rosenknop, omgiven af Torne, Du, der lever et Drømmeliv om alt det Ubekjendte, om denne Verden, Du aner kun." Ibid., 24.

31. Irene Iversen advocates this view on the literature of the Modern Breakthrough: "Frigjøringen av seksualiteten—og særlig kvinnenes—ble sett som nøkkelen til den sosiale frigjøringen" (Sexual liberation—especially that of women—was considered key to social liberation). Iversen, "Et moderne gjennombrudd," 158.

32. Thus Orientalism is used to serve feminism, the underlying dichotomy of which is man-woman rather than Said's East-West. Zonana dates this discursive strategy back to Montesquieu's *Lettres Persanes* (1721)—the precursor to Mary Wollstonecraft's *Vindication of the Rights of Woman* (1792). Zonana, "The Sultan and the Slave."

33. "'Men, Fru Jerichau, det er slet ikke Deres Sag at dømme politiske Forhold,' hører jeg sige. Nej vist, jeg skal ogsaa nu vedblive med mine Smaanotitser om det Oplevede." Jerichau-Baumann, *Brogede Reisebilleder*, 56.

34. Pratt's "monarchic female voice" is related to her depiction of "imperial stylistics" as laid out here in connection with Hans Christian Andersen in chapter 1. "Imperial stylistics" are discussed primarily in connection with male travelers, but the term also applies to female travelers in a particular, gendered variant: "Through irony and inversion, she [Mary Kingsley] builds her own meaning-making apparatus out of the raw materials of the monarchic male discourse of domination and intervention." Women's travelogues are thus marked by *dominating* comic self-deprecation. Pratt, *Imperial Eyes*, 213, 215.

35. "Mange er komne til at holde af mig herhjemme til Trods for al den Rejseuro, der betegner mit bevægede Kunstnerliv; man har vænnet sig til, at jeg, den ikke dansk Fødte, men Danmark Elskende, mine danske Børns Moder, at jeg, mig selv uafvidende og mod min Vilje, er anderledes end Andre herhjemme." Jerichau-Baumann, *Brogede Reisebilleder*, 149. The artist's intense wish to be accepted and appreciated by Danes clearly informs Nikolaj Bøgh's moving biography, written upon her death in accordance with "Mrs. Jerichau's last will." Bøgh works deliberately and thoroughly to convince his reader of the artist's Danishness and concludes his work with the following pathetic obituary: "Now that she is dead and her true essence emerges ever more clearly, authentically and truthfully, one must say to her: "You were born far from us; but you became as honest a Danish woman as, perhaps, few of our own, and we must almost feel ashamed when we hear your praise of and your love for our country; you shall be inscribed into our history with gratitude because you belonged so passionately to us,

NOTES TO CHAPTER 2   253

with double gratitude because you were born so far from us. On your tomb the beech ought to grow; that would not be but what you had honestly deserved when the Danish flag was finally wrapped around your coffin and lowered with it into our ancient soil. You were a loyal Danish woman!" Bøgh, *Elisabeth Jerichau-Baumann*, 282.

36. Anna Rebecca Kledal discusses the context in which Jerichau-Baumann painted her Orientalist and nationalist motifs in two articles: "Mor Danmark mellem haremskvinder og danske bønder," 9, and "Moder Danmark blandt haremskvinder," 41. Jerichau-Baumann, according to Kledal, painted in the style of the Düsseldorf school and considered herself a cosmopolitan. Folsach likewise writes about Jerichau-Baumann's background, and in this context defines the style of the Düsseldorf Academy as a mixture of realism and romantic idealism judged negatively by Danish audiences of the time (as well as by Folsach herself) as saccharine and pathetic. Folsach, *I Halvmånens Skær*, 83.

37. Ryom, "Folket og de nationale symboler," 31.

38. "Rejsens Maal var jo, foruden at gjøre orientalske Studier, at bringe Skatte til Hjemmet, ellers havde jeg som Moder næppe forladt det i saa lang Tid; *thi der er interessante Motiver nok i Norden*." Jerichau-Baumann, *Brogede Reisebilleder*, 42; emphasis added.

39. "I Italien som i Norden have Naturen og dens Fænomener Alt tilfælleds med Menneskene selv, eller omvendt. I Norden have vi Graavejr, Taage, vedvarende Storm og Kulde ... Og Nordboen er saaledes som den Natur, der betegner hans Hjem; Taagens Melankoli dækker Øjets Stjærne ... Forholdet er ganske anderledes hos Sydboerne og i Syden, dette Lidenskabernes Hjem. Sydboerne ere Lidenskabernes Børn ...; her er de glødende, flammende, futtende op, det bruser ud som Torden og Lynild, og stærke ere Regnskyllene, disse Taarernes Oversvømmelser." Ibid., 65.

40. "Kvinden i Norden ligner Viol og Maidenblush, de ligne Liljekonvaller i Skovens Skygge, de ligne Kornblomsten mellem Rugens Ax, den sødtduftende Kløverblomst, de ligne den lyse Forglemmigej ..., Aakanden ...; men Grækerinden ligner den glødende Granatblomst, den purpurrøde Rose, den mathvide Datura, Giftblomsten ... Orkideernes æventyrlige Blomsterfænomener." Ibid., 37.

41. Hans Christian Andersen also uses Jerichau-Baumann's depictions of Danish motifs to convince his readers of her Danishness. He describes *Danske Bønderbørn legende med Faar* (Danish Peasant Children Playing with Sheep, 1852) as a work that "illustrates how rooted she has become in the Danish soil and how ingeniously she succeeds in grasping and representing the national." Andersen, "Jens Adolf Jerichau og Elisabeth Jerichau, født Baumann," 89.

42. "Kvinderne er det, der gaa forrest i Slaget, naar de først ere fanatiserede; det er Kvinderne der ere Forkæmperne, der ere de farligste Propagandister for nye Idéer, naar de først ere grebne af dem." Jerichau-Baumann, *Brogede Reisebilleder*, 58.

43. "Kongen snakkede da Dansk med mig og talte gemytligt om sit Fædreland, om Hjemmet. Den gode, unge, græske Konge! Han har et stort, trofast, dansk Hjærte!" Ibid., 31.

44. "Det af Kong Otto byggede ... Slot er pompøst og tungt i sine Propositioner og sin Udstyrelse og bærer Præget af den tyske, tunge, sig fordybende Aand ... Man

overraskes ved i Dronningens nyindrettede Gemakker at se sig hensat til Paris; dette skyldes Kong Georgs fine Smag." Ibid., 30.

45. In *Nordic Orientalism*, one of my main theses is that Denmark, in the nineteenth century, turned its attention to Paris in order to construct a national identity perceived as light and French, rather than heavy and German. The focus of the book is the appropriation of French Orientalism into Danish and Norwegian literature and culture.

46. "De skjæggede, kraftige, kjære, danske Mænd, hvoraf saa Mange i Krigens svære Tider havde værnet om gamle Danmark." Jerichau-Baumann, *Brogede Reisebilleder*, 35.

47. "[Jeg] følte mig i Samfund med dem, som vare de mine egne Børn." Ibid.

48. "Saa bringer jeg det da trøstigt her hjem, hvor det Hele har Rod... Og lægger med dybtfølt Hyldest det ned for min Konges Fod!" Ibid., from the dedication.

49. "De Kvinder, der ved at afklippe Haaret tæt som Mandens og bruge Hue, Paletot, Spaserestok og Næseklemmer søge at stille sig lige med det stærkere Kjøn." Ibid., 150.

3. The Ironic Traveler

1. Joseph Conrad's *Heart of Darkness* (1902) is often referred to as a turning point in this connection. See, for instance, Melberg, *Å reise og skrive*, 29.

2. "Er det ikke også temmelig godt gjort å stå med sin fot i selve Tyrkiet? tænker jeg videre. Det er ikke alle som har vist dette mot. Tyrken spiser ikke mennesker mere, neivel. Men tør nogen påstå at han er tandløs? Har nogen anden norsk forfatter våget sig hit til dette land? Goethe reiste engang fra Weimar til Italien; men besøkte han Tyrkiet?... Kortsagt, det er temmelig godt gjort." Knut Hamsun, "Under Halvmånen," 261.

3. The excerpt is from Krag's review of Hamsun's *Sult* (1890) in *Fædrelandsvennen*. Quoted here from Ingebretsen, *En Dikter og en Herre*, 59.

4. Wærp, "Knut Hamsun som reiseskildrer," 254.

5. Loria writes: "But Georgians do not like that Hamsun in his book never focuses on our national identity the way we know it. Neither are Georgian literary academics particularly fond of Hamsun's way of regarding all of the Caucasus as one cultural, homogeneous area. Even in the Georgian capital Tbilisi—which in Hamsun's time had many European features—the main character in *I Æventyrland* only sees what is Asiatic, even only what is Muslim. He mixes Georgian letters with Persian and Arabian ones... For the book's 'I,' the Caucasus is the Orient, the East. The way I see it, he deliberately tries to ignore everything that can connect the area to the West. For instance, he completely ignores that Georgians are Christians with a long church tradition." Loria, "Hamsuns kaukasiske mysterium," 82–83.

6. "Under Halvmånen" was first published in *Aftenposten* in 1903 and later in *Stridende Liv* (1905). See Wærp, "Knut Hamsun som reiseskildrer," 242.

7. By using the term Occidentalism I do not mean a total inversion of Orientalism, which would imply that the power structure between the Orient and the Occident had turned around. Like Orientalism, Occidentalism—as I use the term—occurs on

European conditions. The Oriental does not travel to Europe, Occidentalizing the West. Rather, Europeans have traveled to the Orient and have established a recognizable pattern regarding their preference for sights and activities over time. The Oriental guides have noticed this pattern and use it automatically in their encounter with all Western tourists—without differentiating based on individual difference.

8. "The 'good' Orient was invariably a classical period somewhere in a long-gone India, whereas the 'bad' Orient lingered in present-day Asia, parts of North Africa, and Islam everywhere." Said, *Orientalism*, 99.

9. "Det begynder med at vi ser et par av stormagternes gesandtskapshoteller som dominerer ved sin frie beliggenhet og virker hæslig ved sin grove størrelse og sin kasernestil. Så ser vi minareterne." Hamsun, "Under Halvmånen," 266–67.

10. "[Konstantinopel] er efter Sekler igjen bleven tilgængelig for Europas Kultur. Igjen ere kristelige Huse og Kirker byggede paa de vidtstrakte Brandtomter, der amfitheatralsk hæve sig langs Bosporus's Bredder. Englands, Ruslands, Frankrigs og alle andre Nationers Flag vaje i den klare Luft, hvorpaa de slanke Minareter i Tusindtal og tusindfold saa mange Master tegne sig mod Horizonten . . . Det er et dejligt Syn og alle de her udtalte Tanker hvirvlede om i min Hjærne, da Konstantinopel for første Gang fremtonede for mine Blikke." Jerichau-Baumann, *Brogede Reisebilleder*, 8.

11. See Pratt, *Imperial Eyes*, 204.

12. "Alt hvad vi ser er forskjellig fra hvad vi hadde tænkt os. Er vi ikke i Tyrkiet?" Hamsun, "Under Halvmånen," 13.

13. Hvad er tyrkisk tid?

Jo det skal jeg straks si Dem, svarer han og peker op til fortet. De ser den soldat der, han som går bort til flagstangen? Hold øie med ham.

Soldaten gav sig til å stå ved flagstangen.

Pludselig lyder et signalskudd; soldaten stryker flaget.

Klokken er seks, sier japaneren. Det er solnedgang.

Akkurat midt for vor næse! Just som vi var kommet til fortet! Ibid., 261.

14. "Uret som går, billedet går med, billedet er i virksomhet." Knut Hamsun, *I Æventyrland*, 186. Except where noted, all English translations of this work are from Sverre Lyngstad's translation of Knut Hamsun, *In Wonderland*.

15. Ibid., 83. "En dyp og trollsk verden"; *I Æventyrland*, 214.

16. The episode with the watch may also be read in connection with Hamsun's anti-Semitism. Like the watch, the Jew is portrayed as false and perverse. The fact that Hamsun's narrator comes under his influence may function as an excuse and a strategy of innocence in the sense that being unreliable is cast as being Jewish and/or Oriental. This attitude is further confirmed at the end of the journey when the traveler—on his train journey between Baku and Tiflis—is tricked by a modern Mohammedan Tatar. First the narrator is puzzled, but then he remembers having read that "orientalerne iblandt kan drive det kosteligste narrespil med reisende 'englændere' og vil sig under den lydeligste latter når det går godt" (*I Æventyrland*, 280); "Orientals occasionally play the most priceless pranks on traveling 'Englishmen,' writhing with the most delighted laughter when they succeed" (*In Wonderland*, 170). In the end, the narrator jovially admits,

"Ret betænkt er det nu heller ikke underlig om orientalerne holder sig litt skadesløse for al vesterlændingernes påtrængenhet og nysgjærrighet. Selv holder de det for under sin værdighet å vise forbauselse over nogetsomhelst, mens vi glor på en mærkelig ting, viser hverandre den, gir utrop" (*I Æventyrland*, 280); "And all things considered, it's no wonder that Orientals try to requite some of the importunity and curiosity of the westerner. They themselves consider it beneath their dignity to show surprise at anything whatever, while we gape at unusual things, show them to one another and crow over them" (*In Wonderland*, 170–71). On the one hand, the narrator may be considered Orientalist in an episode like this, as he points out fundamental differences between the Oriental and the Westerner—even as he values the former over the latter in the vein of fin-de-siècle Orientalism. The Oriental's alleged lack of curiosity is viewed favorably as opposed to being regarded as a sign of mental dullness, as it was earlier in the nineteenth century. Yet, while the traveler and the Oriental are portrayed as opposites on the plot level, the author and the Oriental are engaged in the same activity. The text turns Oriental (and not Orientalist) in the sense that it fools readers, telling them things they wish to hear about an Oriental essence that does not really exist.

17. Also there was a tradition of describing Constantinople this way. In *En Digters Bazar*, Hans Christian Andersen similarly divides his depiction of the city into sections on "Bazarerne," "Derwischernes Dands," "Kirkegaarden ved Scutari," and so on (2:79–114).

18. "Hvor sandheten ligger er ikke godt å vite—kanske på grund av at vi har en næsten enstemmig europæisk presse til å fortælle os den. Man blir litt mistænksom. Den andre part som også skulde høres er stum... Bare den ene part taler, taler ustanselig og over hele verden." Hamsun, "Under Halvmånen," 265.

19. Porter's exemplary late-romanticist text depicting a perverse traveler is Flaubert's *Voyage en Orient*, based on Flaubert's journey to the Orient in 1849–51. What makes Flaubert's traveler perverse is not that he establishes sexual relations with prostitutes such as Kuchak Hanem, but rather the extreme consciousness and aestheticist detachment with which he observes his own sexual desires. Porter, *Haunted Journeys*, 165.

20. "Haremet, tænker jeg, fårehyrdens harem! Det er da svært med disse østerlændere hvor de ikke kan la være!" *I Æventyrland*, 217.

21. "Et gromt bælte og både dolk og pistol ved siden." Ibid., 215.

22. "Sæt nu at denne mand hadde villet myrde mig her i min store ensomhet og forlatthet." Ibid.

23. "Jeg vilde ha sprunget på ham og lagt mine labber om hans strupe. Og når jeg hadde kvalt ham næsten ihjæl vilde jeg ha holdt inde et øieblik og git ham leilighet til å angre sit liv. Hvorpå jeg vilde ha gjort det av med ham." Ibid.

24. "Jeg skulde ikke hat meget imot at nogen derhjemme hadde set mig i denne frygtelige kamp med en vild." Ibid.

25. "Et lite galant æventyr til min dagbok." Ibid., 218.

26. "Jeg tænkte mig at det var bedst om jeg til en begyndelse skrev noget til hende. En mand som kunde gjøre så rare kroker på papir vilde hun få estime for. Så kommer indholdet av det jeg vilde skrive, og netop her vilde min overlegenhed seire svært." Ibid., 219.

NOTES TO CHAPTER 3

27. "Det går da sandelig ikke an å lyve så grovt?... Og dit ridt ind i bergene fra Kobi tror jeg heller ikke på." Ibid., 251.
28. Lejeune, "The Autobiographical Contract," 216.
29. "Jeg lægger ruten. For det er dog endnu jeg som har litt å si... Men allerede straks fraviker grækeren min rute." Hamsun, "Under Halvmånen," 294.
30. "Det var ikke kvinderne som så på mig, det var eunukerne... De er mandbiske. De går med hårde svøper... Jeg nærmet mig en skjønhet og så på hende... Pludselig hører jeg en ulyd, en rallen, og en svær eunuk luter sig frem mod mig. Han ser stenhårdt på mig og begynder å tygge med kjæverne. Her er det bedst å være forsigtig! tænker jeg og trækker mig bort." Ibid., 301.
31. "Et brøl svarte mig og eunuken slog svøpen av al kraft i disken." Ibid.
32. "Hun skvat litt da svøpen faldt, men vedblev så å se på varer og pludre. Da forlot jeg hende. Når jeg intet betydde for hende hadde jeg ikke mere der å gjøre." Ibid.
33. Montagu, *The Turkish Embassy Letters*, 128.
34. "Det er sælsomt at vandre herinde, fulgt af Bevæbnede, betragtet med vrede Øine af de Bedende, som vare vi banlyste Aander." Andersen, *En Digters Bazar*, 2:84.
35. "De sat og gjorde sig til og var fraværende i koranstudiet fordi de visste at her var fremmede tilstede." Hamsun, "Under Halvmånen," 274.
36. "Men alle læste. De læste uten stans." Ibid.
37. "Retter sit blik like ind i vore ansigter og læser videre med munden... Jeg glemmer det aldrig. Dette brændende blik kom langt borte fra og gik langt forbi os; da han atter så ned i sin bok hadde han næppe set os. Om vi hadde været et kongepar i al sin stas vilde han ha været ligegyldig for vor nærværelse." Ibid.
38. Claude Lévi-Strauss writes about games; as opposed to rituals, games create inequality: "Games thus appear to have a *disjunctive* effect: they end in the establishment of a difference between individual players or teams where originally there was no indication of inequality. And at the end of the game they are distinguished into winners and losers." Lévi-Strauss, *The Savage Mind*, 32.
39. "Gjæsterne er likesom alle enige om ikke å glo på os." Hamsun, "Under Halvmånen," 241.
40. Henrik Ibsen, "Abydos," 344.
41. "Orientaleren holder det for under sin værdighet å vise nysgjærrighet... Vi turister... Vi vesterlændinger, vi barbarer, hvad angår vi ham?" Hamsun, "Under Halvmånen," 269.
42. "Verdens frelse og fremtidens liv bare i jærnbanebygning og socialisme og amerikansk brøl." Ibid., 311.
43. "Vestens og Østens civilisationer blande sine kilder og muligens bringe en ny kultur til å bruse i levende strømme." Ibid.
44. "Oppholdet i Amerika som gav den unge Knut Hamsun en siste modning og jevnet veien for hans litterære gjennembrudd." Tore Hamsun, "Forord," xi.
45. Knut Hamsun, *Fra det moderne Amerikas Aandsliv*, 17. Henceforth cited in the text as *Amerikas Aandsliv*.

46. "De gode Borgere af den store By kunde ikke forsvare for deres Samvittighed at lade være at glo." Ibid., 122.

47. "Om jeg havde været et vandrende Teater, kunde jeg ikke vakt større Opsigt." Ibid.

48. "I amerikanere synes ikke å være tilfreds med lite. I vil være helt ovenpå. I vil ha overflod. Orientaleren står som motsetning hertil med sin nøisomhet, sin medfødte evne til å undvære." Hamsun, "Festina Lente," 140–41.

49. "Orientalerne forekommer mig at stå høit i etisk visdom. De var fra gammel tid de lykkelige innehavere av tilfredsheten med livet, de smilte til occidentalernes rastløse sprell og bøiet sitt hode i kontemplativ ro, de hadde nok med sitt eget." Ibid., 136.

50. "Sheiken uttrykte da sin tvil om at opfindelsen, reisen, hele ideen var verd den sum av *menneskelig sjel som bruktes på foretagendet.*" Ibid.

II. Modern Primitive Travel

1. Adams, *Travel Literature and the Evolution of the Novel*, 280.
2. Bakhtin, "Epic and Novel," 15.
3. As Bakhtin puts it, "The epic wholeness of an individual disintegrates in a novel" (37).
4. According to Bakhtin, "This is not merely a matter of the author's image appearing within his own field of representation—important here is the fact that the underlying, original formal author (the author of the authorial image) appears in a new relationship with the represented world. Both find themselves now subject to the same temporally valorized measurements, for the 'depicting' authorial language now lies on the same place as the 'depicted' language of the hero, and may enter into dialogic relations and hybrid combinations with it (indeed, it cannot help but enter into such relations)" (27–28).
5. Another important point of generic intersection between fact and fiction is that between the travelogue and the historical document. This difference, too, has been studied. Reflecting upon such studies of comparison, Adams concludes that "the travel writer is much closer to the novelist, for he consistently takes departure from present scenes and events and returns to the past only as those scenes and events guide his thinking" (280–81).
6. Clifford, *Routes*, 66.
7. The pressure arose not only from postcolonialism but also from feminism. As Clifford points out, "The work of feminist scholars has played a crucial role in specifying the social body of the ethnographer" (69).

4. Savage Science

1. See Leif Nedergaard, "Forord til 1. udgave."
2. Bent Haugaard Jeppesen, for instance, writes, "What Johannes V. Jensen thought and felt up until the middle of this century regarding imperialist expansion and the

lacking value and integrity of foreign peoples was—despite the subjective couching—extraordinarily typical for the time." Jeppesen, *Johannes V. Jensen og den hvide mands byrde*, 26. Regarding racism as an integral part of imperialism, Henrik Wivel cites some of Jensen's racist thoughts: "In 'The New World' it is the Negro who comes under fire. As JVJ expresses it, not even 'with the same education will [the Negro, HW] be able to be raised to the level of the white man... His brain capacity only reaches a certain limit... The gorilla drives him out of his clothes.'" In addition, "'The Yellow Danger' states that 'a great... anthropoid ape is buried in every Chinese or Mongolian physiognomy.'" Henrik Wivel, *Den titaniske eros*, 158.

3. "En rejsende i antropologi." Quoted in Nedergaard, "Forord til 1. udgave," 154.

4. "Efter udstrakte Rejser i Østen, Malakka, Kina og gentagne Ophold i Amerika gav jeg Anledning til en Frontforandring indenfor dansk Litteratur og Presse, idet jeg indførte Impulser fra amerikansk, angelsaksisk, Aand, til Afløsning af den hidtil dominerende gallicistiske, dekadente Smagsretning." Quoted in ibid., 591.

5. For more on Jensen's race theories in which he placed his own kind—the Jutlander (linked to the Germanic and Anglo-Saxon)—at the height of human development, see Lars Handesten, *Johannes V. Jensen*, 84.

6. Mary Louise Pratt, *Imperial Eyes*.

7. Lars Handesten, *Litterære rejser*, 73.

8. Ole Egeberg, "Ironiske skraveringer," 92.

9. Johannes V. Jensen, "Udenfor Tiden," 172.

10. See Aage Schiøtz-Christensen, *Om Sammenhængen i Johannes V. Jensens Forfatterskab*.

11. Leif Nedergaard emphasizes its stylistic sources of inspiration, pointing in particular to Heine's *Atta Troll*—viewing *Skovene*, ultimately, as a textual cross between Heine and Hemingway (230–31). This type of scholarship constitutes what Said calls a classical humanist approach: "Most humanistic scholars are, I think, perfectly happy with the notion that texts exist in contexts, that there is such a thing as intertextuality, that the pressures of conventions, predecessors, and rhetorical styles limit [an individual author's creativity]." Edward Said, *Orientalism*, 13.

12. In "Ironiske skraveringer," Egeberg reads *Skovene* with a keen eye to its irony, verbal games, and intertextuality.

13. In *Den titaniske eros*, Henrik Wivel places the travelogue within Jensen's oeuvre that, in its entirety, reveals an oedipal complex. Basing his analysis on Freudian as well as Jungian theories of a collective unconscious, Wivel sees Jensen not only as a particular individual but also as a representative of a new, twentieth-century type of man possessing what he calls an imperialistic consciousness (10).

14. Correspondingly, rather than emphasizing Heine as Jensen's major source of inspiration in *Skovene*, Jeppesen points to Jensen's Kipling fascination and translations into Danish (17, 39, 74).

15. The twenty-two chapters are not numbered in the text, but I have taken the liberty of doing so for the purpose of this description.

16. In analyzing *Skovene* one must also take its complicated history of publication into account. Jensen wrote the first half upon his arrival to Chicago, publishing it separately as "Paa Tigerjagt" (1903). He then revised this part and added the second part in a version called *Skovene,* first published in 1904. The final important benchmark in the history of the publication of the text is 1910. Since this year *Skovene* has been published together with three earlier texts: "Forsvundne Skove," "Dolores," and "Louison"—all from 1899—now published with "Skovene" under the collective title *Skovene.* Read within this overall context, the travelogue takes on a new meaning, not just because it ends up being read against two depictions of Paris, but also because the last text, "Skovene," becomes tied to the first text, "Forsvundne Skove." The latter title recalls the former, and the narrator refers to the same mythical figures in both. In one of the final chapters of "Skovene," the traveler compares his guide, Ali, to Korra. The comparison does not make much sense unless one has read "Forsvundne Skove," an allegory—or myth—about the slave trader Korra. In addition, the word "Korra," figuring at the end of "Skovene," establishes a poetic connection to *Skovene*'s beginning—the very opening word of which is "Korra."

17. "Jeg tærer paa min Galde." Jensen, *Skovene,* 153.

18. "Tid og Rum kendes ikke der, Landet har ingen Historie og er ikke et opmaalt Areal men en Evighed, en *Skov* der er dyb og barbarisk dejlig som det gamle Testamente." Ibid., 99.

19. I am admittedly simplifying in order to make a point, not only about the difference between poetry and prose, but also about the difference between the symbolist's romantic belief in transcendental moments as opposed to Jensen's skepticism. One of the things that complicates this simplification is that "Ekbàtana" is written into the travelogue *Valfart,* consisting of both prose and poetry.

20. "Han tænker som uskyldig Malaj kun paa Elskov og foregaar sit Folk med et Eksempel i det Store." Jensen, *Skovene,* 102.

21. "Vaagner til Bevidsthed i et System af strænge Paragrafer og Paabud, der vokser med ham." Ibid.

22. "Saa er det jo, at Profeten i sin Visdom tillader eller vel endogsaa strængelig paabyder Urskovsture en Gang imellem." Ibid., 103.

23. "Jeg agtede at udforske og bestige *Bukit alam,* skydende Tigre til højre og venstre undervejs." Ibid., 109.

24. "Jeg kunde desværre ikke blive fotograferet ved Afrejsen, fuldt udrustet som jeg stod med min *khaki* Dragt lige fra Skræderen i Singapore og uden en Fold, min Patent Korkhjælm og mine Patronbælter korsvis over Brystet. Men jeg lovede mig selv at lade Haar og Skæg staa oppe i Skovene til Fordel for Interviewerne, naar jeg kom tilbage med Tigerskindet og Rekorden fra *Bukit alam.*" Ibid., 113.

25. "Tigren er Fortætningen af den store Natur, den er Skovenes Sjæl, den er inkarnationen af det *Kvindelige,* jeg vil maale mig med den!" Ibid., 121.

26. In connection with *Skovene,* Henrik Wivel explains, "It is obvious that the colossal drive the Jensenian characters possess, aside from being demonstratively aggressively belligerent, also is regressively femininely submissive. JVJ's drive is reactionary,

seeks back, down, and home to the tender prepubescent relations or to the protective and Edenic, maternal womb. Home in the early and primitive vaginal forests." Wivel, *Den titaniske eros*, 81.

27. "Oh, mine Snobber og Monomane, tænkte jeg, mens jeg sad i Alis Baad, og Middagsheden og Rejsens Feber og Fart havde gjort mit Hoved stort. Oh ho, I smaa Sjæle, her kommer en anden Slags Tigerjæger!" Jensen, *Skovene*, 121.

28. "Her var jeg nået så vidt, at jeg havde smidt Bukserne og anlagt *Sarongen* ligesom de andre Skørtemennesker omkring mig, der bekendte Islam! Jeg skammede mig for de to Hvide, skammede mig som en kristen Hund over mit østerlandske Kostume." Ibid., 203.

29. One of Handesten's main points is that for Johannes V. Jensen religion is a thing of the past—of the traditional, not the modern world. What has come to substitute for the old institution of the church is traveling. Traveling becomes a modern ritual (*Litterære rejser*, 88–89).

30. The lengthy depiction of the *makan besar* and its consequences indicates its importance to the narrative. It takes up six of twenty-two chapters—and half of the chapters that are set in the forest.

31. "Whiskyen indvirkede saadan paa Matti og mig, at vi steg ned til det lavere Trin, paa hvilket Aoaaoa og Lidih befandt sig, og Kaffen hævede dem op til os; vi mødtes i en Stemning, der henholdsvis ikke var vor egen og altsaa frisk for begge Parter. Vi byttede paa en Maade Køn, og det var rigtig godt." Jensen, *Skovene*, 173.

32. "Malajen har en Tilbøjelighed til at gaa amok i alle Ting... Jeg tror, denne Tilbøjelighed til at gaa amok skyldes en Ophidselse af Musklerne, det er en Art Kødrus, en Overophedning af Muskulaturen. Malajerne er de kødfuldeste Folk i Verden, de er faste som Buldogge, Kødet trænger sig paa deres Krop. Deres Livsfølelser er derfor nærmest bestemt af det Kraftindtryk, de faar af sig selv; deres Muskler er i Stand til at tage Magten fra dem." Ibid., 114–15.

33. Jensen has actually claimed to be connected to "the instinctual world" of Mongolian Malays, Asians, and Indians on his mother's side. Handesten, *Johannes V. Jensen*, 84.

34. "Tredive umættelige seende Malajer... [dirre] af Tyndhudethed, af Ensomhedsfølelse, af Raseri og Smærte." Jensen, *Skovene*, 138.

35. For further discussion of the schizophrenic scientist, see Kirsten Hastrup, *Viljen til Viden*, 143–46.

36. "Hendes Træk taler ikke for hende, Næsen er brak og bredt ud i et Par store Vige med aabentstaaende Lugtehuller, og Munden er en Flab uden personlig Form. Men dette Ansigt af lav Type er som skabt af Farver i dunkle og underfulde Toner... Grundfarven er glødende brun som rent Kobber, der i Skyggerne ved Næsen og om Øjenlaagene fortoner sig som Bronce og Tin, og de store Læber er lyst skiferfarvede. Tænderne indenfor er røde som Ild af Betel. Frem af disse Farver, der er fuldkomne i Renhed og Lys, træder Aoaaoas Blik fra sortebrune Øjne med en Hvide, der i sin Friskhed næsten er blaa som Himlen. Og bag de violette Øren og om den fulde teglfarvede Hals strømmer det tykke stenkulsorte Haar. Hun sidder ned paa sin ene Lænd med Fødderne trukken op til sig, haarde og tørre Vandrefødder, paa hvis ene brune Taa hun bærer en Sølvring

med en grøn Sten. *Sarongen, der indhyller hendes lange skønne Hofter og slutter tæt over den smalle Mave er af simpelt grønblomstret Kattun, og Overkroppen med det haardføre Bryst dækkes af et svovlgult Skærf.*" Jensen, *Skovene*, 166–67.

37. "Sammen og i og med hende ... faa de svundne Tider, som jeg havde begrædt, tilbage, Ægyptens solrøde Døtre, Biblens messingfarvede Jomfruer, de blaa Piger fra Palmyra." Ibid., 167.

38. "Objektet er trådt i baggrunden til fordel for den subjektive oplevelse i en fetichagtig dyrkelse." Ole Egeberg, *Ironiker og troubadour*, 57.

5. Humor, Gender, and Nationality

1. Knud Sørensen, "Om sproglig interferens i *Den afrikanske Farm* og *Out of Africa*," 297.

2. For the sake of convenience I will refer to the author and her work only in English (i.e., as Isak Dinesen and *Out of Africa*) throughout most of this chapter. However, in sections where I discuss discrepancies between her Danish and English versions, I will distinguish between *Den afrikanske Farm* and *Out of Africa*.

3. After the publication of *Breve fra Afrika* (1978), scholars were particularly eager to point out inconsistencies between the two texts. See Tone Selboe, *Kunst og erfaring*, 33–35.

4. Nina Johnsen, "Poesi, etnografi og sandhed," 78.

5. James Clifford, *Routes*, 67.

6. Ngũgĩ wa Thiong'o, "Her Cook, Her Dog," 133 and 135. This article was first published as "A Tremendous Service in Rectifying the Harm Done to Africa," in *Bogens Verden* (1980). In his "prison diary," Thiong'o portrays Dinesen as an arrogant aristocrat using Africa as an "erotic dreamland" in which "her several white lovers appeared as young gods and her Kenyan servants as usable curs and other animals" (quoted in Selboe, *Kunst og erfaring*, 47). As Susan Hardy Aiken points out, Thiong'o's attitude may be politically correct from a postcolonial point of view, but it certainly is not from a feminist point of view. Thiong'o, among other rather insulting deductions regarding Dinesen's life, presence, and status in Africa, reduces her authorship to a consequence of barrenness. Aiken, *Isak Dinesen and the Engendering of Narrative*, 311–12.

7. Specifically, JanMohammed points to Dinesen's having likened her loathing of carrying an identification card during the Nazi occupation of Denmark with the hatred of squatters' having to carry the *Kipandi* (a passbook).

8. See Selboe, *Kunst og erfaring*, 37.

9. In referring to the work's mythical quality I am thinking specifically of Dinesen's striking creation of a timeless place. While she is precise in mentioning prices and mountain heights, she clearly avoids years. One pattern is that she refers to "my time"; another is that she will cite documents with specific dates—e.g., Ngong, September, 26th—but omit the year.

10. Isak Dinesen, *Out of Africa* and *Shadows on the Grass*, 22.

11. Tone Selboe, *Karen Blixen*, 12. According to JanMohamed, Isak means laughter (77).

12. "Han maa have tænkt: Hvilken lang Række Uheld! Hvor det dog gaar op og ned for mig! Han maa have undret sig over, hvad Meningen vel kunde være med alle hans Prøvelser, han kunde ikke vide, at det var en Stork. Men gennem hele sin Lidelseshistorie holdt han sig sit Formaal for Øje, intet fik ham til at vende om og gaa hjem, før han havde faaet sit Arbejde gjort. Han fuldførte Løbet og bevarede Troen. Den Mand fik ogsaa sin Belønning, om Morgenen saa han Storken. Da maa han have leet højt." Karen Blixen, *Den afrikanske Farm*, 195–96. Throughout this chapter, I will quote *Out of Africa* in the main text and *Den afrikanske Farm* in the endnotes, except in cases that call for a direct comparison in the main text.

13. The laughter produced is a result of the absurdity that life's meaning should somehow be a stork. This approaches the immature type of humor Søren Kierkegaard depicts as the humorist finding "a humorous alleviation in asserting the absurd, just as it can be alleviation to parody the meaning of life by paradoxically stressing the trivial." Kierkegaard, *Concluding Unscientific Postscript to Philosophical Fragments*, 292. As Aiken shows, though, it is also possible to interpret the stork as meaningful—as a "mythic sign of life and generativity" (Aiken, 245).

14. *Out of Africa* is based on the experience of losing the farm, which in turn generates the *story* about the farm, so that experience is transformed into art. Selboe, *Kunst og erfaring*, 34. "The incomplete and failed parts of life become complete and successful in fiction." Ibid., 38.

15. Bo Hakon Jørgensen similarly emphasizes the "later on" *(siden hen)* of Dinesen's poetics, relating it to a three-phase process: the experience, the overview, and the interpretation. Jørgensen, *Siden hen—om Karen Blixen*, 131. "Seeing the stork," for Dinesen, generally means seeing the pattern through which meaning is produced retrospectively (118). The moment of retrospection usually occurs several years later (118), but as Jørgensen points out, Dinesen, in her private correspondence, may also be found confessing to being obsessed with this "later on," worrying that it will not occur at all (129).

16. In Denmark the romantic notion of humor was influenced by Jean Paul, Friedrich Schelling, Friedrich Schlegel, and Karl Solger. Poul Lübcke, *Politikens filosofileksikon*, 197.

17. Kierkegaard, *Concluding Unscientific Postscript to Philosophical Fragments*, 291.

18. These transitional stages *(eksistensmuligheder)* are deduced and constructed based on *Afsluttende uvidenskabelig Efterskrift* (the earlier three on *Enten-Eller*). Lübcke, *Politikens filosofileksikon*, 238. See also Jens Himmelstrup, *Terminologisk Ordbog*, 86–89.

19. Søren Kierkegaard, The Concept of Irony, 329. In this context, Dag Heede's dissertation on Dinesen's "inhumanity" *(umenneskelighed)* forms an interesting parallel to Kierkegaard's view of the humorist. In *Det umenneskelige*, Heede argues that Dinesen's oeuvre at its very core remains antihumanist and antianthropocentric. In

decentering the human being, her texts have continuously disturbed and provoked the modern, bourgeois reader, prompting a huge biographical interest. Heede sees this tendency to constantly read Dinesen's texts in relation to her real life as symptomatic of the reader's refusal to accept Dinesen's fundamental antibourgeois antihumanism: "This 'humanizing' biographism I regard as an invocatory infringement on main efforts in the Blixenian texts... For the individual or the human being is by no means the basic unit or building blocks in her narratives... The Blixenian texts are not 'humanistic literature.'" Dag Heede, *Det umenneskelige*, 24. From a nineteenth-century Christian point of view, Kierkegaard then regards the humorist's deanthropocentric effort as a step that could have led to a theocentric worldview, but instead—tragically—places the human being in the role of God. Dag Heede, on the other hand, from a twenty-first-century postmodern point of view, celebrates Dinesen's deanthropocentric effort, seeing it not as potentially placing the human being in the role of God but as positing a decentered worldview in which our lives revolve around an empty center. Regarding this from a romanticist, philosophical point of view, I am arguing that what is placed at the center of this worldview is not human individuality but rather human relations and sociability.

20. "The humorist makes the deceptive turn and revokes the suffering in the form of jest." Kierkegaard, *Concluding Unscientific Postscript*, 447.

21. Kierkegaard, *Concluding Unscientific Postscript*, 271.

22. "'Ophængt paa Korset, nedtaget og begravet, nedfaret til Helvede, paa den tredie Dag igen opstanden, siddende ved Guds, den Almægtiges højre Haand, hvorfra han skal komme at dømme Levende og Døde.'" Blixen, *Den afrikanske Farm*, 196.

23. "Hvor det gaar op og ned, mere frygteligt endnu end for Manden i Historien. Hvad kommer der ud af det? Den anden Artikel i den halve Verdens Trosbekendelse." Ibid.

24. According to Harald Høffding's view of the humorist, this attitude toward the religious is typical: "As to the humorist, he will hardly be very concerned with whether people call him religious or not. He might have a humorous attitude towards the various attempts at stating what religion 'actually' is." Høffding, *Den store Humor*, 110.

25. The verse is Sully Prudhomme's: "...d'humbles marionnettes / Dont le fil est aux mains de la Nécessité." Bergson, *Laughter*, 75.

26. In *Det umenneskelige*, Heede too focuses on Dinesen's view of humans as marionettes: "The marionettes are used as a strategy both to point out the fictionality of the fiction and as an anti-anthropologizing technique" (236). Yet, while Heede reads the use of marionettes as an example of Dinesen's texts' antihumanism preventing the reader from identifying with the text's characters (235–36), I regard it in the light of humor and comedy, the function of which is that the reader does identify with the characters, achieving on the one hand a sense of self-deprecation and on the other a sense of community as he laughs at the comical with (imagined) fellow readers.

27. "Somali-Humor." Blixen, *Den afrikanske Farm*, 94.

28. For instance, at a ngoma, a song is performed for the old Kikuyu women: "The toothless bald old Kikuyu wives...nodded their heads...[They] beat their thighs, and

threw up big gapes, like crocodiles, at it." Dinesen, *Out of Africa*, 174. "De gamle tandløse og skaldede Kællinger... lyttede med stor Tilfredshed til Sangen og nikkede og smaskede til... De... klaskede sig paa Laarene og slog store glade Gab op." Blixen, *Den afrikanske Farm*, 133.

29. "Deres Ansigter med de høje Kindben og frækt svungne Kæbeben er polerede, svulne, uden en Fure eller Fordybning, deres dunkle Øjne, der intet ser, er indlagt i Ansigtet som to mørke Stykker Sten i en Mosaik." Ibid., 109.

30. This, according to *Den afrikanske Farm* in which they "humper og kravler" (32). This more nuanced depiction of their way of walking is omitted in *Out of Africa*.

31. "Hvorsomhelst man gik gennem Kikuyuernes Shambaer var altid det første, man fik Øje paa, Bagpartiet af en lille, gammel Kikuyu-Kone, der stod og rev og stak i Jorden som en Struds med Hovedet gemt i Sandet." Blixen, *Den afrikanske Farm*, 14.

32. "Saa at de gamle Kvinder var humpet og kravlet den lange Vej til Huset, som de selv siger *buri, omsonst.*" Ibid., 32.

33. "De gamle, indfødte Koner... har blandet Blod med Skæbnen og [genkender nu] dens Ironi, naar de møder den, som om det var en Søsters." Ibid., 7.

34. "Denne Hændelse var sidenhen en Kilde til megen Glæde for de Gamle selv. Undertiden, naar jeg mødte en af dem paa en smal Sti i Majsmarken, stod hun brat stille overfor mig, stak efter mig med en kroget tynd, sort Finger, og med det gamle mørke Ansigt opløst i Latter, saa at alle Rynkerne blev trukket sammen i det, som om de var fæstet til en enkelt, hemmelig Snor, der blev strammet, paakaldte hun Mindet om den Søndag, da hun og hendes Medsøstre i Tombacco havde gaaet den lange Vej op til Huset og der havde faaet at vide, at jeg havde glemt at købe Snus, og der var ikke et Gran—'Ha, ha, Msabu.'" Ibid., 32.

35. "Stod ud paa ham som Knaster paa en Stok." Ibid., 23.

36. "I Køkkenet og den kulinariske Verden havde Kamante alle de Egenskaber, som kendemærker et Geni, lige til Geniets Forbandelse." Ibid., 34.

37. "Hans lille spottende Latter, som blev gjort Brug af under alle Livets Forhold, var ganske særlig rettet mod andre Menneskers Selvtillid." Ibid., 31–32.

38. "Han havde en lille, spottende Latter fuld af Foragt og bedre Viden, som han gjorde Brug af overfor de andre syge Børn." Ibid., 26.

39. "Det var umuligt at tro andet, end at [storken] med Vilje efterlignede hans stive, afmaalte Gang. Deres Ben var omtrent lige tykke. De smaa Vogterdrenge havde Blik for Parodi og skreg henrykt op, naar de to gik forbi dem, og Kamante forstod godt deres Mening." Ibid., 53–54.

40. "'I Kikuyuer er saa fjantede, at I er bange for at røre ved en død Mand,'" but "Kamante slog sin lille lydløse Latter op. 'Du glemmer igen, Msabu,' sagde han, 'at jeg er Kristen.'" Ibid., 52.

41. "Længe efter havde Kamante Fornøjelse af at tænke paa dette Udslag af min Ukyndighed. Han kunde gaa og arbejde i Køkkenet ligesom fyldt med en hemmelig Glæde og pludselig le: 'Kan du huske, Msabu,' sagde han, 'dengang du havde glemt, at jeg var Kristen og troede, at jeg var bange for at hjælpe dig at bære *Msungu Msei,* den gamle hvide Mand?'" Ibid., 52.

42. A further indication that Dinesen feels included through the Kikuyus' humor arises with the Kikuyu women's giving her the Kikuyu name Jerie. Nobody explains to Dinesen why this name is chosen for her, but Dinesen imagines that is an outcome of an inclusive sense of humor. Jerie is the name a Kikuyu gives to a child born long after its siblings: "I suppose that the name has a note of affection in it." *Out of Africa*, 396. "Jeg tænker mig, at Navnet har en særegen, venlig eller spøgefuld Klang." *Den afrikanske Farm*, 294.

43. Kirsten Thisted, "Dead man talking," 110. In *Isak Dinesen and the Engendering of Narrative* (1990), Susan Hardy Aiken similarly bases her reading of *Out of Africa* on Dinesen's shifts in perspective. Like Thisted, she hails Dinesen's sensitivity to the Africans' "art of mimicry," her likening it to her own stance and writing, and her attempt to view herself from the Africans' point of view. The grand example of Dinesen's anticolonialist inversion is her early description of her farm's squatters culminating in her admittance that they, most likely, regarded her "as a sort of superior squatter on their estates" (10) ("som en stormægtig Squatter paa deres eget Land") (*Den afrikanske Farm*, 14). As Aiken points out, Dinesen's viewpoints may be viewed as commendably anticolonialist at the same time as they are made possible only by a political system of colonization: "She evokes alternative ways of seeing and being that ultimately subvert the politics and poetics of the very systems which, paradoxically, had made *Out of Africa* possible" (216).

44. All translations of Høffding into English are my own.

45. "Ali was an old dry Malay with bitter eyes without a penny's worth of jump to his body. His grey chest looked like an old burned-out gridiron with ashes between its bars, and his stomach was as dried up as a rubber ball" (Ali var en gammel tør Malaj med sure Øjne og ikke for to Øre Kild i Kroppen. Hans graa Bryst lignede en gammel udbrændt Kulrist med Aske mellem Stængerne, og hans Mave var saa indtørret som en Gummibold). Johannes V. Jensen, *Skovene*, 111.

46. "Havde de to Malajer da ført mig i en Rundkreds og ikke, som jeg hele Tiden antog, lige ud? Havde Ali, Ali den Hellige, indblæst dem dette Raad som det sundeste baade for dem og for mig? Jeg forskede i deres Miner; de saa fromme ud men kunde kun med en vis Udtryksløshed møde mit Blik... Meget vel. Der havde jeg altsaa, lod det stærkt til, gaaet i flere Timer—for mig en Menneskealder—med Livet i Hænderne som gratis Forlystelse for to Malajer overlegne i Forstillelseskunst... Jeg følte mig som taget i Munden af højere Magter og igen spyttet ud." Ibid., 154–55.

47. "Ironikeren... mener at have indset hulheden i det æstetiske stadie, men har ikke tiltro til, at den etiske alvor kan løse problemet. Med bidende hån og intellektuel skarphed kan han derfor kritisere (ironisere over) alt og alle—inklusive sig selv. Han har et godt humør—men ingen humor." Lübcke, *Politikens filosofileksikon*, 240.

48. Mary Louise Pratt, *Imperial Eyes*, 214.

49. "The quote is from *Den afrikanske Farm* and does not appear the same way in *Out of Africa*: "Det kan også være, at..." (258).

50. I take this to be Dinesen's interpretation, although she does not mention the

word *tisa* (Selboe, *Kunst og erfaring*, 57). *Tisa* resembles words for peeing and penis in Danish and Norwegian, but not—as far as I have been able to find out—in Swedish.

51. "Tanken om dette System beskæftigede mig i lang Tid og voldte mig stor Glæde. Her har vi da, tænkte jeg, endelig engang et Folk, som har Mod og Fordomsfrihed til at bryde med vor egen Talrækkes ældgamle Pedanteri." Blixen, *Den afrikanske Farm*, 212.

52. "Men jeg har endnu paa Følelsen, at der eksisterer et indfødt Talsystem uden Tallet ni, som gaar meget godt, og ved hvis Hjælp man kan finde ud af mange Ting." Ibid.

53. Reading the anecdote "Natives and Verse" as a mise-en-abyme, Selboe arrives at a similar conclusion: "'Natives and Verse' may be read as a poetological commentary on *Out of Africa*: in poetry and art, the poetic is superior to the substance of truth, and it is in the sound, in the form, that the poetic is located." *Kunst og erfaring*, 56.

54. "'Din *Kabilla*—din Stamme—bliver ikke saa vrede som andre Mennesker fra Europea,... I ler ad Folk.'" (279) The statement, as I will discuss in further detail, is omitted in *Out of Africa*.

55. "'Ja, vi tør ikke andet,' sagde jeg, 'vi har en gammel Bwana, som har lært os det, og som holder os i Orden. Der staar han paa Hylden.'" Ibid. As mentioned in the preceding note, this is omitted from *Out of Africa*.

56. Many Danes before Dinesen have regarded humor as a particularly Danish national trait, aligning the Danish with the French—in opposition to the Germans. Johan Ludvig Heiberg, too, traces Danish literary humor back to Holberg's importation of French comedy. In "Digter-Misundelse," for instance, he explains that Holberg has founded "our" (Danish) literature upon a French pattern. Ever since, Danish literature has been characterized by French simplicity, expressing ever greater sympathy toward France and greater antipathy toward Germany. This trend, says Heiberg, is recognizable "by the fact that the comic remains more national in Denmark than the tragic, whether this be caused by the original Holberg-provided impulse, or by the fact that he had correctly perceived the national in us." Heiberg, "Digter-Misundelse," 403–4.

57. "Ismail sagde engang til mig: 'Jeg kan se, at denne Dusk er af samme Stamme som du selv, han ler ad Folk.'" Blixen, *Den afrikanske Farm*, 59.

58. Several readers have pointed to the in-between position into which Dinesen enters. Selboe, for instance, notes that "the colonial roles are simultaneously exploited and negated" and that Dinesen "assumes a position between the whites' [the Englishmen's in particular] dry scientific character and the blacks' magical or mythical world comprehension," concluding that "the I cultivates the role of the outsider." Selboe, *Kunst og erfaring*, 44.

59. As to Oehlenschläger's theories on the attraction between opposite races, see his prologue to *Aladdin* (1805). For an analysis of the drama's Orientalism, see Elisabeth Oxfeldt, *Nordic Orientalism*, 21–54.

60. "Der er... en Forelskelse i Syden og de sydlige Folkeslag, som er Nordboernes Kendemærke." Blixen, *Den afrikanske Farm*, 19.

61. "Var korte for Hovedet, naar det gjaldt deres eget Klima og deres egen Familie, men de tog imod den afrikanske Tørke, de farlige, martrende Solstik, mod Rinderpest

i deres Hjorder og mod deres indfødte Tjeneres Uerfarenhed, med Ydmyghed og Resignation." Ibid.

62. "Selve deres Følelse af Individualitet gik tabt i Forstaaelsen af de uendelige Muligheder, som findes i Samspillet mellem Mennesker, der kan blive eet i Kraft af selve deres Væsensforskel. De sydlandske Folkeslag har ikke denne Egenskab, og den findes heller ikke hos Folk af stærkt blandet Blod." Ibid.

63. Knud Sørensen has this information from Ole Wivel; Sørensen, "Om sproglig interferens i *Den afrikanske Farm* og *Out of Africa*," 297.

64. All translations of Sørensen into English are my own.

65. For the sake of consistency I will continue the pattern of referring to the author as Dinesen in this chapter, letting the title of the book indicate whether I am talking about the Danish text penned by Blixen or the English text penned by Dinesen.

66. "Det var en Fornøjelse baade for ham og mig at tale Dansk, saa vi udvekslede mange Betragtninger om Begivenhederne paa Farmen, bare for at kunne udtrykke os i vort eget Sprog." Blixen, *Den afrikanske Farm*, 49.

67. "En Tid havde jeg en Stork med en knækket Vinge i Huset. Jeg fik Hjemvé af at se paa den, den saa ud, som om den hørte til i Danmark." Ibid., 53; the last sentence in text is my translation.

68. "Det var som en regnvejrsdag i Danmark." Ibid., 272.

69. Carrying out a similar translation study three years later, Elias Bredsdorff also concludes that "her command of Danish was much better than that of English... She was at home with the Danish language in a way she was not at home with English... Karen Blixen was completely at ease when she wrote in her own language." Bredsdorff, "Isak Dinesen v. Karen Blixen," 292.

70. "Var humpet og kravlet den lange Vej til Huset." Blixen, *Den afrikanske Farm*, 32.

71. "Et Tegn af Skæbnen." Ibid., 283.

72. "Stod et Øjeblik, som om den var forlegen og betænkte sig. Saa slog den rask og beslutsom sit Næb ned som en Hammer, og plukkede Kamæleonens Tunge ud." Ibid.

73. As an allegory, the story also indicates the chameleon-like aspect of Dinesen's identity as a person who constantly attempts to fit in. This in turn relates to her different ways of addressing an Anglo-Saxon and a Nordic reading audience. Many other scholars have looked at her chameleon-like qualities in relation to various aspects of her life and authorship: her change of pseudonyms, her relation to men (chameleon vs. cock), her assuming an authorial voice at all (the theme of tongue and voice). See Jørgensen, *Siden hen—om Karen Blixen*, 16–17, 84–85.

74. "Vældige Magter havde leet ad mig, eller til mig, med et Ekko fra Højene." Blixen, *Den afrikanske Farm*, 284.

75. Høffding found that Kierkegaard underestimated humor, a viewpoint that may very well represent that of Dinesen as well (47, 135). Building on Kierkegaard's discussion of humor as a worldview, Høffding traces its origins back to Socrates. He also mentions Bergson, but only in a sentence, indicating that he is less interested in the social function of humor than in its psychological and philosophical functioning (90). While Kierkegaard studies humor in relation to religion and Bergson studies the comic

object, Høffding's object of study is the laughing subject. We might say that Kierkegaard's approach is religious, Bergson's tends toward the phenomenological and sociological, and Høffding's towards the psychological.

76. All translations of Høffding into English are my own.

77. "Den gensidige Illusion." Blixen, *Den afrikanske Farm*, 205. The sentence is not included in *Out of Africa*.

78. "Det virkelige Aristokrati i Verden, og det virkelige Proletariat, de er begge i Forstaaelse med Tragedien og dens Idé. Den er for dem selve Guds Plan med Verden, og Livets Toneart. Heri adskiller de sig fra det Bourgeoisie af alle Klasser, som fornægter Tragedien og grumme nødig finder sig i den, og for hvem det tragiske er ensbetydende med det triste i Verden eller med dens Ubehageligheder. Mange Misforstaaelser imellem de hvide Nybyggere af Middelstanden og de Indfødte kom af dette Forhold. De mørke tvære Masaier var baade Aristokrati og Proletariat." Ibid., 159.

79. Bergson, too, recognizes the humorist as a split individual: "When the humorist laughs at himself, he is really acting a double part; the self who laughs is indeed conscious, but not the self who is laughed at." Bergson, *Laughter*, 132.

80. Aristotle, *On Poetry and Style*, 24.

81. "En Spøg, eller en Skaal Tembu, fik med det samme deres rynkede, tandløse Ansigter til at opløses i Latter." Blixen, *Den afrikanske Farm*, 294.

82. "Kraft, og store Kærlighed til Livet, var for mig ikke alene højst agtværdig, men storartet og fortryllende. Jeg og de gamle Koner havde altid været gode Venner." Ibid.

83. "Taarerne strømmede ned over hendes Ansigt." Ibid., 295.

84. "Hun stod som en Ko, der lader Vandet paa Sletten foran En." Ibid., 295.

6. The Traveler and the Tourist

1. Svein Johs Ottesen, "I tannhjulposisjon til verden."

2. Jan Christian Mollestad, *Trollmannen i Ålefjær*, 97–100.

3. "Så hele denne reisen i 'Ikaros', hvor det bare er én mann, den var vi virkelig to om. Men sånt var for komplisert å beskrive. Per måtte vekk." Ibid., 40. The facts surrounding the journey remain a bit nebulous as Axel Jensen told different versions at different times. In an interview immediately following his debut, he claims to have traveled to Baghdad, Arabia, and Africa with two Swedes. Tom Eide, *Outsiderens posisjoner*, 98.

4. "I 'Ikaros' er det jo meg selv som forteller og fabler mellom sannhet og fantasi." Mollestad, *Trollmannen i Ålefjær*, 12. Jensen found his narrative inspiration in Colin Wilson's *The Outsider*, a work that showed Jensen how to combine the depictions of an inner and an outer journey. Mollestad, *Trollmannen i Ålefjær*, 57.

5. Jensen's kinship with Hamsun has traditionally been noted in terms not of the travelogue genre, but of Jensen's stylistics. *Aftenposten*'s critic, Rolf Nettum, for instance, notes "an expression of a Hamsunian tone, a strange adjective, may occur to his pen... but it does not suit him poorly." Other critics find Jensen's Hamsun style more annoying: "The touches of Hamsun in his style can also be annoyingly obvious." Quoted in Audun Tvinnereim, "En norsk femtitallsroman," 132.

6. Axel Jensen, *Ikaros*, 47. Unless otherwise noted, all English translations are from Maurice Michael's translation. Jensen, *Icarus*, 52.

7. Ole Wivel, "Fem brød og to fisk," 105.

8. Interview with Axel Jensen: "Ikaros på flukt til Delfi—i brukt bil." Tom Eide, in particular, emphasizes Jensen's project in relation to the author's interest in Jungian individuation. *Outsiderens posisjoner*, 51.

9. Tom Eide first listed Axel Jensen's main foreign sources of inspiration as Jungian psychology, the teachings of Gurdjieff and Ouspensky, Oriental mythology and mysticism, the European esoteric tradition, and European mythology. Eide, "Kulturkritikk og utopisme." In his dissertation on the early part of Jensen's authorship, Eide furthermore emphasizes Norwegian psychiatrist Arne Duve's Jung-inspired cultural philosophy as an important source of inspiration. *Outsiderens posisjoner*, 52.

10. Hence, Eide views characters and places as elements of the author's psyche. The characters and places, according to Eide, end up illustrating a split individual whose internal conflicts are ultimately repressed and avoided rather than worked through. Ibid., 125.

11. Eide ultimately views the book from a rather pessimistic perspective: "Everything points toward loss and destruction. Despite all the hero's assurances of the opposite, this seems to be the opinion the novel promotes on a more fundamental level." Ibid., 135.

12. "Det forferdelige ved min galskap er jo angsten for å bli normal. Ordet 'normal' gir meg kvelningsfornemmelser." Jensen, *Ikaros*, 23; *Icarus*, 28.

13. "Jeg hadde tenkt meg Tamanrasset som en dyster, middelaldersk rytterborg på en hylle i fjellet. Gatene skulle være trange...Overalt skulle jeg møte svartkledde tuareger. De skulle gli forbi meg som vesener fra en fremmed klode. To meter høye." Jensen, *Ikaros*, 78.

14. "Hun spiser meg med primitiv glupskhet i øynene." Ibid., 127.

15. "Ved føttene mine gikk grensen mot tomrommet. Og tomrommet voldtok meg og nærmere var jeg aldri kommet det vidunderlige." Ibid., 121.

16. "Og da jeg stod på stupet og så ut over ørkenen ble min bevissthet oversvømmet av noe stort og mektig som var mer enn jeg selv og som skremte meg." Ibid., 143.

17. Torgovnick, *Primitive Passions*.

18. "Den svakheten jeg følte hos Jung var at når han skriver om sitt møte med fremmede kulturer, for eksempel da han var i Afrika, så har han hele tiden tropehjelm på seg, hvis du forstår?...Han klarte liksom ikke å riste av seg den eurosentriske vinterfrakken." Quoted in Mollestad, *Trollmannen i Ålefjær*, 51.

19. "Den menneskelighet som gjør det mulig for oss å sitte her og prate sammen. Eller for å si det rett ut: Den menneskelighet som får meg til å reise i flere døgn gjennom ørkenen for å lappe sammen en fyr som vil finne De Vises Sten." Jensen, *Ikaros*, 188.

20. "Jeg hadde ikke noe å sette opp mot dette. Jeg satt bare og tok imot. Det gjorde litt vondt, men innerst inne likte jeg det." Ibid.

21. "Selv om du føler varme og samhørighet med tuaregene—ja selv da du rørte ved livsnerven, stemte i parringsskriket og kjente strupen skjelve av fremmed ekstase, så ble

NOTES TO CHAPTER 6   271

det likevel et kontinent mellom oss... Vi hadde hver vår skjebnelinje—en hvit og en sort—min skjebne og nomadens skjebne." Ibid., 174.

22. "Jeg følte meg så fri og lett til sinns i samværet med disse enkle naturfolkene. Derfor ble jeg overrasket hver gang jeg oppdaget at de ikke var så enkle likevel. Selv blant tuaregene i Thaza ble jeg altså en fremmed med den fremmedes mangel på finfølelse for de former som har avleiret seg i menneskene gjennom tidene." Ibid., 148.

23. Fussell, *Abroad*, 208.

24. And as the narrator realizes: "En kan ikke skrive det tyvende Århundredes apokalypse i en slik varme" (112); "One cannot write the twentieth century's apocalypse in such heat" (112).

25. In Denmark, Tjæreborg charter travel began in 1951. By 1962 it was Europe's greatest travel agency. The year 1962 also marks the founding of Tjæreborg's Sterling Airways. In Norway, Saga Tours charter travel began in 1959.

26. "Turistene kom med fly. Direkte fra sivilisasjonen. De bodde gjerne på Hotel dal Piaz et par døgn. De spiste fem retter til middag. Slappet godt av i den frodige haven utenfor hotellet. Dormet i liggestoler. Drakk Pernod og ble lystige. Drakk konjakk. Ble søvnige. Drakk isvann. Og ble til slutt syke." Jensen, *Ikaros*, 44.

27. "Hun trodde kanskje det var en overkåt liten turistfaen hun snakket med. Hun så ikke at det var noe ekstra med meg, noe magisk, at jeg levde et symbolsk liv. Ja!" Ibid., 22.

28. In this description, Urry draws on Roland Barthes's chapter on *Guide Bleu* in *Mythologies*. John Urry, *The Tourist Gaze*, 43.

29. In the English translation the phrase is rendered as "Thomas Cook's corner" (37), thus losing the pejorative sense of the word "institution" (bordering semantically, in Norwegian, on the word "asylum").

30. About to flee from Fedallah and Armand, the protagonist thinks, "De ville alltid huske meg som en overspent turist som drar omkring og stirrer på landskaper. De følte ikke stemmegaffelen skjelve i hjertet når de uttalte ordet Tamanrasset" (62); "They would always remember me as an overstrung tourist who travelled round gaping at landscapes. They did not feel a tuning-fork vibrate in their hearts when they heard the word Tamanrasset" (67).

31. "En thargi-kriger med lanse og sverd og skjold, hyllet i svarte, mysteriøse gevanter, sittende på en melkehvit kamel, speidende mot fjell som ikke ville gi slipp på solnedgangen." Jensen, *Ikaros*, 32.

32. Aristotle, *On Poetry and Style*, 10.

33. "– Fy fanker'n te' kvinnfolk! sa han. – Dem står vel der og vil ha en araberjævel på kroken. Fy faen! Bare slør og hvite blonder. Går'e an å bli kåt av slikt?... Nei da var faen salte meg jentene i Le Sphinx sprekere! Han hadde vært der han! Ikke no' slør og lureri med dem. Dem kom fra Frankrike dem. Reale hvite horer som hadde lært seg te' å knulle sia' dem fekk hår på dusken. Tjo san!" Jensen, *Ikaros*, 15–16. The translation does not attempt to capture either the sociolect or the vulgarity of the sailor. Throughout *Icarus*, the English translation avoids compromising scenes and language.

34. "Jeg trudde faen knuse meg jeg sku' pule pikken av ledd jeg!" Ibid., 29. This sentence also is omitted from Maurice Michael's translation.

35. As the terms hypertext and hypotext suggest, Genette prefers the general term hypertextuality to describe the overall broad phenomenon. Intertextuality he uses to describe the phenomenon in a more narrow sense—as opposed to Julia Kristeva and Michael Riffaterre who use it more broadly. Because intertextuality—despite Genette's effort to narrow down its meaning—has become the term most often used by literary scholars, I will continue to use it—also to describe what Genette would rename hypertextuality.

36. The narrator informs us of Port's reflections upon tourism through a voice of *style indirect libre* (free indirect speech) suggesting Kit's point of view.

37. "Tuaregene kalte meg Mustafa. Men siden, for det er gått noen år før jeg ble modig nok til å skrive om det, liker jeg å tenke på meg selv i lys av den greske mytologi, og jeg kaller meg selv Ikaros, han som fløy så høyt mot lyset at voksen i hans vinger smeltet og han styrtet mot jorden igjen . . . Jeg fløy mot horisonten for at jeg skulle fylles av horisonten. Men alt ble så annerledes enn jeg hadde tenkt det." Jensen, *Ikaros*, 195.

38. "For å unngå en altfor nærgående identifisering av de personer forfatterne møtte under sitt opphold i Sahara i 1953, er de fleste av bokens navn forandret." Ibid. This disclaimer is not included in Michael's translation.

39. Eide discusses the difference between the travel letters and the travel novel (*Outsiderens posisjoner*, 105–9). The names, he notes, have changed so that Mineakael turns into Mukazzem, Toikeradh turns into Tehi, and the place-name Tahasah is changed into Tazah (106).

40. "Her i den store kaotiske verden er alt så vanskelig." Jensen, *Ikaros*, n.p.

41. Eide quotes Carl G. Jung, *Psychology and Alchemy*, 99f.

42. M. M. Bakhtin, "Epic and Novel," 7.

43. "Anarkiet er bare umodenhet. Sosialisme er svindel. Kommunismen et bedrag. Kapitalismen en utvekst på jordens rompe og som sådan motbydelig. Velferdsstaten en latterlig feiltagelse og all religion blasfemisk." Jensen, *Ikaros*, 30.

44. Eide furthermore views Mukazzem as constituting the father figure in an Oedipal fantasy in which the protagonist sleeps with his mother and kills off his father (126).

45. Fanon, *Black Skin, White Masks*; Said, *Orientalism*.

46. Right after World War II, the German seems to range above the Arab in abhorrent behavior. Arabs, too, use "German" as a term of abuse. When the protagonist haggles with an Arab in Algiers, the Arab rolls his eyes at him and yells, "Crazy tysker!" (Crazy German!). Jensen's protagonist immediately corrects him by responding in Norwegian (46/51).

47. "Det var nettop fortiden jeg ville til bunns i. Jeg ville se den innerste årsaken til hans brudd med sivilisasjonen." Jensen, *Ikaros*, 139.

48. "Det er så enkelt. Bare en tysker kunne finne på noe så enkelt . . . Den enkleste og billigste måten du kan tenke deg . . . Hele gulvet smurt inn med grønnsepe . . . Alt de gjør er å knuse noen ølflasker . . . Glasskår over hele . . . Du er der inne naken." Ibid., 141.

49. Crawling home on his hands and knees, the hero continually likens himself to William Blake's painting of Nebuchadnezzar (166/164).

50. "Til slutt treffer jeg tyskeren dyktig i brystet." Jensen, *Ikaros*, 163.

51. Peter Madsen, "Kulturkrise, dagligliv og engagement," 107–9.

52. In terms of *Heretica* poetry, Nerval is a figure similar to Ole Wivel's Lazarus in his poem by that name from 1949. Lazarus has also survived and returned from the concentration camps, and the poetic "I" seeks to understand him in all his suffering and vulnerability. In addition, he situates him within a Christian mythology, in which Lazarus is both Christlike and, as his name indicates, is to be compared to Lazarus, who was resurrected from the dead.

53. "Bevissthet begynner med angsten for døden." Jensen, *Ikaros*, 170.

54. "Nerval hadde sett Lyset. Og i konsentrasjonsleiren hadde han også sett inn i det svarteste mørke. Spennvidden i hans sinn var altfor svimlende til at jeg kunne fatte den... Men hvorfor kunne man ikke finne det samme lys nede på jorden? I felleskap med dyr og mennesker? Ja, nettopp med menneskene!" Ibid., 196.

55. "Mukazzem...finner frem det tunge, skarpe tuaregsverdet. Arven fra far. Og fars arv fra Kain." Ibid., 183.

56. "Idiotisk! tenkte jeg. Århundredets største banalitet, å finne seg selv...å flå skallene av sjelens løk til en satt igjen med tårer i øynene og et tomrom mellom hendene." Ibid., 186,

57. "Et land langt, langt borte...et land hvor det er lang høst og kort sommer og hvor kvinnene har lyst hår og sterke blå øyne og norske fjes og spinkle fugleaktige stemmer." Ibid.

58. In his reading of *Ikaros*, Melberg similarly notes the Arabian female stereotypes: "The Arabian women are dirty erotic in a similar way and precisely therefore just as attractive as the men are repulsive" (142).

59. "Jeg er kommet til veis ende." Jensen, *Ikaros*, 196.

60. Høffding, *Den store Humor*, 56.

61. "Å bli dikter var noe stort og forlokkende. Nesten overmenneskelig." Quoted in Mollestad, *Trollmannen i ålefjær*, 129.

62. "Kunstnerens oppgave er å gjøre kunsten overflødig og la selve livet bli en kunst." Jensen, *Ikaros*, 176.

III. Late and Postmodern Travel

1. Peter Hulme, "Travelling to Write (1940–2000)."

2. Clifford, *Routes*, 67.

3. The wilderness category applies less to *Jeg har set verden begynde* and *Jeg har hørt et stjerneskud* than to *Det glemte folk: En rejse i Burmas grænseland* (2004), a tale about the lost tribe of the Karens.

4. Tvedt, *Verdensbilder og selvbilder*, 74–101.

5. In this case, the fall of the Soviet bloc plays a significant role, adding a particular political dimension to Jensen's observations. This fits into a general trend depicted by Hulme: "Given that the world is constantly in flux, there is still a prominent place for the mixture of personal reportage and socio-political analysis which has been a

component of travel writing since its earliest days. The collapse of communism opened up opportunities for travel in Eastern Europe and Central Asia which many writers have been keen to take" (94).

7. From the Personal to the Universal—and Back

1. As Erik Svendsen puts it, "Carsten Jensen is one of the very few Danish authors who write themselves into the Danish literary history without anchoring their authorship in fictional texts." Svendsen, "Carsten Jensen," 348. Recently, however, Jensen has marked himself as a writer of fiction as well, not least with his novel *Vi, de druknede* (2006).

2. See Sven Lindqvist, *Ökendykarna* (1990).

3. "Der var en, jeg havde forladt, før jeg tog af sted. Det var min rejses begyndelse. Det var den samme, jeg elskede. Det var min rejses opdagelse." Jensen, *Jeg har set verden begynde*, 366. The English-language passage quoted in text is from the 2000 translation by Barbara Haveland titled *I Have Seen the World Begin*, 228. Unless otherwise noted, all subsequent English translations are from Haveland's translation. This translation, however, skips Jensen's travels in Russia and Hong Kong. Translations from these passages are my own.

4. "Det eneste, jeg ved om verdenshistorien, har jeg lært ved at se et barn blive født." Jensen, *Jeg har set verden begynde*, 7.

5. Fussell, *Abroad*, 214.

6. "Den skrigende kvinde så ikke ud til at være i nogen individuel neuroses vold. Snarere var det en kollektiv spænding, der rasede i hende. Hendes anfald af vrede bundede i det indre pres, der opstod, hvor for mange mennesker uophørligt levede for tæt på hinanden. Hendes skrig var alles indre skrig." Jensen, *Jeg har set verden begynde*, 128–29.

7. Frits Andersen, "En følsom rejsende," 10.

8. " 'Tag nu f.eks. Deres navn. De hedder Jensen . . . Så nu glemmer jeg aldrig Deres navn igen. Jensen.' " Jensen, *Jeg har set verden begynde*, 517.

9. Jensen's travel letters were published in Scandinavian newspapers: *Extra Bladet, Politiken, Expressen,* and *Aftenposten* (Andersen, 10).

10. "Man skulle rejse, når man var ung . . . Så blev rejsen måske en dannelsesrejse. Når man rejste i en moden alder, rejste man ikke i det håb at blive smeltet om og blive en anden." Jensen, *Jeg har set verden begynde*, 177. In Vietnam, Jensen returns to his speculations on age, travel, and identity: "Rejsen er ungdommens medie, et flydende sted for selvudforskning og begyndelser" (408); "travel is a medium of youth, a floating venue for self-exploration and new beginnings" (247).

11. "Jeg rejste uden nostalgiske illusioner og var ikke på sporet af mit yngre jeg og ungdommens grænseløshed." Ibid., 408.

12. The term "liquid Self" comes from Zygmunt Bauman's notion of a "liquid modernity"—a concept similar to Giddens's notion of late modernity. Bauman, *Liquid Modernity*.

NOTES TO CHAPTER 7   275

13. "Jeg var blevet for meget mig selv og var ikke længere modtagelig." Jensen, *Jeg har set verden begynde*, 176.

14. "Det var et øjebliks uventet ekstase, som efterlod mig underligt forvildet med en følelse af, at denne rejse var alt for uoverkommelig stor til mig, og at den snart ville æde mig op, så at alt det, jeg havde vænnet mig til at kalde mig selv, blot ville blive tilbage som en levning." Ibid., 528–29.

15. "Hele den såkaldte personlighed [er] en fiktion, som kun lod sig opretholde, fordi omgivelserne hele tiden bekræftede den." Ibid., 177.

16. For a view of how this plays itself out on a larger scale in Scandinavian literature of the 1990s, see Per Thomas Andersen, *Tankevaser: Om norsk 1990-tallslitteratur*.

17. "Kvinderne i Sovjetsamfundet... havde måttet omskabe sig til mænd. Man kunne stadigvæk se det. Når de nu under påvirkning fra Vesten eller måske fra et uimodståeligt indre pres forsøgte at erobre deres kvindelighed tilbage, kom de til at ligne ludere eller transvestitter." Jensen, *Jeg har set verden begynde*, 68.

18. The chapter on Cambodia is one of the most text-based. It contains much more background information about the country's history and politics than it does accounts of the traveler's personal encounters with people.

19. Pratt, *Imperial Eyes*.

20. "Saigons forstæder var som alle forstæder i Den Tredje Verden kaotiske med et virvar af huse, der så ud, som om de var vokset frem af sig selv i en anarkistisk knopskydning af facader, halve og hele tilbyggede etager, malet eller nøgen beton, blikskilte og små butikslokaler, der lå hulter til bulter oven i hinanden." Jensen, *Jeg har set verden begynde*, 333.

21. Interestingly, the metaphors have been removed in the translation into English; thus the semantic density in the depiction disappears.

22. "Der var få biler på Saigons indfaldsveje, men ind og ud mellem dem bevægede sig tusinder af små Honda-scootere. Jo tættere vi kom på centrum, jo flere af dem var der, og på mange af dem så jeg unge kvinder iført lange bukser og hvide, højt opslidsede silketunikaer. Deres forfinede ansigter var indrammet af blankt, blåsort hår, der nåede dem til den smalle talje. På mange af scooterne sad der to kvinder, den bageste med benene yndefuldt samlede og den ene arm om taljen på veninden, mens hun i den anden holdt en smørgul parasol som beskyttede mod solen. Som motoriserede blomster snoede de unge kvinder sig ind og ud i trafikken, og jeg glemte alt om arkitekturen for at hengive mig til synet af dem." Jensen, *Jeg har set verden begynde*, 334.

23. "Jeg tror ikke, jeg overdriver, hvis jeg siger, at jeg aldrig har været et sted, hvor min selvfølelse som mand blev så stimuleret som i Vietnam." Ibid., 478.

24. "Orientens mystik var blevet erstattet af robotternes, Østerlandets gådefuldhed af effektivitetens." Ibid., 115.

25. "Alligevel åbnede Vietnam sig for mig som et land af parallelle universer, der hele tiden tilbød mig nye eksistensformer, andre identiteter, en række af mulige jeger. Der var noget andet og voldsommere end ungdommens frihedsdelirium, der greb mig. Det var en følelse af min egen fuldstændig plastiske formbarhed. Jeg kunne være morder, tyv, forfører af mindreårige, landet tilbød mig det hele, og i min anonymitet...

mærkede jeg mit eget svar. Jeg blev forført og fristet... Vietnam var et land, hvor jeg kunne blive væk i mig selv, de indre muligheders land." Ibid., 408.

26. See Dennis Porter, "The Perverse Traveler."

27. "Snarere havde man fornemmelsen af at ligge side om side med byen som efter vellykket elskov. Den hede, fugtige luft, den lette støvregn, der faldt intim som sved på huden, stemmerne, blikkene udgjorde tilsammen en stor generøs berøring, en altomfattende erotisk oplevelse. Det var en hel kultur, der samlede sig om én i et kærtegn." Jensen, *Jeg har set verden begynde*, 424.

28. Jensen's actual criminal behavior consists of illegally purchasing a Buddha head—an act he feels extremely guilty about, but one that also relieves him of his good conscience and thus connects him with a great part of human beings toward whom he had previously felt morally superior (410–13).

29. "Jeg har altid haft en regel, når jeg rejser. Ingen fremmede har lov at røre ved min krop. Mit jeg er i forvejen under så voldsomme angreb, at jeg må trække en grænse et sted, og jeg trækker den der, ved det fysiske, og jeg tror, det er et klogt tabu at have. Men i Vietnam var der hele tiden fremmede, der rørte ved min krop, uden at jeg følte mig truet... For hver berøring faldt et nyt lag af løget, og jeg nærmede mig den overgivelse, som accepten af éns egen anonymitet er. Det gjorde ikke noget, de rørte. De måtte godt, for jeg havde tillid til dem, eller rettere min tillid voksede ud af disse berøringer." Jensen, *Jeg har set verden begynde*, 409.

30. Giddens bases his argument on Erving Goffman's Umwelt theories, explaining that "the protective cocoon is the *mantle of trust that makes possible the sustaining of a viable Umwelt*" (129). A main point for Giddens is to correct a common misunderstanding that the present-day fussing over the corporeal Self is a mere sign of narcissism (7).

31. "'Du ser ud som en mand. Men du er jo ikke en rigtig mand. Du er en kvinde.'" Jensen, *Jeg har set verden begynde*, 419.

32. The one exception to the feminized men with whom Jensen comes in contact is the aggressive cyclo drivers who seem more eager to pick fights than to pick up customers. These, however, are mentioned at the very beginning of the Vietnam section and then disappear from the story (336/205).

33. "Hun lignede ikke de andre i lokalet... Hun lignede en studerende på et universitet i Vesten" (369); "She did not look like the other girls in the bar... She could have been a student at any Western university" (231).

34. "Jeg elskede hende ikke, og hun var for opfyldt af sin egen skæbne til selv at kunne elske nogen." Jensen, *Jeg har set verden begynde*, 387.

35. The structure of the travelogue is chronological in its main sections, depicting one country at a time. Within the main sections, though, the subchapters, generally following the itinerary, are sometimes ordered more thematically to create small, coherent units. This pattern becomes particularly prominent in the section about Tam. In "Mennesket er som et bambusskud" (Man Is Like a Bamboo Shoot), the relationship is depicted from beginning to end. The following subchapter (omitted in the English translation) nevertheless begins with: "Tam havde en vidunderlig evne..." (Tam had a

wonderful ability...) (389). In addition we find out that in earlier chapters in which the traveler is depicted as if touring alone, he was actually accompanied by Tam.

36. "En mødernes usynlige historie, som ikke har noget at gøre med landskabernes diktater eller voldsomme begivenheders lange skygger." Jensen, *Jeg har set verden begynde*, 377.

37. Miserable people sometimes "opfører sig som prostituerede og giver sig selv væk for en smule opmærksomheds håndører. Jeg burde have vidst det. Der har været tidspunkter i mit eget liv, hvor jeg selv har gjort det samme." Ibid., 371.

38. Frances E. Mascia-Lees, Patricia Sharpe, and Colleen Ballerino Cohen, "The Postmodernist Turn in Anthropology," 29. Quoted in Michael Cronin, *Across the Lines*, 135.

39. Arne Melberg also comments on how Carsten Jensen's use of the girl back home novelizes his travelogue: "He frames his account by something that resembles the intrigue of a novel. I mention this to emphasize that while sexuality has been cultivated in the journey depicted in novels, it has practically disappeared from the nonfictive journey; and if it shows up, as in the case of Carsten Jensen, then it is immediately reminiscent of a novel." Melberg, *Å reise og skrive*, 245.

40. "Det, jeg først havde kaldt min skyggekærlighed, blev hele min indre virkelighed, det eneste stabile punkt, midt i rejsens sandskred af steder og mennesker." Jensen, *Jeg har set verden begynde*, 367.

41. Carsten Jensen, *Jeg har hørt et stjerneskud*, 322.

42. "Både mænd og kvinder, så ud, som om de led under et frygtindgydende overskud af mandlige kønshormoner." Ibid., 23.

43. I discussed Clifford's three stages in the introduction to Part II and the chapter on Johannes V. Jensen, where the traveler is exemplary of Clifford's first-stage anthropologist. Perhaps I should rather call this a prestage anthropologist as it refers to the period before the 1920s when the field of anthropology was established as a separate field. As previously discussed, until the 1920s travel writing and ethnographic accounts had been part of one another. During the heyday of anthropology, anthropologists distanced themselves from travel writers, insisting on the serious scientific and objective aspect of their reports. The second stage, then, lasts from the 1920s to the postwar, anticolonial period of the 1950s when ethnographic reports and literary accounts were two separate things. Clifford, *Routes*.

44. "Antropologien er i lige så høj grad et katalog over vore drømme, som den er et katalog over menneskehedens mangfoldighed." Jensen, *Jeg har hørt et stjerneskud*, 15.

45. "Begge køn var meget muskuløse, og selv om vi befandt os midt i en slags by, var det tydeligt at se, at det var omgangen med naturen, der havde skabt deres hårde, kantede kroppe." Ibid., 24.

46. "Endnu mere slående var dog deres knudrede ansigter. De havde dybe linjer ned over kinderne og rundt om munden og panderynker, der lå i folder hen over hinanden og ned over den krogede næse. Det dystre udtryk blev forstærket af de blå tatoveringer og ornamentale ar, mange af dem, både mænd og kvinder, bar forskellige steder i ansigtet.

De fleste mænd havde et kruset fuldskæg, og kvinderne et stort vildt hår, der fik det til at se ud, som om de lige havde modtaget et kraftigt elektrisk stød." Ibid.

47. "Lignede... en rigtig kannibal, der sultent stak hovedet frem for at spejde efter frokosten." Ibid., 25.

48. Sontag, *Regarding the Pain of Others*, 105.

49. "De rugede over den skæbne, det var at have fået meget mere kraft, end de kunne finde forløsning for. Der var noget rådvildt over dem, som om de befandt sig afskårne fra at udøve en naturlig funktion, som fugle i bur, der forhindres i at slå vingerne ud, eller rovdyr, hvis jagtinstinkt er afløst af rastløs traven, mens de venter på signalet til fodring. Det kunne ikke være Port Moresby... der fik dem til at opføre sig, som om de befandt sig i fangenskab. Det var noget inden i dem selv, som havde sat sig fast og var forhindret i at få afløb." Jensen, *Jeg har hørt et stjerneskud*, 25.

50. "Der var noget eftertrykkeligt og pompøst over vejbyggeriet, som om fremskridtet, der havde været så længe undervejs, ville kompensere for sin langsomhed og annoncere sin ankomst med et tordenskrald." Ibid., 202.

51. The narrator generally views the historical time period on the islands as the stone age (20), but adapts the view advanced at the National Museum (PNG Art): "Tiden før 1960 var forhistorisk tid, her endte stenalderen, og den moderne tid begyndte, og selv om det sjældent var til at se forskel på ting, der var lavet før og efter 1960, så var der forskel. For det, der var produceret før 1960, var på en måde skabt i evigheden, det næsten uendelige kontinuum, som strakte sig tilbage i tiden... Om denne tid havde varet 50 år eller 10.000 var på en måde ligegyldigt, for det var tiden før den hvide mands komme... Der var to tidsaldre i Papua Ny Guinea, stenalderen og nutiden, og nutiden begyndte efter 1960" (The time before 1960 was prehistoric; this was where the stone age ended, and where modern time began, and even though it was rarely possible to tell the difference between things made before and after 1960, there was a difference. For that which was produced before 1960 was, in a way, made in eternity, the almost indefinite continuum reaching back in time... Whether this time had lasted for 50 or 10,000 years was, in a way, indifferent, for it was the time before the white man had arrived... There were two eras in Papua New Guinea, the stone age and the present age, and the present age began after 1960). Ibid., 26–27.

52. Holland and Huggan use Pico Iyer as their example of an anti-imperialist, pro-transculturation travel writer (65).

53. "Jeg gjorde det, fordi jeg ved, at store forandringer er på vej, og at vores landsbys skikke måske snart er historie." Jensen, *Jeg har hørt et stjerneskud*, 61.

54. "Jeg var klar over, at det var en handel, jeg var involveret i. De gav mig deres historier, og jeg måtte give dem noget til gengæld. Gazebind og Panodiler var min valuta." Ibid., 76.

55. "Noget autentisk gammelt og noget helt nyt. Det var et åndehus. Men det var også et varehus, og det ville være forkert at se denne kommercialisering af de aktiviteter, som tidligere udelukkende havde stået i ritualernes tjeneste, som et tab af kultur og autenticitet, et udsalg, der også var en åndelig selvopgivelse." Ibid., 124.

56. "De trådte ind i pengenes globale kredsløb, men ikke for at underkaste sig og lade deres særpræg udslette. Der var ikke tale om en kamp mellem gammelt og nyt, men om et møde mellem dem, en syntese, der tillod deres verden at udvikle og udvide sig." Ibid., 125.

57. During, "Postcolonialism and Globalization." Quoted in Holland and Huggan, *Tourists with Typewriters*, 64.

58. This the natives realize as well. When a long hike in the rain turns the traveler sad and downcast, they try to cheer him up with stories about their tribal customs. One of his guides, Michael, "kendte min interesse for antropologiske detaljer og altings navne" (knew my interest in anthropological details and the names of everything) (205). He tries to stimulate the traveler by telling him the name of a bush. It does not quite work, but later that night, being fed by the fire and having an old man show up who "gav sig til at berette om stammens skikke" (began to tell about the tribe's customs) (206), the traveler finally regains his happiness.

59. "Hidtil havde jeg på min rejse levet et dobbeltliv. Jeg sad om aftenen alene på et hotelværelse med mine bøger og min dagbog. Det var en ensomhed, der både skræmte og udmattede mig, men det var også i den, at jeg samlede mig og genfandt mig selv." Ibid., 187–88.

60. "Jeg tilbragte alle mine aftener omgivet af mennesker, der hele tiden ventede på mine udspil, og imellem os var der en kløft i henseende til erfaring og levevis så dyb, at det krævede det yderste af min opmærksomhed og koncentration at sætte over den. Jeg savnede et kendt ansigt, mest af alt mit eget." Ibid., 188.

61. "Mine eneste øjeblikke alene var de timer, hvor jeg sov, eller når jeg stjal mig til at skrive i min dagbog eller læse et par sider i *Don Quijote*, altid omgivet af nysgerrige øjne og spørgsmål, der med de uskyldiges selvfølgelige ret brød min ro." Ibid.

62. "Han havde gråsprængt hår og et rynket ansigt. Hans mavemuskler var med alderen blevet slappe, men hans hud var glat og blank som på en ung mand, og musklerne tegnede sig tydeligt under huden." Ibid., 103.

63. "Det gik op for mig, at han var der for at føre os rundt og rundt i cirkler og holde mig borte fra steder, hvor jeg efter hans mening ikke havde noget at gøre." Ibid.

64. "Det gik op for mig, at det ikke var den gamle mands mening, at jeg skulle nå op på bjerget." Ibid., 106.

65. "Jeg kunne ikke lade være med at give den gamle mand ret. Jeg havde ikke noget at gøre på bjerget, og var dets top for dem et område omgærdet af en mystik, som de ikke ønskede krænket af fremmedes indtrængen, havde jeg ingen ret til at insistere." Ibid.

66. "Når verden kommer til jer, vil I indse, ... at I har mistet noget væsentligt." Ibid., 110.

67. "Jeg fortrød med det samme, hvad jeg havde sagt. Jeg havde ingen ret til at være romantisk på deres vegne." Ibid.

68. "Pludselig gik det op for mig, at det her ikke var sightseeing, og at sætningen 'Jeg vil gerne se, hvordan en minearbejderfamilie lever' ikke var nogen tilstrækkelig

begrundelse for det, jeg var i færd med at gøre. Jeg havde tilbragt hele dagen som tilskuer til disse menneskers tragedie. Skulle jeg nu også trænge ind i deres hjem for at være vidne til deres elendighed? Med hvilken ret bad jeg dem ydmyge sig for øjnene af mig? Forfatterens, journalistens ret? Fordi jeg ikke var her på min egen private nysgerrigheds vegne, men som vidne, på verdens vegne, for at se for andre og gøre dem delagtige i Potosís drama, der nu havde stået på i 400 år og stadig ikke var slut? Var det ikke blot en skinhellig forklaring, som dækkede over en voyeurisme, som troede sig politisk og moralsk legitimeret, blot fordi den ikke rettede sig mod andres kønsliv, men mod deres elendighed?" Ibid., 354. John Urry has noted the "remarkable increase in interest in the real lives of industrial/mining workers," and he views this interest as typically postmodern. The postindustrial, postmodern society has brought about nostalgia for what is perceived as heroic industrial labor as well as a satisfying social life surrounding this type of labor. In addition, postmodernity has brought about a leveling of dichotomous relationships (public-private, inside-outside, back-front), leaving people interested in gazing behind the scenes—and assuming they can gain access to this space. Urry, *The Tourist Gaze*, 97.

69. "Det var i dette øjeblik, jeg besluttede mig til ikke skrive nogen artikel om dem. Verden er i forvejen fuld af journalistik, som under påberåbelse af at ville forbedre menneskers vilkår fratager dem deres værdighed." Jensen, *Jeg har hørt et stjerneskud*, 358.

70. For a more detailed analysis of *Træet i ørkenen*, see Elisabeth Oxfeldt, "Refleksionsrum i den postkolonialistiske tekst."

71. See Flemming Ytzen, "Tragedier i technicolor," and Sigrun Berge Engen, "Geriljaturisme."

8. Futile Journeys

1. Per Thomas Andersen, *Norsk litteraturhistorie*, 560.

2. Parodies on travelogues have existed since Lucian's *True History* written in the first century AD—a work, according to Peter Hulme and Tim Youngs, "so supremely wrought that most subsequent travel parodies are mere variations on its themes." As opposed to *L*, however, these are often based only on an imaginary journey. Hulme and Youngs, "Introduction," 5.

3. Loe, *L*, 36.

4. "Dere sier at den store fortellingen er død?... Dere vil ha små fortellinger?... Det skal dere faen meg få." Ibid., n.p.

5. "I min verden fins det ikke lenger hvite flekker på kartet." Ibid., 9.

6. "Jeg ser ut til å være født relativt sent i menneskenes utvikling, for sent til å påvirke samfunnsstrukturene i nevnelig grad, for sent til å oppdage land eller sentrale fenomener." Ibid., 30–31.

7. "Det er litt som om verden var ferdig laget da vi ble født inn i den. Den er ikke vår. Vi har ikke bygd den. Det eneste som gjenstår er vedlikehold og reparasjoner. Vi er født inn i et oppussingsobjekt. Hvor pirrende er det?" Ibid., 362–63.

8. "Og like før vi går hjem vil Egil ta ordet og si at han beklager at han var litt gretten de siste dagene på øya og når vi nå først er samlet, så har han lyst til å si at han er glad i oss. I hver og en av oss. Hver især. Og han kommer til å si det med et tonefall og et nesten umerkelig smil som gjør at det blir en distanse i det. En distanse som skinner uklart, men tydelig nok igjennom. Kanskje kan vi kalle det ironi. Men det er i så fall ingen liketil form for ironi. Den er ikke som ironier flest. Den er subtil og betyr ikke det motsatte av det han sier. På sett og vis sier han at han er glad i oss, men han åpner for at det også kan bety andre ting. Helt andre ting. Ting som ikke ligger i selve ordene og som ingen vet hvor kommer fra. Utsagnet har nyanser langt utover det vanlige. Det får meg til å smile og føle meg varm og det bekymrer meg lite hva det egentlig handler om." Ibid., 453–54.

9. The Norwegian psychologist Finn Skårderud, for instance, refers to Loe's as the ironic generation. Skårderud, "Skrumpselvet," 126.

10. "Jeg føler meg trygg på at ettertidens sosiologer, psykologer, litteraturvitere og hva har du, vil kartlegge alt slikt på grundige måter. Vi kan bare ta det med ro." Loe, *L*, 454.

11. Hutcheon, *A Poetics of Postmodernism*, 61.

12. Thus, *L* ends up exemplifying what Hutcheon views as characteristic of postmodernism: "Postmodernism questions centralized, totalized, hierarchized, closed systems: questions, but does not destroy... It acknowledges the human urge to make order, while pointing out that the orders we create are just that: human constructs, not natural or given entities" (41–42).

13. The term "Generation X" is usually traced back to Douglas Coupland's *Generation X: Tales for an Accelerated Culture* (1991). Coupland, in turn, based his term on Paul Fussell's depiction of an anticlass category of people referred to as X in Fussell's sociogocial study *Class: A Guide through the American Status System* (1983). Generation X has come to refer to those born between the 1960s and the 1980s. They are people whose teen years in some way coincided with the 1980s. They tend to be overeducated, underachieving, cynical, frustrated, and still living at home. Particularly relevant for this study is that what distinguishes Generation X from previous generations is the transition between colonialism and globalization. See http://en.wikipedia.org/wiki/Generation_X (downloaded April 21, 2006).

In Norway, the term is not as prevalent as in the United States. Henning Wærp, however, uses it in his review of *L*: "The 1980s are the years of their youth, they are a generation often called X, or the ironic generation, and the book writes itself right into this tradition." Wærp, "Erlend Loe: L," 180.

14. The two travelogues bear many resemblances. When Loe devotes much space to outlandish fund-raising tactics, he evokes not only Thor Heyerdahl but also the real-life Axel Jensen, who threw himself at random millionaires as well as the state to raise money for his adventures. Jan Christian Mollestad, *Trollmannen i Ålefjær*, 32, 106.

15. Pfister uses the plural form of postmodernization, seeing Chatwin's work as one of many examples of postmodernizations. Wanting to avoid the postmodern pitfall of

substituting all master narratives with that of postmodernism (as in Lyotard's case) and wanting, like Linda Hutcheon, to emphasize process(es) rather than totalizing abstractions and reified concepts (Pfister, 253), Pfister nonetheless generalizes toward his conclusion when he views the potential of his analysis "for describing some recent developments within the genre of the travelogue" (264). Pfister, "Bruce Chatwin."

16. Pratt, *Imperial Eyes*, 216.

17. In addition to pointing out the travelogue's popular status, its marginal position vis-à-vis official literary histories, and its unsettling status between fact and fiction, Pfister underscores its potential for deconstructing cultural stereotypes: "as a transcultural genre mediating between cultures it can problematize culturally encoded projections of Self and the Other" (265).

18. "Der var grønne, kegleformede skaller, der var røde sneglehuse, der var blå og sorte skjolde, og slæbende på denne brogede beboelse kriblede og krablede krebsene for at komme op ad kokosnøddens stejle inderside." Jensen, *Jeg har hørt et stjerneskud*, 512–13.

19. "Eremitkrebsene på New Ireland havde givet mig en slags svar. Det var måske ikke de mest anskuelige svar, men det var, hvad jeg havde med hjem fra min rejse, og jeg kunne ikke finde på nogen bedre." Ibid.

20. "Vi [er] så å si omringet av eremittkreps... De minste er omtrent på størrelse med en liten svensk köttbulle, men de fleste er store som knyttnever og helt røde... Det er hundrevis, kanskje tusenvis av dem... Lyden av tusen er ubehagelig og skremmende. De krafser og leter etter noe som kan spises. De spiser hva som helst, totalt ukritisk. De spiser bæsj, om så skal være." Loe, *L*, 257.

21. Thor Heyerdahl, *Kon-Tiki*, 211. Except as noted, all quotations in English are from F. H. Lyon's translation.

22. You may of course say that while Loe shies away from romantic symbolism, he nonetheless also portrays his meeting with hermit crabs in a manner that may serve as an allegory. While Jensen's symbolic allegory indicates closeness and unity through a sense of romantic, monistic universalism, Loe's allegory ends up representing the postmodern cynicism of an ex-centric generation, thoroughly alienated from nature.

23. "Jeg hadde altså kjøpt en Fox og kom ut av butikken og der sto, som jeg allerede har vært inne på, Roar og denne andre fyren og oppsummerte helga." Loe, *L*, 105.

24. "Når man sier melkeglass så snakker man ikke om noe lite glass. Når man drikker melk, nipper man ikke. Man spiser en skive kneippbrød eller to og hiver i seg glass etter glass med melk. Store glass. Et melkeglass er ikke et lite glass. Det er helt på det rene. Og denne festdeltakeren fylte det altså." Ibid., 106.

25. "Han var neppe klar over det selv, men han var med på å legge listen veldig høyt for oss andre. Hvis det var melkeglasset man skulle strekke seg etter, kom man til å føle seg temmelig mislykket i mange år fremover. Jeg husker følelsen av avmakt fra den dagen utenfor butikken. Det føltes umulig, og det gjør det fremdeles." Ibid.

26. "Jeg føler meg som en voksen gutt og ikke som en mann." Ibid., 133.

27. "Jeg knytter meg raskt til dette brødstykket. Vi blir venner. Jeg later som om brødet er et levende vesen... Etterpå lar jeg det sitte på skuldren min og se ut gjennom vinduet." Ibid., 198–99.

28. "Det er klisjéen av sydhavsøya som ligger foran oss. Den som er en del av vår alles kollektivt ubevisste. Uransakelige smil er den eneste fornuftige reaksjonen." Ibid., 223.

29. "Vi er fjetret av synet som møter oss. Av øya. Den er fantastisk vakker." Ibid., 227.

30. Ibid., 41. In F. H. Lyon's English translation, Heyerdahl's language is normalized so that "green-green" becomes "bright green." Thus Heyerdahl's enthusiastic allusion to a "primitive" language structure is lost.

31. "Stranden er ca. 20 meter bred og består av en blanding av sand og istykkerslåtte koraller. Den skråner nedover mot lagunen som ligger der, vekselvis blå og grønn, med spredte samlinger av koraller over og under vann. Et par hundre meter fra stranden ligger selve revet. Vi kan se bølgene slå mot det så vannet står høyt til værs." Ibid.

32. "Bak oss ligger skogen, eller jungelen. Jeg vet ikke helt hva som skal til for at noe skal kunne kalles en jungel. Det er i hvert fall mange trær her." Ibid.

33. Gumbrecht, *Production of Presence*, 82.

34. Or, as Linda Hutcheon puts it, postmodernism queries the relation of reality to language (*A Poetics of Postmodernism*, 15). The narrator of *L* constantly dwells on language—especially on the idiomatic expressions of Heyerdahl's generation, such as "å skyte seg gjennom" (to shoot one's way through) (69) and "å ha vært ute en vinternatt før" (to have been out one winter's night before) (70–76). Both expressions are used in *Kon-tiki ekspedisjonen*, and Erlend dwells on them as signs of a macho generation that still had important things to do, defend, and discover. Eirik Vassenden carries the study of Loe's preoccupation with signs and objects at face value further, claiming that Loe's novels, especially *L*, constitute a serious examination of the surface. See Vassenden, *Den store overflaten*, 75–76.

35. I am thinking, for instance, of Georg Simmel's depictions of the blasé urbane type from 1903: "The essence of the blasé attitude is an indifference towards the distinction between things." Epitomizing this type is the person in whom "the nerves reveal their final possibility of adjusting themselves to the content and the form of metropolitan life by renouncing the response to them." Simmel, "The Metropolis and Mental Life," 329, 330.

36. "The narrating and travelling 'I' largely recedes into the background . . . He is a pose rather than a subject." Pfister, "Bruce Chatwin," 263.

37. Genette, *Palimpsests*, 8.

38. For instance, Eirik Vassenden and Kaja Korsvold refer to "'L' for 'Learning'" (Vassenden, 80). Kaja Korsvold, "Erlend Loes siste roman slippes i dag. 90-tallets bokkomet." Barbro Bredesen Opset dwells on this comparison a bit longer: "By using the international traffic sign for 'learning' as its title, the book may be attempting to call attention to people in society who are not quite sure of the 'traffic rules.' Some lack direction as to where the boundary between play and seriousness traditionally is drawn. The book claims that there are some people out there who do not just want to learn the rules of society; they also want to understand them thoroughly, perhaps question them and reject them once in a while." Opset, "Generasjon O fag," 60–62.

39. Wærp suggests L may simply stand for Loe (181).

40. Klein, *No Logo*, xx.

41. Geelmuyden, "Marco Po Loe," 88.

42. "Man har sendt kunnskap videre. Gjennom generasjoner. Jeg lærer dette til deg, så bruker du det i en femti-seksti år og gir det videre til dine barn. Og skulle du finne på noe nytt underveis, så skader ikke det." Loe, *L*, 19–20.

43. Typically, Generation Xers are fascinated not with the generation of their parents but with that of their grandparents—the post–World War II generation.

44. "Vi baserer oss med andre ord veldig på Heyerdahls tur." Loe, *L*, 19–20.

45. "Jeg føler meg sikker på at denne skøytelyden gjenspeiles i musikken fra Polynesia den dag i dag." Ibid., 37.

46. "Egil har altså ikke sugd det fra eget bryst, men, sier han, vi må ta i betraktning at den tiden er over. I dag er det ganske lite som kan suges helt fra eget bryst. Det er ikke mulig lenger. Folk har tenkt tankene før. Vår oppgave blir å raffinere dem." Ibid., 122.

47. The quotation from Eco is a paraphrasing from Hutcheon, *A Poetics of Postmodernism*, 39.

48. "Det betyr jo ikke at Heyerdahls teori blir noe dårligere. Tvert imot. Dette er to sider av samme tese. Heyerdahl fulgte sin idé. Jeg må følge min. Andre kan jo ha dratt over havet i balsaflåter senere, da isen forsvant. Det er ingenting i veien for det. Da hadde de jo noen å besøke... Dette ser ut til å henge godt sammen." Loe, *L*, 36–37.

49. "Spesialisering er lite tiltrekkende. Jeg vil heller vite noe om alt. Renessansemennesket. Universalgeniet. Som trekker linjer hit og dit. Ser helheten. Det er slik jeg helst vil bli sett." Ibid., 31. The statement echoes Heyerdahl's in *Kon-Tiki*: "Modern research demands that every special branch shall dig its own hole. It's not usual for anyone to sort out what comes out of the holes and try to put it all together" (19). In his afterword from the 1994 edition (not included in Lyon's translation), Heyerdahl states it even more adversarily: "It was actually specialization within science that was the worst barrier to overcome," and, "Science has become so specialized today that the experts attain their knowledge in depth at the expense of their overview in breadth. That way an incredible lack of knowledge is accommodated among specialists, and great gaps between them and in their collective knowledge, without our being able to deny that they are authorities" (230, 233; my translation).

50. Linda Hutcheon, *A Theory of Parody*, 10. In *A Poetics of Postmodernism*, she writes: "The postmodernist novel puts into question that entire series of interconnected concepts that have come to be associated with what we conveniently label as liberal humanism: autonomy, transcendence, certainty, authority, unity, totalization, system, universalization, center, continuity, teleology, closure, hierarchy, homogeneity, uniqueness, origin" (57).

51. Genette writes: "By hypertextuality I mean any relationship uniting a text B... to an earlier text A... upon which it is grafted in a manner that is not that of commentary" (5). These relationships, however, are not mutually exclusive in *L*. Yet, Genette also writes: "One must not view the five types of transtextuality as separate and absolute categories without any reciprocal contact or overlapping" (7). "The hypertext, too, often acts as a commentary" (8).

52. It is interesting to note that just as in Inger Christensen's systematic poetry—such as *Alfabet* (1980)—the system ends up going haywire. Instead of being followed

by "9. bål," "9. dag" is followed by "10. dag," and from then on all the days are followed by a depiction of the previous day's bonfire. This pattern remains stable for another ten days, until, finally, the twenty-third day is followed by "22–32 bål" and a depiction of arriving back home.

53. Including the report card is not without its irony as Erlend is "touched" that a fifth-grade teacher observed his actions so closely and took pains to record them (43). Living in a country where one is attended to so carefully and so well taken care of, and in which one is forced to think collectively rather than individually is a privilege *and* a curse.

54. "Poenget med gruppearbeid er at det ikke fins snarveier. Man kan ikke lure seg unna på samme måte som man kan det når man jobber alene. Man må lytte til alles meninger. Snakker man tull, vil noen arrestere en. Det er en trygghet i systemet. Snakke. Snakke. Evaluere. Kvesse kompetansen. Åpne seg for andres forslag. Også de som er helt på jordet. De hører også med til gruppen. Over tid vil de gode forslagene sannsynligvis seire... Allerede på skolen hatet jeg gruppearbeid. Jeg var elendig på samarbeid. Jeg syntes det gikk for sakte, at de andre var tosker, at ingenting ble gjort hvis jeg ikke gjorde det selv." Loe, *L*, 30.

55. Borchgrevink, "Noen tanker omkring engasjement," 17.

56. "Vi klarer ikke å ta det helt alvorlig. Vi gjør så godt vi kan, men lykkes ikke helt. Men det er naturligvis alvorlig. Mii og Tuaine tror på Gud. Det må vi respektere. Hver eneste dag lærer vi noe om oss selv og andre." Loe, *L*, 233.

57. Tvedt, *Verdensbilder og selvbilder*, 75.

58. Arguing that there is no irony in Kjærstad's trilogy is a matter of a subjective reading with which one may agree or disagree. Still, the overall issue of whether the goal of turning into a humanitarian great power should be viewed as generous or expansionist remains relevant.

59. "Om hundre år vet man alt om dette. Da vet man hvem vi var." Loe, *L*, 454.

60. Andersen, "Loe," 40.

61. Tønnessen, "Dannelsesprosjekt i to generasjoner," 132.

62. Homi K. Bhabha, "'Race,' Time and the Revision of Modernity."

Conclusion

1. Engdahl, "Modernismen er død," 8.
2. Two recent examples are *At rejse er at skrive* (2006), edited by Poul O. Andersen and Knud Michelsen, and Jørgen Alnæs's *I eventyret* (2008).
3. "Hvad denne universelt udbredte kulturform, som går under navnet amerikanisering, egentlig står for." Jensen, *Jeg har set verden begynde*, 534.
4. Giddens, *Modernity and Self-Identity*, 242.

Bibliography

Adams, Percy G. *Travel Literature and the Evolution of the Novel.* Lexington: University Press of Kentucky, 1983.
Aiken, Susan Hardy. *Isak Dinesen and the Engendering of Narrative.* Chicago: University of Chicago Press, 1990.
Alnces, Jørgen. *I eventyret: norske reiseskildringer fra Astrup til Aasheim.* Oslo: Cappelen, 2008.
Andersen, Frits. "En følsom rejsende: Retorisk realisme og orientalistisk slør i Carsten Jensens rejsebøger." *Kritik* 132 (1998): 1–10.
———. "Felix Arabia." *Kritik* 162–63 (2003): 4–14.
———. "Felix Arabia." *Weekendavisen* 33, Aug. 15–21, 2003, 3rd section Books, 1–2.
———. "Ørkenspejlinger." *Weekendavisen* 3, Jan. 21–27, 2005, 3rd section Books, 2.
Andersen, Hadle Oftedal. "Loe." *Syn og segn* 106, 2 (2000): 31–40.
Andersen, Hans Christian. *Dagbøger.* Vol. 2. Edited by Helga Vang Lauridsen. Copenhagen: Gads forlag, 1973.
———. *En Digters Bazar.* 2 vols. Copenhagen: Lademann, 1975.
———. "Jens Adolf Jerichau og Elisabeth Jerichau, født Baumann." *Folkekalender for Danmark,* 80–91. Copenhagen: Lose & Delbanco og Iversen, 1854.
Andersen, Jens. "På gat med verden." *Berlingske Tidende,* May 2, 2004, 2nd section Magasin, 1.
Andersen, Per Thomas. *Norsk litteraturhistorie.* Oslo: Universitetsforlaget, 2001.
———. *Tankevaser: Om norsk 1990-tallslitteratur.* Oslo: Universitetsforlaget, 2003.
Andersen, Poul O., and Knud Michelsen. *At rejse er at skrive.* Copenhagen: Gyldendal, 2006.
Anderson, Benedict. *Imagined Communities: Reflections on the Origin and Spread of Nationalism.* London: Verso, 1991.
Aristotle. *On Poetry and Style.* Translated by G. M. A. Grube. Indianapolis: Liberal Arts Press, 1958.
Baggesen, Søren. "En rendestensunges dannelse: H. C. Andersen." In *Dansk Litteraturhistorie.* Vol. 5, 2nd ed. Edited by Peter Holst, 124–56. Copenhagen: Gyldendal, 1990.
Bakhtin, Mikhail M. "Epic and Novel." In *The Dialogic Imagination.* Translated by Caryle Emerson and Michael Holquist, 3–40. Austin: University of Texas Press, 1981.

Barthes, Roland. *Mythologies*. Translated by Annette Lavers. London: Paladin Grafton Books, 1973.

Bataille, Georges. *Erotism: Death and Sensuality*. Translated by Mary Dalwood. San Francisco: City Lights Books, 1986.

Bauman, Zygmunt. *Liquid Modernity*. Cambridge: Polity Press, 2000.

Bergson, Henri. *Laughter: An Essay on the Meaning of the Comic*. Translated by Cloudesley Brereton and Fred Rothwell. 1914. Copenhagen: Green Integer, 1999.

Bhabha, Homi K. "The Commitment to Theory." In *The Location of Culture*, 19–39. London: Routledge, 1994.

———. "'Race,' Time and the Revision of Modernity." In *The Location of Culture*, 236–56. London: Routledge, 1994.

Blixen, Karen. *Den afrikanske Farm*. Copenhagen: Gyldendal Paperbacks, 1986.

Bøgh, Nikolaj. *Elisabeth Jerichau-Baumann: En Karakteristikk*. Copenhagen: Forlagsbureauet, 1886.

Borchgrevink, Aage Storm. "Noen tanker omkring engasjement." *Bøygen* 3–4 (2000): 12–17.

Bowles, Paul. *The Sheltering Sky*. 1949. New York: Penguin Books, 2000.

Bredal, Bjørn. "Hos araberne." *Politiken*, Aug. 19, 2003. 2nd secton: 1.

Bredsdorff, Elias. "Isak Dinesen v. Karen Blixen: *Seven Gothic Tales* (1934) and *Syv fantastiske Fortællinger* (1935)." In *Facets of European Modernism*, edited by Janet Garton, 275–93. Norwich: University of East Anglia, 1985.

Buzard, James. "The Grand Tour and After (1660–1840)." In *The Cambridge Companion to Travel Writing*, edited by Peter Hulme and Tim Youngs, 37–52. Cambridge: Cambridge University Press, 2002.

Carr, Helen. "Modernism and Travel (1880–1940)." In *The Cambridge Companion to Travel Writing*, edited by Peter Hulme and Tim Youngs, 70–86. Cambridge: Cambridge University Press, 2002.

Clifford, James. *Routes: Travel and Translation in the Late Twentieth Century*. Cambridge, Mass.: Harvard University Press, 1997.

Cronin, Michael. *Across the Lines: Travel, Language, Translation*. Cork: Cork University Press, 2000.

Dinesen, Isak. *Out of Africa* and *Shadows on the Grass*. New York: Vintage Books, 1985.

During, Simon. "Postcolonialism and Globalization." Meanjin 48, 2 (1992): 339–53.

Egeberg, Ole. *Ironiker og troubadour: Studier i Johs. V. Jensens Skovene*. In *LÆS: Litteratur, æstetik, sprog*, 15. Århus: Institut for Nordisk Sprog og Litteratur, Århus Universitet, 1993.

———. "Ironiske skraveringer: Om Johs. V. Jensens *Skovene*." *Passage* 8 (1990): 89–95.

Eide, Tom. "Kulturkritikk og utopisme: Om kulturfremmed innflytelse i Axel Jensens tidlige forfatterskap." In *Scandinavian Literature in a Transcultural Context*: Papers from the XV IASS Conference, Washington, August 12–18, 1984, edited by Sven H. Rossel and Birgitta Steene, 120–35. Seattle: University of Washington, 1986.

———. *Outsiderens posisjoner: Axel Jensens tidlige forfatterskap*. Oslo: Universitetsforlaget, 1991.

Engdahl, Horace. "Modernismen er død." Interview by Anders Ehlers Dam. *Weekendavisen*, Feb. 20–24, 2004. 3rd section Books, 8.

Engen, Sigrun Berge. "Geriljaturisme." *Adresseavisen*, May 26, 2004.

Eriksen, Thomas Hylland. "Been There, Seen This." *PROSA* 3 (1996), http://folk.uio.no/geirthe/Reiselitteratur.html (accessed Nov. 26, 2007).

Fanon, Frantz. *Black Skin, White Masks*. London: Pluto Press, 1986.

Folsach, Birgitte von. *I Halvmånens Skær: Eksempler på skildringer af Den Nære Orient i dansk kunst og litteratur omkring 1800–1875*. Copenhagen: Davids Samling, 1996.

Foucault, Michel. *The Order of Things: An Archaeology of the Human Sciences*. New York: Vintage Books, 1994.

Fried, Michael. *Absorption and Theatricality: Painting and Beholder in the Age of Diderot*. Chicago: University of Chicago Press, 1980.

Fussell, Paul. *Abroad: British Literary Traveling Between the Wars*. Oxford: Oxford University Press, 1980.

Geelmuyden, Niels Christian. "Marco Po Loe." In *Gud og hvermann*, 81–89. Oslo: Schibsted, 2001.

Genette, Gérard. *Palimpsests: Literature in the Second Degree*. Translated by Channa Newman and Claude Doubinsky. Lincoln: University of Nebraska Press, 1997.

Giddens, Anthony. *Modernity and Self-Identity: Self and Society in the Late Modern Age*. Stanford, Calif.: Stanford University Press, 1991.

Gumbrecht, Hans Ulrich. *Production of Presence: What Meaning Cannot Convey*. Stanford: Stanford University Press, 2004.

Hamsun, Knut. "Festina Lente." In *Fra det moderne Amerikas Aandsliv*, 135–41. Oslo: Gyldendal, 1962.

———. *Fra det moderne Amerikas Aandsliv*. Oslo: Gyldendal, 1962.

———. *I Æventyrland: Oplevet og drømt i Kaukasien*. In *Samlede Verker*, vol. 3. Oslo: Gyldendal norsk forlag, 1976.

———. *In Wonderland: Experienced and Dreamt in the Caucasus*. Translated by Sverre Lyngstad. New York: Ig Publishing, 2004.

———. "Under Halvmånen." In *Stridende liv, Samlede verker*, vol. 4. Oslo: Gyldendal, 1976.

Hamsun, Tore. "Forord." In Knut Hamsun, *Fra det moderne Amerikas Aandsliv*, vii–xxii. Oslo: Gyldendal, 1962.

Handesten, Lars. *Johannes V. Jensen: Liv og værk*. Copenhagen: Gyldendal, 2000.

———. *Litterære rejser—poetik og erkendelse i danske digteres rejsebøger*. Copenhagen: Reitzel, 1992.

Harbsmeier, Michael. "Introduction." In Carsten Niebuhr, *Rejsebeskrivelse fra Arabien og andre omkringliggende lande*, vol. 1, 9–32. Translated by Hans Christian Fink. Copenhagen: Forlaget Vandkunsten, 2003.

Hastrup, Kirsten. *Viljen til Viden*. Copenhagen: Gyldendal, 1999.

Hauge, Hans. *Post-Danmark: Politik og æstetik hinsides det nationale*. Copenhagen: Lindhardt og Ringhof, 2003.

Heede, Dag. *Det umenneskelige*. Odense: Odense Universitetsforlag, 2001.

Heiberg, Johan Ludvig. "Digter-Misundelse." In *Prosaiske Skrifter*, vol. 3, 397–406. Copenhagen: Reitzels Forlag, 1861.

Heltoft, Kjeld. "Introduction." In H. C. Andersen, *En Digters Bazar*, vol. 2. Copenhagen: Lademann, 1975.

Heyerdahl, Thor. *Kon-Tiki: Across the Pacific by Raft*. Translated by F. H. Lyon. New York: Tess Press, 2004.

———. *Kon-Tiki ekspedisjonen*. Oslo: Gyldendal, 2002.

Himmelstrup, Jens. *Terminologisk Ordbog*. In Søren Kierkegaard, *Samlede Værker*, vol. 20. Copenhagen: Gyldendal, 1964.

Høffding, Harald. *Den store Humor*. Copenhagen: Gyldendal, 1967.

Holland, Patrick, and Graham Huggan. *Tourists with Typewriters: Critical Reflections on Contemporary Travel Writing*. Ann Arbor: University of Michigan Press, 1998.

Houe, Poul. *En anden Andersen—og andres: Artikler og foredrag 1969–2005*. Copenhagen: C. A. Reitzel, 2006.

Hulme, Peter. "Travelling to Write (1940–2000)." In *The Cambridge Companion to Travel Writing*, edited by Peter Hulme and Tim Youngs, 87–101. Cambridge: Cambridge University Press, 2002.

Hulme, Peter, and Tim Youngs, eds. "Introduction." In *The Cambridge Companion to Travel Writing*, 1–13. Cambridge: Cambridge University Press, 2002.

Hutcheon, Linda. *A Poetics of Postmodernism: History, Theory, Fiction*. New York: Routledge, 1988.

———. *A Theory of Parody: The Teachings of Twentieth-Century Art Forms*. New York: Methuen, 2000.

Ibsen, Henrik. "Abydos." In *Samlede Verker*, vol. 15. Oslo: Gyldendal, 1930.

Ingebretsen, Herman Smitt. *En Dikter og en Herre: Vilhelm Krags Liv og Diktning*. Oslo: Aschehough, 1942.

Iversen, Irene. "Et moderne gjennombrudd." In *Norsk kvinnelitteraturhistorie*, vol. 1., edited by Irene Engelstad et al., 155–67. Oslo: Pax Forlag, 1988.

JanMohamed, Abdul R. *Manichean Aesthetics: The Politics of Literature in Colonial Africa*. Amherst: University of Massachusetts Press, 1983.

Jensen, Axel. *Icarus: A Young Man in the Sahara*. Translated by Maurice Michael. London: George Allen & Unwin, 1959.

———. *Ikaros: Ung mann i Sahara*. Oslo: Stenersens Forlag, 1999.

———. "Ikaros på flukt til Delfi—i brukt bil." Interview with Axel Jensen. *Aftenposten*, Nov. 13, 1957.

Jensen, Carsten. *Det glemte folk: En rejse i Burmas grænseland*. Copenhagen: Aschehoug, 2004.

———. *Jeg har hørt et stjerneskud*. Copenhagen: Rosinante, 1997.

———. *Jeg har set verden begynde*. Copenhagen: Rosinante, 1996.

———. *Træt i ørkonen: En resje i Niger*. Copenhagen: Aschohoug, 2003.

Jensen, Johannes V. *Kongens Fald*, 7th ed. Copenhagen: Gyldendal, 2001.

———. *Skovene*, 7th ed. Copenhagen: Gyldendal, 2001.

———. "Udenfor Tiden." In *Skovene*, 172–85. Copenhagen: Gyldendal, 1953.

BIBLIOGRAPHY

Jeppesen, Bent Haugaard. *Johannes V. Jensen og den hvide mands byrde.* Copenhagen: Rhodos, 1984.

Jerichau-Baumann, Elisabeth. *Brogede Reisebilleder.* Copenhagen: Forlagsbureauet, 1881.

Johnsen, Nina. "Poesi, etnografi og sandhed: Karen Blixen og 'Den afrikanske Farm.'" *Tidsskriftet antropologi* 26 (1992): 77–89.

Jørgensen, Bo Hakon. *Siden hen—om Karen Blixen.* Odense: Odense Universitetsforlag, 1999.

Jung, Carl G. *Psychology and Alchemy.* London: Routledge & Kegan Paul, 1980.

Kierkegaard, Søren. *The Concept of Irony.* Translated by Howard V. Hong and Edna Hong. Princeton, N.J.: Princeton University Press, 1989.

———. *Concluding Unscientific Postscript to Philosophical Fragments.* Translated by Howard V. Hong and Edna Hong. Princeton, N.J.: Princeton University Press, 1992.

Kittang, Atle. *Luft, vind, ingenting: Hamsuns desillusjonsromanar frå "Sult" til "Ringen sluttet."* Oslo: Gyldendal, 1984.

Kledal, Anna Rebecca. "Moder Danmark blandt haremskvinder: Om dansk orientalisme og dannelsen af national identitet i 1800-tallets romantiske billedkunst." *Kvinder, Køn & Forskning* 3 (2000): 39–49.

———. "Mor Danmark mellem haremskvinder og danske bønder: Om dansk orientalisme og dannelsen af national identitet i 1800-tallets romantiske billedkunst." *Tidskrift för mellanösternstudier* 2 (1999): 7–15.

Klein, Naomi. *No Logo.* London: Flamingo, 2001.

Korsvold, Kaja. "Erlend Loes siste roman slippes i dag: 90-tallets bok-komet." *Aftenposten Morgen,* Sept. 15, 1999.

Krag, Vilhelm. Review of Knut Hamsun's *Sult* (1890). In *Fædrelandsvennen,* Sept. 1890.

Lejeune, Philippe. "The Autobiographical Contract." In *French Literary Theory Today,* edited by Tzvetan Todorov, 192–222. Cambridge: Cambridge University Press, 1982.

Lévi-Strauss, Claude. *The Savage Mind.* Chicago: University of Chicago Press, 1966.

Lewis, Bernard. *The Emergence of Modern Turkey.* London: Oxford University Press, 1961.

Lewis, Reina. *Gendering Orientalism: Race, Femininity and Representation.* London: Routledge, 1996.

Lindqvist, Sven. *Ökendykarna.* Stockholm: Bonnier, 1990.

Loe, Erlend. *L.* Oslo: Cappelen, 2000.

Loria, Kakhaber. "Hamsuns kaukasiske mysterium." *Syn og Segn* 3 (2005): 80–85.

Lübcke, Poul, ed. *Politikens filosofileksikon.* Copenhagen: Politikens Forlag, 1983.

Madsen, Peter. "Kulturkrise, dagligliv og engagement." In *Dansk litteraturhistorie,* vol. 8, 107–9. Copenhagen: Gyldendal, 1985.

Mascia-Lees, Frances E., Patricia Sharpe, and Colleen Ballerino Cohen. "The Postmodernist Turn in Anthropology: Cautions from a Feminist Perspective." *Signs: Journal of Women in Culture and Society* 15, 1 (1989): 7–33.

Melberg, Arne. *Å reise og skrive: Et essay om moderne reiselitteratur.* Translated by Trond Haugen. Oslo: Spartacus, 2005.

Melman, Billie. *Women's Orients: English Women and the Middle East, 1718–1918; Sexuality, Religion and Work.* 2nd ed. Basingstoke: Macmillan, 1995.

Mills, Sara. *Discourses of Difference: An Analysis of Women's Travel Writing and Colonialism.* London: Routledge, 1991.

Mollestad, Jan Christian. *Trollmannen i ålefjær: Axel Jensen om Axel Jensen.* Oslo: Cappelen, 1993.

Montagu, Mary Wortley. *The Turkish Embassy Letters.* London: Virago, 1994.

Müller, Sigurd. *Nyere dansk Malerkunst: Et Billedværk.* Copenhagen, 1884.

Nedergaard, Leif. "Forord til 1. udgave." In *Johannes V. Jensen: Liv og Forfatterskab*, 2nd expanded ed. Copenhagen: C. A. Reitzel, 1993.

Niebuhr, Carsten. *Rejsebeskrivelse fra Arabien og andre omkringliggende lande*, vol. 1. Translated by Hans Christian Fink. Copenhagen: Forlaget Vandkunsten, 2003.

Nielsen, Torben Hviid. "'Den menneskelige Kløgt' og 'de stærke Natur-Aander.' H. C. Andersen om den eventyrlige teknologi." In *H. C. Andersen—eventyr, kunst og modernitet.* Edited by Elisabeth Oxfeldt, 115–43. Bergen: Fagbokforlaget Vigmostad & Bjørke, 2006.

Opset, Barbro Bredesen. "Generasjon O-fag: En lesning av Erlend Loes *L.*" *Bøygen* 4 (1999): 60–62.

Ottesen, Svein Johs. "I tannhjulposisjon til verden." *Aftenposten Morgen*, Sept. 11, 1998.

Oxfeldt, Elisabeth. "'Han er jo næsten hvid.' Race, identitet og iscenesættelse i H. C. Andersens *Mulatten*." *Spring* 22 (2004): 28–53.

———. *Nordic Orientalism: Paris and the Cosmopolitan Imagination 1800–1900.* Copenhagen: Museum Tusculanum Press, 2005.

———. "Refleksionsrum i den postkolonialistiske tekst: Ord og billede i Carsten Jensen og Tine Hardens *Træet i ørkenen*." *TijdSchrift voor Skandinavistiek* 30 (2009): 49–81.

Pfister, Manfred. "Bruce Chatwin and the Postmodernization of the Travelogue." *LIT (Literature, Interpretation, Theory)* 7 (1996): 253–67.

Porter, Dennis. *Haunted Journeys: Desire and Transgression in European Travel Writing.* Princeton, N.J.: Princeton University Press, 1991.

———. "Modernism and the Dream of Travel." In *Literature and Travel*, edited by Michael Hanne, 53–70. Amsterdam: Rodopi, 1993.

Pratt, Mary Louise. *Imperial Eyes: Travel Writing and Transculturation.* London: Routledge, 1992.

Rasmussen, Inge Lise. *Øjets sekraft og billedets fødsels: Artikler om H. C. Andersen.* Copenhagen: C. A. Reitzel, 2000.

Ryall, Anka. *Odyssevs i skjørt: Kvinners erobring av reiselitteraturen.* Oslo: Pax Forlag, 2004.

Ryom, Peter. "Folket og de nationale symboler." In *Bogen om Danmark*, edited by Me Christensen et al., 31–32. Copenhagen: Danmarks Nationalleksikon, 2001.

Said, Edward. *Culture and Imperialism.* New York: Vintage Books, 1994.
———. *Orientalism.* New York: Vintage Books, 1979.
Schiøtz-Christensen, Aage. *Om Sammenhængen i Johannes V. Jensens Forfatterskab.* Copenhagen: Borgens Forlag, 1956.
Seierstad, Åsne. *Bokhandleren i Kabul: Et familiedrama.* Oslo: Cappelen, 2002.
Selboe, Tone. *Karen Blixen.* Oslo: Gyldendal, 2001.
———. *Kunst og erfaring: En studie i Karen Blixens forfatterskap.* Odense: Odense Universitetsforlag, 1996.
Simmel, Georg. "The Metropolis and Mental Life." In *On Individuality and Social Forms: Selected Writings,* edited by Donald N. Levine, 324–39. Chicago: University of Chicago Press, 1971.
Skårderud, Finn. "Skrumpselvet: Retretter." *Samtiden* 5–6 (1998): 123–26.
Sontag, Susan. *Regarding the Pain of Others.* New York: Farrar, Straus and Giroux, 2003.
Sørensen, Knud. "Om sproglig interferens i *Den afrikanske Farm* og *Out of Africa.*" *Blixeniana* (1982): 296–307.
Svane, Marie-Louise. "Moderkroppen tegner sig: Analyse af nogle af Elisabeth Jerichau-Baumanns tegninger." *Kultur og Klasse* 1 (1985): 52–66.
Svendsen, Erik. "Carsten Jensen." In *Danske digtere i det 20. århundrede,* vol. 3. Edited by Anne Marie Mai, 338–48. Copenhagen: Gads Forlag, 2000.
Thiong'o, Ngũgĩ wa. "Her Cook, Her Dog: Karen Blixen's Africa." In *Moving the Centre: The Struggle for Cultural Freedoms,* 132–35. London: James Currey, 1993.
Thisted, Kirsten. "Dead man talking—om tale og tavshed og repræsentationens ambivalens hos Karen Blixen og Thorkild Hansen." *Spring* 22 (2004): 102–30.
Tønnessen, Elise Seip. "Dannelsesprosjekt i to generasjoner: En krysslesning av Dag Solstad og Erlend Loe." *Norsk litterær årbok* (2001): 121–38.
Topsøe-Jensen, Helge. "Efterskrift." In H. C. Andersen, *En Digters Bazar,* vol. 2, 223–46. Copenhagen: Lademann, 1975.
Torgovnick, Marianna. *Gone Primitive: Savage Intellects, Modern Lives.* Chicago: University of Chicago Press, 1990.
———. *Primitive Passions: Men, Women, and the Quest for Ecstasy.* Chicago: University of Chicago Press, 1997.
Tvedt, Terje. *Verdensbilder og selvbilder: En humanitær stormakts intellektuelle historie.* Oslo: Universitetsforlaget, 2002.
Tvinnereim, Audun. "En norsk femtitallsroman: Axel Jensens 'Ikaros.'" *Norsk litterær årbok* (1970): 130–41.
Urry, John. *The Tourist Gaze.* 2nd ed. London: Sage, 2002.
Vassenden, Eirik. *Den store overflaten: Tekster om samtidslitteraturen.* Oslo: Damm, 2004.
Wærp, Henning. "Erlend Loe: I.." *Nordlit* 7 (2000): 179–82.
———. "Knut Hamsun som reiseskildrer: *I Æventyrland.*" In *Hamsun i Tromsø II: Rapport fra den 2. Internasjonale Hamsun-konferanse,* edited by E. Arntzen, N. M. Knutsen, and H. H. Wærp, 239–61. Hamarøy: Hamsun-Selskapet, 1999.

White, Hayden. *Metahistory: The Historical Imagination in Nineteenth-Century Europe.* Baltimore, Md.: Johns Hopkins University Press, 1973.

Wivel, Henrik. *Den titaniske eros: Drifts-og karakterfortolkning i Johannes V. Jensens forfatterskab.* Copenhagen: Gyldendal, 1982.

Wivel, Ole. "Fem brød og to fisk." *Heretica* 2 (1948): 98–105.

Woolf, Virginia. *Orlando: A Biography.* San Diego: Harcourt, 1956

Ytzen, Flemming. "Tragedier i Technicolor." *Politiken*, May 8, 2004.

Zonana, Joyce. "The Sultan and the Slave: Feminist Orientalism and the Structure of Jane Eyre." *Signs: Journal of Women in Culture and Society* 3 (1993): 592–617.

Index

Adams, Percy G., xxi, 82, 244n17, 258n5
afrikanske Farm, Den. See Blixen, Karen; Dinesen, Isak
Afsluttende uvidenskabelig Efterskrift. See Kierkegaard, Søren
Aiken, Susan Hardy, 125, 127, 131, 134, 262n6, 263n13, 266n43
Albertine (Krohg), 48
Alnæs, Jørgen, 285n2
Andersen, Frits, xi, 178, 187, 190, 203, 243n
Andersen, Hadle Oftedal, 230
Andersen, Hans Christian, xiv, xxiii, 4, 6–30, 82, 233–34, 236–8, 243n2; in relation to Carsten Jensen, 183, 190, 191, 199, 201, 203; in relation to Dinesen, 106; in relation to Hamsun, 58, 62, 63, 67–69, 71, 256n17; in relation to Jerichau-Baumann, 37, 42, 44, 47, 250n11, 254n41; in relation to Johannes V. Jensen, 88, 92
Andersen, Jens, 12–13, 247n21
Andersen, Per Thomas, 275n16, 280n1
Andersen, Poul O., 285n2
Anderson, Benedict, xxvi
anthropology, xxi, xxv, 84–86, 173, 234–37; in relation to Carsten Jensen, 190–97, 199, 203; in relation to Dinesen, 107, 264n26; in relation to Johannes V. Jensen, 87–89, 92–95, 98–105. *See also* ethnography

anti-conquest, 14, 84, 89, 90, 105, 168, 187. *See also* seeing-man
Arabian Nights, 26. *See also Thousand and One Nights, A.*
Aristotle, 140, 152, 216, 224
autoethnography, xix, xxvi, 109, 132, 134, 237, 244n12. *See also* transculturation
Aya Sophia, 25, 71–72, 76, 234

Baggesen, Søren, 245n3, 246n15
Bakhtin, Mikhail M., xxii, 82–84, 86, 160, 234, 244n17
Barthes, Roland, 90, 151, 168–69
Bataille, Georges, 94–95, 237
Bauman, Zygmunt, 274n12
Baurenfeind, Georg Wilhelm, xi–xii, xxv, xxvi, xxvii
Bergson, Henri, 114, 117–21, 123–24, 128, 135–36, 237, 269n74, 269n77
Bhabha, Homi K., xvi, xviii–xix, 75, 122, 124, 231, 241
Bible, the, 103. *See also* Old Testament, the
Blixen, Karen, xiv, 106, 109, 132–34, 238. *See also* Dinesen, Isak
Bøgh, Nikolaj, 252n35
Borchgrevink, Aage Storm, 226, 230, 232
Bowles, Paul, 152, 154–58
Bredal, Bjørn, 243n4
Bredsdorff, Elias, 268n68

295

296 INDEX

Brogede Reisebilleder. See Jerichau-Baumann, Elisabeth
Burton, Richard, 29
Buzard, James, 244–45n2

Carr, Helen, xxii, 245n7
Chatwin, Bruce, 209, 213–15, 281n15
Christian IX, 50, 55
Christianity (Christian), 234; in relation to Axel Jensen, 164; in relation to Dinesen, 112–13, 121–22; in relation to Hamsun, 60–62, 71–73; in relation to Hans Christian Andersen, 24–25, 30; in relation to Johannes V. Jensen, 93, 99
Claussen, Sophus, 92
Clifford, James, 84–85, 98–100, 107, 173, 191, 236, 237
Concept of Irony, The. See Kierkegaard, Søren
Concluding Unscientific Postscript. See Kierkegaard, Søren
Conrad, Joseph, 59, 254n1
Constance Ring (Skram), 48
contact zone, xii, xxvi, 16, 83–84, 86, 89, 105, 216, 228
contestatory genre, xviii. *See also* autoethnography
cosmopolitanism, 16–17, 51, 53, 57, 131, 174, 230, 238–40

Darwinism, 81, 85, 87, 234, 244n12
diary: in relation to Carsten Jensen, 188, 196–97; in relation to Hamsun, 68–69; in relation to Hans Christian Andersen, 8, 26; in relation to Johannes V. Jensen, 91
Diary of a Seducer, The (Kierkegaard), 94
Digters Bazar, En. See Andersen, Hans Christian
Dinesen, Isak, xiv, xv, xvi, xxiv, 85–86, 106–42, 235–38; in relation to Axel Jensen, 146, 147, 166, 168; in relation to Carsten Jensen, 179. *See also* Blixen, Karen
Don Quixote, 197, 244n17
During, Simon, 196
dystopia, 74–77

Egeberg, Ole, 89, 91, 103, 259n12
Egypt, xi, xiii, xvii, 4, 32, 35, 39–42, 48, 103, 166, 186
Eide, Tom, 145, 152, 159–60, 162, 165, 272n39
"Ekbàtana" (Claussen), 92, 260n19
Engdahl, Horace, 233, 236, 244n18
Engen, Sigrun Berge, 280n73
epilogue, 50, 55–57
Eriksen, Thomas Hylland, xix
Erotism. See Bataille, Georges
ethnicity. *See* ethnography
ethnography, xxii, xxiv, 84–85, 236, 243n2; in relation to Carsten Jensen, 190–92; in relation to Dinesen, 106–7, 109, 115, 130, 132; in relation to Hans Christian Andersen, 11; in relation to Jerichau-Baumann, 31–32, 34, 35, 39, 45, 53; in relation to Johannes V. Jensen, 89, 98, 103. *See also* anthropology; autoethnography
exoticism, xi, xiii, xxiii, xxiv, xxvi, 81, 83, 234, 238, 240; in relation to Axel Jensen, 150, 160; in relation to Carsten Jensen, 194, 195, 203; in relation to Hans Christian Andersen, 7, 11, 23, 26, 30; in relation to Jerichau-Baumann, 31, 39, 42; in relation to Johannes V. Jensen, 88; in relation to Loe, 214, 227, 228, 231
expressionism, 87, 92, 102, 103, 198

Falconbridge, Anna Maria, 127
Fanon, Frantz, 75, 162
feminist Orientalism, 33–34, 46, 48–49, 57, 67, 127, 236
"Festina Lente" (Hamsun), 77

Finch-Hatton, Denys, 109, 115
Flaubert, Gustave, 37, 67
Folsach, Birgitte von, 22, 26, 250n11, 251n16, 253n36
Forførerens Dagbog (Kierkegaard), 94
Foucault, Michel, xvi, xvii, 66, 77, 127
Fra det moderne Amerikas Aandsliv (Hamsun), 74–75
Freud, Sigmund, 81, 121, 231, 259n13
Fried, Michael, 39
Fussell, Paul, 178, 243n6, 244n19, 281n13

Geelmuyden, Niels Christian, 283n41
Genette, Gérard, xxiii, 155–56, 159, 217, 221–22, 237, 272n35
George, King, 54
Giddens, Anthony, 177, 179, 181, 185–87, 190, 196, 199, 237, 240
Gide, André, 93, 108–9
glemte folk, Det (C. Jensen), 202–3, 273n3
Goethe, 8, 59
Gone Primitive (Torgovnick), 88, 99
Gothic Renaissance, The (J. V. Jensen), 88
gotiske Renæssance, Den (J. V. Jensen), 88
"Grecian Urn" (Keats), 40
Greek mythology, 85, 144, 154, 155, 158
Gumbrecht, Hans Ulrich, 216

Hagia Sophia. *See* Aya Sophia
Hamsun, Knut, xiv, xvi, xxiv, 4–5, 58–77, 82, 83, 85, 233–34, 237–39; in relation to Axel Jensen, 144, 147, 154, 158, 164, 269n5; in relation to Carsten Jensen, 179, 180; in relation to Dinesen, 106, 126; in relation to Johannes V. Jensen, 87–88, 91–92, 95–97, 104; in relation to Loe, 205, 224
Hamsun, Tore, 74
Handesten, Lars, xx, 89–90, 245n4, 247n21, 259n5, 261n29

Harbsmeier, Michael, 243n1
Harden, Tine, 202
harem: in relation to Hamsun, 67–68, 70; in relation to Hans Christian Andersen, 19, 21, 22; in relation to Jerichau-Baumann, 32, 38, 44, 48
Hastrup, Kirsten, 261n35
Hauge, Hans, 244n14
Heede, Dag, 263n19, 264n26
Heiberg, Johan Ludvig, 267n55
Heltoft, Kjeld, 26, 247n22
Heretica, 144, 145, 164, 165, 273n52
Heyerdahl, Thor, 175; in relation to Carsten Jensen, 191; in relation to Loe, 204–5, 212, 214–15, 217–22, 224, 226–29, 231, 283n34, 284n49
Himmelstrup, Jens, 263n18
Høffding, Harald, 123, 135–38, 140, 168, 237, 264n24, 268n74
Holberg, Ludvig, 129, 130, 134, 138, 267n55
Holland, Patrick, 191–92, 196–97, 203
Homer, 3, 18
Houe, Poul, 245n2, 247n24
Huggan, Graham, 191–92, 196–97, 203
Hulme, Peter, xxi, 3, 173, 174, 273n5, 280n2
Hutcheon, Linda, 206–9, 220–22, 224, 226, 237, 281–82n15, 283n34

I æventyrland (Hamsun), 58–73, 91, 95, 97, 104
Ibsen, Henrik, xix, 72, 154, 166, 189, 205, 239
Icarus. *See* Jensen, Axel
I have seen the world begin. *See* *Jeg har set verden begynde* (C. Jensen)
Ikaros. *See* Jensen, Axel
imperial eyes, xix, 14, 203. *See also* imperial gaze
Imperial Eyes (Pratt). *See* Pratt, Mary Louise

INDEX

imperial gaze, 72. *See also* imperial eyes
innocent eyes, 22. *See also* seeing-man
In Patagonia (Chatwin), 209, 215
intertextuality, 175, 235, 237, 238, 240; in relation to Axel Jensen, 146, 150, 154–56, 164, 166, 167; in relation to Dinesen, 134; in relation to Jerichau-Baumann, 35; in relation to Loe, 207, 208, 214–16, 221, 231
In Wonderland (Hamsun). *See I æventyrland*
Islam, 19, 24–25, 31, 61–62, 72, 99, 244n8. *See also* Mohammedanism
Iversen, Irene, 252n31

JanMohamed, Abdul R., 108, 122, 129, 138, 139, 263n11
Jeg har hørt et stjerneskud (C. Jensen), 174–75, 176–80, 187, 190–203
Jeg har set verden begynde (C. Jensen), 174–75, 176–90, 191, 201, 202, 203, 285n3
Jensen, Axel, xiv, xv, xxiv, 85, 86, 143–69, 235, 237, 238; in relation to Carsten Jensen, 176–77, 179–81, 187; in relation to Loe, 208, 217, 221, 224, 226
Jensen, Carsten, xiv, 174–75, 176–203, 235–37, 239–40; in relation to Loe, 209–11, 216, 220, 230
Jensen, Johannes V., xiv, xvi, xxiv, 85, 87–105, 233–34, 236–38; in relation to Axel Jensen, 148, 158, 164; in relation to Carsten Jensen, 179, 187, 190, 192–94, 196–98; in relation to Dinesen, 108, 109, 123, 126, 131; in relation to Loe, 224
Jeppesen, Bent Haugaard, 90, 258n2
Jerichau-Baumann, Elisabeth, xiv, xvi, xxiii–iv, 4, 31–57, 82, 233–34, 237–38; in relation to Dinesen, 106, 126–27, 131–32; in relation to Hamsun, 58, 62

Johnsen, Nina, 107, 110
Jørgensen, Bo Hakon, 263n15, 268n72
journalism, xiv, xxi, 174, 233, 235, 241; in relation to Carsten Jensen, 178, 190, 200–1, 203; in relation to Hamsun, 66, 74; in relation to Johannes V. Jensen, 96
Jung, Carl G., 93, 108–9, 145, 148, 149, 154, 160, 259n13, 270n8, 270n9

Keats, 40
Kierkegaard, Søren, 6, 94, 112–14, 123–24, 138, 165, 237, 263n13, 263n19, 264n20, 268n74
Kingsley, Mary, 49, 126, 141, 252n34
Kittang, Atle, 60
Kledal, Anna Rebecca, 51, 57, 253n36
Klein, Naomi, 217
Kongens Fald (J. V. Jensen), 87, 103
Kon-Tiki (Heyerdahl). *See Kon-Tiki ekspedisjonen*
Kon-Tiki ekspedisjonen (Heyerdahl), 204, 217–19, 222, 226–27, 284n49
Koran, the, 72, 95
Krag, Vilhelm, 59, 63, 74
Krohg, Christian, 48

L (Loe). *See* Loe, Erlend
Laahne, Elmer, 202
Laughter. See Bergson, Henri
Lejeune, Philippe, xxiii, 69, 179
Lévy-Strauss, Claude, 257n38
Lewis, Bernard, 246n18
Lewis, Reina, 32, 34, 36, 37, 53
"lille Pige med Svovlstikkerne, Den" (H. C. Andersen), 20
Liszt, Franz, 9–10, 11, 17, 30
"Little Match Girl, The" (H. C. Andersen), 20
Loe, Erlend, xiv, xxiii, 59, 161, 174, 175, 204–32, 235, 237, 239
Loria, Kakhaber, 60
Lyotard, Jean-François, 205, 207, 223

Madsen, Peter, 164
Malinowski, Bronislaw, 84, 88, 98, 191
Mascia-Lees, Frances E., 189
Mead, Margaret, 191–92
Melberg, Arne, xx, 155, 233, 254n1, 273n58, 277n41
Melman, Billie, 32–34, 48, 50, 243n6, 246n18
Michelsen, Knud, 285n2
Mills, Sara, 33–34, 39
Modernity and Self-Identity. See Giddens, Anthony
Mohammedanism, 19, 23–24, 92–94, 99, 255n16. See also Islam; Muslim
Mollestad, Jan Christian, 144, 161, 269n4, 281n14
Montagu, Mary Wortley, 33, 71
Moravia, Alberto, 183
Mor Danmark (Jerichau-Baumann), 51, 53, 54, 56–57
Mother Denmark (Jerichau-Baumann). See *Mor Danmark*
Mulatten (H. C. Andersen), 22–23
Mulatto, The (H. C. Andersen). See *Mulatten*
Müller, Sigurd, 249n3
Muslim, 25, 42, 60, 61, 71–72, 73, 94, 116. See also Mohammedanism

Narrative of Two Voyages to the River Sierra Leone (Falconbridge), 127
Nazili Hanum, 44–45, 48
Nedergaard, Leif, 259n11
Niebuhr, Carsten, xi–xiii, xvi–xvii, xix, xxv, 13
Nielsen, Torben Hviid, 245n8
Nietzsche, Friedrich, xx, 154
Nightingale, Florence, 48
nostalgia, xi, 4, 10, 85, 104, 235; in relation to Axel Jensen, 168; in relation to Carsten Jensen, 179, 180, 193, 199, 280n70; in relation to Dinesen,

114, 137, 138; in relation to Hamsun, 61, 73

Old Patagonian Express, The (Theroux), 183
Old Testament, the, 18, 92, 154, 166. See also Bible, the
Om Begrebet Ironi. See Kierkegaard, Søren
Opset, Barbro Bredesen, 225, 283n38
Orientalism. See Said, Edward
Otto, King, 54
Out of Africa. See Blixen, Karen; Dinesen, Isak
Oxfeldt, Elisabeth, 248n35, 267n58, 280n72

Palimpsests. See Genette, Gérard
paratextuality, xxiii, 174, 175; in relation to Axel Jensen, 158–59, 169; in relation to Jerichau-Baumann, 50; in relation to Loe, 217, 222–23. See also epilogue
Park, Mungo, 15, 17–18
Peer Gynt (Ibsen), 154, 166, 185–86, 189
Pfister, Manfred, 208–9, 212–16
poetic realism: in relation to Carsten Jensen, 199, 203; in relation to Hans Christian Andersen, 18–26
poetics, xxvi, 7, 9–10, 18–22, 201, 263n15, 266n43
Poetics of Postmodernism, A. See Hutcheon, Linda
political correctness, xi, 30, 187, 188, 227, 229, 262n6
Polo, Marco, xiii, 3, 223
Porter, Dennis, 37, 38, 67, 250n12, 276n28
Pouplier, Birgit, 31
poverty, 19–20, 24, 42, 184, 191, 199–202

Pratt, Mary Louise, xii, xvi–xix, xxv–xxvi, 33, 83, 84, 86, 173, 236–38, 252n34; in relation to Carsten Jensen, 182–83, 187–88, 194, 197; in relation to Dinesen, 126–27, 129, 141; in relation to Hamsun, 63, 72; in relation to Hans Christian Andersen, 14–15, 17, 24–25, 29; in relation to Jerichau-Baumann, 49, 55; in relation to Johannes V. Jensen, 88–90, 102–3; in relation to Loe, 209–10, 215, 229
Primitive Passions (Torgovnick), 88, 93, 108
primitivism, xxi, xxiv, 81, 85, 234, 237–38, 240; in relation to Axel Jensen, 144, 147–49, 164, 166, 167; in relation to Carsten Jensen, 181, 184, 188, 191, 194, 199; in relation to Dinesen, 108, 139; in relation to Jerichau-Baumann, 42; in relation to Johannes V. Jensen, 88, 90, 91–95, 97, 98–104; in relation to Loe, 204, 227–28, 231
prostitution, 41, 100, 150–54, 169, 181, 187–89, 256n19

Rasmussen, Inge Lise, 248n45
reciprocity, xii–xiii; in relation to Carsten Jensen, 181, 182, 197; in relation to Dinesen 125, 130, 137–38; in relation to Hamsun, 71; in relation to Hans Christian Andersen, 13, 15–16, 29; in relation to Johannes V. Jensen, 102; in relation to Loe, 220, 229
Regarding the Pain of Others. See Sontag, Susan
Reisebeschreibung nach Arabien und andern umliegenden Ländern. See Niebuhr, Carsten
Rejsebeskrivelse fra Arabien og andre omkringliggende lande. See Niebuhr, Carsten

religion: in relation to Axel Jensen, 161; in relation to Carsten Jensen, 178; in relation to Dinesen, 111–13, 122, 138, 264n24, 269n74; in relation to Hamsun, 71; in relation to Hans Christian Andersen, 13, 23, 25, 26, 247n21; in relation to Johannes V. Jensen, 92–95, 99, 261n29
reportage. *See* journalism
Robinson-ekspeditionen, 217, 222
Routes (Clifford). *See* Clifford, James
Rule Britannia (Jerichau-Baumann), 57
Ryall, Anka, xvi, 233

Said, Edward, xvii, 237, 243n8, 259n11; in relation to Axel Jensen, 163; in relation to Hamsun, 60, 61, 66, 74, 75; in relation to Hans Christian Andersen, 14, 18, 24, 29; in relation to Jerichau-Baumann, 32, 33, 38, 47, 252n32;
Salvador (Didion), 173
Schiøtz-Christensen, Aage, 259n10
seeing-man (seeing-men), 14, 88, 89, 238. *See also* anti-conquest; innocent eyes
Seierstad, Åsne, 241
Selboe, Tone, 111, 114, 126, 262n3, 262n8, 263n11, 267n52, 267n57
Seven Gothic Tales (Dinesen), 132–33
"Shadow, The" (H. C. Andersen), 11
Sheltering Sky, The. See Bowles, Paul
Simmel, Georg, 283n35
Skovene (Jensen). *See* Jensen, Johannes V.
Skram, Amalie, 48
"Skyggen" (H. C. Andersen), 11
slave, 22–23, 41, 116, 260n16
Socrates, 122
Sontag, Susan, 193, 200, 237
Sørensen, Knud, 133–34
store Humor, Den. See Høffding, Harald
Sultan Mahmud, 16, 25

INDEX

Survivor. *See* Robinson-ekspeditionen
Svane, Marie-Louise, 250n10
Svendsen, Erik, 274n1

Theory of Parody, A. See Hutcheon, Linda
Theroux, Paul, 183
Thiong'o, Ngugi wa, 107, 262n6
Thisted, Kirsten, 122
Thousand and One Nights, A, 9, 18, 116, 246n13. *See also Arabian Nights*
Tønnessen, Elise Seip, 231
Topsøe-Jensen, Helge, 246n14, 246n17, 247n23
Torgovnick, Marianna, 237; in relation to Axel Jensen, 148; in relation to Dinesen, 108, 129, 131, 138, 139; in relation to Johannes V. Jensen, 88, 90, 93, 99
Tourist Gaze, The (Urry). *See* Urry, John
Træet i ørkenen (C. Jensen), 202
transculturation, xxv, 55, 194, 202, 237, 244n21. *See also* autoethnography
Travels in the Interior Districts of Africa (Park), 15
Travels in West Africa (Kingsley), 126
Turkish Embassy Letters, The (Montagu), 33
Tvedt, Terje, 174, 230
Tvinnereim, Audun, 145, 269–70n5

"Udenfor Tiden" (J. V. Jensen), 91
"Under halvmånen" (Hamsun), 60–74, 77
Urry, John, 151–53, 237, 279–80n70
utopia, 73–77

Vassenden, Eirik, 283n34
Vindication of the Rights of Woman (Wollstonecraft), 48, 252n32

Wærp, Henning, 60–61, 65, 254n6, 281n13, 283n39
Weekendavisen, xi, xxvi
welfare state, xiv, 160–61, 166–67, 208, 226
Which Tribe Do You Belong To? (Moravia), 183
White, Hayden, xxii
whore. *See* prostitution
Wivel, Henrik, 101, 259n2, 259n13, 260n26
Wivel, Ole, 270n7, 273n52
Wollstonecraft, Mary, 48
Woolf, Virginia, 67

Yeats, William Butler, 10
Youngs, Tim, xxi, 3, 280n2
Ytzen, Flemming, 280n73

Zonana, Joyce, 48–49, 252n32

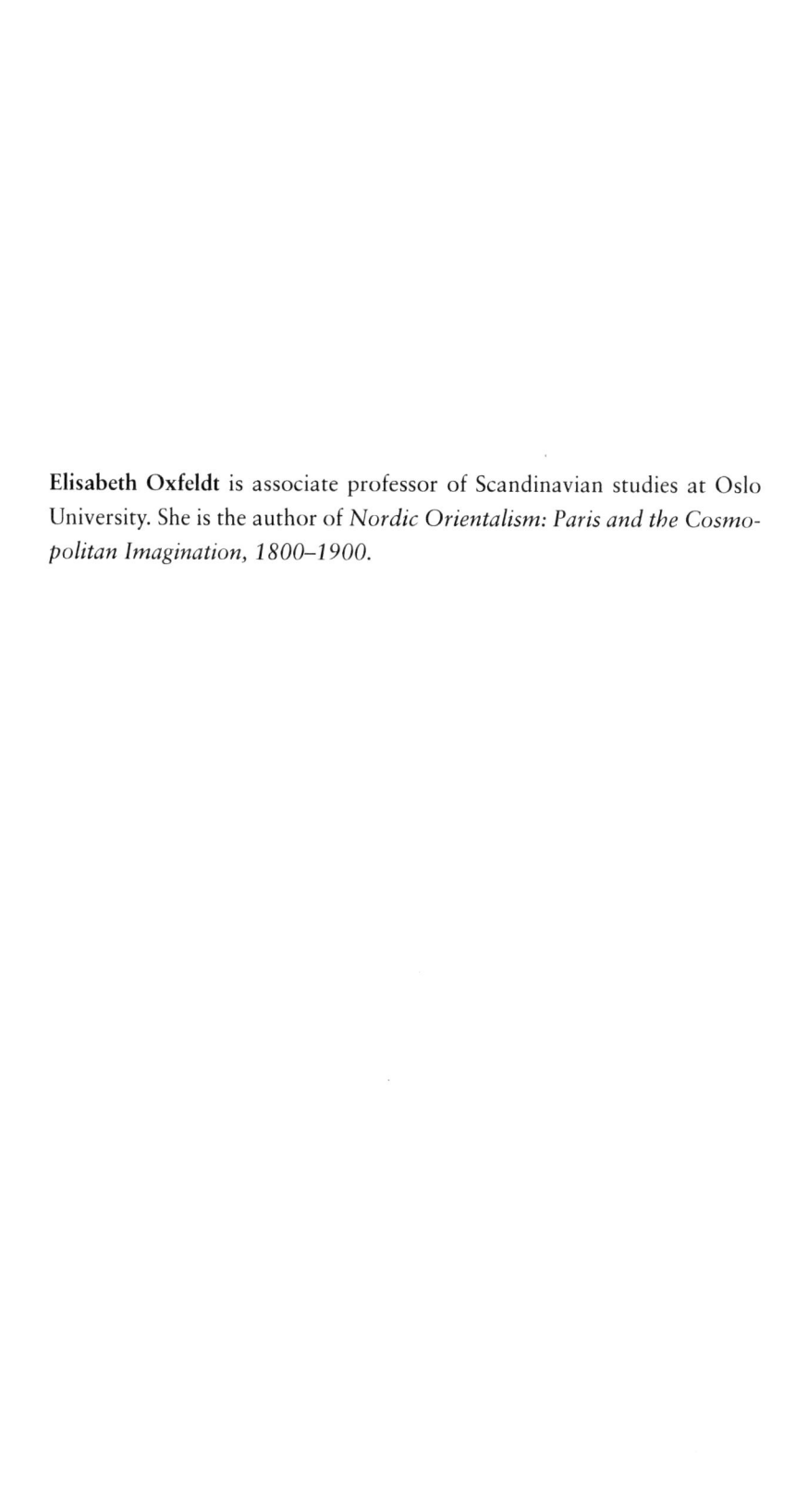

Elisabeth Oxfeldt is associate professor of Scandinavian studies at Oslo University. She is the author of *Nordic Orientalism: Paris and the Cosmopolitan Imagination, 1800–1900*.